The Walrus on My Table

The Walrus on My Table

Touching True Stories of Animal Healing

Anthony Guglielmo *and* Cari Lynn

St. Martin's Press ⚏ New York

www.stmartins.com

Library of Congress Cataloging-in-Publication Data

Guglielmo, Anthony.
    The walrus on my table : touching true stories of animal healing /
Anthony Guglielmo and Cari Lynn—1st ed.
        p.   cm.
    ISBN 0-312-26267-1
    1. Guglielmo, Anthony.   2. Animal massage therapists—Biography.
 3. Massage for animals—Anecdotes.   4. Animals—Anecdotes.
 I. Lynn, Cari.   II. Title.

SF613.G85 A3 2000
636.089'5822'093—dc21
[B]   00-031819

First Edition: November 2000

10 9 8 7 6 5 4 3 2 1

To my wife, Cathy, for all her patience, support,
and encouragement, and to my parents,
who taught me to show love and respect for
all of God's wonderful creations.

—Anthony Guglielmo

To Jason.

—Cari Lynn

Contents

Acknowledgments

Our first and foremost thank you must go to Jeff Kleinman, whose vision was the impetus for this book.

This project also would not have been possible without help from numerous other people, including all the staff at the Dolphin Research Center, the Jenkinson's Aquarium; Patricia Whalen-Shaw of Integrated Touch Therapy, Inc.; Mike Sorentino, Jr.; and the staff at the New York Aquarium.

For their time and insight, we'd like to thank Cassandra Batson, L.M.T. (Providence, Rhode Island), Dr. Judith Ray Swanson, Robert Altman, Mike Scott of Equine Massage/Muscle Therapy, Will Green of the International Massage Association, Dr. Joyce Harmon of the American Holistic Veterinary Medical Association, the American Massage Therapy Association, Barbara Joel and the New York Society of Medical Massage Therapists, Briah Anson, the Rolf Institute, the Asso-

ciation of Massage Therapists and Holistic Practition-
ers, the American Zoo and Aquarium Association, the
International Marine and Aquatics Trainers Associa-
tion, Stacy Smalls of the International Alliance for An-
imal Therapy and Healing, Dr. Warren and Anita
Ugent, Todd and Staci Zellen, Alan Goldsher, Dr.
Deena Schaffert, David Everett of the Johns Hopkins
University, and Adam Rand.

Many, many thanks to Heather Jackson Silverman
and the rest of the wonderful staff at St. Martin's Press,
including Ellen Smith, Joan Higgins, and John Murphy.

And last but certainly not least, to those really re-
sponsible for this book: Champ, Cindy, Rudy, Kathy,
Tab, Presley, Mickey, Wanda, Reddog, Molson, Sadie,
Baby, and, of course, Nuka.

Prologue

Animal Kneads

The field of massage therapy has gained acceptability in America only within the last fifteen years or so—even though it's been practiced on humans for the past 4,600 years, and for nearly as long on animals. Although no official record exists, animal massage is believed to have begun in ancient Thailand, where it was used on tigers and leopards: in fact, the royal family had their own animal massage therapist. Massage quickly caught on and spread throughout most of Asia.

In the United States, animal massage has been used sporadically (although it's rumored that the Barnum and Bailey circus animals have regularly received massage for decades). Anyone who has ever handled an animal has probably, to some extent, used some massage techniques—except horse trainers might call it "grooming," and cat owners might call it "petting." The truth is, animals' bodies require maintenance just like our own—

especially animals who are in captivity and who "work" for a living by performing.

In my animal practice so far, I have done massage therapy on over a dozen different species—from mammals, to birds, to fish. One very dear dolphin named Cindy is the animal that's mostly responsible for my work in this field. If it wasn't for Cindy, and for the empathy I felt for her, I may never have pursued animal massage.

But it was a long road to get to Cindy—I had to prove myself first. I did that with another of my favorites, Nuka, a nearly two-thousand-pound, middle-aged walrus who had lost the use of her rear flippers. Nuka's dramatic, documented response opened the door for me to work on other ailing animals.

After Nuka, I was able to fulfill my boyhood dream of working with dolphins, some of the most elegant creatures on this earth. I massaged Tab and Presley, two very rambunctious, energetic male dolphins who often took to one-upping the other; then I worked on the "Golden Girls," two female dolphins in their forties (old for dolphin years) who had lived through shark attacks.

There were plenty of horses along the way, including one racehorse who consistently placed poorly—until his owner discovered the benefits of massage.

Then there's Kathy, the oldest beluga whale in the world living in an aquarium, who has given hope to this nearly endangered species; plus, many other animals, including Rudy the penguin, Reddog, and Baby the shark.

I receive calls from around the world to help injured or traumatized animals, or to lecture. I recently gave a lecture to a group of veterinary students at Cornell University; I spoke to a packed lecture hall, filled with students who were there out of their own interest (none had been assigned my lecture as part of a class). After I spoke and showed slides of some of the animals I had worked on, I was bombarded by questions. When the professor of the next class began flicking the lights on and off, I was followed out of the room by a line of students, asking when I would be back again. It made me optimistic to see the next generation of veterinarians so curious about alternative forms of therapy.

On the flip side, the traditionalists can often be quite close-minded. Immediately after the lecture at Cornell, a woman silently handed me a piece of paper, then turned and hurried away. It was a notification from a veterinary society that warned that it was illegal to treat animals without a veterinary degree. I knew I had nothing to worry about—I always work on animals under the supervision of a veterinarian. Yet, the refusal of some to explore new, nontraditional methods continues to frustrate me.

Luckily, some of the nation's best zoos and aquariums are open-minded and have contacted me to work on everything from an elephant who couldn't lie down to a shark with a back condition called scoliosis.

I'm still amazed how similar the animal world is to our own. I never thought I had much in common with a shark or a ferret—but I do, we all do. Regardless of the creature, there is the universal language of touch. Touch is one of the simplest pleasures we know; it is also one of the most underestimated. Science fails us when it comes to the power of touch, of contact between living beings. No study can precisely explain or document the effect touch has, but we all know that it is powerful, healing, and that, above all, it feels good. After all, who—great or small—doesn't love a back rub?

The Walrus on My Table

1

Champ: Nag'in Pain

About a year after I opened my own medical massage practice—humans only—I receive a phone call from the mother of one of my patients.

Debbie's mother, Sylvia, has been in my office a few times with her daughter so I have met her briefly before, but her call is still out of the blue.

"Anthony," she says. "Could you take a look at Champ?"

"Who's Champ?" I ask, trying to remember if her husband or son has such an unusual name.

"My horse."

"Your *horse*?"

"Oh, he's beautiful, you'll love him—everybody loves Champ—he's a big bay, white socks, a real sweetheart—"

I try to interrupt. "Sylvia, I'm sorry, but I don't—"

"Champ was abused. Severely."

I don't know what to say.

In a pinched voice, she goes on, "I didn't know when

I bought him, but his previous owner had tied him up and beat him before competitions. Don't ask me why; we don't have any idea. It sure isn't a way to train a horse. But he's so tense when I ride him—I thought that maybe a massage could help him relax. Anthony, I don't care if he ever becomes a top show horse. I just don't want him to feel scared."

My heart goes out to Champ, but what can I do?

"Sylvia," I say, "I'm sorry, but I don't know how to massage a horse."

"I think you'd be great at it," she says, her voice perking up. "I'll call you next week after you've had a chance to mull it over."

I hang up the phone, knowing full well the next time we speak my answer will still be no.

True to her word, a week later, Sylvia calls me.

"Champ has been asking about you," she says.

Little do I realize, but there is a whole world out there devoted to horses and massage therapy. In equine circles, massage therapy is not necessarily viewed as cutting edge or alternative—it is an accepted, and even relatively standard, practice.

That night, as I flip through the *American Massage Therapy Association Journal*, I catch an advertisement I've never noticed before: "Become certified in equine massage. Learn how to practice the art of horse massage for performance and well-being."

I can't believe there is actually a school for this.

The next day I call the number in the ad to find out more.

"Equine massage has been practiced for years," the

school spokesperson says. "It gives the horse the edge in competition. Think of it this way: in your human practice, if you treat an athlete or a dancer they will find that massage enhances their performance—why wouldn't the same hold true for a horse?

"We feel our program is one of the top in the country. We offer a certification course and teach you how to set up your own equine massage practice—how to recruit clients and market yourself."

I certainly am not interested in the business plan aspect—I want to help Champ and then get back to my human practice. Still, the notion that my field is practiced on animals intrigues me, so I arrange for the school to send me a brochure and a videotape.

The massage I see on the video is not what I hoped it would be. I don't know a lot about horses at this point, but I don't like how they are fidgeting back and forth. The therapists seem competent enough, giving thorough explanations as they work; maybe this is how animal massage is supposed to be. If it is, I don't like it. The horses are pulling to the ends of their lead lines and pushing away from the therapists, as if trying to avoid the contact.

On the video, the massage therapist is pressing firmly into the muscle groups—so firmly that it seems impossible for the massage not to be uncomfortable—even painful—for the horses. I picture a person on my massage table who jumps when I hit a sore spot. Do I keep pressing into that spot? Of course not. So why are these therapists?

Every massage therapist has a different mind-set toward therapy and toward treating pain. Many therapists—like many athletes and their trainers—subscribe to the "no pain, no gain" philosophy: you know things are improving when it hurts, or at least is uncomfortable. For me, massage therapy is a tool used to solve problems; but the problem can't be solved if the patient is tense, or avoiding contact, or is unhappy or uncomfortable while I'm trying to treat him or her. Even if that patient is hurt—with a torn ligament or pulled tendon, for example—my massage will not be about pain: it will be about relaxing, smoothing away the tension or the spasm, so the patient isn't bracing against the hurt anymore. And once the patient isn't bracing—be it physically or mentally—the healing can begin.

As I watch the video, I start wondering if there are similar schools of thought for horse massage therapy. Do other schools teach a different, gentler philosophy? A few nights later, I flip through my massage therapy journals and find another advertisement for an equine massage school in Ohio. As I'm copying down the number, the phone rings. Cathy appears in the doorway.

"Guess who?" she says.

I put the number of the school on top of my stack of things to do first thing tomorrow.

"Our main interest is in the nurturing and care of the horses," Patricia Whalen-Shaw, the owner of Integrated Touch Therapy, says when I call. "It's a week-long intensive class where the goal is not necessarily to help animals perform better, but to help them recover from injuries and feel better."

"I want to help one specific horse who's been abused," I explain. "I don't want to cause him any more pain, though."

"We don't believe that a massage should be about pain. We practice applying massage with a gentle technique. The focus first and foremost is on relaxation. We want our horses to enjoy their massages."

We speak for a half hour, and unlike the other school, Patricia doesn't once give me the pitch about how they can help me set up my own practice, or how much money this certification will translate into. This is appealing because I don't want to start a new business venture—I want to help Champ.

I encountered a similar situation when I was figuring out where to apply for regular massage therapy school. Many schools I had looked into had very stringent attitudes—they taught that there was only one right way of doing massage, and that was *their* way. Of course, I knew that wasn't true: I knew of at least forty different massage techniques; to really master them, and use them effectively to develop your own style, is an art. I eventually made the choice to go to a school that was farther away from my home but was also open and nurturing.

Patricia's school also seems small and personal, not a cookie-cutter type of place like the other. The only problem is that it's in a small town in Ohio, about an hour from Columbus, and that means a pretty hefty investment of time and money—all for one horse and one persistent woman.

That night, over dinner, I discuss the situation with Cathy.

"I've never known you to pass up a chance of being with animals," she says, and we decide I should enroll.

It's a ten-hour drive from Long Island to Circleville, Ohio. When I arrive in Circleville, I check into the Travel Lodge, and the next morning, bright and early, I follow the map the school had sent me. At the entrance of a long driveway off the main road is a small wooden sign: Synergy Farm. I follow the drive past green fields, around to a white barn next to a two-story farmhouse. It looks like a well-kept farm, not a school.

I turn off my car and sit staring at the barn. Reality has hit: I am in the middle of a farm in the middle of nowhere. No, correction: there is one main road (with traffic lights), a Long John Silver's, a Wal-Mart, and an interstate highway exit toward Columbus, which is an hour away. And I am here to learn how to—what else?—massage a thousand-pound horse.

There is no sign of any other human life as I get out of the car and grab the bag with my notebook and pens out of the backseat. I walk toward the barn and notice a side door with a plaque: "OFFICE." It is the only indication that there might be a real school here. I pull open the door. Two women are sitting at a folding table.

"Are you here for the massage therapy class?" one asks.

I nod, then remember my manners and stick out my hand. "I'm Anthony Guglielmo."

"We're your classmates. I'm Lisa and this is Heike. We're from Wisconsin." Three students? The owner had told me they only allowed small classes, but this is personal attention at its finest.

Neither Lisa nor Heike has training in massage therapy, but both work as stable managers, so they have extensive experience riding and taking care of horses. As they talk about their jobs and the people and horses they know in common, I feel more and more out of my element. About the most experience I've had with horses was when I was a little kid at a neighborhood fair and I kept hunting for quarters so that I could have just one more ride on a horse who was being led back and forth down a chalked-in line.

Just then, the door opens and a woman in her forties wearing jeans and a T-shirt walks in. She introduces herself as Patricia, our instructor and the owner, the woman with whom I spoke on the phone. She tells us about herself and the other instructor—both are licensed massage therapists and sports equine massage practitioners—and about the farm, which is her home where she lives with her husband, daughters, cats, and dogs (which she admits to regularly massaging, too—she even offers classes in feline and canine massage).

She then hands each of us a three-ring binder. I am alarmed at first by the massive amount of material, but as I flip through the pages I realize it is mostly basic information on massage, such as the techniques of effluerage, petrissage, tapotement, all things that I know inside out and practice daily. As I watch Lisa and Heike try to soak up the massage definitions—all of which are new to them—I feel that I just might be able to hang in there.

What surprises me most, however, is that the equine massage techniques are quite interchangeable with the techniques I use on people. I haven't actually thought about it before, but now it seems to click into place: living beings are not all that different from one another.

Included in the binder are numerous drawings of a horse's anatomy, complete with lists and descriptions of the muscles and how they all work together. I thought that after I had graduated massage-therapy school, I would be done memorizing muscles. I didn't anticipate that this would be anything but hands-on training—but here I am, again staring at a list that we are going to be tested on.

"It's absolutely vital to know how a horse's body works and to understand the intricacies in order to understand the problems," Patricia says. As I look over the diagram, I realize she is right. It's a common misperception that a massage is just rubbing. A medical massage is something far beyond, and in order to help serious problems you've got to really understand the location of the muscles, and which muscle affects what, and how the entire system is connected. There really is no way a person can just go in and start massaging a horse, or any animal for that matter, without understanding its anatomy.

Then Patricia passes out colored pencils. "The best way to learn the horse's muscles," she says, "is by coloring."

We begin corresponding the numbers to the various muscles on the diagram and color them in so that we can distinguish one muscle from the next. I am familiar with the coloring lesson—we did the same in massage-therapy school with a special anatomy coloring book.

We spend the rest of the morning at the table, learning about the muscles—specifically synergists and antagonists, muscles that work with each other and muscles that work against each other. We also learn about the skin—the largest organ on a horse—and the unique nervous system (not present in humans) that controls the skin. If you've ever seen a fly land on a horse and noticed that the horse's skin twitches, then you've seen that nervous system specific to the skin working—a horse's skin can move on its own, unlike ours.

The class is as intricate as my anatomy and physiology class in massage therapy for humans, and the horse's muscles and bones and movement are just as detailed.

After our lunch break, it is time to venture into the barn. Lisa and Heike are excited; this is their area of expertise. I am a little nervous—if I get stuck with a horse who is in a bad mood and decides to bite off my finger, there goes my career.

Patricia leads us through a side door and into the main barn. On either side of a center aisle, five horses wait in their stalls.

"Anthony, you take Lacey," Patricia says, motioning toward a white mare with peanut-sized brown spots. "Lisa, you've got Sonata, and Heike, you take Zantana."

I walk over to the far stall and stare at the horse. She stares back. She is quite unique-looking, with a yellowish-white mane and a black-gray patch on her nose. Lisa tells me the horse is an Appaloosa.

"The first thing you are going to want to do," Patricia says, "is to size up your horse and evaluate its personality. If you are describing the horse's size, you don't do it in feet and inches as you would a human, you do it in 'hands.' An average measurement for a horse is about 15.2 hands, which is what Lacey is."

Lisa and Heike are already patting their horses on the neck and between their eyes, and talking to them as if they were old friends. I am still standing a good two feet away from Lacey's stall door, my hands intentionally behind my back.

"Next," Patricia continues, "you look at five different characteristics: the eyes, the profile, the nostrils, the mouth length, and what's called the whorls or swirls. Nice round eyes indicate friendliness."

Lacey does have nice round eyes. Phew.

"If the profile is straight, as opposed to something called a Roman nose," Patricia says, pointing to another horse whose nose bulges out in a comically Roman slant and hook, "then that indicates an uncomplicated horse."

Lacey's profile is nice and straight.

"Long nostrils tend to mean the horse is intelligent."

Again, Lacey checks out okay.

"And the last thing to look for is the markings on their forehead. Whorls and swirls look like pinwheels. You don't necessarily want to be working on a horse that has more than one marking."

I peer at Lacey's forehead—only one pinwheel; a good first horse. I find it odd, yet amazing, that you can tell so much from a horse's face alone. If only humans had those same characteristics, imagine how different dating would be: the two-swirl men or women would be found out right off the bat, and there'd be no surprises, no "I thought she was different," or "I thought I could change him"—there'd be far less divorce, that's for sure.

"Now after you size up the horse, you want to greet it," Patricia says, walking over toward Lacey and me. "First, you can't be standing across the room."

Lisa and Heike titter as Patricia takes my arm and leads me up to the stall door. "Then, you breathe into the horse's nostrils." She leans forward and exhales into the horse's nose. The gesture looks odd to me, but Lisa and Heike are quite familiar with it and do the same. "This is how the horse gets a sense of you. Amazingly, they can know you by your smell."

"Which may be unfortunate for them," I say, "I had some pretty strong coffee this morning." Patricia laughs as she moves out of the way so I can greet Lacey. I lean in and, mimicking the motion, breathe into the nostrils. The horse breathes out on me, her breath smelling sweet and rich.

Our next lesson is putting on the halter and lead rope. Of course, Heike and Lisa can do it in their sleep, and they try to stifle a laugh as they watch me struggling, trying to be gentle, trying not to bend the horse's ears. Finally, Patricia comes over and turns the halter around. "It works better if you put the horse's nose through the small hole, and buckle it over the top."

I practice leading the horse out of the stall into the open center aisle, called the breezeway. From the wall hang "cross-ties": two chains with snaps at the end; these attach to metal circles on Lacey's halter. The cross-ties aren't tight enough to prevent movement, but will keep the horse from walking or running off.

"Let's start at the mandible," Patricia says.

Tentatively, I rub my hand over the horse's jaw to get

the feel of it. Then I slowly begin moving my fingers in soft circles so that the horse's skin moves with me.

Usually, when I work on a person, I don't look at my hands. I often close my eyes and use my fingertips to "see." The hands can detect the slightest abnormalities that the eye, just looking at a body, never could. But now, with Lacey, I am scared to even blink. Will this horse sense my fear and turn around and bite me? Exactly how much latitude will these cross-ties allow? I wonder if, by the end of the week, I will still be nervous.

Each day is broken up so that we're in the classroom in the morning, then go into the stable to practice what we've learned. We move section by section: the neck is one lesson, then the shoulders, chest and foreleg, then the hindquarters. I identify each spot on Lacey, then do gentle massage, not deep-tissue, just surface rubbing to warm up the horse and to get a feel for the different muscles. Lacey stands as still as a statue and I figure she is always the horse assigned to the novice of the class.

Back in the classroom on the third day, we cut out strips of felt shaped like the muscles and stick them to a diagram of a horse taped to the wall: an adult version of pin-the-tail-on-the-donkey (er, horse). We go through each and every muscle, layer by layer. Then we head out to the stable and put what we've learned together, until we've covered the entire horse, mane to tail.

For our final test, we write all the muscles on Post-it notes and are led into the stable. It is a stifling hot

day, ninety degrees indoors at least. Patricia has a large
fan going but it seems to hardly stir the thick air.

Instead of getting to work on Lacey, I am assigned
Sonata: a black mare, 15.3 hands, with a white star on
her forehead. A "star," I note, has nothing to do with
swirls—which can indicate that a horse may be trouble.
A star is just a white spot, a color marking. Sonata has
big round eyes and nice long nostrils, although she does
have a Roman nose—is that going to mean she'll be
somehow complicated or even difficult?

"All right, you've got to work with me," I whisper as
I breathe in Sonata's nostrils. The horse stands motionless as I pull off the first Post-it note—easy, the pastern.
I bend down and stick the note to the horse's ankle.
I walk round and around, locating the muscles, and
pressing the Post-it notes onto the horse. I am acing the
test. Suddenly I see the Post-it stuck to the flexor tendon slide off. I walk back around to restick it when the
Post-it stuck to loins slides to the ground. Suddenly they
all start sliding off and I am standing in a puddle of
yellow Post-its. Patricia is snickering.

"I guess Post-it notes don't adhere that well to a
sweaty horse," she says, mopping off her own brow with
a bandanna. "Don't worry, I've been watching you. Con-
gratulations, you labeled everything correctly."

Later, I work on Audi. Audi is a thoroughbred—the kind
of horse that races on the flat, like in the Kentucky
Derby. He is sleek, with well-defined muscles that show
that he is made for running—and he's tall: 17.2 hands,

which means that his back is higher than the top of my head.

Audi fails Patricia's checklist for determining if a horse is going to be easy to work on. His eyes are beady; his face is long, with a Roman nose; and he has two swirls on his head—so he'll have a tendency toward unexpected emotional reactions.

What is worse, Patricia asks me to massage Audi in his stall rather than leading him into the breezeway where I'd have more room to work, and—more importantly—room to get out of the way if he decides to bite or kick.

"I know it's unsettling," Patricia says, "but you are going to have to work on a horse just like Audi one day and this is the only way you'll learn how."

I muster up my courage and enter Audi's stall. I know I can't show him how nervous I am so I stand tall, take a deep breath, and, under the watchful eye of Patricia, begin the massage. I push my thumbs into his crest (at the top of the mane, where the mane meets the neck) and make tiny circles in the muscles. Suddenly someone a few stalls away drops a bucket and it clangs against the cement floor. Audi is startled, his forefeet come off the ground in a rear kick. I fly out of the stall. My heart is racing. Patricia runs over.

"Are you all right?" she asks.

I nod. I am fine—unhurt, just shaken.

"Good. Now go back in there and finish," she says.

My chest is still pounding as I shake my head.

"You've got to show that you're in command. You cannot—hear me?—*cannot*—allow a horse, or any other animal, for that matter, to think he's got the upper hand. You don't have to be nasty about it, but you do have to show them that you're the boss."

Reluctantly, I take another deep breath, compose myself, and walk back into the stall. I do a hurried job with the massage, but I still finish, although I vow that I will never again work on a horse I feel I can't trust.

"For today's lesson," Patricia says on our fifth day, "we're going riding." Lisa and Heike grin; they are used to riding every day and have been missing it.

"That's really not necessary for me," I say, but Patricia shakes her head—no way I can weasel out of this.

"It's important to be able to detect problems when you ride. Then, after you massage the horse, we're going to ride again so you'll feel the difference."

"But I'm really never going to be—" I try again.

Patricia cuts me off. "You'll be amazed at what you're going to feel, Anthony."

No doubt about it, I am scared. I'm paired with Lacey again and I hoist myself onto her back, mimicking only what I know from watching *The Lone Ranger*. I feel like I don't belong in the saddle. Suddenly Lacey begins walking, and I know that Lacey knows exactly who is in control. I have "rookie" written all over me.

"Just let her follow the others around the ring," Patricia calls.

We all walk around the outside of the ring. After a few minutes I realize that this isn't so bad, after all. Lacey's brown-spotted ears keep flickering back as if she is listening to me. She *is* listening: when I tug on the reins to turn left, she turns left; when I tug right, she goes right.

"OK, now kick the horse to get her to trot."

"I can't kick her."

"It won't hurt her."

But I still can't bring myself to do it. Besides, I don't want to trot. Walking is just fine by me.

"Now see if you can detect areas of stiffness or places where the horse is not getting a full stride," Patricia says.

I am more concerned about falling off than I am about trying to figure out where massage might be useful. The others are off trotting or cantering while Lacey and I walk around in a circle. The only part of the horse's stride I can concentrate on is making sure it isn't going to go above a brisk walk. Forget about the horse being tense, my whole body is clenched until the moment I finally get Patricia's okay to climb off Lacey.

On the last day of class, we pile into Patricia's station wagon and drive to a barn about a half hour away. It is here that I meet the first two extremes that will go on to characterize a lot of my work with animals. It's here that I'm scared out of my wits, and that I fall in love.

We have already each massaged all five horses at Synergy Farm: a workhorse, a thoroughbred racehorse, two quarter horses, and a pony. Although each one has a different personality, they are all quite accustomed to massage, and are easy to work on. The horses at this new barn are different.

I thoroughly enjoy the first horse I massage: Brandy, a twenty-year-old trail horse with a stiff neck. This is a common problem with some horses who are used for riding: it's sort of the equivalent of human lower back pain—an annoying condition that's the direct result of repetitive behavior. In a horse's case, it's from the tugging of the reins while they're being ridden.

Before the massage, Brandy holds her neck rigidly—she can't move her head up or down, or from side to side, fluidly. For twenty minutes, I do petrissage—deep massage on the muscle that starts behind her ear and travels down to the shoulder. With elongated fingers I make big loops—swooping up, then circling down to create invisible ovals.

After, I watch with a proud smile as the stable hand leads Brandy out of her stall. She holds her neck regally and swings it easily and gracefully. If she were a person who'd come to see me for lower back pain, she'd now be touching her toes.

It is so rewarding to see the near-immediate benefits of massage—even more so on animals than on people, I realize, because there is no placebo effect. When I massage a person, I never quite know how much of the benefit is from the massage or from the simple fact that the person is relaxed. For some people, just *knowing* that they are going to get a massage is cause enough for them to feel better. That's the placebo part—where our brains tell us that something is going to work and because we think that, it actually does. But with animals, there is no advanced thought process going on. There is no power of suggestion. They don't know that their sore muscle *should* feel better after I've massaged them.

So to do a massage, and then to see firsthand that a horse is actually taking a longer stride because I've worked his flank and stifle joint, or that it's holding its neck with proper posture, is proof that the massage is effective.

But then my day turns sour. Enter Rose—and don't be misled by her sweet name. Rose is a miniature Clydesdale, the type of big cream-colored draft horse with the long white "feathers" on its lower legs that the Budweiser commercials have made so famous.

"Where's the miniature?" I ask Patricia, eyeing Rose dubiously.

"Hey, she's about a hand or two smaller than a standard Clydesdale," Patricia says. I am not comforted.

A stable hand pokes his head into the stall as I am greeting Rose. "Just an FYI," he says. "Rose is in a downright nasty mood today, a real tizzy."

It is another stifling hot day, especially in the barn, and especially in jeans, which we have to wear because of the flies. Cautiously, I begin working on Rose. As I make my way down her back and start to squat, I take my hands off the horse so that I can pull up my jeans, which are sticking to my legs.

Since my hands are momentarily off Rose, I have no advance notice as to what is about to happen. Normally, with my hands in place, I will feel the horse's muscles contract, and be alerted to get out of the way.

Suddenly Rose is lifting her hind leg and swinging it straight toward me—a full-blown cow-kick, the most dangerous and powerful kind, aimed right for my knees. By sheer luck, and because my hands are on my knees, my reflexes take over and I catch Rose's leg in my hand. I give it a yank before I let go.

Patricia is watching with wide eyes. "That was a good save."

"No," I say, "that was a lucky save."

I head toward the stall door, but Rose moves directly in front of me to block my way. I push my fist into her rump—which won't hurt her, but which will make her listen and pay attention to me. "You want to push me?" I say. "Watch, I can push back." I am annoyed now. Rose pushes at my hand; I push back. I brace my leg against the wall for extra leverage. Finally, Rose backs off and I quickly maneuver around her and out of the stall. "I gave you a massage and this is how you thank me?" I mutter as I shut her stall door.

After Brandy and Rose, I want to call it quits. But there is only one left to go: a palomino named Chester, who was used in roping and riding competitions and has been here ever since a steer-roping contest when he was gored by the steer; that was Chester's final competition. He now lives out his days in this boarding stable. As I study the six-inch-long jagged scar on the horse's chest, my heart goes out to him. Despite his injury, he stands tall and has maintained his muscle tone even though he no longer works. I spend much time poring over his sore muscles. When I reach the scarred area I gently place my fingertips on his skin. He twitches and I back off for a few seconds before gently replacing my hand. He flinches again, but I hold my hand there, letting him know it is okay, that I am aware this is a sensitive spot, and that I'll take it gently. Chester lets me delicately massage around the scars. He is patient and gentle. If I could fit him in my Honda, I would take him home with me.

But instead I leave Circleville alone. I think about the two extreme situations you can encounter when dealing with animals: you can absolutely fall in love, as I did with Chester; or you can be terrified, as I was with Rose. Each animal has the ability to affect humans in either of these ways; likewise, humans can have the same effect on animals. Despite some of my experiences today, I like to believe that dealing with animals is sort of like looking in a mirror—if you show respect, respect will be reflected back.

I drive through the night back to Long Island and, at long last, to Champ.

After I return home, I call Sylvia to tell her that I am now a certified equine massage practitioner. She lets out a high-pitched "Well, bless your heart!"

A couple of days later, I embark on the true test. I pull on jeans and a T-shirt and drive out an hour east on Long Island to a small town called Wading River. As I pull into the lot at the stable, I see Sylvia standing out front, waving furiously. She is wearing jeans and a blouse and riding boots and I think she is going to tackle me with a hug when I walk over. Instead, she just grabs my hand and holds it.

"Thank you from the bottom of my heart for coming, Anthony," she says. "I can't wait for you to finally meet Champ."

She leads me into the stable. On each side of the aisle, over a dozen horses stand in their stalls munching on hay or dreamily gazing off into space. At the far end is a large riding arena. Sylvia stops in front of a stall halfway down.

"Here he is," she says; I am not exactly sure if she is talking to me or to Champ.

Champ is a chestnut bay, about 15.3 hands, who looks as if he were ready for a night on the town. Sylvia had him freshly bathed, groomed to the hilt, with his mane and tail brushed and even braided.

"Grooming relaxes him," Sylvia says, "and besides, I wanted Champ to make a good impression."

Champ has nice round eyes, a white diamond on his forehead—with only one swirl—and white socks on all four legs. Overall, good signs that he'll be pleasant to work on. As I was taught in school, I approach Champ by breathing into his nostrils so that he can get a general feel for me, the horse version of a handshake.

But as I lean close to his face, my stomach drops; there are the telltale signs of abuse: a scar across the bridge of his nose and jaw where his mouth had been wired shut.

"No animal should have such scars," Sylvia whispers. "Besides the beating, I also heard that Champ had been tied up, but I have no idea where or how."

I have a strong suspicion I will find out.

"I'm going to leave you two boys alone now," Sylvia says. She leans in close to me, "I'll be watching from down there. I don't want to distract Champ," she murmurs, as if she doesn't want the horse in on her little plan.

As Sylvia walks away, I place my hand on Champ's forehead, between his eyes, and gently rub.

"Here goes," I whisper, feeling uneasy and excited at the same time—it is just me and this horse, no instructors to guide me. I pick up Champ's lead line and lead him out of the stall and into the breezeway. If there is one thing I came out of school feeling strongly about, it's that I don't like massaging horses in their stalls, no matter how big or roomy. In the breezeway, neither of us will feel penned in; Champ will be able to see what's going on, have more room to move around, and still be under control at all times. And it will be easier for me to get out of the way if there are problems.

As I'd been taught at school, I clip the cross-ties onto Champ's halter, which will keep him from running off, but will still allow him enough slack so that he can move; I keep them loose so that he won't feel as if he is trapped or tied up—this is important: I don't want Champ to have any memory or association of his days of abuse during the massage.

I start massaging the back of Champ's neck using effluerage, a basic circular motion that works the surface of the muscle to warm up the area. Almost like a kitten, Champ begins to melt under my touch. As I rub, he stretches his neck, pulling it down, then lifting his head—it is as if he knows this will enhance the massage. I work his neck up to his mane, then head down his back. I take my thumb and glide it into the muscle. If I feel a tight spot—a sign of tension—I press my forefinger and thumb and slide them back and forth. Champ lets out a huge sigh, yawns, stretches his head, then shakes.

Sylvia is standing far off to the side, but I can still

hear her mutter to herself: "I have never seen that horse so relaxed."

I work the top of his head—the poll—right between his ears. Most animals, especially dogs, love this spot; I know that since dressage horses spend so much time tucking their chins toward their chests, the poll is often very tight. I massage down to the crest, through the mane, into the neck, all the way down to the withers. I then move back to the jowl, just underneath his jawline, and run my palms straight down the length of his neck to get a good myofascial stretch. Then I do something to increase the circulation called "angel wings" or "V-wings," where I put my hands flat against the horse, my fingers touching, and keeping my fingertips in place, I push my palms outward, making an inverted V. I do the angel wings all up Champ's shoulder, then on the bicep and tricep muscles in his front legs.

And then something amazing happens: Champ turns his head and begins grooming me, nibbling on my hip, using his soft lips to gently pull at my jeans. I know horses groom each other as a sign of affection and re-spect, but in all the work the instructors and my fellow students did at school, I had never seen a horse groom a human. As I move down his back, he stretches to groom my back. Sylvia, from the corner, gasps.

I move my way down to Champ's legs. It's always amazed me how a 1,200-pound animal can stand on legs like spindles, but it's the massive muscle in the hip that really supports them. As I massage down, Champ gives a little shake, as if he were concerned about where I am headed. Could this be a trigger of a memory of being tied up? I concentrate solely on his right leg and he stands still as a statue. I give his leg a good stretch by placing my hand behind the knee joint, holding the pastern in the other hand, and leaning my body weight forward, I can feel the tension release.

Then I do a circular motion with the leg, called circumduction, which will open the shoulder joint and allow a greater range of motion. If you place your hand behind a horse's knee and rub down the leg, a horse oftentimes will lift up his leg. Holding the leg, I draw it to the side, making a circular motion, first clockwise, then counterclockwise. After the stretch, I let go of Champ's leg, but instead of placing it back on the ground, Champ lets his bent leg just hang there, as if it is too relaxed to support his body.

Champ allows me to move him around at my will. He seems lost in a faraway place, as if he's turned himself over to me and has completely stopped paying attention. On his hindquarters I use a chopping motion called tapotement, which is like karate chops, only instead of just using my hand, I use my entire forearm. Then I take his tail, and without grabbing or yanking, I wrap my fingers around it at the very base and pull. It's as if someone cupped you under the base of your skull and gently pulled upward, so that your entire spine stretched—it is a form of traction.

In Champ's case, it works: Champ's spine actually straightens. Many therapists don't watch body language, which is a mistake. This is why working on animals is so difficult—you've got to watch their bodies because that's all you have. Champ can't communicate that the stretch felt good, but by being tuned into the subtleties of his body, I can see the positive effect.

I want to try a back stretch, lifting from the belly. This is a feel-good stretch, sort of like arching your back, and I have a strong sense that Champ will be willing to try it. I squat, as if I am about to lift something heavy, then reach my arms under Champ's gut. With my hands securely wrapped around his belly, I try to straighten my legs. Champ takes to it immediately and arches his back.

For the very last portion of the massage, I walk around front to do his face. His eyes look heavy, as if he has just woken up from a nap. I rub in a circular motion around his cheeks, nostrils, and lips. You don't usually notice a horse's lips because their big teeth tend to overshadow them, but their lips have this almost primordial softness, like velvet.

I let Champ's head hang over me as I work down the front of his chest, the pectoral muscles. Then Champ lifts his head and gently rests it on top of mine. This is the most endearing gesture—I can almost hear Champ whispering: "I'm yours, you won me over, I'm your friend for life." Champ is no longer a 1,200-pound horse. He's become a family dog. He is breathing nice, long sighs. His head, like a sleeping baby's, grows heavier and heavier against mine. I learned a lot at the certification school, but this reaction, this emotion, was never in any of the material we covered.

I am through with the massage, yet Champ is still in a sort of meditative state, so when I gently move my head from under his, he shudders, as if I have jolted him awake. I unhook the cross-ties and lead him back to his stall.

As of yet, there has been no indication of Champ's traumatic past. There is only one more exercise I want to do that is a nice way to end because it induces the horse to stretch on its own—but it is also a little risky because it's done in the stall, not out in the open, and the horse can't be tied or restrained with cross-ties.

The exercise requires a prop and I reach into my bag to pull out a carrot. I slide it into my back pocket, careful not to let Champ see. Then I lead him into the stall, make a circle, and have him step sideways so that his left side is against the wall. I take the lead rope and draw him back so that his rump is up against the back corner. Then I hold up the carrot, allowing him to take a bite so that he knows it will, eventually, be his to eat. As he is chewing I bring the carrot down to the ground, luring his head to follow. Little does Champ know it, but I'm not teasing him so much as getting him to do a neck stretch. I bring the carrot back up to knee height, then slowly move down so that Champ stretches his head all the way down in between his hooves. Upon successful completion, he gets to finish off his reward. I nab another carrot from my bag and hold it near his flanks so that he turns his head to the right, stretching his shoulder, neck, pectoral, latissimus dorsi. This completes the stretch on Champ's entire right side, so I lead him over to the opposite wall to line him up for the left-side stretch.

As I try to back him into the corner, he suddenly, and for the first time today, refuses. Something has triggered a memory—I knew it would come out, and here it is.

He fidgets and is no longer calm, but flustered. He won't follow the carrot, but instead walks forward. I back him up and he walks forward again. I back him up again and he does a bit of a dance showing that he doesn't want to cooperate. I don't know if I should continue—should I respect the fact that this horse has been abused and was traumatized?

I decide the only way for him to get over his anxiety is to help him work through it.

"Champ, back up," I say firmly. "Let's go, boy." Reluctantly, he backs up and we stretch the left side, the one that must have taken the brunt of abuse. I want to break the cycle of memories. This is obviously the position he was in when he was tied up. I want to show him that the abuse is over, that he can be in this position and nothing is going to happen, he's just going to get a good stretch.

Even though the massage is technically over—we have worked every aspect of his body—I don't want to leave Champ on this negative note, as I know that animals remember what you do last. So I begin to gently work his back again, doing the strokes in the areas that he enjoyed.

"No one's going to hurt you ever again," I whisper.

When Champ is relaxed again, I leave the stall and gently close the door behind me. Sylvia walks over and says, "I just want to let you know that I've never seen Champ act that way with anyone other than me, and even then, it's rare that he'll show that much affection."

Not only is the massage beneficial for Champ, but I feel an incredible sense of accomplishment. I performed an entire horse massage without needing a teacher standing over me. I knew what to do and I had allowed my hands to do what came naturally.

I continue to massage Champ on a weekly basis. Soon, Sylvia allows me to come to the stables without her, she knows she can trust me to be alone with Champ. One day, when I walk into the stable, there's only Champ and one other horse I have never seen before. The other horse is a large, very dark brown, almost black, mare who's a little overweight. She's in the stall directly across from Champ's. Since I am going to be working on Champ in the breezeway, right next to where her head hangs out of her stall, I figure I should go say hello. I walk over to give her a little pet on the head, but as soon as I extend my arm, she immediately spins around and bounces her rear legs as if she is going to kick me. I jump back. I don't understand, have I scared her?

As soon as my heart stops pounding, I go over to Champ's stall, lead him out, and set him up in the breezeway. The dark horse has turned back around and again has her head sticking out of the stall. One of the hooks from Champ's harness is right next to her stall, only a few inches from where her head is. I know she can sense my fear, so I decide to try one more time to make peace. I reach my hand toward her head and again she spins around. I back off, quickly hook Champ's clip to the wall, and walk around to Champ's far side.

I start working on Champ's neck, but as I massage, the mare leans her head over, takes the cross-tie in her teeth, and pulls, drawing Champ toward her. I yank it back, and continue massaging. Again, the horse pulls at the cross-tie. Again, I yank, and it becomes a tug-of-war between me and a very mean horse.

Through all this, poor Champ—who's trying to stay out of it—is caught in the middle, being pulled back and forth. There's nowhere else for me to hook the cross-tie to, so I try to ignore the other horse. She continues to antagonize us and Champ continues to sway— he's drawn toward her when she pulls, then back toward me when I pull. Despite all the distraction from the other horse, Champ is letting out deep sighs and nuzzling my shoulder, proof that he's still enjoying the massage.

I finish the left side, but I hesitate before moving. I need to work Champ's right side, but that means I will have to have my back to the other horse. I know that when you're in the company of a distrustful horse, you never turn your back to it. My only option is to try once again to make friends with the mare. Holding my breath, I go over to her, talking gently, "Hey, girl, that's it, I just want to say hello." She allows me near her and cautiously I blow into her nostrils and touch her forehead, rubbing in between her eyes. She lets me stroke her jowls and I can't believe this is the same horse that not more than twenty minutes ago had tried to slam me. I play with her chin, letting her feel my hands and see what they are doing. Is she at ease with me because she has seen me working on Champ and has seen him enjoying it?

A stable hand walks in and sees me near the mare.

"Be wary around Cocoa," he cautions. "She just had her ovaries removed. Cysts. She's fine now, but suspicious of everyone because she's had nothing but needles for the last couple days. I wouldn't go near her myself."

So that explains it. Once she saw what I was up to, and that I wasn't a threat to her and that Champ was actually enjoying what I was doing, she was okay.

I go back to massaging Champ and Cocoa doesn't pull the tie once. I make a mental note to never forget this incident, for it is a strategy that I can use in the future: if ever I have to massage more than one horse at the same stable, I will know to take the one with the nicest personality and massage it first, in plain sight of the other horse. By the time I am ready to work on the more difficult one, they will both have been eased— either that or the second one will succumb to what I believe is sort of like animal-peer pressure (if Champ was nice and sweet, then I can be too). Animals, either through communication or instinct, understand—here is the evidence, in black and white.

I continue to massage Champ on a regular basis. Champ returns to the show ring, although it's not likely he'll ever be the top show horse that he once was. No matter, he is more relaxed, less jumpy, and his posture and stance are much improved.

Sylvia is no longer pestering me. She is so pleased, however, that she has given my name to everyone she knows. So all her horse-owning friends are calling . . . calling . . . and calling.

2

Helping Cindy
Part I

I had only touched a dolphin once before, when I was a teenager and we were visiting Sea World. I was chosen from the audience to hold a rope and the dolphin dived over it in a graceful arch—I was so close I was able to see the dolphin's muscles flexing. Afterward, I got to pet Shamu—but just a pet seemed like taking a bite out of a candy bar and having the rest yanked away.

And now, here I am, feeding herring to a dolphin who is anxiously bobbing in the water just a couple inches from the edge of the pool where I'm kneeling.

Spending time with these beautiful sea mammals had been my dream—so much so that when Cathy and I were planning a vacation to the Florida Keys, I called several dolphin programs—from Sea World to the zoo. If I could do massage therapy on a horse, and the horse could benefit, then why not try massage on other animals? Unfortunately, not many of the dolphin programs saw it from my point of view.

"If you want to swim with the dolphins, you have to pay to swim with the dolphins," was the general response I received.

The Dolphin Research Center was different. I had read that they are a not-for-profit organization that has a program where terminally ill children can swim with the dolphins. I spoke with Lynne, the Center's medical director. "Your dolphins act as therapists for much of the day," I said. "Take it from me, there's no doubt that therapists themselves need a little T.L.C. every once in a while."

Lynne agreed and told me they had one dolphin in particular, Cindy, who was in great need of massage therapy. Lynne invited Cathy and me to come for a tour and to meet the dolphins. I was ecstatic—I was going to be able to do hands-on work with dolphins. I had no idea at that point, however, just how much Cindy actually needed healing.

I also had no idea that the sight of this one ailing dolphin would literally change the course of my life, fueling a career I had never even thought existed—let alone was possible for me to do.

———

We arrive at the Dolphin Research Center first thing in the morning. It is nestled right on the coast of Grassy Key, and the dolphin pools are in the Gulf of Mexico. Long underwater gates section off the pools from the rest of the Gulf. The gates are not so much to keep the dolphins in, but to keep predators—namely, sharks—out. On our tour of the Center, Lynne, who is tall and tan and has a gentle, yet enthusiastic, way with the animals, introduces us to the seventeen dolphins that live there. She calls each one over by his or her name and a special whistle signal.

"Tursi!" she says, following it with a long tone on the high-pitched whistle that's much more audible to dolphins than to humans. Suddenly Tursi breaks through the water.

"Well, hello there," Lynne says. Tursi is the daughter of Mr. Gipper, who is better known as a stand-in for Flipper in the original movie. She's also the oldest dolphin born here—she'll be turning twenty-six soon. "We lovingly call her 'Whopper' because she happens to be—how should I say it—a plus size. She's nine feet long and weighs over five hundred pounds. Tursi, say 'hi' to Anthony and Cathy."

Tursi waves her flipper.

Next up is Tursi's son, Talon, who's nine years old. "Talon has had to deal with a very overprotective mother," Lynne explains. "Tursi wouldn't let him out of her sight until he was nearly two years old. He had to wait until he was four before he was allowed to play with the other young dolphins in the lagoon." Lynne gives Talon a hand signal and he obediently lifts himself straight up and begins "walking" on the water with his tail. This defiance of gravity seems almost magical to me.

"The apple doesn't fall far from the tree," Lynne says. "Tursi has always been our fastest tail walker, but her boy is catching up." Lynne tosses Talon a fish and he does an impromptu flip. "Just like Mom, you show-off, you!"

The trainers—mostly tanned women, their sun-streaked hair pulled back in ponytails—begin to feed the dolphins the first meal of the day, pulling fish out of plastic buckets.

"We have the best staff," Lynne says. "We're a non-profit organization so no one here works for the money; we do it for love of the animals, first and foremost."

It's obvious in the way the staff greets the dolphins; Dana, for example, who works in the PR department but who trains the dolphins on the side, makes her rounds, saying hello to each and every dolphin. She can tell the dolphins apart in a split second, sometimes, just by their voice as they click and squeal.

"How do you know who's who?" Cathy asks.

"I had a feeling that's what you were going to ask," Dana says. "Actually I will grant you that they all look very, very similar, but once you get to know them and you spend a significant amount of time around them, they look as different from each other as we do. See, Delphi's on the right, he's larger. He also has white scarring on his snout. That's sort of indicative of older age. Being so curious by nature, they don't have any appendages to probe around for things so they do all their probing with their snout. Little nicks and dings here and there builds up that scar tissue, so it's not uncommon for a dolphin in a natural environment to have a whitish snout."

"Oh, I see it," says Cathy, "there on his nose."

"It's actually not called a nose," Lynne says.

"Mother Nature gave dolphins a nose job," Dana says.

"She moved the nose to the top of the head to facilitate breathing. And that's where dolphins make noise from as well."

Delphi lets out a series of clicks, as if on cue.

"So if that's the nose, where's the blowhole?" Cathy asks.

"The nose is the blowhole," Lynne says. "It's a common misconception, but they are one and the same. Of course, it doesn't help that they are called the bottlenose dolphin when they really don't even have a nose."

We all chuckle as if we're caught in a game of Who's on First? Delphi imitates us with more squeals.

"They have fantastic hearing too," Dana says. "That tiny dimple behind their eye is their ear, yet they can hear even when they're underwater."

"But what I think is most amazing," says Lynne, "is their echolocation, their sonar."

Dolphin communication is still a great mystery. Dolphins, like whales, project sound waves through the melon, their forehead. The sound waves will bounce off an object and come back to the dolphin in the form of echoes. By analyzing these very sophisticated echoes, they can tell the size, shape, and density of the object. The U.S. military has tried desperately to mimic echolocation, but cannot quite figure it out.

"In a sense," Lynne says, "they can see without even opening their eyes. So on a day like today, when the waters are murky, they can just flip on the echolocation switch and navigate."

A teenage girl, one of the first guests of the day, walks by and points to the dolphin hovering in the water. "Is he sleeping?" she asks.

"That's Rainbow, he's watching. Quite possibly resting," Lynne says.

"How do they sleep?"

"Dolphins don't sleep—not in the unconscious way that we do. If they did, they'd have to have some sort of autopilot that would float them to the surface for air, and then submerge them again."

"So what do they do?"

"Dolphins don't breathe involuntarily. They have to be conscious, or at least partially conscious, in order to breathe. So what they do is hold their breath—for up to ten minutes—submerge, and rest on the bottom. Then they come back up for air."

"That's incredible."

"Some scientists believe that the dolphin brain is made up of two identical parts. Half shuts down to rest while the other half stays alert. If you look at a dolphin closely while it's 'resting,' you'll see that its eyes are open and it's looking around."

Lynne gives three short signals on her whistle and a smaller dolphin swims over, then, like a firework, leaps and does a spiral high in the air. The sunlight creates diamond sparkles on the spray of water from her tail.

"Oooh," Cathy and I coo.

"That's Aleta," Lynne says. "She's our most famous resident. She's been in so many commercials and music videos that she has her own portfolio. She absolutely adores the attention and even pushes other dolphins out of the way so she can be sure to be on film. Aleta's also a gymnast—she's even invented her own move. We call it the Famous Flying-Forward-Tail-Walk-Alligator. I'll have her demonstrate later, but in the meantime, Talon wants to play a game with you."

We walk out onto a pier, then step on a floating platform that juts into the dolphin pool. At the very edge, we kneel; the platform, like a boat, bobs and dips with our weight.

"Okay, hold your hand out," Lynne instructs. I outstretch my arm and hold my hand flat. "Now, whatever you do, don't move your hand."

I can see Talon in the distance, swimming over—his mouth is wide open.

"He's not going to bite me, is he?" I ask.

"Just don't move your hand."

The closer Talon gets, the more apparent it becomes that he's not going to close his mouth. My mind is racing: this dolphin's going to bite me—a hundred teeth can do serious damage. Cathy lets out a little gasp as the dolphin's gaping mouth hovers over my hand. My hand is in his open mouth now, and he encircles it, like he's teasing—or torturing. Then, in a split second, he turns and swims away.

"So this is a game of chicken!" I say.

"You got it. Now Talon's going to want to go again. Remember, don't move your hand."

We play one more round. Talon's open mouth traces my hand.

"Okay, now, on this last time, pull your hand away."

"Anthony," Cathy says, "you heard that, right? Pull your hand away."

I smile, hold out my hand, and as Talon's mouth approaches, I pull back—just as all one hundred teeth come clashing down.

"Now I'd like to know how you discovered that the third time was the charm?" I ask.

"You can ask the thumbless guy over there," Lynne jokes.

Our mood becomes more somber as Lynne leads us to Cindy's pool. Cindy is the newest addition to the Center. She came from another facility in Florida that went bankrupt and was forced to give away their dolphins.

The sight of Cindy makes me flinch. She is all hunched over, as if she has a terrible stomachache and can't straighten up. The muscles on her sides are so contracted, they're rippled. She is also very skinny— weighing in at around four hundred pounds, which, although it sounds hefty, is underweight for a dolphin, which usually weighs at least a hundred pounds more. It tears at my heart—her awkward, labored swimming, the way she just bobs with the current around the pool.

"Do you think you could try to help her?" Lynne asks.

"I'd have to study up on dolphin anatomy, and then I'd love to try."

"How long are you in the area?"

"Only another two days."

Lynne's face drops. "Cindy's incredibly shy," she says. "That was actually one of the tip-offs that something was wrong. Usually dolphins live and play together in what we call 'pods.' They also tend to associate easily with people. Cindy's different. Because she's in pain, she doesn't warm up to people well. Since you've never worked on any dolphins before, I'd want you to spend at least a week getting to know her so that she can feel comfortable enough to allow you to touch her. I'm sorry."

As sorry as Lynne is, I am more so—not only because it has been my dream to work on dolphins, but because this animal could use my help. I watch Cindy as she bobs in the water, her body contorted in its arch. I know that until she's helped, I won't be able to rid her from my mind.

When Cathy and I return home from Florida, I begin reading everything I can about dolphin anatomy. I also call every aquarium along the East Coast. From Massachusetts to Connecticut, the answers are the same: "You want to *massage* our dolphins? No. We don't let people *massage* our dolphins." *Click.*

But at the New York Aquarium, the senior animal trainer isn't so curt. "I'm sorry," she says politely. "We won't be able to allow that now, but I'll keep your name in our files in case an opportunity does arise."

I figure this means I'll never hear from them again.

Not even two months later, the phone rings. It's the New York Aquarium's animal supervisor, Hans Walters.

"I know you called about massaging a dolphin," Hans says. "But we have another animal here that I think could use your help."

3

The Walrus on My Table

I awake in the middle of the night from a dream that I am being smothered by two thousand pounds of blubber. I sit up abruptly. A few weeks ago, the dream would have seemed absurd, just as surreal as a dream where aliens landed or where I could fly. My clock glows 4 A.M. In two and a half hours I'll be on the road, making the trip to Brooklyn's Coney Island from my home on Long Island. By 9 A.M., when I pass through security at the New York Aquarium, my dream may not seem so off-the-wall.

I am going to do what no one else has ever tried: I am going to massage Nuka, a walrus whose rear flippers are impaired.

The day that Hans called, I thought it was a joke that my friend Bill was playing on me.

"We have a troubled walrus here," Hans said. "Nothing conventional seems to be working. She's having difficulty using her back flippers and can't swim or move normally. We were wondering if you might be able to help her."

I actually laughed at him. "So you want me to rub your walrus?" I said. But when he didn't laugh back, it began to sink in that his request was real.

Nuka, a fifteen-year-old walrus—which is middle age in walrus years—had a tusk removed when it became infected. It's a common occurrence—at some point, many walruses in aquariums have their tusks extracted—sort of like the walrus version of getting wisdom teeth pulled. For Nuka, it was nothing new: her other tusk had been taken out a couple years earlier. Since the infection caused by the remaining tusk was still in her bloodstream, she was supposed to be taking antibiotics with her meals—the pills were hidden inside a slit in the herring. But at feeding time, she would turn her head away from fish she normally relished. The aquarium veterinarian had to give her the antibiotics by injection.

Injecting an over ten-foot, 1,800-pound walrus is not a simple task. Because of Nuka's weight, she had to be given several darts of medication for a dosage strong enough to work. The veterinarians used a syringe on the end of a long pole so that they could give the shot while standing a safe distance away.

After the surgery, Nuka would sit on the rocks all day, hardly moving. When the other walruses would splash her or try to play, she would turn away. The aquarium staff became concerned and moved her inside to what they call a dry holding area—a private cement pen just off the exhibit—where Nuka could be monitored. For over a month, she was served herring and squid, but she refused it. The antibiotic shots, along with frequent, nourishing IVs, also continued. Finally, after forty-two days, the infection cleared. Only now, Nuka's hip muscles—where she had been injected over two hundred times—were tight and contracted.

Because she was in pain, she was sluggish and stiff. The veterinarians tried everything: exercise, anti-inflammatory drugs, muscle relaxers, painkillers. Nuka didn't respond. By the time I received Hans's phone call, Nuka weighed about 1,300 pounds—down over 500 pounds from her normal weight.

In the week after I'd talked to Hans, I tried studying everything I could on walrus anatomy. I needed to locate an anatomical drawing of a walrus so I could figure out which muscles were involved and where they were situated—but it seemed that no drawing of a walrus existed. Marine biologists and veterinarians had done necropsies—the technical term for an animal autopsy— of walruses and recorded their results, but none had taken pictures or made drawings of what they saw. I asked Hans for help in my search and he called the Bronx Zoo. They began searching, too. Finally, in the zoo archives, someone found a faded, brittle drawing of the muscles of a walrus. The drawing was done in the year 1827; it appears to be the only one ever made.

On a brisk January morning in 1997, I pulled into the aquarium lot. I was going to meet Nuka and observe the extent of her problem. Hans, the animal supervisor, had made arrangements with the aquarium security to let me in. A tall, lanky man in his mid-thirties with a head of wild sandy hair, Hans was waiting for me at the main entrance along with Joanne, the senior animal keeper, who oversees the walruses. We shook hands.

"Thanks for coming," Hans said, then handed me a photocopy of the anatomical drawing. I scanned it quickly: I would need to study it in detail before I could attempt what they were asking of me. He opened a door marked STAFF ONLY and we followed the winding concrete hallway to the back of the walrus exhibit.

I had only seen the aquarium during business hours—kids bouncing from exhibit to exhibit, parents trailing after them with cameras and video recorders; school and day-camp groups winding along, hands linked to form a chain of children who can't get lost or wander away. Now, there was a surreal quiet—no laughter, no oohs and ahhs—just the sound of trickling water from the waterfall at the walrus exhibit, echoing off the stone walls.

The smell of fish grew stronger, becoming as pungent as if we were standing at a wharf with fishing boats coming in.

"We've moved Nuka back into the exhibit," Hans said. "We want to get her reacquainted with the other walruses."

The exhibit is made of rough red rock that simulates a walrus's typical arctic home. Before walking through the entrance, we stepped in a tray of mouthwash-colored antiseptic so that we didn't track any germs or bacteria near the animals. Trays sit out front of most entrances that lead to the animals. The aquarium staff wear high rubber boots and they slosh in and out of the trays dozens of times a day. I was wearing sneakers—Joanne said I didn't have to step all the way in, but that I should wet the bottom of my shoes.

"Nuka! Nuka!" Hans called. "Come."

A walrus turned its head, and slowly made its way to the ledge where we were standing. Scrunching up its face, it strained to heave itself out of the water and onto the rocks. The sight reminded me of an old woman who was slowly, arduously, trying to lift herself from a wheelchair. The walrus spread out in front of me in an awkwardly bent mass.

"Hello, Nuka," I said.

Normal posture for a walrus is much like that of a person lying down—the spine should be straight. At Nuka's hips, her spine suddenly took a sharp turn to the right. She was literally twisted in an "L." If she'd been human, she'd have had third-degree scoliosis—a condition that's not easily fixable.

I didn't tell Hans or Joanne that I thought there was nothing in the world I could do to help this walrus. They stared at me, anxiously awaiting my verdict. Even though I'd learned it was aquarium policy that staffers try to keep emotional distance from the animals—they don't play with them unless it has to do with training, feeding, or basic care; and they don't coo or gloat over cute traits—I was positive by looking at the both of them that emotional distance was impossible.

"I'll at least be able to relieve some aches and pains," I said. "I'll work on her twice a week for two months. If we don't see any improvement, I'll stop."

They nodded, then, after stepping in the antiseptic, led me out of the exhibit and down the steps of the main building to the dimly lit hallway where public observation windows allow you to watch the walruses and other animals in underwater action.

There are four other walruses beside Nuka at the aquarium. They were named by Inuit schoolchildren living in the region where the walruses were found: Ayveq means "walrus"; Uupa means "sea peach"; Kulusiq (or Kulu for short) means "iceberg"; and Tiipaq means "little country girl who went to the big city and came back a woman." The walruses thrust through the water with surprising elegance, considering their massive size.

"See the way they swim, it's called sculling," Hans said, referring to how a walrus rotates its hips side to side to propel itself through the water. "Instead of using her hips, Nuka uses her front flippers—which are normally only used for steering or altering speed."

"So she's relying entirely on those front flippers to move," I said, "and it's causing a tremendous strain on her upper body." They nodded.

"When Nuka's on land, she also resists using her back flippers," Joanne said. "Instead, she drags her entire body with her front flippers."

I told Hans I wanted to take time to study the drawing and we made arrangements for me to come back next week.

Like a horse or a dolphin, a walrus's anatomy is very similar to human anatomy; walruses have hamstrings, quadriceps, biceps—and all in relatively the same locations as a human. So the techniques involved in the massage do not intimidate me. It is Nuka's size that worries me most: if I touch a sore spot and she decides to turn on me . . . I envision a cartoon scene where Wile E. Coyote is standing directly on the X when a piano comes falling through the air and—*splat!*—flattens him.

The following week, Hans meets me at the front entrance and leads me back behind the exhibit. Joanne waits at the exhibit door. She's in her mid-thirties and always wears her red, sun-streaked hair pulled back. She holds a shiny silver pail of herring and squid that she'll try to feed Nuka while I attempt to work.

I look at Hans, then Joanne. "Well," I say, "here goes."

Nuka is already out of the water, waiting.

"Nuka, tuck," Hans says gently, using a verbal command the walruses are trained to know. Slowly, Nuka inches into position: on her stomach, back arched, flippers at her side. She winces; her breathing sounds strained, as if getting into the simple position is an exhausting feat.

"I'm going to feed her so that she'll be slightly distracted and more relaxed," Joanne says, squatting down next to Nuka's face with the bucket of fish. "Thatta girl," she says softly. She dangles a fish and Nuka slurps it. I rest one hand on top of Nuka's back—a safety precaution: if Nuka is going to move abruptly, I will feel the muscles tense and will be given a slight warning to get out of the way.

Before I massage a human patient for the first time, I run through a list of standard questions: Are you feeling pain or soreness? What is the degree of pain? Is it radiating, shooting, dull? What areas are tender? How long have you been having symptoms? Any history of pain or injuries? I also try to gauge how tense or relaxed the patient is, how open they are to being touched, and what areas are more sensitive than others. Of course, with Nuka, getting any of that information up front is impossible. I have to glean it through trial and error.

I decide to work on Nuka's side first, slightly above where her hips are bent. That way, she can get used to me touching her—and *I* can also get used to touching her—without getting too close to areas that might send her reeling.

I'm worried that I won't be able to feel any muscle tone under her inch and a half of blubber. I reach out and rest my hand gently on Nuka's side. She seems not to even notice. Although I'm wearing surgical (or plastic) gloves, I can tell her skin is cool and moist and rubbery. I press a little harder. Nuka continues slurping fish. I had expected the blubber to be loose and jiggly, but instead it's firm and shifts easily under my pressure. Amazingly, I feel muscle.

Unlike in humans, the fat on a walrus—the blubber—is an entire separate layer that sits between the muscle and the skin. When I press, the blubber displaces—as if I were to dunk my fist in a bucket of water, the water level would rise on each side. In humans, fat cells are interspersed between muscle cells; there's no displacement, so it's actually difficult to get at the muscles of an overweight human—more difficult, I realize, than that of a hefty, blubber-encased walrus.

"She's used to people touching her," Joanne says.

"She's been here, around people, since she was three weeks old."

When I massage humans, I have a certain sense of control, as if there is an unstated agreement that they relinquish their muscles to me. I assure all my patients that I believe in gentle massage—that it should feel good, not painful. The challenge of massaging an animal is somehow communicating this philosophy to them.

I begin rubbing Nuka's side in a gentle circular motion, applying enough pressure so that she knows I'm there, but still being gentle enough so that I communicate, "This is supposed to feel good; this is going to help you."

"Nuka was abandoned when she was just born," Hans says, "off the coast of Alaska, in the Prudhoe Bay. There could have been a storm and she got separated from her mother, or maybe there was a polar bear ambush and the mother ran one way and the calf ran the other. Whatever the reason, she was literally left there to die. The U.S. Fish and Wildlife Service does regular aerial surveys of the region, and they spotted her. If we hadn't brought her back here, she'd have starved."

The aquarium staff had asked me not to draw attention to anyone regarding Nuka, at least in these initial days of treatment. It seems that whenever an animal there or at the zoo is sick, animal-activist groups come out in record numbers to protest or picket, shouting that this is what happens when animals are kept in captivity. I had heard this many times before from the Dolphin Research Center as well.

The truth is that many of the animals in the aquarium

were abandoned by their mothers in the wild or—like the beluga whales and some species of seals—are protected species. The aquarium has actually kept them alive and is fostering their species by mating them.

Crouching beside Nuka, I work my way down her side.

"What does her name mean?" I ask.

"Nuka means 'little sister,' " Hans says.

"Okay," I say. "I'm ready to try her flippers."

Joanne glances at Hans; he nods. Cautiously I place my hand on Nuka's hip. I feel her tense and I immediately lighten my touch so that my hand is just brushing her skin.

This is an animal's way of communicating to me— and I've learned how to listen. Nuka's giving me a signal: when she tenses, she's telling me she feels pain. When I lighten my touch, I communicate back to her that I have understood.

Before I know it, I'm moving my hands across her bent hip and flippers—this walrus is letting me massage her! I rub in small circles for another fifteen minutes. Then Joanne says, "Feeding time is almost over—I've got about five fish left." I can't believe it—I have been massaging a walrus.

Nuka's next feeding time is at eleven-thirty; we decide that I should attempt more massage then.

In the meantime, I stroll around the aquarium, which is open to the public now. I pass the penguins and the pools with the beluga whales—which are a protected species—then the seals and the sea lions, and then the dolphins. I wander indoors down the dimly lit halls where you can watch the animals in the shark pool. Different-sized sharks circle through the water while sting rays and various sea turtles float among them. It's like a conveyor belt of exotic sea creatures looping around and around. Nursing sharks gather in a corner, grazing the tank floor. In the center of the tank rests an ancient-looking safe, coated with barnacles, that was taken from the *Andrea Dorea* shipwreck. In what seems like slow motion, algae sways in the current as sharks swim by. A sea turtle inches right up to the window I'm standing at. It tries to figure out how to move forward but keeps bumping into the glass. I'm directly on the other side, yet the glass is so thick, I don't hear a sound.

I walk down the corridor to the underwater viewing windows of the walrus pool. Occasionally, a walrus will stop and stare through the window at the humans. The walruses, despite their size, aren't at all threatening; in fact, they seem playful, even mischievous. They forage on the bottom of the pool with their faces and come up with whiskers full of algae. They cover their eyes with their flippers and play what seems like a game of peekaboo. I observe how they "scull," making sure to memorize what I see so I can contrast it to the way Nuka moves.

Two walruses swim right up to the window and, eye to eye, wrap their flippers around each other and bring their heads together. At the same time, a group of two dozen schoolgirls in plaid uniform jumpers saunters over. They gasp at the sight of the walruses, then they shriek: "Grrrosss! They're KISSING! Ewww!" The girls are right, the two walruses are—literally—sucking face.

People's bodies are stiffest when they wake up in the morning; Nuka is no exception. As I start to massage her during the second feeding, I feel a difference. She is much more relaxed and limber than she was earlier. I position my legs so that I'm straddling her rear flippers, then I inch my way up, kneading her spine as I go, until my legs can stretch no farther. I work my way back down her hips, completing the massage; her posture doesn't change.

I leave the aquarium smelling like raw fish. Even after I shower—and rinse the bottom of my shoes—the odors linger. The stench in my car, too, is a testament to the fact that, today, I have massaged a walrus. Twice.

The other walruses are taking turns playing in the jet spray of water that shoots off and on throughout the day. They are like little kids, pushing each other under the sprinkler and racing to see who can get there first. One walrus is off to the side, gingerly treading water— it's Nuka.

I walk around to the back of the exhibit where Hans, Joanne, and three other animal keepers are waiting by the door.

"Hi, Anthony," Joanne says. She speaks softly, yet exudes a sense of confidence and control around the animals. "The other walruses are going to be fed at the same time, so when they are done, we've got to wrap up too."

A lot of psychology takes place at the aquarium; many of the trainers and keepers have psychology degrees rather than marine-biology backgrounds. Psychology is important especially around feeding time. All of the animals naturally develop their own hierarchies—so the dominant animals might try to interfere with the more submissive ones' eating. The trainers and keepers make sure that all the animals are fed at about the same pace. This way, too, each animal can be fed its individually prepared diet.

During the first week's initial massage, I wanted to get Nuka used to my touch; now, I am going to get down to work. On one side, Nuka's hip muscles are severely contracted; on the other side, her muscles are very stretched out. As Nuka makes her way onto the rocks and into the tuck position, I decide I'll massage her contracted right side to try and loosen those muscles up, then I'll exercise her stretched-out left side to see if I can get those muscles to pull back the spine a bit.

Again, Nuka is a good patient. It seems strange to describe such a big creature with such bristly, long whiskers as "sweet," but no doubt, as walruses go, Nuka is sweet and friendly. She slurps up fish, and as we're nearing the end of the twenty minute feed time, she gives me what Joanne refers to as "a present"—Nuka has a bowel movement on my hand.

"It's a good sign, Anthony," Joanne says with a laugh. "It means she's relaxed."

I continue massaging Nuka twice a week. Three weeks pass. On an overcast day in the beginning of April, I decide to walk through the corridor where you can view the walruses underwater before I go outside to meet Hans and Joanne. I spot Nuka immediately—singling her out by the shape of her head, which is rounder than the others'. Suddenly I do a double take: that can't be Nuka—that walrus is using its rear flippers to swim. I lean closer to the glass. Nuka also has a bigger build than the others; it is—without a doubt—Nuka.

I race outside, through the hall, to the back of the exhibit. I see Hans pulling on his boots.

"Hans, Nuka's swimming with her back flippers!"

Hans shakes his head. "That can't be Nuka. You're probably mistaking Tiipaq for her."

We step in the antiseptic tray and walk out onto the exhibit.

"Nuka!" Hans calls. Nuka's head pops up from under the water. "Nuka, come!"

Nuka begins swimming over—using her rear flippers.

"I don't believe it," Hans says. He breaks into an astounded smile.

———

By the end of May, Nuka's spine has straightened just enough so she has some use of her rear flippers, but it's still severely bent and she isn't sculling, or swimming, the way she's supposed to. She's also regained some weight—about three hundred pounds—but she's by no means cured.

I call a friend of mine who's a chiropractor and who has a special certification to work on animals to see if he can suggest anything.

"Do a good stretch," he says. "Twist and flex the hip."

"How do you stretch a 1,600-pound walrus?" I ask.

He chuckles. "That one I can't help you with."

When I arrive at the aquarium for Nuka's massage, I pose the hip stretch to Hans. He raises his eyebrows, contemplates for several seconds, then says, "Let's give it a try."

We walk into the walrus exhibit and Hans calls Nuka over. Slowly, she eases her way onto the rocks.

"How about if you push her left side down and I'll grab her right hipbone," I say.

We face each other on either side of Nuka's hips. Hans pushes down while I position myself squarely—my legs bent as if I'm posing to lift something heavy. I slide my hands under her and grab onto the anterior-superior-iliac spine—the pointy part of her hipbone.

"Ready," I say. "On the count of three. One . . . two . . . three!"

I use all my strength to lift her hip. Hans pushes down on her opposite hip to provide the counterforce. Suddenly Nuka's head shoots up. She whips her neck around and lets out a bark that echoes off the rocks. Then she raises herself up with her front flippers. I immediately let go and jump back.

"You all right?" Hans calls.

Hans gives her a command and Nuka barrels back into the water and swims away as best she can.

When I return three days later, Nuka will have nothing to do with me. As I go to put my hand on her, she waves her front flippers and fidgets to the point that I can't even touch her. She even barks at me.

"I'm sorry," I tell her. Of course, that doesn't make a difference. "She doesn't want her massage," I report to Joanne, who ends up having to feed Nuka while the walrus is in the water.

"Do you want to try to massage her at the next feed?" Hans asks.

"No," I say. "I guess she's very sore. I don't want to touch her—I don't want her to associate pain with a massage."

I walk around the aquarium in a daze. Was the stretch too much for Nuka?

I do stretches on people all the time, but usually I have them push into me as much as they can. There's a level of communication: they know to push until they've reached their limit. A "limit" is something that's difficult to gauge with an animal. Had I gone past Nuka's?

At home that night I can't concentrate. Cathy can sense I'm troubled. "Don't worry," she says. "It's common for people to be sore after a massage—so why not a walrus?"

"But I don't believe in making people sore—that's not how I do massage."

She puts her hand on my shoulder. "I know."

The next day is booked with appointments, yet I can't take my mind off Nuka.

At night, I hear Nuka's bark echoing in my head. Walruses have deep, reverberating voices, which you've heard if you've seen the movie *Jurassic Park*. Steven Spielberg recorded the sounds walruses make and used them for the dinosaurs' roars.

I hardly sleep, and decide to drive back to the aquarium early the next morning. I arrive at eight-thirty, just as the staff is preparing the animals' food in the "kitchen"—a stainless-steel room that's sparkling clean. Large basins line the wall and the faucets are more like shower heads—elevated, with a powerful spray. The fish is stored in huge coolers and is fresher than fish in most restaurants. It's top of the line quality too—everything in the aquarium is; even the water in the tanks, which is brought in from the Atlantic Ocean, is funneled through large filters to remove all impurities.

Suddenly I hear a familiar voice. "Anthony."

It's Joanne. Her eyes are wide. "Have you seen Nuka?"

My stomach drops.

"Is . . . is she okay?" I stammer.

"Come with me," Joanne says. I'm trying to read something—anything—in her voice but it's the same soft-spoken tone as always. I follow her to the walrus exhibit. My heart is racing. *Please let Nuka be all right.*

Joanne pulls on her boots and stomps in the antiseptic tray. I dip my sneakers in. We walk out onto the rocks.

"Nuka!" Joanne calls. I hold my breath. A wavy brown form emerges just under the surface of the water and sculls over to the ledge. It can't be Nuka—she's too bent to scull.

"Nuka, come!" Suddenly Nuka's head pops up like a periscope. She hoists herself onto the ledge—first her

front flippers, then her rear ones, and then, I see it—
although I don't believe it.

"Joanne . . ." I say, before I'm rendered speechless.
Joanne is beaming.

I stare in disbelief. Nuka is spread out right in front
of me and her hips are—unmistakably—straighter.

Joanne gives Nuka the command to roll over and the
walrus lounges on her back as Joanne feeds her squid.
Nuka slurps them down, one by one—looking like the
walrus version of Cleopatra draped on a chaise, a servant popping grapes into the queen's mouth.

4

Boys Will Be Boys

While working with Nuka, I had asked the director of animal training every week when I'd be able to work on the New York Aquarium's dolphins. I felt like a little kid with a one-track mind, pestering "Are we there yet?"—but I couldn't help it. Working on the aquarium's dolphins—who were very healthy—would be my ticket to working on Cindy.

For nine months, the aquarium's answer to my constant plea was: "Not yet." Then, one warm September day, after I had given Nuka her massage, "not yet" finally became "yes."

As I walk the length of the New York Aquarium's outdoor dolphin tank, The Boys pay me no mind. Martha, the senior dolphin trainer, has called them over with a hand signal—first Tab, then Presley.

Tab and Presley are Atlantic bottlenose dolphins. Tab was born in Florida and is now seventeen years old, middle-age for a dolphin; Presley was born on the other coast—California—and is twelve, an adolescent (and it often shows). Both dolphins were born in aquariums and met when they were put together in a petting pool in California.

Before Tab and Presley came to live in New York, the aquarium had three good-natured, very easygoing female dolphins. The females lived there until they reached breeding age. Normally, the aquarium would have bred them, but that takes much time and supervision, and the aquarium was already occupied breeding their beluga whales, which are a protected species.

So a breeding loan was arranged. The aquarium would swap its females for two males in California who were already accustomed to being in the same pool together. The females would have a good, new home in a tropical climate, with plenty of male dolphins around— female dolphin Shangri-la, it seemed.

The dolphins on each coast were suspended on stretchers made specifically for transporting dolphins. Using a crane, the stretchers were hoisted into the air and carefully lowered into large crates filled with just enough water to support the animals. Then the crates were loaded onto cargo planes, along with a crew of trainers and veterinarians, who constantly monitored the dolphins.

When Tab and Presley arrived, the aquarium was in for a slight surprise: the female dolphins had been sugar and spice—but The Boys were an entirely different story: each male dolphin was trying to show up the other. Martha generally used clinical terms—"Each dolphin was trying to express his dominance"—although one day I heard her mutter: "Typical males."

It was happening even in the training sessions: Martha and the other trainers would be giving hand signals and Tab or Presley would lunge and seem to rough house.

Ironically, this type of misbehaving or aggression is common in dolphins who've had human audiences, like Tab and Presley. Let's say a child is standing at the petting pool dangling a capelin in the air to feed to the dolphin. As the dolphin swims over, it opens its mouth for the fish to be dropped in. Suddenly the child sees one hundred teeth—each a half an inch thick—coming straight at him.

The child's natural reaction? To pull away.

The dolphin's natural reaction? To lunge toward the fish.

Even if there's no fish around the petting pool, the dolphins often get what the trainers refer to as "positive reinforcement." When the dolphins show their teeth, onlookers ooh and ahh or clap. When the dolphins splash, onlookers laugh. When the dolphins lunge, onlookers shriek. The dolphin is getting attention—reactions to its behavior, even though it's not exhibiting the desired behavior.

On the other hand, when a dolphin is being good—swimming quietly, minding its own business, staying out of trouble—it's ignored by the onlookers; there are no shouts, cheers, or jeers. Thus, Tab's and Presley's acquired philosophy: it's no fun being good.

———

The New York Aquarium had already spent almost a year training The Boys when I first met them. The trainers noticed improvement, but The Boys still had a long way to go. Martha had been putting off my request to work on the dolphins because she feared they would nip at or bite me. But finally, she gave in to my suggestion that maybe massage would relax the dolphins and curb their aggression.

When Martha told me that I could finally work on the dolphins, I did something I never do: I canceled my scheduled appointments with my human patients.

"I'm sorry," I explained, "but I'm going to have to reschedule. I just got a once-in-a-lifetime opportunity. I'm going to massage a dolphin . . . No, that's right, like Flipper, a real dolphin."

I was like a giddy child who had finally been allowed to get what he wanted. Every patient I rescheduled was excited for me and made me promise to call and let them know how the dolphin massage went.

I hang around the aquarium, standing in the very back of the packed arena to take in the last demonstration of the day. A lone dorsal fin appears above water, then dips back under. Children jump up and down in their seats. "Look, Mommy! There's one!" The water ripples where the dolphin had briefly taken in a breath of air. If you had blinked, you would have missed it; the children keep their eyes glued for another sighting.

One dorsal fin after another pokes through the water, as if the dolphins know it's almost time to begin and they're warming up the audience. Suddenly a dolphin's in the air, doing a pre-show bow; it's like fireworks: the crowd erupts in unison, "Ooooh!"

"I want to be a dolphin—that would be awesome," one little boy sitting near me says. His mother smiles. "How about a marine biologist, honey? Then you can work *with* dolphins."

"No," the little boy insists, "I want to be a *dolphin.*"

The demonstration begins: Tab and Presley alternate doing nose dives—jumping over ten feet into the air. Martha explains to the crowd that dolphins do these jumps to escape from sharks. "Since they are mammals," she says, "they need to come to the surface of the water to get air. A dive is a great way to grab a quick breath of air without losing speed, plus they can disappear momentarily from the shark's view, and then reappear with amazing force—enough to make a getaway."

Next up are the back floats, where Tab and Presley slap their tails against the water. Then they leap back into the air and back flop with big splashes. Martha explains that these are ways that dolphins communicate. The sound that a back flop makes can travel for miles underwater and warn other dolphins of danger—the original form of long-distance communication.

"Speaking of communication," Martha says, "dolphins don't have vocal cords; all the sounds they make come from their blowholes." She gives a hand motion and Tab and Presley start talking it up in chirps and whistles. The kids in the audience begin imitating.

For the finale, the dolphins launch into the air, gracefully twist, then belly flop back into the pool. The crowd goes wild. People proudly wring out their T-shirts as they herd out of the arena; the water signifies—for all to see—that there had been contact with a dolphin—*they* had been splashed by a real-live dolphin!

Records of human-dolphin interaction trace back all the way to Greek mythology. The story goes that Odysseus' son was drowning in the sea when a dolphin came to his rescue and brought him safely to shore.

I have often wondered just what it is about dolphins that fascinates us humans so much. Is it the surprising similarities—the apparent language and communication, the shows of affection, the intelligence? A fascinating study revealed that if a dolphin is given a mirror, it begins to become focused on its image, or—scientists went so far as to say—on its looks. For the study, a black circle was stuck to the dolphin's side. When a mirror was placed in the water, each dolphin would stare at the circle as if it were quite disturbing. Could this be a demonstration of the very human quality of vanity?

Or maybe our intrigue with dolphins is more one-sided—could it just be that we humans love the eternal smile a dolphin wears, the joyful clicks and back flips and other antics that make a dolphin appear as if it's always having so much fun?

The large arena that had been filled with roaring laughter and anticipation is now silent. The first several bleachers are still damp from the spray of water. I'm standing at the head of the dolphin pool, where the trainers had stood. Martha raises her hands and blows two quick tones on her whistle. In response, one wavy, gray, underwater form appears, followed by another. Each breaks through the water, flashing that perpetual dolphin grin.

I am still surprised how big and intimidating the dolphins appear up close. I had figured after working on the 1,800-pound Nuka, a 600-pound dolphin would seem puny; but they are solid muscle and I can see it flexing and tensing under their shiny skin. Tab is slightly larger than Presley, although Presley has a bigger head. The easiest way to tell them apart is that Presley has light pink splotches on his lips and belly.

A large water-covered step leads into the pool, and for this first massage, the dolphins will come out of the water and lie on the step. Presley is directed over to the side, where another trainer occupies him with a bucket of fish. Martha hoists her hands through the air in a signal, and suddenly, in one swift move, Tab bounces out of the water and onto the step, right at my feet. The salt water runs smoothly off his body.

As I kneel down in several inches of water, I grow nervous. I have been hearing for months how rough The Boys can be, and now, here I am, a total stranger, about to touch them in a way they have never been touched. I hear Cathy's voice in my head: "Are you crazy?" Yet I firmly believe that because my intentions are good, these dolphins, no matter how unruly, will know that and treat me with respect.

Besides, this is my ticket to helping Cindy in Florida.

I gently place my hands, palms down, on Tab's back. I don't rub or create pressure yet, this is just my initial way of saying, "Hi, nice to meet you," with touch. Tab's back is solid. His skin feels cool because the water is only in the upper sixties.

Tab jerks his head around to try to see what's going on, then he wiggles like an antsy child.

"Okay, Anthony," Martha says calmly. "Why don't you slowly back off."

I lift my arms up, away from Tab. Martha allows Tab to slide back in the water. I back away a couple feet from the edge of the deck, and we wait, watching the two dolphins circle the pool.

"I'm going to let him stay in the water, where I think he might be more comfortable," Martha says. I lie down on the pavement on my stomach, my arms and chest leaning over the edge of the pool. Martha directs Tab to line up in front of me, his body parallel to the pool's edge. I take a deep breath and gently put my hands on him. Again, he shimmies, but I keep my hands in place. Slowly, I begin moving them down his side. Although I have been studying books on dolphin anatomy for the past week, he doesn't feel at all like what I expected. His body is like hard rubber, and his muscles are better-tuned than any I have ever felt. He's just a typical dolphin in an aquarium, without an ocean to swim in, yet he is built like an Olympic athlete. I move down his back to get a sense of a dolphin's body and the movement of the muscles. The muscles feel normal—tight, yet not contracted. This means there are no spasms.

After a couple of minutes, Martha instructs me that it's Presley's turn. Because there are only two dolphins, the aquarium must be very conscious of not ignoring one or seeming to favor the other. I know that Presley is the more aggressive of the two, but still fair is fair, and each has to have his brief round of massage for the day.

Without any hassle, Presley lines up next to me

alongside the edge. I lie back down. He has seen what I have just done with Tab, and he allows me to put my hands on him, only he twists his head around. He wants to keep my hands in view at all times. I slowly move up and down his back. His black eyes follow me closely.

"I know this doesn't seem like much," Martha says, "but let's stop here and pick it back up next week." She gives the whistle signal and Presley swims away.

A few days later, before the dolphins' second massage, I walk into the aquarium past the underwater viewing section. I see Tab swim by the window, but where's Presley? Suddenly I notice a large gray form lying motionless on the pool floor. I run up the stairs and outside to the arena where Martha is unlocking the entrance gate.

"Martha," I call, out of breath. "It's Presley, I . . . I think he's dead."

Martha narrows her eyes. "Is he lying on the floor?"

"Yes, and he's not moving at all."

She breaks into a smile. "Anthony, it's all right," she says, her smile turning into a laugh. "He's resting.

"I'm thinking let's try ten minutes of massage on each," Martha says.

I nod. "Sounds good." I kneel down on the step. "I'm going to start at the fluke," I say.

The fluke is the dolphin's tail. It's actually made up of two parts—that is, each side of the tail can move individually, or they can both move together to propel the dolphin through the water. The fluke, along with the flippers, is used as a sort of rudder to turn or direct the dolphin. The fluke is really the power source for the dolphin—it's where propulsion, stabilization, and steering originate. Surprisingly, this integral and powerful body part has no bones, it's pure muscle, tendons, and fibers. Like the walrus, the dolphin's body structure is similar to our own. They have shoulder blades, off which span the flippers—their "arms"—then the tail, coming down into the split fluke, reminding me of legs and feet. The fluke also has many veins; that's where veterinarians go if they need to draw blood from the dolphin.

I want to start at the fluke so that the dolphins won't be able to easily reach around and nip at me. This way, I can get them used to my touch, while at the same time allotting myself a small window of time to roll out of the way if one does turn on me.

Tab waits patiently as I move my hands down his fluke, which feels like an inch and a half of hard rubber. I begin adding more pressure, expecting that as I press, Tab will buoy slightly. But he doesn't move. I imagine pushing into a standing person, like when you brush up against someone's shoulder in a crowd. The person's shoulder—unless it belongs to a world-class weight lifter—will give slightly, sort of move and then bounce back. But Tab doesn't give at all, despite the fact that the water is his only grounding. Using the padded part of my palm, I knead my hands across his spine. Tab occasionally turns his head, more out of curiosity than concern; he's not flinching or eyeing me as if he's getting ready to bolt. I begin to press harder, holding the fluke with one hand and pushing with the palm of my other. I continue with this stroke and the ten-minute massage flies by.

Presley's turn. Again, he doesn't allow me out of his sight. He holds himself at a curve so he can keep his eye on me. He squints and follows, as best he can, my every move. But still, he lets me massage his fluke for the whole ten minutes.

It's the morning of the dolphins' third massage, and I follow Martha into the arena. She is a good ten steps ahead of me, and as she walks around the pool, Tab and Presley—who are on the other side—seem not to even notice she's there. But as I begin to walk around the pool, something amazing happens: both Boys swim over and follow me around to the spot where we had conducted the massages. Do they actually recognize me? Is this their way of communicating that they want my touch? That they enjoy it?

Tab is called over for his massage. He immediately presents himself at my feet. Neither dolphin has yet to be mean; they are just curious. I feel like I am really starting to get to know them. Tab and I seem to be bonding more. He's much more cooperative and laid-back than Presley, who will often purposefully flip buoys at the trainers.

I decide to start working my way a little up the fluke, concentrating on his sides. I do a technique called "thumb glides," where I make small circles along each vertebra with my thumbs. I can feel Tab relax as I'm massaging—the tenseness in his muscles is melting at my touch. Yes! he's finally starting to let go. He even lets his eyes close during the massage.

Presley, on the other hand, is accepting the massage, but still keeps a close lookout. His muscles remain slightly clenched. He's not quite ready to give himself over yet.

"Next time," Martha says, "would you like to start moving closer to Tab's head?" I nod eagerly.

———

It's an overcast day as I kneel down in front of Tab and begin working my hands in a circular motion up to his pectoral fin. Suddenly he lets out a chirping noise from his blowhole. It sounds like a child giggling.

"You hit a tickle spot!" Martha exclaims.

Again, I touch the spot, which is right under his flipper, and Tab wiggles his head, splashes the water, then blows bubbles from his blowhole. I can't help but laugh—it's contagious—plus, the simple fact is funny: I'm tickling a dolphin's armpit.

I notice that from the blowhole forward, they seem to be much more sensitive. As I move closer to his head, Tab begins to completely give himself over to me. He becomes so relaxed, his fluke curls under his body, his head dunks slightly underwater, and his mouth quivers. His breaths are slow and in a rhythmic pattern, like he is sighing, "Ahhh."

Presley still isn't keen about total relaxation. I can feel him start to relax—his muscles loosening and giving, his posture slumping a bit—but then, just as he's getting very comfortable, he suddenly tenses back up, as if he's consciously not allowing himself to let go. If Presley were a human, he'd be a definite Type A.

For the next several weeks, I continue massaging the dolphins. I find certain muscles that are tight from the dolphins' daily work—from the back flips, aerial maneuvers, forward flips, and belly flops that they would perform in the wild, but do on command for the summer demonstrations. They strain their bodies the same way a gymnast would. Martha has noticed that Presley has a slight twist to his jump. I take a look and, sure enough, his muscles on one side are tighter than on the other. I begin to use a technique called wringing, where I line my hands up along their spines and while I gently push with one hand, I pull with the other. Tab has even taken it upon himself to present different spots to me— he'll tilt up his hip, or roll over on his side, or hand me his fin, as if to say: "Right here, massage here."

It's October now and The Boys have recently been moved to the inside pool for the winter. Just moving pools is a very involved process. The outdoor pool is drained until there's only about a foot of water left. Then, the dolphins are placed in the stretchers, which are hooked to a crane, donated for the day by a local crane company. Slowly, the dolphins, cradled in the stretchers, are hoisted into the air. The crane only raises them a few feet off the ground so that the veterinarians can walk along with the dolphins and monitor their vital signs throughout the entire move. The indoor pool has a canvas top that opens; the crane lifts the dolphins and maneuvers through the opening, gently depositing the stretchers into the pool, where trainers are waiting to unhook them.

Because of the excitement from the move, coupled with the change of scenery, The Boys are much more energetic and meddlesome than usual. They're splashing and dashing about. They are sneaking up behind each other, then zipping off. Tab sees me and swims over, wanting to play. Presley doesn't want to play, he just wants attention and he continues to splash and dart from side to side.

I lie down on the pavement on my stomach, my chest and arms leaning over the edge of the pool. Martha directs Tab to line up in front of me, his body parallel to the pool's edge. While I massage Tab, Martha calls Presley to the side of the pool to run through his drills and to give him his daily inspection. She motions for him to turn over so she can make sure he has no cuts or infections on his stomach. Reluctantly, he rolls onto his back, but he splashes at Martha. She tosses a pink plastic hula hoop into the pool and gives Presley the signal to dive through it. Instead of diving, he pushes the ring around with his snout.

"That's it," Martha says. "Time-out!" The dreaded time-out. The animal version of being sent to the corner. I've heard the trainers use it with the dolphins and the beluga whales, but I've never actually witnessed one. As soon as Martha announces time-out, all the humans immediately get up, turn their heads, and walk away.

"You too, Anthony," Martha says.

Tab has been enjoying his massage. Lost in a state of relaxation, he seems stunned as I lift my hands. "Sorry, buddy," I whisper. "Better go talk to your friend over there." I turn away, careful not to look back, and follow Martha down the ramp and out of sight from The Boys.

"I have a feeling it's going to be like this all week with Presley," Martha laments. "He's all excitable from the move."

I sneak a glance over the ledge. Tab and Presley are swimming side by side, back and forth along the length of the pool.

"I think they're having a heart-to-heart," I joke to Martha.

Dolphin communication is amazing. Martha told me that every couple of months, a researcher visits the aquarium in hopes of learning more about how dolphins interact. Once, as I was walking into the arena to do a massage, a short, dark-haired woman was leaving, recording notes into a dictation machine. She had been running an experiment on echolocation, a dolphin's sonar and possible way of communicating. It's likely to take years to collect enough data to really figure it out, the researcher said when I asked what the outcome had been.

After a few more minutes of time-out, we return to the pool side. Tab immediately lines up along the edge so I can continue, and amazingly, Presley presents himself to Martha, eager for her next command. She tosses in another ring. Without missing a beat, Presley gracefully jumps through and turns back to Martha. Spiral swim, she orders. Presley does a beautiful spiral swim.

"So you've decided to be a good boy, after all?" Martha asks him. She pumps her fist (a visual command) and Presley nods.

"Okay, bye, bye," Martha says. Presley waves with his flipper as he swims on his back, toward the other side of the pool.

Martha walks over to me. "Seems Tab here has lectured Presley to knock it off." It was the behavior modification we have all been hoping for—the proof that the work I'm doing is paying off. Martha squats toward Tab. "Was he disrupting your massage?" Tab blows bubbles through his blowhole.

5

Mambo Point and Other Electric Horses

Sylvia has made sure that my name is circulating quite well in the equine world; at the same time, many massage therapists are also familiar with my work on horses and other animals. So it is by word of mouth that I soon receive a call from Mike Sorentino, Jr., who races several horses at Yonkers Racetrack.

"I've got this horse, Mambo Point," Mike says. "He's had a lousy year and we've got a big race coming up. Do you think massage could help my horse win?"

Massage is certainly respected in the human sports arena—every sports team employs massage therapists. The Chicago Bulls, as well as most other sports teams, have at least two full-time massage therapists on staff.

"I can't assure you it will make him win, but it certainly will help him to perform at his best," I say.

The four-year-old Mambo Point is one of Mike's prize racehorses. Mike has bred Mambo himself, using a former champion racehorse and a mare he already owned. At the time the horse was born, Mike was taking dance classes and was learning the mambo.

In Mambo Point's year-and-a-half career, he has raced about twenty times, and has won several of them. Mike feels that he has a tremendous amount of potential; he's just a classic underachiever. By the time I receive Mike's call, Mambo Point hasn't won, placed, or showed in any race for the past four months. Mambo's now set to run in a $40,000 stake race and Mike knows the horse can do it—Mambo's already been entered—but he's exasperated because Mambo *could* have won a lot of races in the past year that he hadn't. Mike can't figure out why Mambo has become so lax.

"When is the big race?" I ask, checking my calendar to see when I can fit Mambo in.

"Soon," Mike says.

"How soon?"

"Three weeks."

That's definitely pushing it. Massage can create quick results, but to really see significant improvement, it needs to be done over time. The body has to be trained—while muscles can stretch and joints can loosen up, the body needs to become accustomed to the new positioning and feeling. This typically takes longer than three weeks. Still, Mike wants to try, and I'm curious to see what kind of results massage can have on this type of horse, so we arrange for me to come to the racetrack twice a week, right up until the day before the big race.

The type of racing done at Yonkers is standardbred racing where the horses are called trotters and the riders sit on a two-wheeled cart, called a sulky, that's strapped onto a harness that fits around the horse's back. It's much slower than thoroughbred racing, which is where the jockey rides horseback.

The two types of racehorses are very different as well: standardbreds, like Mambo, are sturdy and can withstand injuries that would send thoroughbreds to the pastures. They are fuller animals, more meaty, whereas thoroughbreds are leaner and high-strung, like greyhounds—animals born to run, and at high speeds. Mambo and the other trotters may race up to forty races a year, but thoroughbreds and their jockeys won't enter in more than ten races a year.

Equine massage is just as common in the horse-racing world as it is in the show-horse or dressage world (where Champ performs). Massage can help show horses move more gracefully, such as jumping the poles without clipping them. With a racehorse, massage can help to open up a horse's stride so it can perform at its full potential. Massage therapy on a horse can make a difference—even if it's just by that all-important fraction of a second.

It is a cold, rainy February day when I first arrive at Yonkers Racetrack. I sign in at the gate and then I walk down the gravel path to Barn 2A, a green building with a tin roof. I wear several layers and heavy gloves, which I know will have to come off once I begin the massage. In the stable, there are ten stalls lining each side wall. Each stall has a window. The stable floor is covered with hay, and buckets hang from ropes on hooks so that stable hands can fill them with feed. Birds fly in and out, nestling in the rafters. A portable radio is blaring Top 40 music.

Mike comes in from the track, perched on the back of a sulky pulled by a horse he's training. He hops off the back as the stable hands come over to remove the harness from the horse. Mike is in a one-piece, rain-resistant jumpsuit and he sloshes over to me in mud-splattered boots. He's in his mid-thirties, and has short, dark hair and a muscular build.

"Cold enough for you?" he asks as we shake hands. I follow him to the other side of the stable.

"Here's Mambo," Mike says, holding out his hand to the chestnut-colored bay horse standing in his stall, minding his own business. His neighbor in the next stall wants attention, and eagerly bobs its head up and down as I pass by.

"How long will it take for Mambo to show improvement?" Mike asks.

"That's hard to determine, every animal's different. My goal would be to get his muscles to reach full stretching motion."

Mike pats Mambo on the neck.

"He's a good boy. Never gave anyone any problems. He's so easygoing I let my little kids around him."

I size Mambo up: he has soft round eyes, long nostrils, and only one swirl—all good signs. Since my early days at the school I've learned that another way of judging a horse's mood is to watch its ears, which can perk up and swivel from side to side. You have to be careful when their ears fold flat back, which is a sign to get the heck away.

"You'll be fine," Mike says. "I'll check back with you after I jog another horse." He turns and sloshes out of the stable. Right outside the door, a horse is being hosed down and Mike disappears in the rising steam from the hot water hitting the cold air.

Here at Yonkers there is a lot of action in the barn: trainers and grooms leading the horses in and out, tossing them hay, brushing them down, hosing down their legs, trotting past in the carts. There isn't room in the aisle to conduct a massage, so I'll have to do it in the stall. Besides, with so much going on, Mambo will be too distracted if he's in the middle of the commotion.

But working in the stall makes me nervous. The only thing that eases my mind is that I see there are portable cross-ties hanging from hooks in the wall inside of the stall. This way, it will still be close quarters, but the cross-ties will keep Mambo steady, only allowing him to take tiny steps forward, back, or to the sides.

Slowly I enter Mambo's stall and he looks up at me, pricking his ears forward curiously. I greet him by breathing into his nostrils. Then I place my hand on his forehead. He seems jittery. I move my hand up toward his ears and he begins to pull his head away, as if rejecting my touch. Some horses are like this—it's called "head-shy"—sometimes there's a reason for this, like a groom has pulled on the horse's ears, or the horse suffered some sort of traumatizing event; sometimes horses just don't like being touched around the forehead and ears.

Forgoing the rest of the greeting, I hook the portable cross-ties to Mambo. The chains snap into the halter and extend to screw eyes embedded in the wall; I begin working on the poll, which is the area directly behind the ears. Mambo's fine with me touching his head here, it's only when I tried to come at him from the front to touch his forehead that he felt threatened. I head down the mane.

If I met Mambo Point anywhere other than a race-track, I would still be able to tell he is a racehorse: the muscles on his left side are severely contracted from running around the circular track. The horses go around the track counterclockwise, which leads to an imbalance of pulling around the circle—the left side, which is toward the center, takes the brunt of the force. The cart, or sulky, also causes additional tension in the shoulder. It sits right behind the withers, creating a lot of sensitivity and stiffness.

Whenever I touch a tight spot, Mambo flinches and walks a couple steps sideways. Unfortunately, he has plenty of tight spots—he is flinching so much it looks almost like he's dancing. Each time he steps sideways, I step with him. I can tell that my touch is not causing him pain: if the muscle had twitched when I touched it, I would have known that caused pain. But instead Mambo is fidgeting more for the simple reason that he's wary of me. I have to stick with him because it's important that I communicate to him that he isn't going to win; he isn't just able to walk away. And in establish-ing this, I'm also reassuring him that what I'm doing is okay. I know he'll settle down as soon as he feels com-fortable with my touch.

I also know why Mambo has so many sore spots up and down his neck: he's a short-track racehorse. There are two types of racetracks for trotters, the long track, which has two turns (because it's shaped like an ellipse); and the short track, which has four sharper turns. Mambo doesn't have much speed, but he has the agility to turn, which is where he makes up his time. Because the short-track runners are cornering more turns, the left side is constantly pulling and those inside muscles are going to be contracted; in contrast, the right side is overstretched.

One of the reasons Mambo may not be racing well is that his muscles are too tight to have a full, open stride. The more open the stride, the more ground a horse is going to be able to cover, and the faster the horse will race. I press my thumbs into the sore spots. Loosening up Mambo's left side will be the best way to improve his time.

After a few minutes of massage, our power struggle has played itself out and Mambo actually begins leaning into my hands to increase the pressure.

As I massage, a strange thing happens. Little shocks, like static electricity, tingle through my fingertips, only I'm not rubbing in a way that should produce much static. For a fleeting second I wonder if it might be ticks or fleas, but nothing's there—and besides, ticks don't bite so quickly, and I don't think horses even *get* fleas. I chalk the weird shocks up to my imagination and continue working.

I move down to Mambo's front leg, using a technique that looks like a modified version of wringing out a towel, where I move my hands in opposite directions. Then I do something called compression, where I squeeze the muscle between my fingers and palm. I work all the way back up to the inner part of the back leg called the stifle, which is equivalent to the groin muscle on a human. This is a muscle that gets pulled and strained very easily, but it's also an area that horses are very protective of. As I bring my hand near the stifle, Mambo steps away. This reaction is typical. I try again; again, he moves back. This keeps going until he's backed himself into the corner and can move no farther. I'm determined to work that area because Mambo's reaction tells me it's sore and tight. But I need to figure out a way to get there—some massage therapists would just force the massage, but I want to find another technique that won't cause Mambo pain. So I try a different method: I put my right hand on his croup—the place just above his tail—and begin to work the fingers of my left hand into the stifle.

Suddenly I feel a whack on my hand. I glance down: Mambo's four hooves are on the ground, and the whack certainly didn't feel like his tail. I start working again and—*whap!*—am whacked again. I can see all his legs except for the right hind leg. Out of the corner of my eye I catch his right hind leg, at lightning speed, swinging up and knocking my hand. Luckily, this isn't a cow kick, which can be really dangerous and powerful—if that had been the case, I would have been out of there—this was a sharp tap, making it very clear that the therapy was not being appreciated by my patient.

"All right," I sigh, "I get it, this is a very painful area." Time to quit. I switch to his right side to give him a break and repeat the same strokes I did on his left side. As I work my way toward his head, I feel a knot emanating heat—definitely a muscle spasm—near the shoulder.

Mambo turns his head, and for a second he looks like he's had a friendly change of heart and is going to nuzzle me, like Champ did. I'm doing thumb gliding around his scapula, pressing my thumb into the muscles to release them. "Does that feel good, boy?"

But rather than giving me a grooming, Mambo holds out his velvety lips and bites my arm. I jump back with a yell. Startled, Mambo jumps away, and scoots as far from me as the chains will allow. I get out of the stall and in the aisle pull up my ripped sleeves to see if my arm is bleeding. Because of the cold, and knowing that I'd be in an unheated barn, I'm wearing several layers: a thermal shirt, a sweatshirt, and, over that, a flannel jacket. Even with all those layers, his bite has left a red welt, although it didn't break the skin. I've never been bitten by a horse before. During school, I remember the way Patricia directed me after the scare with Audi; I can hear her voice in my head now: "Anthony, get back in there and make it clear to that horse that this isn't the end, that he isn't going to win."

Without allowing myself time to reconsider, I march right back in, place my hands on Mambo's shoulder, and continue with the massage exactly where I'd left off. He brings his head around again, but I'm ready: I stiff-arm him, sort of like a football player who does a strong-arm block. My arm is straight and locked so that his head movement is restricted and he can't reach me. I'm making it very clear that I'm the one in control here; Mambo had better give up. He got me once, but he isn't going to get me twice.

After ten more minutes, Mike pokes his head into the stall. "So how is he?"

"Well, he's tight and sore, and he nipped at me."

Mike scrunches his face in disbelief. "He's never tried anything, not even with my kids."

"Your kids probably never hit a sore spot, especially in the stifle."

Mike nods. "Yeah, those stifles can get pretty sore with these harness-racing horses."

"There was also something else I noticed." I walk Mike around and point out the swelling and inflammation on Mambo's left side, close to his rear.

Mike nods again. "I'm left-handed," he said, "so when I ride I use the whip on the left side and that's where it catches. I just trained Mambo yesterday so that's why the area is tender. Most horses will be sore on the right side since the other trainers are right-handed."

I don't tell Mike about the little shocks I felt when touching Mambo. That I keep to myself, in case I was truly imagining it.

Two days later, when I'm back massaging Mambo, I feel the shocks again. Even when I just rest my hand on Mambo's back, it feels like little pins pricking me.

Mike has asked me to massage two of his other horses—each a different size and temperament. When I start working on another of Mike's horses, Max Table, I feel the shocks too. Max Table is a five-year-old bay mare who is seventeen hands tall—so she's pretty big. She isn't the swiftest, and often has trouble holding her own among the virile young males. She can only run the big track because she has difficulty with the turns— she bangs her knees. Because of this, her legs are always wrapped in poultices made of a medicated mud therapy that will reduce swelling—over the poultice, her legs and knees are wrapped with cotton bandages.

When I walk into Max's stall, she acts as if I've been coming there for years. I introduce myself by breathing into her nostrils and she allows me to place my hand on her forehead. She bows her head as if to say, "At your service, do as you please."

I begin working on the crest of her head. She relaxes immediately, her body becoming as malleable as putty. Unlike Mambo, she seems to recognize I'm here to do something enjoyable for her. Max has the typical problems of a racehorse—contracted left side, stretched right side, sore stifles. But she's a long-track runner so her condition is a little different from Mambo's—she doesn't do as much turning, so her neck isn't as constricted. The main goal with Max is to lengthen her stride, to increase her speed.

Mike told me that Max has a hair-loss condition that the veterinarian said is not harmful, but not fixable either. As I rub Max, her hair sheds like crazy and the cool winter breeze blows the stray hairs around the stall.

Max is very sore at the withers, the base of the neck where her shoulder starts, precisely where the harness sits and rubs. Since Mike and the other trainers ride her, she is tender on both her lower haunches because of the whip. Even though she is sore, she accepts my touch. When I move toward the stifle, she winces, indicating the area is tender, but she doesn't move or dance around as Mambo did.

Because her legs and forecannons, or knees, are wrapped, I can't work on those areas, even though I think it is probably where Max needs massage the most. So I work down to the knee, skip the rest of the leg, resume at the pastern, which is like the ankle. I'm sure they are sore, but she has no objection to me touching her legs.

When I reach under her belly for the final exercise, she gives a nice good stretch, as if that is relieving to her. She seems to enjoy it.

That evening, after I return home, I call Patricia from the equine massage school.

"I have a strange question," I say. "I started massaging a couple racehorses and when I touch them, I feel little shocks. Am I imagining this?"

Patricia laughs. "No, you're not going crazy," she says. "It can happen when you work on horses outside. When you rub your hands, you increase the electrical charge and the charge just keeps firing. You're also not the only one who's feeling the shocks—they go both ways, so the horses feel them too."

"Which explains why the horses were jittery," I say.

"Bingo."

On Monday, I arrive at Yonkers Racetrack carrying an odd item: a box of Bounce dryer sheets. I hook up Mambo to the cross-ties, and before I start massaging, I wipe him all over with a dryer sheet. Then, I rest my hand on his back. Nothing. I begin rubbing. No shocks; just powdery spring freshness.

As I work, I begin to feel that Mambo has finally

accepted me—this is his third massage and he doesn't keep turning around to see where I am or what I'm doing, he just lets me do what I want, except for touching him between the eyes, which, for whatever reason, he isn't crazy about. He even lets me work on his stifle. He is no longer uppity, and he remembers me—he remembers that this is okay and that he doesn't have to suspect me or give me a hard time. But the true test will be the race—that's next week.

The third horse I work on is Ahoy Mate. I am feeling confident because I have won over Mambo, and Max Table has expressed enjoyment from the start—so I don't hesitate to try this new horse. Until I see him.

Ahoy Mate is very dark brown, almost black; his deep-set eyes look mistrusting, and he has a Roman nose. He also has two swirls.

From the moment I walk into his stall, I wonder if there's even a third swirl hidden somewhere. Immediately Ahoy Mate lays his ears flat against his skull and glares at me.

"You've got to watch this one," Mike says, sticking his head in. "Ahoy Mate has a rotten personality, he's always miserable—you look at him and his ears go back. But he can run like the wind, at times. Other times he runs like mud. That's why you're here."

This horse is going to put me to the test.

Now I have already been bitten by Mambo, who Mike thinks is an angel, so his warning catches me off guard. I watch Ahoy Mate closely as I hook him up to the cross-ties. His ears are flat lines on his head: a clear order to get away, and fast. He positions himself so that I am blocked from fully entering the stall. I reach my hand to his forehead to greet him, and suddenly I see his teeth coming at me. I yank my hand away. I need to take a different approach, so I reach toward his jaw. His mouth swoops around, his teeth barely missing my hand. I feel like walking right out, but I think a healing touch will be the best thing for a horse like this.

I move away from his mouth and, standing alongside of him, rest my hands on his mane. I begin doing a push-pull: my right hand leaning into the muscle, my left hand pulling it back. Then I switch directions, right pull, left lean. I do this, walking my hands down his neck from the top all the way to the withers. Muscle spasms—knots and the telltale warmth—are every-where I touch. Ahoy Mate tries to pull away, but he can't go anywhere, so he swings his head around, un-successfully trying to bite me. As I work toward his shoulder, he gets a better idea: he raises his front left foot and sends it straight down on top of mine. Since I have my hand on his back, I feel the action before it actually happens—I feel the muscles contracting and lifting—and I'm able to move my foot slightly so that his hoof only brushes the tip of my sneaker.

I can't let him have the last laugh. I can't leave with him thinking he won. So I decide to work the leg he just stomped. I squat down, but he reaches his neck down to try to take a nip at me. I want to yell at him, "What do you think you are doing, I'm trying to help you here!"

Frustrated, my only option is to tighten his cross-ties so that his movement will be restricted even more. Ahoy Mate doesn't like this and he starts to dance and move around. I speak nicely and calmly, as if nothing has changed, "Come on now, boy, it's all right." I keep talking to him in as soothing a tone as I can muster.

As I work my way down to his hindquarters, he raises his leg to cow-kick, shooting his hoof straight out to the side. I remember the motion I was taught to prevent this kick—the one I learned while working on Rose: I take my fist and push it into Ahoy Mate's hindquarters, knocking him slightly off balance and forcing him to put his leg down to steady himself.

Ahoy Mate even has another trick—he starts walking sideways, pushing me toward the wall. This massage is now getting risky.

When Mike returns from warming up another horse, he pokes his head in. "Is he giving you trouble?"

"You could say that," I answer.

"Don't be afraid to show him who's the boss," he says. "If you need to, cup your hand and give him a whack on the forehead. This will get his attention but won't hurt him."

Despite the fact that I know it won't hurt Ahoy Mate, doubled by the notion that this horse is trying to hurt me with every chance he gets, I can't do it. Bopping an animal on the head makes it harder to reach my goal, which is to ease the horse, improve his well-being, and make him relax. But in this case, with Ahoy Mate, nothing's working. I try to do some more massage strokes, but give up in a matter of five minutes and leave the stall.

Later that week, after I have worked on Mambo and Max, I muster up my courage to try to work on Ahoy

Mate again. As I walk over to his stall, a stable hand is coming out.

"Watch out," he says. "His Highness just bit me."

"So it isn't just me he tries to bite?"

The stable hand gives me an "are-you-kidding?" look.

Ahoy Mate relays no sign of recollection as I enter his stall. I target the same areas, the shoulders and the neck, which are his major sore spots. He is tight and flinches often. When I get to the stifle, he tries to kick my hand. After twenty minutes, I throw my hands in the air and leave his stall.

Once in my human practice, a patient of mine bought a gift certificate for her husband. He was so rigid and tense that after fifteen minutes I stopped and said, "This is defeating the purpose, why don't we just call it a day?" The man was so relieved, he jumped off the table, smiling and casual, as if he had suddenly transformed into a totally different person. This was how it is with Ahoy Mate. He genuinely doesn't want to be touched. It is not my job to force him.

———

On Mambo's third treatment, he finally allows me to work on the stifle. I have devised a new way: I take my hand and begin on his back side, moving down his leg to relax the entire area. Then, I glide my hand up into the coveted stifle. I keep my other hand on his rear, to steady myself. Mambo's willingness does not come a moment too soon: the practice race for the big tournament is tomorrow.

Before I leave for the day, I watch as Mike trains

Mambo. Onto Mambo's harness, he hooks a heavier training cart; that way, when they race with the real one, which is lighter, they move faster. Mike runs Mambo once around the track, then turns him around and jogs him, which is a fancy way of saying he runs him in the opposite direction around the track so that the horse's muscle tone is kept even.

That night, I call Mike to find out how the practice race went. Mike's report: Mambo felt really good coming out, but got stuck behind two others. If he hadn't gotten stuck, he had it in him to win.

The next day I head out to Yonkers for Mambo's final massage before the big race. Now that I am able to get to the stifle, I can do more serious work that will open up Mambo's hind legs, which is where a horse's strength originates.

I work on Mambo during the day, then drive back to Yonkers that night with Cathy to watch the first race in the tournament. We pay the few dollars admittance at the gate, then take the escalator up to the restaurant. At the desk, we ask for Mike's table and the hostess immediately leads us over to a long table with ten chairs next to a full wall of windows overlooking the track, about twenty feet below. Mike's father and a couple of friends are at the far end of the table and we introduce ourselves. From our chairs, we look right over the finish line—the best seats in the house. Speakers are propped everywhere and the announcer comes on, gearing up for the race. I feel as if I were about to watch a child of mine perform the lead role in a school play. My palms are sweating.

Unlike thoroughbred racing, the trotters don't line up in starting gates, but right on the track behind a car connected to a retractable fence. Earlier, when the riders randomly drew starting numbers, Mike picked number six (out of eight)—not the best position considering number one starts the closest to the rail, a definite advantage. The car with the retractable fence starts up, and the horses, pulling the sulky, follow. As the car speeds up, so do the horses—sort of a running start. At thirty-five miles an hour, the gates go up and the car drives off the track.

"And they're off!" the announcer shouts. Cathy and I lean forward. Mambo comes out of the start sixth, but little by little, funnels toward the inner circle, inching his way past the others. Suddenly, as if someone has picked Mambo and Mike up, they are in the lead. I have to double-check the number—number six—it is definitely Mambo. They round the last corner in the first lap. Mambo is leading by a mile.

Suddenly another horse, number two, comes up from behind.

Mambo is still ahead by a full body length.

Then by a nose.

Then they are neck and neck. The finish line is only two hundred yards away. I am afraid to blink. It is a blur across the finish line. Cathy and I leap up, as does the rest of the crowd in the restaurant. When the dust from the track clears, we see Mike turn and lead Mambo to the Winner's Circle. Cathy and I jump up and down, screaming. He won! Mambo has won!

Then the voice comes over the loudspeaker: "The winner, number two, Nose Twitch."

Everyone at the table starts murmuring. I pull Cathy

over to the television monitor and we wait, along with others who are eagerly clutching their tickets.

The replay comes on in slow motion, there is Mambo, there is number two, and at the finish line, it is true—number two has beaten Mambo by an inch.

After the race we find Mike in the stable. He is still pleased. Mambo has gone from the verge of washed-up to a near first-place winner.

"Keep doing whatever it is you're doing," Mike says.

I can't go to the second race, but first thing the morning after, I run out to the corner store to pick up a newspaper. Before I even make it to the register, I have flipped to the sports section and the stats. I run my finger down the list of scores.

Mambo has won.

The store is a couple blocks from my home, but I call Cathy on my cellular phone from the checkout line, yelling with excitement. The other customers turn to give me weird glances.

The tournament is set up in such a way that there are ninety-six horses total. They're divided up so that they each compete against seven different horses in a total of three races. The horses are then assigned points by their performance: three points for a win, two points for a place, one point for a show. Then, the eight top horses compete in the final race for the $40,000 stake. So far, Mambo has five out of a possible six points. Not bad, although there is one horse, English Tudor, who has won both races so far. There still is one more race left to go.

I watch the third race from my friend Bill's home in upstate New York, where I am spending the weekend. In all the years Bill has known me, he never once saw me even remotely interested in races or gambling. Yet now, Bill and his wife Lori, and Cathy and I, sit in front of the television with popcorn and drinks, watching and cheering as Mambo and Mike line up behind the starting cart.

"And they're off!" The horses funnel toward the inside circle because the closer you are to the rail, the shorter the distance, so everyone moves in.

Mambo makes it over—he pulls to the front—he is in the lead as they round into the second lap.

I am standing at this point—jumping, actually—eyes pasted to the screen. This time, there is no question: a cloud of dust blows between Mambo and the second-place horse as he crosses the finish line. I give Cathy a big hug; Bill hugs Lori.

The winner of the next and final race wins the $40,000 purse. Mambo has eight out of nine points. The only horse going into the final race with a perfect score is English Tudor, a beautiful gelding, known for his speed and agility. The odds are against Mambo.

That next weekend, Cathy and I set up in front of the television for the race (it's a wavy, snowy picture because we don't have a satellite like Bill and the race isn't broadcast on commercial stations). We even turn off the phone so nothing can distract us.

"And they're off!"

"Come on, Mambo!" Cathy shouts.

The horses funnel toward the inside, but Mambo is boxed in, trapped behind a slower horse so that he can't

get over. I am screaming at the TV, "What are you doing?" Cathy is screaming too. We are both yelling, yet
there is nothing to be done, Mambo is stuck.

Mike has to slow down for Mambo to get by, but by
then it is near impossible for Mambo to catch up.

English Tudor wins. Mambo comes in fifth out of
eight.

"I'm sorry, Anthony," Cathy says, as if Mambo were
my horse.

Finally, after a half hour of long faces, Cathy snaps
out of it. "Your job wasn't to get Mambo to win," she
says. "It was to get him to perform his best. He did that.
Mambo was a losing horse, and now he's a winning
horse."

Cathy is right. We go out to dinner to celebrate.

———————

Every week, I continue to massage Mambo and Max
Table. I even stick it out with Ahoy Mate and everyone
has noticed improvement. Mambo Point continues to
run well—winning far more often, and seeming much
happier about it. Although from time to time I wish he'd
won that race, and would keep winning all the races, I
realize that it doesn't much matter: what matters is that
the massage helps, and makes him a quicker, better athlete.

6

The Five-and-Dime Ferret

I am standing in line at the pet store, Animals Alive, in Wantagh on Long Island, waiting to pay for fish food. In front of me is a woman holding a baby ferret who is only about a foot long. "This store sold me a defective ferret," the woman complains. "I had it for three days and now it's not walking right."

The pet-store worker, a teenage girl with glitter on her eyes, takes the ferret and sets it on the counter. Sure enough, as the ferret takes two steps, it drags its back legs. I've never much cared for ferrets, mainly because of their odor. It's like a b.o. that, much like the *Seinfeld* episode, has the rare ability to transfer from the original "b" and attach itself to any and everything else it touches. I learned this firsthand when my friend handed me his ferret right before I was leaving to go out to dinner with my wife's family. Throughout the rest of the night, I stank. I could smell myself, it was so bad.

"What did you do?" Cathy hissed at me when her parents weren't listening.

"It's the ferret."

"The *what*?" But now, looking at the ferret as he drags himself along, I feel nothing but sympathy for it.

"Did anything happen to it?" the pet-store worker asks.

"Of course not, what would have happened?" the woman snaps. "It's defective and I'd like my money back."

"Are you sure it didn't get dropped or stepped on?"

The woman is becoming agitated and answers just a bit too defensively: "I bought it for my son. He never, ever would have done that. Impossible."

"Ma'am, I'd like to take it back, but we wouldn't have sold you a ferret that couldn't walk, and you wouldn't have bought it either."

"It wasn't like that when I left here, but it *became* like that—all on its own." The woman's voice is starting to rise and the line behind her is growing, so with strained agreement, the girl behind the counter takes back the ferret and refunds the woman's sixty dollars.

I am next up and I quickly lean over the counter. "I work with animals," I say. "I'm a massage therapist and I think I can help this ferret. Do you mind if I take a look?"

The girl raises a glittered eye at me, then hands the ferret over. I cradle it in my arms and it leans its head against my forearm.

"Is it a male or a female?" I ask.

The girl peers at the ferret. "Boy."

I nod. While I hold the ferret with one arm, I take my other hand and begin to glide my thumb up and down his spine. When I do this with people, my thumbs will glide rhythmically along the vertebrae, sort of like going over road bumps—unless there's a problem. In this case, the ferret is no different: my thumbs glide along until—*thump*. My thumb hits a jagged spot, a misalignment, right above his hip.

I know I need to first loosen up the muscles around the hip, which are strained from the trauma. I do effluerage on the surface, then move into deep tissue work. The ferret sits in my arm, completely surrendered. After his muscles are warmed up, I take his hips and gently rotate them, hoping to stretch the muscles.

Suddenly I hear a click. Then, as if the joint has just popped back in the socket, the ferret begins moving his legs, wiggling them as if he were making sure they are still there.

I massage his back muscles for another ten minutes, then hand him back to the girl. She has been helping the line of customers behind me, so she sets the ferret back on the counter to see how it is. Sure enough, the ferret is walking on all fours, without dragging. The girl looks at me with wide, sparkly eyes.

"How'd you do that?"

"Massage."

She calls over the owner and tells him what happened. He is in his mid-thirties and is friendly and genuinely concerned about the animals. I show him exactly what I did and give him instructions to continue daily for a week: first, gentle circles, then push deeper, then

take the hind leg and do a range of motion, just rotate
it in the hip socket. The owner asks for my card.

He gives me a discount on my fish food.

By the next week, the ferret is sold.

7

Rudy the Humpbacked Penguin

It's autumn and there are new babies at the New York Aquarium: six tiny, squirmy penguins, called chicks, each covered with a layer of charcoal-gray down, and each weighing only a few ounces. The smallest of the chicks—the runt—is Rudy.

When penguins are born it is impossible to tell their gender, so when Rudy hatched, the aquarium veterinarians didn't know yet if it was male or female, but they did know Rudy was not healthy. Rudy had a rare condition called kyphosis, or in lay terms, a humpback.

Because of Rudy's bent-over condition, breathing, for the baby bird, was difficult. Most of the time, birds born with malformations such as a humpback don't survive very long.

Penguins are the largest group of flightless birds. They mostly live in antarctic regions and divide their time between water and land. Their bodies have unique features that enable them to do this: because of an ingenious network of blood vessels, penguins are able to get out of the water and walk around on the ice without their wet feet freezing.

Hans leads me down the back hall, then through a corridor I've never been in before. Suddenly I'm seized by a scent that smells like we've just entered an overused public bathroom.

"What *is* that?" I ask, wincing.

"That," says Hans, "is the lovely aroma of penguin guano."

When I say penguin guano smells, I don't mean smells like zoo animals or like a barn. I've been in many a dirty stable on a hot, humid day when it does not smell too pleasant, but even that is nothing compared to the penguins. This guano reeks—a putrid ammonia-based odor that seems to seep into your hair, your clothes, your skin. It amazes me how something so small and cute can create something that smells so badly.

"No one breathes through their nose around here," Hans informs me. He unlocks a heavy door and pulls it open. Suddenly we are in the midst of the penguin exhibit—surrounded by smooth brown stone, lush green plants, a pool of water, and dozens of feathered heads that turn inquisitively toward the door.

Despite the noxious odor, the penguins are adorable. Curious to the point of being nosy, they wobble around, hopping up and down on the rocks, occasionally losing their footing on the slick stone and sliding into the water.

When penguins are in the water, they either tuck their wings so that they resemble ducks swimming in a pond, or they stick their wings out, which is how they cool themselves off. Their dense waterproof feathers retain much of the heat generated by their high metabolisms—which protects them against antarctic winters—but the downside is they grow very warm in the summer. The coolest place on their body is their armpits. When they lift their wings, the breeze or the cool water against their underarms is refreshing.

An aquarium worker is cleaning the penguin exhibit. She's donned a wet suit and is wielding a large hose, spraying off the rock with a forceful stream of water. Her nose is crinkled from the stench. The penguins gather behind her, enjoying the mist from the hose. They lift up their wings as if to say, "Mist my armpits, please."

Hans turns to me. "Are you ready to meet Rudy?"

He leads me out the door and back down the hall to a little room that is directly behind the exhibit. There, a penguin keeper, Lisa, is sitting at a desk, a silver pail of fish to her right, and three neat piles of vitamins to her left. She picks a herring out of the pail, and with the dexterity of a surgeon, she slits it lengthwise with a tiny knife and inserts one vitamin from each pile: vitamin B, vitamin E, and Stress Complex—after all, living the life of a penguin takes energy. She drops the "laced" herring into another pail at her feet. The supplements serve not so much as an added boost or a new-age ritual, but simply as a means of replenishing the vitamins and minerals that were depleted in the freezing and thawing process of the fish.

Behind Lisa is a makeshift playpen lined with fake green grass mesh, the kind you find at outdoor pools. In the far corner stands Rudy, a gangly six-week-old South African black-footed penguin, who's less than a foot tall. Rudy hasn't yet grown into his wings or webbed feet and he wobbles toward us, practically tripping over himself. Rudy's back is so rounded, he looks like a little old man.

A heat lamp shines down on the playpen, and in the other corner is a stuffed toy—a plush walrus snatched from the aquarium gift shop. Hans leans over to check on the baby penguin.

"Rudy is not that talkative," Hans says. "At least not like the last baby, Gomez, who would just chatter all day long—only penguin chatter is like short, mournful cries."

"I like the silent ones," Lisa says as she conceals a vitamin in a fish. She drops the fish in the pail and pushes her chair back. "Feeding time," she announces. Against the wall are what look like rows of cubbies, each one marked with a number. Lisa takes the bucket of fish in one hand, and in the other she dangles a key with a little penguin key chain. Turning the key in the lock of cubby number nineteen, she opens the door and there sit two full-grown penguins, Linus and Cameron, carefully guarding their nest of rocks and strips of plastic mesh and their egg. The cubby is their home—from the exhibit, it looks like an authentic penguin burrow, but from the other side, each one can be individually accessed through the cubby doors. Linus and Cameron are a couple, they live together monogamously, as many adult penguins do, just like they are married. In penguin land, the divorce rate, as well as the adultery rate, is slim to none.

The aquarium takes pains to prevent inbreeding, although on rare occasion, nothing can come in the way of love: Linus and Cameron are actually uncle and niece, as well as husband and wife. Unbeknown to them, their egg was replaced several weeks ago with the egg from another couple, Kip and Summer, who are notoriously bad parents. Kip and Summer don't sit on their eggs to keep them warm the way that Linus and Cameron do. So far, several of Kip and Summer's babies have died, and many of their eggs have never hatched. So the aquarium staff intervened, secretly taking Kip and Summer's egg and adding it to Linus and Cameron's nest. In order not to upset Kip and Summer, their smuggled egg was switched with a decoy—a ceramic egg that looks and feels exactly like a real one. Kip and Summer will haphazardly sit on the decoy all season, then assume it died, as did their others. Linus and Cameron, two very conscientious nesters—"good incubators" as Lisa calls them—will hatch the baby and raise it as their own; planned parenthood at its finest.

Rudy awkwardly cranes his neck as I reach over to pet him. Penguins enter the world featherless, with only a soft charcoal-gray, down coating. I rub Rudy's tiny head; the fluff is so soft, like a plushy teddy bear. In a few weeks, Rudy will start getting waterproof feathers, but then will molt. It isn't until over one year of age that penguins get their full set of feathers.

Petting Rudy instantly reminds me of when I was a child and my father brought home three abandoned baby ducklings. Rudy is just like those babies, fragile and helpless. I'd like to be able to help Rudy, to straighten out his back in one swoop, but I know that's impossible. In fact, the degree of the humpback makes me quite concerned; Rudy's is extremely pronounced.

People with hunchbacks can have problems with their ribs not opening and closing during breathing since the muscles involved are so constricted. I worry about Rudy's chances of survival.

In the wild, when penguin chicks reach two or three months old, they are kicked out of the nest and forced to fend for themselves. The aquarium eases this process a bit by taking the month-old chicks and bringing them into an indoor playpen to hand-feed them and insure that each penguin has the skills to survive on its own. One by one, the chicks prove their independence and are sent back to the exhibit—except for Rudy. Out of the entire litter, Rudy was the only penguin left in the playpen.

Rudy is quite used to people and to being touched and handled. Lisa has become Rudy's parent figure; she checks and weighs, as well as feeds and pets, Rudy every day. There's even a photo pinned to a bulletin board of Lisa with Rudy, taken a few weeks ago when Rudy weighed only several ounces—as compared to Rudy's current two pounds.

I climb inside the playpen, careful where I step.

"Sorry," Lisa says, "I just cleaned, but . . ."

"Accidents happen," I say. I plant my feet alongside Rudy and squat down. With one hand, I cup Rudy's chest in my palm to hold it steady. When I massage infants in my human practice, I do very gentle touching; their bodies are fragile and their bones are soft. Rudy's a baby too, so I begin by gently stroking his back, working the muscles in a downward direction with only the lightest of pressure.

Penguins have bands of muscles extending down their backs; Rudy's are all stretched out—I can feel how loose and sinewy they are. In contrast, Rudy's chest muscles are too tight; this is pulling Rudy's back down.

At first Rudy is a little nervous and plants a few pain-less pecks on my hand.

"The pecks won't start hurting until they are adults," Lisa says. "Then you've got to watch out. Most adult penguins are not that people friendly—and their beaks are strong, and sharp enough to slice your skin."

Rudy quickly gives up the fruitless attempt to peck, and after a couple soft massage strokes, I've actually won the penguin over. Rudy sits in my hand, seemingly enjoying the contact. I feel like I'm massaging a teddy bear. I continue with the gentle rubbing for a few more minutes, until I feel Rudy is used to my touch. Then I begin doing a technique on Rudy's back called friction. It's a subtle motion, but it creates heat and stimulates the muscles. I place my index and middle fingers on each side of Rudy's back. I rest my palm on the lower back just above the tail, so that I have a solid base to stabilize Rudy, then I draw my fingers down, drawing the muscles down as well.

After several strokes, I prepare to do the other side, the chest muscles. I reverse the process, wrapping my palm around Rudy's stomach to hold Rudy steady. Rudy's a bit shaken by the change and tries to flap his wings to shoo me away. I gently begin rubbing his chest, and again, Rudy is quickly appeased.

I do a different stroke on the chest, since the goal is not to stimulate, but to stretch. I want to try to increase the length of the muscles. As I work, I explain exactly what I'm doing to Lisa, so that she can conduct mini-massages in between my visits.

"The ultimate goal is to relax and increase the length of the breast muscles, while contracting and encouraging the loose back muscles to tighten up," I say. Lisa nods.

"I should do this every day?" she asks.

"Yes. Rudy's just like a child, nice and impressionable. Think of it as shaping a bonsai tree. By doing the massage every day, we will be encouraging the way the muscles and bones form." I set down the little humpbacked penguin who wobbles on unsteady webbed feet. "Hopefully," I add.

Lisa nods solemnly, then quickly changes the subject.

"Did you work up an appetite?" she asks Rudy, who stands there blinking, only it's not a blink like humans do; rather, a membrane sweeps the eye horizontally, from right to left, rather than up and down—much like a windshield wiper. Lisa holds the fish in front of Rudy, and Rudy slurps it up.

"Is the food staying down?" I ask.

"Sometimes," Lisa says. She holds another piece at head level and Rudy scarfs it up.

"I've got an idea," I say. I take a piece of the raw fish, and instead of placing it at Rudy's mouth, I hold the fish up, above Rudy's head. Rudy awkwardly stretches for the fish, and finally manages to pluck it out of my hand.

"See what Rudy's doing? He's reaching in a way he never would—those muscles that are all constricted are getting a nice good stretch."

Lisa smiles. "So from now on, I'll hold the food up above Rudy's head, right?"

I nod. "And you also can try cutting up the fish even

smaller. Remember, it's hard for Rudy to digest because many of his organs are cramped." Lisa immediately takes out her tiny knife and begins cutting the pieces of fish in half.

————

When I return for Rudy's second massage, I am shocked to see how much the little penguin has grown in one week. I can still comfortably wrap my hand around Rudy, but his scrawny body has started to fill out.

"Well it looks as if Rudy's eating well," I say.

"Oh, yes, so much better," Lisa says. "Rudy has kept down everything this entire week."

I smile proudly.

"And look," says Lisa, "doesn't Rudy's posture seem to be a little bit straighter?"

Sure enough, the humpback looks slightly less pronounced, although it is very clearly still there; Rudy is not yet free from danger.

I can tell that Lisa has been massaging Rudy daily because the penguin's muscles are nice and supple. I step into the playpen and squat down. Rudy wobbles toward me. "Well hello there, boy—I mean girl—I mean, when exactly are we going to know what Rudy is?"

"Not for another couple months," Lisa says. "We can't tell until they are fully matured." Matured—and only then when the penguins pair off. They do that when they're about two years old. "If the pair produces an egg, then we know at least one of them's female. Usually, in the pair the larger penguin with the bigger bill is the male."

I rest my left hand along Rudy's chest and begin to massage the breast muscles, taking my thumb and forefinger and moving all the way up to the base of the wings. At the same time, I use my right hand to massage Rudy's back with friction. I do two fifteen-minute sessions, then watch as Lisa feeds Rudy, dangling the fish above the penguin's head. Rudy's stretch comes much easier than last week. With only moderate effort, Rudy slurps the fish from between Lisa's fingers. I feel as if I'm a parent, and my baby has just taken his first steps.

Each week when I come to the aquarium to give Rudy a massage, I notice improvement. Rudy's posture is straightening out—Rudy's head no longer is parallel with the ground, but is more erect. The medical verdict, Hans informs me: Rudy's going to make it.

As Rudy matures, I can see the cartilage in his back forming and taking shape—Rudy will likely never be perfectly straight. As the weeks pass, Rudy looks more and more like a full-grown penguin, getting in some feathers, filling out the tuxedo. Rudy also starts secreting a saltwater solution. This is normal for penguins, it's their way of eliminating excess salt from the fish they eat. A major source of these secretions is located around the beak, and the salt solution collects there until it is shaken off. Now, as I massage Rudy, I have to be on the lookout for the quick head shake—I've learned the hard way: last week

I got a splash of sweat in my eye; the week before, even worse, a salty shot right in my mouth.

It is now the tenth week of treatment and Rudy, for the first time, will be put out on the exhibit with the other penguins. This morning, Rudy earned a black name tag engraved with his ID number so the aquarium can keep track. The tag is clasped, like a bracelet, around the top of his wing. Lisa lifts Rudy out of the playpen, then with a piece of fish, coaxes Rudy to follow her through a doorway onto the exhibit. I brave the aroma to witness the momentous event.

"Go on," she says to Rudy. I feel like a proud, yet nervous, father who's dropping his kid off at kindergarten for the first day. Will Rudy be able to fit in with the other penguins? Will Rudy be ostracized because of the humpback? Rudy teeters out, cautiously. Waddling over to a group of penguins, Rudy lifts his wings. The other penguins size Rudy up for a couple seconds and then they go back to picking at their fish—and that's the call; that's it—Rudy is "in." I want to cheer—what was once a helpless bird, destined to suffer, is now a matured penguin, blending right in with the others.

I hang out at the aquarium for a while, keeping my eye on the humpbacked bird. One penguin even approaches Rudy and "bills" him, which is the penguin version of a handshake, where they tap their beaks.

An exhibit keeper begins the daily routine of cleaning the penguin exhibit. I can't get over how frequently the exhibit is cleaned—and how badly it still smells. Cathy is always able to tell the minute I walk in the door if I have been with the penguins.

One penguin in particular is following the keeper around as she hoses off the rocks. The penguin's hopping with both feet to keep up. I lean against the rail, watching. A family is next to me and a little boy is giving voice to the nosy penguin, narrating the moves in a high cartoon pitch: "Hello, I'm Mr. Penguin, wait, wait, wait for me!" Then, in beat with the penguin wobbling after the worker: "Can I help, can I help, can I help?"

When I arrive at the aquarium for Rudy's next massage, Hans leads me directly onto the exhibit.

"Rudy!" he calls. Suddenly, from among a group of penguins, a head turns. Slowly, one humpback penguin emerges and waddles over, placing itself directly at my feet, as if to say: "I know the drill, massage away." Amazed, I kneel down and begin.

The special attention continues week after week— when I walk out onto the exhibit, Rudy leaves the group and hops right over to me, as if I'm a long-lost friend.

"Do we know yet what Rudy is?" I ask one day as I massage.

"I think it was just determined on Rudy's recent checkup," Lisa says. "I'll find out."

Word comes back later, through several staff members: Rudy's a girl.

To massage Nuka's severely constricted hip muscles, I have to push through a thick layer of blubber. Unlike fat on overweight humans, the blubber on a walrus is a separate layer that sits between the muscle and the skin and displaces to surrounding tissue when an area is massaged. (Photo by Catherine Guglielmo)

Pulling gently on Nuka's rear limbs gives her hip a deep stretch, helping the muscles to eventually loosen so that she can move and scull easily. (Photo by Catherine Guglielmo)

I finish up Nuka's rubdown with relaxing shiatsu massage. Well . . . it's relaxing for her! (Photo by Catherine Guglielmo)

Nuka says "Thank you." After more than two months of massage therapy, her spine is nearly straight and she is able to scull normally. (Photo by Salvatore P. Guglielmo)

Tab's first massage begins with a "getting to know you" session on a low step at the edge of the pool. (Photo by Catherine Guglielmo)

Because the trainers have noticed that Presley has a slight twist to his jumps, I use a technique called "wringing" to massage the tension away. (Photo by Lou Bernstein)

I begin Mambo Point's massage with *effleurage*, gentle surface strokes to calm and relax the patient. (Photo by Julian Murray)

Mambo Point relaxes into his rubdown. (Photo by Julian Murray)

At six weeks old, Rudy is covered with charcoal-gray down. Her severely humped back, caused by a condition called *Kyphosis*, makes it difficult for her to breathe. (Photo by Catherine Guglielmo)

Rudy comes running toward me, eager for her massage. (Photo by Anthony Guglielmo)

Rudy on exhibit. Though a trace of her humpback is still visible, she is much improved and doing fine. (Photo by Anthony Guglielmo)

Reddog sits patiently as I massage and stretch his strained muscles. (Photo by Catherine Guglielmo)

Mickey, the "falling feline," lounges in her living room following a session. (Photo by Dina Van Vuren)

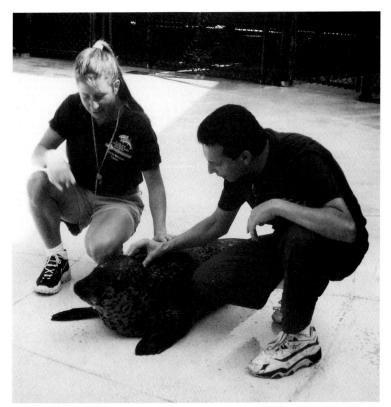

As Martha and I visit with Bernie, a seal who lives in the New York Aquarium, I give him a quick rub on the back of the neck. Everyone loves a massage! (Photo by Catherine Guglielmo)

For her massage, Baby is placed in a specially designed harness that will keep her submerged, within my reach, and immobilized for safety. Though sand tiger sharks are not usually aggressive toward humans, I'm glad for the precautions. (Photo by Catherine Guglielmo)

The view from my perspective as the first-ever known shark massage is about to begin. To my amazement, Baby calmly allows me to massage her for more than forty minutes. (Photo by Catherine Guglielmo)

"We think Rudy has a mate," Lisa announces when I finish up a recent massage.

"Go, Rudy!" I say.

Lisa shakes her head. But there's a problem: competition with Celia. Celia can't make up her mind: she's been running around with two males, which is very atypical for penguins. Celia will spend the day with Arthur—who appears to be Rudy's mate—and the night in Simon's den.

"You're going to have to claim your man," I advise Rudy. She lifts her wings.

I no longer massage Rudy once a week; she doesn't need it. She lives, eats, and even looks like a normal penguin; weighing in at an average seven pounds. Usually, I can pick Rudy out of the crowd by the faint curve that still remains, only today, as I lean against the rail, I can't seem to find her.

It's feeding time and Lisa walks out onto the exhibit in her big rubber boots, a pail of fish in each hand. Three penguins surround her, standing at attention.

"Lisa," I call, "where's Rudy?"

Lisa scans the plastic ID tags. "Here she is," Lisa says, and taps the beak of the full-grown penguin to her left. That penguin has no trace of a humpback that I can see from here. "Are you sure?" I ask. Lisa checks the tag again.

"It's definitely our Rudy."

8

Every Dog Should Have Its Massage

Reddog is not allowed on the bed. He knows this. He also knows that when his owners, Lisa and Phil, leave there is no one in the house to shoo him off the bed. What Reddog doesn't know is that Lisa and Phil have him all figured out. When they come home from work every day, there's always a still-warm indentation on the down comforter, the perfect size and shape of a seventy-five-pound boxer, scattered with indisputable evidence of brown hair.

One lazy Friday, Reddog loses track of time. He is deep in sleep, dreaming of digging up the backyard, when suddenly the rattling of keys in the front door jars him awake. Usually, he's up like a lightning bolt at the first sounds of the car pulling into the driveway, but today, the sun through the window is so toasty and the blanket is so soft and smells so clean, and the bones in the dream are so scrumptious . . .

Reddog knows he's in for a big scolding if he is caught on the forbidden bed. He hates being scolded, the way Lisa's brow furrows and her finger wags in his face, "No, Reddog, no," she'll say sternly. He hates having to mope around after being scolded, feeling like he has to hang his head so that his owners will know he is truly sorry he disobeyed.

There is still hope, though, and as the keys turn in the lock, Reddog hoists himself up and with one powerful flying leap, he launches his body from the bed. He paddles through midair, aiming himself directly for the knit area rug that covers the hardwood floor.

Only, his aim is slightly off.

One foot lands on the area rug, the other on the floor, and in a clash of his footing, he slips and does the splits. Reddog quickly realizes that far worse than being scolded is doggy splits.

Lisa and Phil open the door, toss the keys on the front table, and then look at each other bewilderedly. Where is their greeter, the pup who "innocently" comes bounding from the direction of their bedroom to say hello? Where is their Red?

Suddenly they hear whimpering. They know exactly where to find Reddog and head straight to their bedroom. There he is, sitting with one leg raised so as not to put pressure on it; the area rug has slid clear across the room.

Reddog's veterinarian prescribes painkillers and muscle relaxants. Reddog reluctantly takes the pills, which make him sluggish and sleepy. During the rare times Reddog is up and moving around, he's still limping.

Phil is a patient of mine, and during his weekly massage he tells me how concerned he is about Reddog. "He's not his usual self," he says. "And it seems obvious he's still in pain, the medication is not working."

"I'd love to take a look at him," I say. "Maybe massage would help."

Phil's face lights up. He goes home and calls Reddog's veterinarian who says that massage may be a good idea. Then he calls me back, "Can you come tomorrow?" he asks.

Lisa and Phil had adopted Reddog from a boxer rescue foundation. He is a great family dog—quiet, protective, and polite. Although he sometimes is too polite. He never barks or jumps on people (which is good), but he also never shows much affection. He isn't the type of dog who'll lick your face or follow you around with a tail wagging a hundred miles an hour.

When I walk in the door of Lisa and Phil's home, Reddog hobbles over. His eyes are droopy. One look at him and you can't help but lament, "Poor Red."

I kneel down next to him and put my hand on his pectoral muscle. Immediately I can feel the heat—a sure sign of inflammation. With just my simple touch, Red gives a slight flinch and looks up at me with those sad eyes as if to say, "That's sore, can you please help me?" I gently run my hand over his legs and they radiate heat. I know the X rays from the veterinarian came back showing no broken bones. I can piece it together to figure out that Red overstretched his pectoral muscles, biceps, and triceps and likely pulled some tendons. The medication the veterinarian prescribed has helped Reddog to rest and to stay off the sore leg, but the downside is that Reddog isn't actually healing. Because Reddog is holding the area stiffly, there is little circulation. Micro-tears and pulled muscles need fresh blood and oxygen in order to heal.

There, on Lisa and Phil's living-room floor, I begin with a technique called circular effluerage, which is a basic stroke in Swedish massage where you stimulate the upper surface, the skin and upper layers of muscles, not pressing in very hard. I start in the center of Red's pectoral muscle and work my way outward, trying to move the fluids out of the muscle tissue. I don't exactly know what to expect from Reddog, especially since he is in pain. But instead of pushing my hand away, he begins pushing *toward* me, as if he is trying to help. As I work, I am able to feel that the surrounding muscles are also tight—a tight muscle on a dog feels the same as it does on a person: when relaxed, muscles should be pliable, if there's a lump, that's a tight muscle. I've felt enough muscle throughout my career to be able to distinguish immediately. It's quite common for the muscles around an injury to be tight—and it happens in people too—when one area is hurt, you hold it in a stiff position that causes everything around it to stiffen up.

I switch to a form of massage called trigger-point therapy where I press my fingertips into the muscles at specific points—these points differ on each individual. Every person has trigger points on their body, but they will be in slightly different places. Even identical twins don't have the same trigger points. On some people, a common trigger point is at the back of the neck—it's that spot that when touched, makes you flinch or jump or curl your shoulders up toward your ears. But a trained massage therapist knows how to press into the trigger point slowly so that the urge to flinch goes away, and steady pressure can be applied. After twelve to fifteen seconds, the trigger point will begin to release, and the person will feel what's described as a "good pain"; that's when the body automatically eases up, sort of reeducating the muscle, sending signals for it to relax, so that the spasm will go away.

As I near Red's armpit area, he instinctively raises his paw. It is as if I were holding a doggie treat and asking for his paw—only he isn't handing it to me on command, he is holding it up so I can ease my hands onto the spot I need.

"You've got one very helpful and intuitive dog here," I say.

"He takes after me," Lisa jokes.

From his underarm, I move my way toward his belly. Usually, when a person starts to rub a dog's stomach, the dog automatically lies down or rolls over. Red, however, is not budging. He just sits there, not wanting to roll over, likely because it is painful.

"Come on, boy," I coax. But I have no such luck. Red does not, under any circumstances, want to lie down.

"He's also a bit on the stubborn side," I say.

"He gets that from you too, sweetheart," Phil says, nudging his wife.

I have to devise another way to get to the dog's underside. Since he isn't going to lie down, my only other option is that I lie down. I roll onto my back and slide underneath Red. With my arms raised, I begin massaging his abdomen.

"I can't say I've ever had a view like this before," I say.

My arms quickly tire and I start to slide out for a little break. But as soon as I stop rubbing, Red sits down right on top of my chest, as if to say, "Nope, you're not going anywhere."

So I massage some more, and then some more. Forty-five minutes have passed and my arms are killing me. It is time to devise a plan: Lisa appears with a doggy treat in her hand and as soon as Red looks her way, I quickly slide out. I sit on the floor and Reddog, forgetting the treat, swings around to stare at me. We are eye to eye. I am by no means scared of Reddog—he is gentle and has never been known to bite; and besides, we have a connection, I know that. But I also know that Reddog doesn't make a habit of interacting much with people. Suddenly Reddog leans over, sticks out his tongue, and gives me a lick from chin to forehead. It is the sloppiest "thank you" I have ever received.

Lisa's sister, Jen, has been there the entire time watching the massage and suddenly she lets out a jealous protest: "Hey, I've been trying to get that dog to give me a kiss since he was first brought home!" She leans her face close to Red's.

"Come on, Red, baby, give me a kiss." Nothing.

"Reddog, you know your Auntie Jen loves you, give me a kiss." Red just sits there.

"Pleeease, just one little kiss."

Reddog turns to me and gives me another lick across the face.

The next week, when I walk through Lisa and Phil's front door, Reddog comes right over, as if presenting himself to me. He still is walking with a limp, but it is not as pronounced. I rub my hands across his pectoral muscles—the inflammation is reduced, the area is not burning up like it was last week.

I spend a half hour going over the same massage techniques and pressure points to get the circulation going. Afterward, he seems more mobile and as I watch him mill around the backyard, he seems to have more flexibility when he walks—yet his movements are still slow.

Despite Red's improvement, however, he still isn't completely his old self. He does a little running in the yard, but he doesn't have much desire to play. Usually, the neighbor's cat, Raisin—Reddog's nemesis—can get an instant rise out of him, but even Raisin doesn't pique Red's interest.

Week three: Lisa and Phil are having a barbecue, and although the yard is filled with people, when I walk in, Reddog weaves his way through the crowd and comes right up to me. After lunch, I lead Red inside and work on him. When I am done I let him out through the back door. Suddenly we hear a howling from the backyard. Reddog is up against the fence, chasing Raisin back and forth—who is safe on the other side.

Several months later, Lisa's sister, Jen, gives me a call.

"It's our terrier, Molson," she says. "He's hurt."

She tells me what happened: "The doorbell rang and Molson bolted from the other room toward the front door—like he always does. Only he slipped on the wood floor. He looked like Scooby Doo, his legs just shot out from under him and he slid across the room. I know you were able to help Reddog—"

"I'll be right over."

Jen saw the benefits of massage firsthand with Red, so rather than going to medication as the initial round of therapy, she opted for massage. This is a concrete example of how the alternative medicine field is blossoming—massage is one of the most complementary ways to help heal. If there's a chance it may work in a specific situation, why not try it as the first line of therapy?

Molson is a golden-colored ball of energy that Jen and her husband Matt found wandering their street on a stormy day. The dog had no tags and no one responded to the posters they put up around the neighborhood. It was a good thing, too, because they had fallen in love with the dog. Molson is around sixty-five pounds, but thinks he's much bigger. He'll drag Jen when she takes him for walks. Unlike Reddog, Molson is a face-licker—and a drooler. He'll sit right on top of you and just drool all over you. He's also a sneezer. He will sneeze so hard he sometimes hits his face on the ground.

Molson's favorite thing in life is to dig holes in the backyard. Jen knew he was really hurt when she let him outside and he wasn't even tempted by the ground.

His second favorite thing in life is Jen. Molson is a complete momma's boy and will follow Jen around, sitting right next to her or walking so close by that he sometimes gets tangled in her legs. He loves playing with Matt, too—especially a game where Molson holds a stick in his mouth and Matt grabs the stick and swings the dog until Molson is in the air.

When I arrive, Molson is limping and whimpering. He is walking sideways, as if his hind legs are trying to go first. I run my hands across his body, checking for anything that feels out of the ordinary. Luckily, everything feels normal, except for some strained and pulled muscles. I make up an ice pack and hold it on Molson's leg to reduce the inflammation. Usually animals don't sit still, especially when you are holding an ice pack on them, but it is as if Molson knows he is hurt and that this is going to help him. He sits still and, unlike Reddog, he flips over on his back when it is time for the massage. I do petrissage, trigger point, range of motion, and then, as with Champ the horse and the ferret, I do a technique called circumduction, where I take the limb and rotate it, simulating the muscle's movement. This way, the muscle is moving, it's going through the normal range of motion, but it's not engaged, so there's no strain. This is one of the best ways to get an animal— or a person for that matter—to regain movement.

Molson must have also injured his mid to lower back because he wrinkles up, a twitch reflex, when I touch there.

It takes three massage sessions until Molson is back to normal.

Reddog, however, will never be fully back to normal. His injury is more severe and is prone to flare-ups. Red likely stretched the tendons; tendons, unlike muscles, don't have a rubber-band quality. You can't stretch a tendon and then expect it to eventually go back to normal. It's like a bad back in a person—if someone throws out their back once, it never seems to be the same after that. If Red moves wrong, he's open to re-injuring his shoulder and I get a phone call from Lisa: "Anthony, are you free for dinner tonight?"

"Dinner and a massage?"

9

The Falling Feline

M assage is a most versatile therapy. It has to be or a feline would never, ever go for it—especially not Mickey.

Mickey is a seventeen-year-old charcoal-gray striped cat. She was given to Dina, the daughter of a friend, when Mickey was a kitten and Dina was just a little girl. As a child, Dina would carry Mickey everywhere. "I'm careful not to squeeze her," she'd inform everyone, mimicking her mother's warning.

I've known Mickey for almost her whole life and she has always acted as if she wanted nothing to do with me. I would walk into a room and Mickey would shoot in the other direction.

After I started working on animals, Mickey's behavior began to frustrate me. How could I have such rapport with horses and walruses and penguins and still have this one cat avoid me at all costs?

So I decide to set up an experiment: I ask Dina to hold Mickey on her lap. As I approach, Mickey squirms, but Dina hangs on.

I begin to massage the cat's neck. At first she seems annoyed, like she's wondering, "Just who does this guy think he is?" But suddenly her stance changes, her body loosens up as if she begins to realize, "Hey, this actually feels kinda nice."

Suddenly she's purring. I begin to intensify the massage.

"Does Mickey have any problems?" I ask Dina.

"Not that I know of, but she doesn't really like people touching her back."

I work my way along the spine, one side at a time. When I get to the lower vertebrae, Mickey flinches.

"There it is," I say.

"There what is?" Dina asks.

"A nice big knot."

Dina scrunches up her nose.

I do a deep circular petrissage on each vertebra, drawing the muscles in and up. I use the same strokes I used on the dogs, only with a much gentler touch since cats are smaller and their muscles are more delicate.

Mickey stops flinching and arches into my hands, as if she's telling me to go deeper.

Dina begins growing impatient. "Hey, when's it my turn?"

I stop massaging Mickey and move onto Dina's sore elbow that she strained in a game of tennis.

Mickey begins rubbing up against my feet. Then, when she sees that's getting her nowhere, she jumps up and begins rubbing up against my hands, which are busy working Dina's elbow.

Dina starts laughing.

"Oh, I see, Mickey," I say. "Seventeen years of the cold shoulder and now you're my best friend?"

"Best friend" is putting it mildly. These days Mickey can't get enough of me and runs to me the moment I walk in. She'll jump on my lap, purring—and it almost sounds like, "Please massage. Please massage."

Mickey has favorite spots: just above the hind legs, the hip, and the place where the abdominal and back muscles meet. Whenever I touch those spots, she goes limp. If she's standing, she will literally fall—it's like a hypnotic reaction: I touch the spot, she leans over and collapses.

It's the funniest thing to see. Dina falls over with laughter every time it happens.

10

A Beluga Tongue Scratch

I'm staring at a foot-long, pale pink tongue that belongs to a nearly one-ton whale named Kathy who's anxiously waiting—mouth agape—for me to make a move.

"Go on, scratch it," Kristin, a trainer at the New York Aquarium, says.

"Scratch the whale's tongue?"

"It's their version of a back scratch. They love it."

"I don't believe I'm doing this," I mutter as I roll up my sleeve and extend my hand out. The beluga whale's mouth is open and she's got rows of smooth, one-inch-long teeth. The tongue feels dry and sandpaper rough on my fingertips as I give it a scratch much like I would a furry spot under a dog's chin. With one split-second swoop, Kathy the Whale could easily eat my hand for lunch; yet, I feel a certain ease that this whale would never have it in her to chomp on people.

"Thatta girl," I say as I scratch. Kathy leans in and sticks her tongue out farther as if to say, "More."

"What? You want a tongue *massage*, too?"

Kathy, like all beluga whales, looks like an oversized albino dolphin; in fact, the name 'beluga' is derived from Russian for "large white animal." Unlike dolphins, however, beluga whales don't have a dorsal fin; instead, they have a dorsal ridge, a slight ramp on their backs that almost looks as if a fin had been sanded down or trimmed off. The ridge is solid and strong; and the whales, in their natural arctic habitat, use it to break through ice. The ridge is so durable, it can smash a four-inch-thick ice slab so that the whale can come to the surface of the water and grab some air. Since whales are mammals, they breathe through their lungs and cannot stay underwater longer than fifteen minutes without coming up for a breath. Conveniently, whales do not breathe through their mouths, but rather through their blowholes, a nostrillike opening on the top of their head that has an airtight flap for when they are underwater.

The whale's stark white color serves as camouflage, helping it to blend in with its icy, snowy surroundings, and protecting it from its predators, the polar bear and the killer whale.

Of course, none of the whales living in the New York Aquarium have to worry about predators or glaciers, which is a good thing because Kathy and the four others—Casey, Maris, Natasha, and Marina—are some of the last in a species that is at risk of extinction, because of hunting and pollution. Although humans are probably the main culprit, beluga whales are not extremely resilient. Their immune systems are delicate and, to make matters worse, their infant mortality rate is exceedingly high. Baby beluga whales have all the odds stacked against them—their innate abilities for swimming and nursing are not very fine-tuned, and first-time and even second-time mothers are often inept. The aquarium is one of the world's few breeding grounds for whales and boasts the oldest beluga whale in an aquarium—Kathy—and the oldest beluga born in an aquarium—Kathy's son, Casey, a rambunctious six-year-old.

Up until this point, I had mostly been concentrating on animals who were ill or injured. But the philosophy "if it isn't broken, don't fix it" is especially risky when dealing with animals because problems are often not detectable until they become quite severe. It's similar to problems in babies—a baby can't say, "I think I feel a cold coming on, I better bulk up on vitamin C and take a nice long nap."

In my human practice, I follow a different cliché: an ounce of prevention is worth a pound of cure. I know it's important to treat the human body pro-actively, so why not an animal's?

With this in mind, I went to Kevin, the director of marine mammal training at the New York Aquarium. He is known and well respected by everyone in the marine mammal field, yet when I asked him if I could work on the whales, his first instinct was old school: "But they're all healthy, knock on wood."

I knew I was venturing into brand-new territory—to

do massage on animals for the sole sake of keeping them healthy would be difficult for someone with a hard-core scientific background to digest.

Around the time I was inquiring, Casey was acting quite finicky during feeding time. Kristin, his trainer, would put a fish in his mouth and he would spit it out, catch it, then spit it out again.

At first, it was entertaining to watch him. "Stop playing with your food," Kristin would scold. But by the second or third time, it wasn't funny anymore. Kristin wondered exactly how you made a thousand-pound whale sit there until his plate was clear. Besides, it was pretty atypical for a whale to be a picky eater since they tend to eat fifty-five pounds of food a day and will devour just about anything—herring, capelin, squid, octopus, crabs, clams, and even sandworms. Kristin thought that maybe massage could distract and relax him. Belugas love tactile work and the massage would be an enjoyable way to take Casey's mind off of playing with food.

I began studying diagrams of beluga whales in preparation for my first massage session. I once again found similarities between this species and humans. If you look at an X-ray of a beluga whale's pectoral flippers, you will see bones similar to those of a human hand. Despite the fact that the flippers are extremely small compared to the whale's robust body, they are amazingly effective in steering and even stopping.

Like most people who've ever seen a whale, I'd only done so through the viewing windows at aquariums, watching, along with all the children whose noses were pressed up against the glass, as a mammoth white form moved heavily, yet silently, through the water then disappeared into the bubbles of the current.

But now, here I am, dunking my shoes into the tray of fluorescent antiseptic and following Kristin up the stairs. In the pool is a floating platform. As we step onto the platform, it dips and bobs under our weight. We kneel down at the edge and the platform angles, making me envision, for a split second, sliding off into the pool—not a pleasant thought since the water is kept purposefully frigid to simulate the whales' natural arctic habitat.

The whale exhibit consists of three different pools that are all interconnected, but can be sectioned off. In the pool to the far right, I catch a glimpse of a big white head popping up, then disappearing under the rim. A couple seconds later, there it is again, the round part of the top of a whale head—called the melon—bobbing up, then sinking down.

"That's Kathy," Kristin says. "She's spy-hopping, trying to see what's going on. Nosey, huh?"

While Kristin prepares the fish I watch as Kathy continues to bob, the sliver of white appearing, then disappearing, then appearing again.

"It looks like she has something in her mouth," I say, narrowing my eyes to get a better view.

"Go see what she has," Kristin offers, knowing full well what I will find. I walk over to the adjacent pool and step out onto the floating platform. Kathy immediately swims over and presents her open mouth to me.

There, resting on her long tongue, is a crinkled blue Nestlé Crunch wrapper.

"Go on, take it," Kristin says. "Kathy's our little housekeeper."

"Take it right out of her mouth?" I ask.

"Uh-huh."

"You mean reach right in there?"

"Uh-huh."

I stick my hand into her mouth and quickly pull out the wrapper.

Kathy's reward for cleaning the tank is positive reinforcement—in this case, a tongue scratch: a whale's version of bliss.

After I'm done scratching Kathy's tongue, I return to the platform in the center pool where Casey is. Kristin calls him over with a few quick tones of her whistle. He presents himself readily at the platform edge.

Despite their large size—at least five hundred pounds bigger than a dolphin—belugas appear soft and graceful, and even cuddly. They have cartoonlike round heads and permanent goofy grins. Their soft, sleek lines and round bodies make them look like humongous stuffed animals that you just want to reach out and hug.

The skin on beluga whales is smooth and flawless, like white leather, and as I reach out and touch Casey I'm surprised by how squishy he seems on top and how firm underneath, like a layer of Jell-O over solid muscle.

Casey is the most forward of the belugas at the aquarium. He has a tendency to position himself right in your face. From almost the day he was born, he would go to the center of the pool to swim upside down, a whale's version of showing off. He loves to play with the toys—

plastic buoys and hula hoops, and when the trainers come for play session, Casey is always ready and waiting at the floating platform.

At the age of two, Casey was weaned from his mother, and like a rambunctious little boy, he wanted his independence. He tried to stay as far away from Kathy as possible and refused her help or nurturing whenever she offered. Marina and the two other males that lived there at the time, Winston and Newfy, viewed Casey's behavior as disrespectful and often gave Casey the cold shoulder by nudging him.

With the unconditional love of a mother, Kathy would come to his rescue. But Casey didn't want to be rescued. He wanted to rebel, to fend for himself. Then, things changed in the whale pool: Winston and Newfy were transferred to other aquariums so they could mate, and a new baby, Maris, was born to Marina.

Maris and Casey play second-grade chasing games, although Maris is usually the one doing the pursuing. Casey often acts not-so-thrilled with Maris's advances, but no one's quite sure what he's really thinking—boys will be boys, after all.

Kristin says I should begin massaging Casey at the base of his fluke. My fingers travel along his spine; I reach around to press my middle finger on his left side, which is farther away from me, and my thumb on his right side, which is facing me. I do little grips, which is where you grab the spine with your four fingers on one side and your thumb on the other and you start wide, then squeeze together.

Belugas are perfect candidates for massage. They are known for their curiousity—they have a reputation for following boats for miles—and they are also quite touchy-feely. They will swim together, almost as if they are dancing, looking elegant and nimble despite their size; they touch their bodies together, sometimes face-to-face, sometimes intertwined. It's like watching an underwater ballet.

I expect that Casey will remain stationary and that I'll inch my way down the platform to reach different places, but Casey has a better idea: he is going to help me with the massage by positioning himself where he wants the massage done. He inches himself along, as if he is on a slow conveyor belt that allows me to work evenly on each area—in this case, the vertebrae—with equal amount of time. When I reach the end of the vertebral column, at his blowhole, Casey inches forward and presents himself for another round.

Kristin's mouth drops as Casey positions himself next to the platform.

"I've never seen him act like this before, he loves it!" she says.

He swims back and forth five times; I massage up his spine, down his spine, up his spine, you get the idea—five times. The trainers stop what they are doing and gather to stare. Never before have they seen a beluga act this way.

I'm laughing at this point, even though my hands are killing me—it's hard work digging into inches of blubber. This huge whale is acting like a cat or dog who wants your attention and keeps nudging your hand so you'll pet it.

Then, the moment of truth: Kristin presents the shiny silver pail of herring and capelin. Casey opens his mouth and Kristin drops a fish in. Down it goes. Whales don't chew their food, but swallow it whole—they actually don't even swallow, the fish just slide down their tongues and slip into their stomachs.

Because of the success with Casey, the trainers decide to let me work on Kathy. Kathy is to be the first animal I'll massage who doesn't have any health problems or issues—my first pro-active animal massage.

The belugas are the aquarium's prize—they are such rare, beautiful creatures and for the aquarium to entrust me with their care is a huge accomplishment.

Kathy is the oldest beluga whale living in captivity today. She was born near the Churchill River in Manitoba, Canada. At thirty, Kathy is getting up there in whale years, although she is in incredible health. Because of medical advances, animals in aquariums are long outliving their wildlife counterparts. As a result, geriatric veterinary medicine is becoming quite a popular field.

Kathy knows she's the sage of the group and has become a very stubborn and dominant female. She's the mother figure and is set in her ways. The trainers call her the Queen Bee, because she likes to be in control.

Despite her dominating nature, she is quite affectionate and likes her tongue, neck, and back rubbed—all day long. She loves bucket baths. This is where the trainers take buckets of water and throw them into her mouth.

Still, she lets everyone know she's boss: when toys are in the pool, she hovers over her buoy or hula hoop and everyone else knows to steer clear. In addition to the typical candy wrappers or newspaper she cleans up from the pool, every once in a while she'll find an even stranger "treat." The trainers came in one morning to find Kathy swimming with a bag of Spanish rice under her pectoral fin. When they tried to take the bag from her she started teasing them—swimming up close to the edge of the pool, then just as the trainers reached out to grab the rice, swimming quickly away, as if she were saying, "Nah-nah, you can't have this, it's mine."

Kathy presents herself to me as if we've known each other for years. I begin doing gentle circles to warm up her skin and get her used to my touch. She starts maneuvering her body, leaning more on her side, inching forward, inching backward, as if she is instructing me where to put my hands—only, it seems as if she isn't going to leave any area untouched. In massage school we called a person like that a massage pig, where they just can't get enough of a massage and are anxious for you to massage this spot, and that spot, and some tightness over here, and some soreness over there.

For days after, the staff talks about how much the belugas enjoyed the massage sessions.

"It's no surprise," Kristin says. She and several other trainers now visit my office for their own massages. "I'm just like Kathy, a massage pig."

Marina, my next "patient," is the sweetheart of the belugas. Her four-year-old daughter, Maris, is not. Maris is nicknamed The Screamer. She often puts her face right up next to whomever is near and lets out a piercing shriek. She even squawks at the seagulls that fly up on the deck. You can hear her screaming across the aquarium—"That's Maris," the trainers at other exhibits will say, rolling their eyes.

It's not uncommon for belugas to be extremely vocal; in fact, they are often called "sea canaries." The sound comes through the blowhole and when the whales are producing it, the shape of their melon changes. At least eleven different beluga tones have been documented, ranging from high-pitched whistles and squeals to clucks, chirps, grunts, snorts, squeaks, and barks. Each sound likely has a different function and researchers think that the squawking, like what Maris does, is purely social.

The vocals are often so resonant, they've been heard through the hulls of ships. Maris has the most annoying of sounds down pat. But it's not just the screaming that makes her a handful—she grabs the toys in her mouth and tosses them back on deck, sort of like a child in a stroller who keeps throwing their toys out just for the sake of getting attention. Then, when playtime is over, Maris tries to jump up and snatch the toys from off the deck.

"Time-out!" Kristin will shout when Maris is bad. At the time-out, the trainers all stop what they are doing and walk off the deck, out of sight from the whales. Unfortunately, the others are always getting punished for Maris's little antics. Her mother, Marina, takes constant grief from Maris; but Marina is patient—probably the most patient of all the belugas.

Marina's massage is a joy to perform because she's so easygoing. She also has overcome a great obstacle— she's nearly blind. All commands are given to her both verbally and with touch signals. The loss of vision is

caused by a degenerative eye condition that often forces
Marina to be put into a separate holding pool so that
she can receive special therapy or treatment. When she
is away from the other belugas she gets depressed, mop-
ing around the pool, unenthusiastic about playing with
toys, unresponsive to the trainers; but the moment she's
put back with the others, she becomes her old self
again.

This is typical of belugas; studies and observations
suggest that they have strong emotions and that their
friends and family are very important to them. In the
wild, motherless belugas have been observed carrying
floats or buoys, or even skeletons on their backs. It's
believed this is a surrogate behavior, or sort of like a
child carrying around a doll or a blanket. This is especially common if a mother has recently lost a calf.

Unfortunately, the wild beluga colonies that were
studied are in danger. The large colony in the St.
Lawrence River in Manitoba, Canada, is so polluted
that many of the belugas are developing cancer. Couple
that with the fact that arctic natives still hunt belugas
for food and other raw materials, and you're left with a
struggling species. If it weren't for breeding and educational programs like the aquarium's, belugas could
someday be an endangered species.

11

Massage Marathon

The Dolphin Research Center in the Florida Keys has a colorful history. It was started by a fisherman named Milt Santini in the late 1950s. The property was his home, the lagoons his backyard. One day Santini found a dolphin caught in his fishing nets. He thought he had hurt the dolphin so he brought her home to the shallow water in his backyard and nursed her back to health. In those days, there were no laws protecting dolphins, so it wasn't illegal for a person to just bring a dolphin home; in fact, it was rather common in the Keys to go out and collect dolphins. Santini's goal was to eventually set the dolphin free, but he became attached and started training her. He named her Mitzi. Later, she was better known as *Flipper*.

Santini acquired more dolphins and they all became stand-ins for Mitzi in *Flipper*. One of Santini's dolphins named Little Bit was great with kids so he would do all the shots involving children; another dolphin, Mr. Gipper, would do the tail walk because Mitzi didn't know how.

For nearly thirty years, Santini lived with his dolphins and bred them. But when Mitzi died in the early seventies, Santini sold out to an entertainment conglomerate that converted the land to a roadside dolphin show called Flipper's Sea School.

Ten years later, the facility changed hands again; this time, the new owner was a Frenchman, John Paul, an independent whale conservationist who closed the place to the public. He wanted to achieve a ban on commercial whaling, but since whales weren't that accessible, he thought if he could do research on a similar species—dolphins—and prove to the world how intelligent they were, then he would be able to attain his goal. Some amazing research went on under John Paul—oil detection studies, language studies using computer-generated tones, mother-calf studies.

The ban on commercial whaling was eventually passed. After some celebration, John Paul had to face the moment of truth: yes, he had achieved his goal, but the price was that his dolphin center was broke. He left the place to the head trainers, Armando (Mandy) Rodriquez and Jayne Shannon, and went back to France.

The year was 1984, and Mandy and Jayne had to dodge fish companies in order to feed the dolphins. They would order from one company and the next time order from another company because they hadn't yet paid off the first bill. They were near the brink of having to close down and give the dolphins away when they turned the center into a nonprofit corporation and opened the doors to the public. Today, the center runs a very successful breeding colony—they are on their third generation of little Flippers—and are responsible for a lot of cutting-edge research. Some of the costs of running the center are offset by the swim-with-the-dolphin program, the walking tours, and a week-long college accredited course called Dolphin Lab. They also routinely host children with terminal or serious illness who would like to spend time with dolphins.

On my second trip to the Dolphin Research Center, I feel as if I have come full circle. Throughout this past year, I never forgot the image: I was standing on the pier looking out into the water where the dolphins were playing, circling round each other and diving gracefully—but Cindy wasn't among them. She was the dolphin off to the side swimming awkwardly, since swimming's difficult to do when one side looks like an accordion, all buckled and folded.

Pat, the center's current medical director, greets Cathy and me at the front gate. She's a petite woman dressed in a T-shirt, shorts, and sandals.

"Let's go say hi to the rest of the family," she says. I think Pat is talking about the staff members—the trainers, the veterinarians, the animal supervisors—but she isn't. She's talking about the seventeen dolphins that live at the center.

As she leads us to the lagoons a tour is just being started and we blend in with the group.

"I realize they probably didn't tell you this up front when you signed up for my tour, but you all are actually here to entertain the dolphins," the guide, a tanned twenty-two-year-old with blond-streaked hair, says. "I certainly believe that the dolphins are studying us every bit as much as we are studying them. Only they probably have us all figured out while we still have a whole lot of unanswered questions." A dolphin swims by, stops, and stares.

"Hi, Delphi. This one in particular is an avid people watcher. The big question around here is, who's training whom?" Delphi lets out some chirps and the crowd laughs.

"See, he vocalizes, you all laugh, and he's probably saying, 'HAH! Just trained some more!' "

As the crowd moves on, Pat pulls us aside. "Want to practice on Delphi?" she asks.

"Sure," I say, with an expression much like those on the faces of the little kids on the tour.

Pat continues with the agenda: "We'd like you to work on Cindy on your last day here," she says. When I was first there, they wanted me to spend a week getting to know Cindy. Since then, they'd implemented various techniques, including laser acupuncture, which made her more approachable to strangers. "In the meantime, we want you to get to know the other dolphins and to just sort of 'be around' so that Cindy can get accustomed to seeing your face. How would you like to massage all the other dolphins here?"

I feel like I've hit the jackpot.

Delphi is nicknamed The Fox because he's very popular with the ladies. He's responsible for a good number of the calves who have been born here. It's odd because even when the female dolphins are not specifically paired with Delphi, they all just seem to willingly flock to him. Time and time again, Delphi proves that when you've got it, you've got it. Trainers speculate that maybe it's his bulging eyes that the females find attractive—a dolphin version of "bedroom eyes"; or maybe it's the fact that he's got a double chin (although in humans that would likely work against him). Or maybe it's not physical at all, but based on personality, for Delphi is truly the most innovative of all the dolphins and consistently makes up new moves and new imitations, or adds a little spice to the old ones. He developed an alligator impression where he snaps his jaw open and closed. He also does an amazing shark impression: unlike swimming the normal dolphin-up-and-down way, he swims through the water thrashing his tail from side to side. You can almost hear the *Jaws* music. He also does human laughs. He can do one of the trainers—who has a high-pitched cackle—to a tee. Delphi was never taught any of these behaviors. He just started doing them and then gets positive reinforcement in the form of fish to keep doing them. But no matter what behavior Delphi is doing, he cannot put his face under the water; a self-absorbed male in full, he's always got to show his face to the crowd: as if to say, "I know I'm talented, but don't forget how handsome I am, too."

Delphi's son, Talon, is a chip off the old block. He's imitating the crowd now with his "rude noises"—quite typical for a nine-year-old male, even if he's a dolphin. The crowd goes wild at Talon's raspberries, burps, and other unmentionables.

Delphi also exemplifies a trait common in dolphins: pair-bonded males. This is where two males—in this case, Delphi and Kibby—create a serious bond just like that of mother and calf. Males, once they're sexually mature, are ostracized from the group by the matriarchs. This is nature's way of preventing inbreeding. So the males go off on their own and form partnerships with other males.

There are seventeen dolphins at the center and each one has a very unique personality (what the center calls a dolphinality). After massaging Delphi, I move on to the Old Gals, or the Golden Girls, otherwise known as Molly and Josephine. Both Gals are around forty years old, which is pretty up there for dolphin years—sort of like the equivalent of a human living into the late nineties. Both dolphins have seen and been through a lot in their four decades and they have the scars to prove it.

"Shark attacks," Pat says. She calls Josephine into position. We are kneeling on a deck that's jutting out into the lagoon. Obediently, Jo swims up and floats so that her body is parallel to the deck. I lean over and place my hands on her. I begin doing basic techniques. When I brush my hands over one of her scars, she flinches. I know there isn't any pain, she just doesn't want them touched. The amazing part is that I'm all the way down by her tail, so she can't see that I'm touching the scar—in fact, she can't even see the scars, and unless she caught a reflection of herself at some point, she may *never* have seen the scars. Yet somehow, the moment my fingers hit scar tissue, she knows.

I back off and work another area, yet my hands keep gravitating back to the scar tissue—it's pretty natural for me because my hands are trained to focus on areas that are abnormal, or that feel different. After fifteen minutes, Josephine swims away, clearly not enamored with the massage.

Molly's next. She's had a colorful past: for years she was in a traveling road-show circus; at one point in the sixties, she was being trained to wear a camera apparatus to go in search for the Loch Ness Monster, but she never ended up making it to Scotland. She then fell into the hands of an animal-rights extremist, before finally arriving at the Dolphin Research Center.

"If only she could talk—our language, that is," Pat says as she motions for Molly to line up alongside the dock.

"Yeah," Dana agrees. "If there was anybody here that I could just sit on a bar stool and have a few beers with and just listen to, it would definitely be Molly."

I begin the massage and Molly, like Josephine, doesn't want her scars touched either—she squirms. Fifteen minutes later, as if exactly following Josephine's example, Molly swims away.

So we move on. The next dolphin up is Buck. He was a Navy dolphin, and like Molly, he had a run-in with an animal-rights extremist. The extremist lured Buck and another dolphin onto his boat, then he took them six miles off of Key West and dumped them over the side, saying, "Be free!"

Being "free" in the wild blue ocean isn't exactly a dolphin's version of freedom after it's been living in human care. It's more like a dolphin's worst nightmare. They are not adept at finding food or fending off shark attacks, especially when they are on their own and away from a pod of dolphins. Buck began following boats, begging for food. By the time the two dolphins were found, several days later, they were not only emaciated, but Buck had also been hit by a boat and was injured. Another seventy-two hours in the wild and the marine mammal veterinarian who examined them said they might have been dead.

As I begin to massage Buck, he takes to it like no dolphin I've ever seen. Just like Kathy the beluga whale, Buck is a massage pig—someone who just can't get enough. Only he's even more over the top, rolling over, draping his head back, practically screaming "More!" I find that spot that if he were a dog, would make his leg twitch; it's just behind his pectoral fin. I'm having tremendous fun with him. When a person—or animal— enjoys the massage, it makes me enjoy it even more. Buck completely gives himself over to the massage. He lets his tail, or fluke, hang, and I feel flattered—his tail is his power source and to relinquish that power to me, well, it's like a game of trust and Buck has fallen straight back into my arms, knowing I'll catch him.

Then Buck surprises us all: he willingly flips over onto his back and presents his underbelly. The underbelly is a very vulnerable, protected area on a dolphin. Usually, dolphins keep their underbelly in the water. Buck is the first dolphin I've ever seen who has fully turned over, like a dog rolling onto his back. I start working the underbelly, where the pectoral muscles are.

Dolphins use their "pec" muscles quite frequently to jump and turn. As I work through some of the tightness, Buck shakes and waves his flippers, letting me know which spots are tender, but he never once breaks position. I move down his abdomen and he begins to really relax, so much so that his jaw starts quivering. Suddenly Pat lets out a little shriek. Buck is so relaxed he's just let loose a stream of urine that hits Pat in the chest.

"The ultimate sign of relaxation, eh?" Pat says, blotting her shirt with a towel.

We move onto a baby dolphin, Pax, who's one of Buck's roommates . . . er, lagoonmates. I can tell that they probably get along well together because, like Buck, the baby takes to the massage instantly. He's adorable, only five feet long and around two hundred pounds, which still looks very tiny when compared with a full-grown dolphin. The baby's mother, however, is not so thrilled with the massage. She keeps swimming over and trying to push my hand away.

"Quite protective," Pat says.

Cathy melts over the baby. "Can we fill up our trunk with water and sneak him home?"

Even though Pax is just a baby, he can zip right through the water. A dolphin's silky skin is specially designed to allow them to swim up to thirty miles an hour. When a human moves through water, little swirls called eddies form around the skin and create friction, which slows a person down. But a dolphin's skin has tiny folds called dermal ridges that prevent eddies from forming so that the body can glide right through the water. A dolphin's skin also stays smooth and slick because it is almost continually shedding and regenerating. In a human, the skin cells regenerate every eighteen hours, but in a dolphin, it's every two hours. While I massage, I can feel the skin slough off—the dolphin version of shedding.

The more I work, the more excited I become about working on Cindy; yet I know there's going to be a huge difference: none of these dolphins are in need of treatment, and Cindy most definitely is.

By the end of my marathon massage day I am ready to collapse.

The next day, Pat suggests I try working on the Old Gals again. We walk out onto the deck, and before I can even kneel down, Josephine presents herself, right in position, as if she knew me and I had been massaging her for years.

I begin right away. This time I'm careful not to touch her scars, but Josephine keeps inching her body toward my hands so that it's difficult for me to avoid them.

Finally, I touch one. She wiggles, but stays put. So I work the area until I can feel some of the scar tissue release some of the muscle.

It's approaching fifteen minutes since I began working on Jo. Suddenly Molly comes swimming up from behind and, with her snout, scoots Josephine right out of the way.

I look at Pat and begin to laugh. So I work on Molly, rubbing her scars. Fifteen minutes fly by, and—on the dot—Josephine swims up from behind and pushes Molly away.

Pat smiles wisely. "I bet the old girls were up at night gabbing about you and how good that massage felt."

Back and forth, like clockwork, it goes on—Molly gets her fifteen minutes—exactly—then pushes Jo. For over an hour. My neck, back, and knees are killing me.

"I'm being done in by the Golden Girls," I lament.

On my way back, I pass a swim-with-the-dolphin session. A family is in the water and a dolphin, AJ, is swimming up to each person and giving him or her a kiss.

Every human is cooing, talking to the dolphin as if they knew him, calling him sweetheart and precious. I cannot get over the sparkle in their eyes. Dana walks past and I call her over.

"What do you think it is about dolphins that stirs this in people?" I ask. "Is there anyone who doesn't like dolphins?"

"Dolphins are these creatures that have the ability to look back at you, straight in the eyes, when you look at them. And it feels good to have this smart, fantastic creature notice you. I can't tell you how many people come up to me and tell me it's been their lifelong dream to swim with dolphins."

Around the bend I pass a private swimming session. It's with a six-year-old boy who has cerebral palsy and came here from England as part of the Make-A-Wish Foundation. The boy's father and sister are in the water too, laughing and playing with the dolphin. The little boy rests in the trainer's arm, limp like a rag doll; it's difficult to tell if he understands what's happening when the dolphin kisses him on the cheek. His sister understands, though, and squeals with delight when the dolphin kisses her.

"Smile at the camera, sweetheart," the mother calls from the deck as she snaps a picture.

I head back to my hotel room; tomorrow is my big day.

12

Cindy
Part II

I stand on the pier looking over the lagoon where Cindy lives with four other dolphins. It's still painfully easy to pick her out. One look and anyone—whether they are trained in dolphin anatomy or not—can tell that there is still something definitely wrong. The telltale sign: she's oddly hunched over—her side is folded, and she swims awkwardly.

"It hurts to see Cindy like this," Dana, who works in the public relations department and who is also a dolphin trainer, says. "I've worked here for twelve years, and after that long you really start sharing the same emotions with these dolphins as you do with your own human family."

Dana smiles. "Like when Merina gave birth to Pandora, it was every bit as exciting for me as when my brother had my niece. It's the same thing with Cindy—she's struggling, and we're struggling to make her comfortable and make her well, and it's hard. It's like watching a family member who's ill, and it's tough—you feel very helpless. That's why we're so open to massage therapy."

No one can figure out what exactly is wrong with Cindy. She's been examined by several veterinarians, and Pat has been in contact with animal experts in the marine mammal field. They're still perplexed.

Since I last saw her, Cindy seems to have declined in physical condition, although her spirits are a bit more alive. A year ago she was spending more time alone and often wouldn't eat or socialize with the others, which is very rare for this social species. Now, Cindy is more involved with the other dolphins and trainers. She is eating better, although still not normally, and is allowing laser acupuncture to be done.

Still, one look at her is enough to tear your heart. She looks like she's doing side crunches and can't straighten up. It almost looks like she has shark gills, the way her side is rolled and folded over.

I follow two trainers onto a small boat, a Carolina skiff. The back of the boat is open, since it's made especially for rescuing and transporting injured animals. This is where the massage is going to take place. Pat, the medical director, and Mandy, the center's owner, are in wet suits, along with four other trainers. They sit on the dock and lower themselves into Cindy's lagoon.

"Welcome to the Florida Keys," Mandy says, bracing against the cold water. "Oooh, baby!"

"It never gets any easier, does it?" asks Pat as she wades out. They direct the other dolphins, Theresa and Aphrodite, to swim through the open gate and into the

other lagoons. Theresa is reluctant to go. She is nicknamed Hot Lips because she's always giving kisses—
especially to men with facial hair. She will scout them
out, follow them, and, of course, kiss, by gently pressing
her snout to men's furry cheeks. Now, she hovers near
the mustached Mandy.

"Come on, sweetheart," Mandy says, "in the other
pool. Come on." Theresa doesn't budge. Mandy lowers
his voice, "Sweetheart, let's go." He swings his arm, directing Theresa. Finally, she swims off and Mandy
closes up the gates, sectioning off the lagoon so no
other dolphins can come in.

Two trainers set what looks like a floatable gymnas-
tics mat onto the water. The trainers join Mandy and
Pat in the lagoon and walk the mat out to the center.
Then the trainers carefully climb onto the mat. "Getting
on this thing is like trying to balance two wet bars of
soap on top of each other," the trainer says.

Mandy and Pat guide Cindy along by her snout
toward the mat and line her up so that she's parallel
to it.

"Ready?" Mandy asks. The trainers lean forward on
the mat, allowing water to come up onto it and weigh
it down. Then, Mandy and Pat guide Cindy onto it. In
a move of perfect coordination, as she rolls on, the
trainers roll off the other side.

Everyone in the water carefully moves the mat—with
Cindy on it—over to the boat where I'm waiting.

"On the count of three," Mandy says. "One, two . . ."

They hoist the mat up and slide it onto the boat.
Cindy is lying directly in front of me. This is the first
time I've ever seen a dolphin out of water, lying on its

side. It's an odd sight, and the way Cindy is curled up is not comforting.

But Cindy has a soft look on her face—her eyes are trusting. She emanates gentleness. Ask anyone at the center to describe her, and they'd likely all use the word "sweet."

A trainer hovers over Cindy with an umbrella so that the strong tropical sun doesn't dry her out or burn her. Another trainer kneels at her side with a bucket of water and a sponge to soak her down every few minutes, so that her skin stays moist.

"Anybody got a book they want to read to her out loud?" one trainer jokes.

I kneel over Cindy and place my hands on her side, right on the ripples just below the dorsal fin. I pray that my touch won't be painful to her. Suddenly it feels as if everything I've learned over the past year about animal massage has finally come together. It's as if each animal were watching over my shoulder, coaching me.

From Tab and Presley, I know what a healthy dolphin should feel like, so I close my eyes and let my fingers try to detect what's wrong with Cindy. I keep my right hand near her chin, so that if she decides to swing toward me, I'll know it's coming—this I learned from my work with the horses. Every animal—like every person— has a different personality. Although I've never met a dolphin I didn't like, my work with the horses, Rose, Audi, Ahoy Mate, and even Mambo Point, reminds me that animals can be in bad moods and, at times, are just downright nasty.

I gently slide my fingers along Cindy's side, following her rippled muscles. I make sure to use the entire length of my fingers along her skin, tracing in and out of the folds.

She allows my touch and after a few minutes, I let down my guard and begin to use both hands in the massage. I try to put the pieces together: the muscles on Cindy's abdominal side are all contracted, so the muscles on the opposite side are all stretched out. This is the same situation that I dealt with on Nuka—both animals' bodies were curved unnaturally.

Both of Cindy's sides are lacking circulation and have atrophied muscles. All the other dolphins I've worked on have had tight muscles, but Cindy's, because they've atrophied, feel like a balloon that's only halfway filled with air. When I touch, her muscles literally sink in.

I test the area by giving a little squeeze. There's not a large margin for trial-and-error with animals. With Cindy, it is important that I don't do anything that's going to hurt her.

Cindy doesn't like the squeeze and swings her jaw down to hit my knee. I immediately ease up and my right hand automatically goes up to her jaw so that I can be forewarned if she has anything else in mind. Still, she hasn't opened her mouth to show her teeth, so I know she's not severely discomforted.

I start back up again, this time talking to her in a calm voice, explaining what I am doing—not that she can understand a word, but it feels natural to talk to her, to reassure her as I go along. She curls down occasionally and hits me in the leg: it's her signal to back off, and I listen.

I move around her body and discover that her underbelly, which is not visible when she's in the water, is riddled with spasms, tight bands of muscle. Normally, I would have written off her underbelly as too sensitive, but Buck had clearly demonstrated that the underbelly was indeed a place that could be massaged. I carefully work my way through. I use a gentle version of friction, which I've used on most of the animals so far. I press my fingertips into the spasm. I move in a circle, then push outward to release the grouped muscles. But with each spasm I smooth out, there's another one waiting. There are also adhesions, where a muscle group that travels vertically is stuck to a muscle group that travels horizontally. They get "stuck" when there's a buildup of lactic acid. The body creates lactic acid, which is the burn-off from normal energy. A healthy body is able to effectively circulate the lactic acid so that it doesn't build up. But with an injury, the lactic acid is not expelled properly. As a result, the muscles stick so that when one group contracts it pulls the other muscle group, which resists—the end result is pain. I use what's called cross-fiber friction right at the borders of the muscles to break up the lactic acid underneath. I massage with the direction of the muscle fiber, then once an edge is free, I begin massaging across the fiber.

All the while, Cindy is being doused with water to keep her wet and cool. I feel like I need a dousing too. I'm sweating, and not just because of the blaring sun. It seems that there is no end to Cindy's spasms, adhesions, and soreness. I'm quickly growing overwhelmed.

"I'm going to try a stretch," I announce.

Much like I did with Champ, I cross my arms—right arm past the rippled muscles; left hand underneath, right at her dorsal fin. Then I press and push away at the same time. Suddenly I can feel something happening. I feel the muscles elongate. It's as if I hit some sort of magic button that allows her to unfold. But as soon as I release the stretch, she contracts again.

I repeat the exact same movement. Again, she stretches—only this time, Cindy herself is helping me out: she arches her back to get an even better stretch.

I place my hand on the crest of her spine and turn my wrist back and forth to stretch between each vertebrae. As I release, she continues to arch, with greater flexibility each time. I stop to explain to Pat what I'm doing, using my hands to gesture. As I'm talking, Cindy nudges my arm with her snout as if to say, "Stop talking and massage me!" We all laugh.

I continue with the stretch and Cindy continues to arch. The arch is a normal movement for a healthy dolphin, but Cindy has never been able to do it. She makes clicking noises through her blowhole.

"That means she's loving it," Mandy says.

"I've never seen her stretch that far," Pat says.

We're closing in on a half hour, which is about the maximum amount of time that Pat felt Cindy should be out of the water. So I finish up with gentle tapping. As soon as I stop, Cindy nudges my arm again.

"No more for today. Sorry," I say.

Then the trainers slide the mat right off the back of the boat and Cindy slips back into the water. She swims, and although she's far from normal, her range of motion is definitely increased. She then eats some fish, which is also a good sign.

The other dolphins are let back into the pool and Cindy swims over to them in a rare moment of interaction. Pat smiles proudly and, if I'm not mistaken, blots her eyes.

————

I leave Pat with a detailed write-up of the session and of the techniques to use to continue Cindy's massages. Plus, there's a videotape of me working on Cindy. Pat diligently learns the motions and teaches them to Mandy.

Three times a week, Pat and Mandy wade into the pool to work on Cindy. They don't, however, initiate the massage, it's up to Cindy—if she wants a massage that day, she'll swim over. Almost every time, she swims over.

When they massage Cindy she's in her lagoon—her home—and has the freedom to swim away at any moment; but she doesn't. She stays put. Pat follows my instructions and works the muscles, stimulating the bulging ones and kneading and massaging the contracted ones.

The other dolphins know to give Cindy her space and to not interrupt during the massage. While they patiently wait, they communicate with Cindy through echolocation—sending her sound waves through the water. Perhaps they are trying to give reassurance or praise, although we'll never know for sure. Even when the other dolphins are sectioned off from Cindy, they will press up against the gates and echolocate. Pat and Mandy know the dolphins are echolocating because they can feel the vibrations in the water. Mandy describes it as: "Suddenly being immersed in champagne with all the bubbles."

When Cindy's massage is complete, the other dolphins always swim over and end up getting massages by default ("We don't want them to feel left out," Mandy says) but he knows the dolphins have it all calculated—those animals know there are no default massages.

After Cindy's massage, the difference is clear: she eats, she swims up to the trainers, and she plays with the other dolphins. Her condition hasn't disappeared—and it may never—but anyone can see she's happier. The end result with Cindy is not exactly as I had imagined it would be. I wanted to see her healthy and pain-free. Massage is not a miracle cure. Nothing is. But I can't underestimate the strides Cindy has made. Although they seem small compared to what I would have liked to do, they are big achievements for Cindy. For a dolphin who has been struggling for so long, eating a good meal and playing with friends really is quite an accomplishment.

Now, the rest of the dolphins in the center have started something—whenever they see Pat in the water they race up to her and give her their tails. It's their way of saying, "Rub me." Their tails are one of their most sensitive spots, rubbing it is like the dolphin version of a foot massage.

The Dolphin Research Center was so proud of the work on Cindy that they presented her case, on video, during a conference of marine mammal experts. "All the people in the room who knew dolphins and how their bodies and personalities function were amazed," Mandy says. "They couldn't get over how Cindy was not only allowing us to do this, but actually working *with* us."

————

If you go on a tour today at the Dolphin Research Center, you'll be told how Misty and her daughter Aleta are the pranksters of the group and take special delight in playing tricks on new trainers. You'll also learn that AJ and Kibby like to roughhouse, and that the marks on Kibby's back correspond exactly to the shape and size of AJ's teeth, only in the dolphin world, these marks— or rakes—are signs of affection. Then, if you come around the bend you'll be introduced to Cindy.

"Cindy gets three full body massages each week," the guide will say. "She absolutely loves it. She'll swim into your arms and let you massage her whole entire body." You and the crowd will likely sigh, and then follow the guide down the path to get a lesson on conserving the natural environment, followed by a big dolphin belly flop by Delphi the Fox that soaks everyone.

13

Between a Rock and a Hard Place

I receive a call from the director of another aquarium, Anita. Her voice sounds desperate. "I was wondering if you'd be able to help us," Anita says. "We've got a walrus here who's seriously ill."

She says she heard me speak at the annual International Marine Animal Trainers Association convention, which was held in Baltimore. Because Nuka had responded so well to massage therapy, the aquarium had me present her case during the conference. As part of my presentation, I showed slides and detailed the massage treatment to dozens of top experts in the field.

"What's wrong with the walrus?" I ask.

"She's not eating," Anita says. "There seems to be some type of blockage in her GI tract. As far as we can tell, her symptoms began three days ago."

Without a second's hesitation I tell her I'll be there first thing tomorrow. Anita thanks me profusely, then asks me to pledge strict confidentiality—she says I can't divulge the name of the aquarium or the location to anyone. Confidentiality is, unfortunately, too often necessary in situations like these—if animal-rights activists learn that an animal is sick, they are liable to picket at the front gates, demanding that the animal be released back to the wild. At each zoo and aquarium I've worked at, I've seen the fear they live in from extreme activist groups.

Anita is waiting for us right inside the main gate and quickly ushers us in. "Thank you so much for coming," she says. "The staff first noticed earlier in the week that Wanda was very lethargic. During the feeding demonstration, she wasn't waving or blowing kisses to the visitors. Then, she stopped eating. Our veterinarian first thought that Wanda had swallowed something that would give her indigestion until it passed."

I knew, as does everyone else, that walruses are not picky eaters and will slurp up just about anything they see. Like a two-year-old child who puts everything in his mouth, a walrus can only be given toys that are too big to swallow. The problem is, it's difficult to control the litter or debris that blows into the pool—or what people toss into the pool, despite the numerous "PLEASE DO NOT FEED THE ANIMALS" signs.

To make matters worse, this aquarium is right near a busy section of town so the wind will pick up all types of candy wrappers and plastic bags and popcorn buckets and blow it all over the fence and into the aquarium. Or children might toss coins or toys over the ledge of the exhibit—*maybe Mr. Walrus would like my Barbie doll or a lick of my lollipop?* I've even seen guests litter purposely—they are too lazy to throw their trash where it belongs and they have no idea of the possible consequences—that they could be seriously endangering an animal.

This is not just a problem for animals in aquariums and zoos either. Animals in the wild can just as easily fall victim to litter. I don't know how many times I've read stories about the dolphins that are choked when they eat plastic bags (they look like a jellyfish to a dolphin) or the plastic rings that hook six-packs of soda.

It's amazing all the things that aquariums retrieve. Most of it turns up in the animals' waste material—coins, screws, plastic bags (which can blow up and block everything), Matchbox cars. A lot of times the staff members will come in the morning and see foreign objects on the rocks and not know which walrus swallowed it and if it did internal damage while it was passing through.

Anita continues, "The aquarium veterinarian did what's normally done: gave Wanda mineral oil and kept a close eye on her. But Wanda's symptoms worsened.

"She's scheduled tomorrow for an endoscopy, but she just seems to be in so much pain, we thought you could help." I knew that an endoscopy—where they take a camera down the throat and into the stomach—might well reveal what the animal ate.

"We wanted to bring you in earlier," Anita says, her voice lowering. "But our veterinarian, well, let's just say he's pretty traditional. Unfortunately, he doesn't give alternative medicine the credit it deserves."

Anita leads us around back, past staff trailers and clotheslines where water shoes and wet suits hang to dry.

"Wanda hasn't slept or eaten in days," Anita says, "and she's a walrus who normally slurps up sixty-five pounds of fish a day—not to mention anything else that comes near her mouth. Sorry to be graphic, but Wanda hasn't passed anything through her bowels either. I know that you spoke about how you were massaging Nuka and that she was often so relaxed she'd just sort of release, well I was hoping—we're all hoping—you might be able to do the same for Wanda."

If the situation weren't so dire, I could have thought of a dozen jokes about my "area of expertise," but the truth is, I have no special secret—that's just a natural phenomenon when an animal is relaxed.

"I'll do my best," I say.

Wanda is being kept in a holding room similar to the one where Nuka had been, where the staff and the veterinarians can monitor her closely. Anita leads us down a tiled hallway to the open-ceiling, cement room with a steel-gated door and an emergency exit large enough for a person to fit through, but not for a walrus.

Wanda is lying on her side in the center of the floor. Her flippers are curled and she looks like a child hunched over with an enormous stomachache. Her voice—one that would typically be so loud it would reverberate off the stone, letting everyone know she's there—is now nothing more than a low, strained whimper.

We move into the room very slowly, almost tiptoeing, so as not to startle or alarm Wanda. The walrus turns her head in our direction, and her eyes look so sad, it's as if she's calling out, "Help me, please."

"How do you want to begin?" Anita asks, careful to keep her voice quiet.

"Since it's abdominal work she needs, let's take her over to the side of the room and roll her onto her back."

Anita gently gives Wanda a command, and despite the pain, Wanda arduously inches to the corner. Before she's all the way there she stops and looks up, exhausted.

"Is this far enough?" Anita asks, and even though it's not exactly what I had in mind, neither of us wants to make Wanda move any more.

"That's fine," I say. "I'll be able to reach her stomach."

Anita gives Wanda the command to lay out—a familiar position since it's used every week when the keepers do routine checks to make sure the animal has no injuries, cuts, rashes, or shows anything abnormal. Walruses can't lay flat on their backs, so Wanda rolls over as far as she's able. Her round belly sticks up into the air.

I take a deep breath, then place my palms right on Wanda's belly.

Generally, when I begin working on a patient, I start by doing palpatory work—I want to get an overall feel for what's going on and I want to get the patient used to my touch. My initial touch is extremely light because I know how sensitive the abdomen can be. When your stomach hurts, you want to curl up. So to get Wanda all laid out, belly exposed, is already putting her in an uncomfortable position; plus, the abdomen, especially for animals, is a very protected area, so the response is going to be quite heightened. If I touch a sore spot on a person's stomach, the reaction might be a groan or the person might suck in, or even jump. But when you touch a sore spot on a walrus's stomach, the reaction is unforgettable.

Apparently, even the surface of Wanda's abdomen is sore because my simple touch causes her to let out a whimpering howl that sends chills down my spine. Suddenly Wanda swings around so fast, the movement is a blur. She flips her head back, and in the midst of it all, she pushes Anita. Wanda and I are now face-to-face—more like eyeball to eyeball. She is so close, my eyelashes brush against her forehead. I am frozen.

I stare at her, afraid to even blink. Yet, there's something there that bewilders me: looking straight into her soft brown eyes, I feel a strange connection.

I barely notice her tusks, which, even though they are small, can easily crack me in the head. Instead, I'm drawn to her eyes. Her piercing gaze erases any fear I had. I know she's not going to hurt me; I truly know this. I had touched a sore spot, that much is clear; but it's also clear that she knows I am here to help.

"Wanda, I'm sorry," I say quietly. "I'm here to help you, it's all right, everything's all right." Slowly, Wanda lies back down.

Anita is shaken, but walks back over to Wanda's head, saying, "It's okay, we're going to make you better."

I have seen many injured animals in my career, but never like this. Whatever Wanda has swallowed is causing serious trouble.

"Anthony, what exactly happened?" Anita whispers.

"I'm not really sure, I hardly touched her, but I must have hit the jackpot—I probably landed on the exact spot where the blockage was."

"Are you okay?"

"Shaken," I say, although I'm trying not to let on; I need to camouflage my fear so as not to alarm Wanda any more than she already is. "You?"

"Same," she says. "Do you think we should try it again?"

Without any hesitation, I nod. I have no other choice. Once again, Anita and I resume our positions. I take a nice deep breath and, again, place my hands, even more gently, on Wanda's abdomen. This time, I don't move, just keep my hands still, hoping she'll accept my touch.

So far so good. But as I inch my hands slightly—boom! Wanda pushes up, spins around. Anita is shoved, and Wanda and I are eye-to-eye.

I, once again, look deep into her eyes and it's like I can feel her pain, only for me it's in the form of help-lessness—what can I do to help this animal?

Wanda is not afraid to show me her agony, it's pierc-ing her face, she's desperate for help. I calmly reassure her, "It's all right, I promise I won't touch there again." After a minute or two she lies back down.

"We're going to have to try something different," I say and Anita nods. "Maybe if we move her into the center of the room she won't feel so closed in. It won't leave us with as much leeway, but she may be more relaxed."

Anita agrees and asks Wanda to move. Wanda strug-gles, but complies and lays herself out. Now, I use a little animal psychology: I need to change my position as well; if I vary the angle at which I'm approaching

Wanda, she'll be less likely to associate what I'm doing with the pain she just felt. So both Anita and I walk slowly around to Wanda's backside. This way, if Wanda decides to spin around, she can, and neither Anita nor I will be blocking her.

Anita cradles Wanda's head and does her own little massage, rubbing from Wanda's cheek down her neck. I'm gearing up to try a new technique, a shiatsu movement called Kambiki. It's a rocking/rolling motion that helps relax the muscles. I start at Wanda's flippers, with the goal of beginning as far away from the abdomen as possible so that I can get her relaxed before I work my way up. I gently roll the flippers, then rotate them. I used it on Nuka when I first started working on her. It's a good technique to use because a walrus's large body will sway as I roll it, and it creates a sort of hypnotic, rocking-chair effect.

The motion is slow and measured and it takes me forty-five minutes until I inch up to Wanda's abdomen— I want to be sure the rocking keeps her relaxed, and that her breathing is slow and steady.

Wanda begins to show good signs: she whistles in a low tone, like she's sighing; she closes her eyes and leaves them shut for a few moments at a time. The Kambiki is working.

"Are we ready to try the abdomen again?" I whisper to Anita.

She nods. I ease my hands toward Wanda's belly. As I reach the sensitive area, Wanda lifts her head—it's not anywhere near the forceful reaction from before. I wait, my hands resting on her stomach, until she lowers her head. Then I gently press into the blubber on her stomach.

I want to follow the pathways of the large intestines because that's where, in people at least, blockages tend to occur most. I'm hoping that by using friction I can help to loosen things up. Since I'm quite familiar with walrus anatomy, I've got a mental map of where the intestinal pathways are.

I keep my hands very rigid and use my fingertips to do small circles, working up from the sigmoid area all along the descending colon. When I get to the top of the descending colon, I do a sweeping motion that looks like I'm brushing something off a table, only I'm pushing in with my fingertips as I sweep. This loosens up whatever's in the intestines and draws it down to the sigmoid, which can expel it out.

In a person you don't have to push that hard to affect the organs this way; I usually give a decent amount of pressure, but not to the point that it's uncomfortable for the patient. But with a walrus you need to push so that your fingers sink into the tissue almost two inches. That's why it's so important to relax the area, you can't just dig into a walrus like that. I'm leaning in with my body weight, but there's a fine line—I can't push too hard. I have to feel the muscles, but not hurt them.

Wanda is accepting the movement so I continue along the length of the colon, moving into the transverse colon, going back over repeatedly, doing the circles, then doing the sweeping motion. I work little by little, sort of like shoveling a driveway full of snow: you shovel a little bit from here and a little bit from there, and then you go back over what you just did to really clean it up. You can't just clear it out of the way in one big swoop—your shovel would fill up and you'd have nowhere to dump all the snow.

I'm getting very close to the central area that initially sent Wanda reeling. I nod to Anita, then place my palms on the exact spot. Wanda just lays there and Anita and I both breathe sighs of relief.

Then I move to the small intestines and perform the exact same technique I'd use on a person if I was trying to relax the same area. I use the palms of my hands to make large circles, sort of like the "wax-on, wax-off" movement from *Karate Kid*, only both my hands are moving in the same direction—clockwise, which follows the flow of the intestinal tract.

By this time, an hour and a half has passed. Suddenly I smell a faint, yet familiar, odor that instantly becomes more pungent. I look down and there, on my shoe, a small sign that the massage is working. I've never been so happy to see *that* before.

I know, though, that in the big scheme of things, this small amount is relatively insignificant—it's a start in the right direction but for such a large animal, it's no indication that the blockage has cleared.

The veterinarian assistant, Ana, arrives with vials and needles, all set to take Wanda's blood to continue to monitor her. Ana's amazed that we're still doing the massage—it's been two whole hours, compared to the twenty minutes that I would typically spend on one animal. Seeing Wanda so relaxed makes Ana reconsider.

"This poor animal has been writhing in pain all weekend," she says. "If she's finally resting now there's no way I'm going to disturb her."

Anita turns to me, "Do you think we should try to see if she'll sleep?"

I nod and Anita and I both stand, our knees and backs aching from squatting for so long. We quietly leave the holding pen.

I know I did what I could, but I also know a condition like Wanda's is gravely serious.

We walk past the back door of the walrus exhibit. There, up against the gate, is another walrus, who looks like he's searching.

"Ever since we moved Wanda into the holding pen the others have been coming to the gate looking for her," Anita says. It's remarkable, I think, and enough to tear your heart out.

All that night I can't sleep. I'm tossing and turning and thinking about Wanda, who's scheduled to undergo endoscopies in the morning so that they can see—and then extract—whatever is causing the blockage. Finally, the next morning, my phone rings. It's Anita.

"Wanda just got out of the endoscopies. You're not going to believe this but she swallowed a plastic shopping bag *and* a handball. Now the doctors have to figure out how to remove it all."

I know the handball was probably the main culprit and I also have an idea how Wanda got ahold of it: when I drove out of the aquarium parking lot I passed by a huge park—playground, basketball nets, *and* a handball court—all just a few blocks away. Someone must have whacked the ball and it bounced over the fence and into the walrus exhibit.

Anita tells me the handball has blocked the muscle opening between the stomach and small intestines—an area called the pyloric sphincter. Because of this blockage, Wanda's symptoms are quite understandable.

The veterinarians have already removed the plastic bag using the equipment from the endoscopy. Now, the challenge is: how do you remove a handball from a walrus's intestine?

"Wanda is not in great shape," Anita says. "She's very weak. I wish I had better news, but I'll call you as soon as I hear anything. We're all praying that she pulls through."

For the rest of the day I have difficulty focusing on anything. All I can do is replay the image of Wanda's soft brown eyes pleading with me for help. Every time the phone rings I race for it—"Anita?" But it's a patient, or my wife, Cathy, calling to see if I heard yet.

Finally, at 10 P.M., the call comes.

"Wanda's going to be all right. She's going to make it."

Wanda remains at the animal hospital for several days to recuperate. Once she begins to eat, the veterinarians release her.

She's gently directed into an aluminum cage that is then hoisted by a forklift onto a flatbed truck. A large canvas is draped over the cage, and Wanda is driven back to the aquarium, about twenty minutes away. There, another forklift pulls out the cage and drives it to the back door of the walrus exhibit. The cage door is opened and Wanda is led—on all fours—down the hallway, through the door, and onto the rocks of the exhibit. Wanda slowly eases her way into the water. The other walruses rush over to see their friend. They rub against her, welcoming her back home.

14

The Bunny Hop

Snuggles is a long-eared lop rabbit, with brown and white spots, a long white tail, and brown feet. He's big by rabbit standards: a full nine pounds. Snuggles belongs to a patient of mine, Ilene, whom I saw every week after she had been in a car accident. After seven months of massage work, Ilene improved, but, she told me, her rabbit was getting worse: Snuggles has a kidney problem and the veterinarians tell Ilene that Snuggles doesn't have very long.

"I know you've worked on some pretty exotic animals," Ilene says when she calls. "Do you think you could work on a rabbit?"

I know that massage won't adversely affect Snuggles's kidney condition, but I also know that it won't likely help it.

"I'd be happy to," I say. "But I've got to be honest— massage isn't going to make Snuggles better."

"I know," Ilene says, her voice soft. "I just want to do whatever I can to ease his pain in his last weeks."

Cathy and I used to own a rabbit many years ago so I'm quite familiar with their build and movement. After a little bit of searching in the library, I find a diagram of rabbit anatomy and study it in preparation for the massage.

When Ilene brings in the rabbit cage, Snuggles is lying in it on his side. This is an awkward position for a rabbit because they are usually on all fours—even when they're sleeping.

I gently take Snuggles out of the cage and set him on my lap. I start at the top of his head, making small circles. He slowly closes his eyes, as if he's starting to relax. I use the sides of my thumbs to go up his shoulder blades and then down his legs.

It's an easy massage because I can detect no spasms or muscular problems.

"The best thing you can do for Snuggles is to continue to massage him on your own," I tell Ilene. "If you can keep his circulation moving, it may help him to have more energy."

I switch to using my whole hand to gently rake from his back all the way up to the scruff of his neck. Then I do compression along his spine, giving a little squeeze with my pointer and my thumb. I do compression on his legs, then friction. Snuggles is so relaxed, his body is limp and heavy.

That night Ilene calls. The happiness in her voice is intoxicating.

"Snuggles is hopping all over the place!"

I know the massage is helping Snuggles, but it's also

helping Ilene—she now has interaction with her rabbit that she can feel good about; she no longer feels like she is waiting around for Snuggles to finally give out.

She continues doing the massage every day. A month passes. Then two, then three. Snuggles has long outlived the veterinarian's prognosis.

After four months, Snuggles's kidneys fail. I don't hear from Ilene for several weeks. Then, one day, she shows up in my office. "Meet your new patient," she says. She holds out her palm and there is a bunny so small and sweet I melt. "Snuggles II, say hello to your massage therapist."

15

The First Successful Shark Massage (But Don't Try This at Home)

I had now proven to myself and others that massage could work on any mammal, regardless of size, shape . . . or smell. This made me optimistic for my next patient—my most difficult one to date: a fish.

A very large fish, with rows of very sharp teeth.

Jenkinson's Aquarium is on the boardwalk in Point Pleasant, New Jersey, a summertime tourist town on the shore that empties out once Labor Day passes. It's November when I drive out, so the place looks like a ghost town, all the shops have CLOSED FOR THE WINTER signs in the windows and all the summer homes with the big porches are locked up and dark.

When I arrive at the aquarium, the only other guests there are fifth-graders on a class field trip.

I'm met at the main entrance by the director, Cindy

Claus, and the aquarium veterinarian, Dr. Paluch. "Thank you so much for coming to take a look at Baby," Cindy says to me.

Don't be misled by the delicate name: Baby is seven feet, four inches long and weighs 186 pounds. She's a sand-tiger shark, which is a mildly aggressive shark. Unlike the great white—like Jaws—sand-tiger sharks generally don't attack people. Then again, people generally don't go around massaging sharks. As far as I know, after today I will be the only person on record to ever massage a shark (a fact that my wife is not so keen about—"And how many people, for the record, have tried unsuccessfully to massage a shark?" she asked).

Baby was given her name because when she was brought to Jenkinson's Aquarium she was the smallest of their three sharks. Since then, she has grown to the same size as the other two sharks, who are both males.

Cindy and Dr. Paluch first noticed there was something wrong with Baby a year ago; she was swimming awkwardly, in little spirals, rather than in a straight line. Then they saw there was a bump in her back: it was very round, almost like a bubble underneath the skin. They thought that maybe Baby had been bit or had knocked into something. They put Baby on medication, but nothing changed; instead, she got worse.

One morning Cindy came in to find Baby lying on the bottom of the tank. The only type of shark that does that is the nurse shark, who practically lives on the bottom of the tank or the ocean floor, sucking in water and passing it through the gills. Baby, who's a sand-tiger shark, shouldn't be doing that. Sand-tiger sharks come up to the surface to take gulps of air. The air stays in their stomachs and is used to control their depth—they can release a bit of the air to go deeper into the ocean, or retain the air to stay near the surface. Baby wasn't swimming; she was lying there as if she were exhausted and Cindy could see her laboring and gasping to suck in the water.

I was aware of a shark who had a similar problem: Hans had told me about a shark who lived at another aquarium and had a bump on its back and a spinal deformity called lordosis, where the natural arch of the spine is exaggerated. I would later learn that both this shark and Baby originally came from the same area off the coast of Long Island. I frequently treat people who have lordosis, and a similar spinal deformity called scoliosis. I tried to get in to see that shark, but couldn't. A few weeks later Hans told me he had heard the shark was put to sleep.

I learned about Jenkinson's Aquarium when I met Cindy on the television set of Barbara Walters's show, *The View*. I was demonstrating animal massage and Cindy had brought Checkers the penguin and a mini two-foot alligator from the aquarium (I only ended up massaging the penguin, not the gator). During a commercial break, Cindy and I struck up a conversation.

"Have you ever worked on a shark before?" she asked.

"No, but I've wanted to," I said and told her about the shark I had heard of with lordosis. She listened to me with her jaw dropped.

"There's no known way to help Baby. And we don't want to euthanize her. When can you come see her?"

———

We arranged for me to visit Jenkinson's Aquarium. In the meantime, Dr. Paluch sent me a package of information—diagrams of the shark anatomy, reports on shark lordosis and scoliosis, and a videotape of Baby.

I watched the video with Cathy, and even though she was not enthusiastic about me massaging a shark, I saw her softening at the sight of Baby's awkward swimming. The shark clearly needed help.

I studied up on sharks extensively in preparation for the massage. I learned that sharks in general are very misunderstood animals. They are not really the predators we make them out to be; in fact, sharks don't even care much for the taste of humans. When a shark does attack a human, it's usually because the shark has mistaken the person for a sea lion—a shark's favorite dish. Surfers are mostly prone to shark attacks because from underwater, the shape of a surfer sitting on a board, limbs dangling in the water, resembles a sea lion—especially on days when the water is murky or during twilight. Studies have been done where two dummies were strapped to surf boards. One dummy had no limbs, so the shape from under the water was just the outline of the surf board. The other dummy has limbs that dipped into the water. When sharks were released they only attacked the dummy with limbs; the other went unnoticed. However, as soon as the sharks realized their target wasn't a sea lion, they backed off. It's the same with humans—there may be shark attacks, but after the shark tastes that this isn't the dish he wants, he swims away, even though the shark has forty rows of serrated teeth and could easily engulf an entire person.

As for the shark's anatomy, it's a common misconception that fish have bones. Neither sharks, nor any fish, actually have bones—what we call their "bone" is really cartilage.

A shark's muscles act just as ours do, by contracting and relaxing, only a shark's muscles have a different texture, with peculiar striations—almost like a basketweave pattern—or as I like to refer to it, as "Charlie Brown stripes," because they look just like the black zigzags on his yellow shirt. The muscles that start from behind the gills and travel all the way back toward the tail are stacked and zigzagged. These are incredibly strong muscles and allow the shark to swim by thrashing its tail from side to side—unlike a dolphin, which moves its tail up and down.

While I was still at home studying, the staff at Jenkinson's was trying to figure out exactly how to stage a shark massage. They needed to devise a way to have Baby immobilized but still in the water so that she could "breathe" by way of passing water through her gills. Of course, no sedation or drugs of any sort were going to be used—sedation would relax the muscles too much, so that I wouldn't be able to get an accurate feel of where the problem areas might be—which added to the challenge.

They decided the only way to work on Baby was to move her to a private tank. There was a large holding tank in the basement that would serve the purpose. But how do you get a shark into the basement?

The aquarium staff spent days going over the plan. They purchased a special harness that looked like a stretcher and mapped out the exact route. Then they had a practice session. A senior keeper, Pete, was the shark. The harness was a piece of heavy-duty canvas attached to two long poles. The canvas was set on the ground and Pete laid on top of it. Four staff members lifted the poles and brought them together, wrapping the canvas, like a taco shell, around Pete. Then, with synchronized steps, the four men walked the stretcher down the hall toward the stairwell. Now came the real challenge: walking a "shark" downstairs. They slowly, but successfully, delivered Pete downstairs to the basement pool. But when they inspected the stretcher afterward, they noticed that both poles had bent. They immediately bought stronger poles and ran through the practice session again. Everything went smoothly. Pete actually weighed a few pounds more than Baby, so the aquarium felt confident that they wouldn't end up with a shark on the floor. Baby was to be moved four days before I arrived. This way, by the time I began working on her, she would be accustomed to her new tank.

For the massage, Baby is directed back into the stretcher, which is being held in shallow water by the four staff members. Her face is covered so that she can't see— while this would be terrifying for a human, it's actually more relaxing for an animal. Since they can't think and wonder and anticipate like we can, sight is only a distraction in unusual circumstances.

I hold out my hand and slowly bring it toward Baby. This will be the first time this shark has ever been touched therapeutically by human hands.

I can't consciously think, "This is a shark, I'm about to touch a shark," or else I'd probably run the other way.

Instead, I have to think, "This is an animal who's hurt, this is an animal who needs me."

I rest my hand on Baby's side and rub gently. I stroke downward—from nose to tail. The skin is smooth, like felt. My hand just glides over it. Rubbing in the other direction is a different story: from tail to nose the skin is like sandpaper. Long ago it actually used to be used as sandpaper, and was very durable. As I rub, it feels like the shark's skin is actually exfoliating a couple layers of my skin. Baby seems to not even notice there's a human touching her. She stays very still.

I start with the typical surface massage strokes, the ones I do every time I massage an animal or human, just to get the patient relaxed and used to my touch. Baby takes well to the effluerage. She is completely co-operative. Without any sedation, this shark is even docile. I slowly work my way toward the lump on her side.

When I reach the area, I look up to Cindy and Dr. Paluch. They nod approvingly and I place my hand on the lump. Baby flinches and it causes a chain reaction: I flinch, and the four divers holding the harness tense up to keep the harness steady.

"OK, it's all right," I say.

We wait a few seconds, then I place my hand a couple inches away from the lump and begin massaging there. Slowly, I work my way back toward the lump. This time, I touch it a bit less tentatively. Baby thrashes from side to side.

I pull my hand back; the divers steady the harness. I had only felt the spot for a couple of seconds, but what I felt surprised me: it didn't feel solid, like bands of muscles; it felt soft, almost like a pillow.

"It feels like air," I announce.

Dr. Paluch is amazed. "You think it's just an air bubble?"

"That's definitely what it felt like. I'm going to get her more relaxed so that I can work the area."

It's no pun when a massage therapist says it's all in the touch. We can figure things out with our hands—what's normal, what's not normal. We don't diagnose, but there is nothing that can replicate hands-on work. Frequently, tumors in people are first noticed by massage therapists.

I continue to massage Baby, mostly along her side. I can see and feel her breathing, the way she's abnormally gulping the water, and it helps me to gauge a pattern. At first, she was gulping water every ten seconds, which is extremely fast. But now, shorter, shallow breaths turn into deep breaths, and she's gulping every twenty seconds, half as much as before. I know it is time to try again.

I move toward the lump, and this time Baby lets me know it is sensitive by flinching, but she doesn't thrash like before. I palpate the spot.

"It's definitely air," I say.

"An air pocket in her stomach," Dr. Paluch says.

"I don't think it's in her stomach," I say. "It seems like an air pocket between the skin and the muscles, not in the stomach. If it was her stomach, she wouldn't be digesting."

"A surface air bubble would make sense," Cindy chimes in.

"Yes," I say, "it would explain the awkward swimming and the scoliosis because added trapped air would change the buoyancy in her body."

Dr. Paluch retrieves a stethoscope from his bag and leans in toward Baby. He presses the stethoscope to the lump, and listens. Then, still listening, he thumps his fingers against her side as if he were testing the ripeness of a melon. He nods his head as he removes his stethoscope.

"The way the sound reverberated shows it is definitely air," he says. "I'd like to do an ultrasound soon."

I go back to work and try to move the air pocket by gently rubbing it to see if any air bubbles will come out. Nothing.

Around the lump, however, are numerous muscle spasms, so I begin working those, performing deep tissue massage. Baby squirms, but I'm still able to hold my position.

"I'd like to try a stretch now," I say. I place my right hand on Baby's right side and I slide my left hand down toward her tail. With my arm spaced like this, I now have leverage. I push my hands in opposite directions and as I do this, it's like stretching out Baby's side so that she's able to release the muscles instead of contracting them.

As I do the stretch again, I have one of the divers take his hand and run it along the muscle so that we can lengthen it even more. I then use a myofascial technique where I am able to push down and in—this releases frozen muscles and allows the blood to circulate more efficiently in that area.

I don't even realize it but almost forty minutes have already passed—I'm amazed that this shark has been allowing me to work on her for that long. I finish up the massage, then I slowly take my hands out of the water and dry them off. My fingers are red and tender from the shark's rough skin.

After Dr. Paluch performs the ultrasound, Cindy calls me at home.

"You were right," she says. "The ultrasound confirmed an air bubble just under the skin. Here we were thinking it was a complicated problem, now it seems there may be a simple solution."

A week later Dr. Paluch draws out the air with a long needle. Almost immediately Baby's back is noticeably straighter. She's still swimming awkwardly, but now there is hope for her to recover.

I return to work on Baby because I know it's going to take a while to reeducate her body on maintaining normal posture. It was a similar situation with Nuka; it took six months before she was on her own. I teach the staff how to do the massage so they can work on Baby in between my visits.

"Anthony, this type of thing would *never* take place at numerous other aquariums," Cindy tells me one day. Her voice gets low. "Many aquarium directors prefer euthanasia to trying new therapies," she says.

We stare down at the shark in the pool. Baby's swimming more like a normal shark, whipping her tail from side to side. Her spine no longer has to compensate for the pressure from the air pocket and is much straighter. Her buoyancy is almost back to normal. Hopefully, in a matter of months, Baby will be slicing through the water again with speed, agility, and grace.

16

Where Do You Put the Towel
on a Turtle?

I've worked on over a hundred different animals from
seventeen different species and have seen some dramatic results. Rudy the Penguin is alive and well, Baby
is swimming, and Nuka can use her rear flippers.
There's no question in my mind that massage—carefully
performed by a licensed practitioner, under a doctor's
or veterinarian's supervision—can be a wonderful tool
to heal *all* living bodies: from sharks to infants, penguins to dogs.

I view the entire animal kingdom differently now. It
took me a while to figure out exactly what it meant that
I could get an 1,800-pound walrus or a shark to allow
me to touch them. My conclusion is that the great divide between the human and the animal kingdom isn't
all that great. Animals are more "human" than we realize. My work with them has proven to me that they
have emotions and intuitions and, above all, that they

respond to—and crave—the same things we do, namely personal contact and interaction.

I know that massage is not a technique that will bring health in all circumstances. Often, the benefits of massage are more subtle. With Wanda, massage allowed her to get some rest, which was something she hadn't done in days. With Champ, massage alleviated his deep-rooted fears of abuse. With Cindy, it allowed her to stretch her crumpled body.

Sometimes massage is solely about the frame of mind—many of my human patients have terminal illnesses; no, massage won't cure their diagnosis of cancer, but it will help them to relax, and it's wonderful to be able to give people a sense of ease that they haven't felt in a long, long while. The same holds true with my animal patients. Sure, massage is great for muscle spasms, contractions, and adhesions, it will do its job on those almost every time; but often, life's problems are not that simple. That's when massage is an unexpected gift—it's a respite from pain, it's like a gentle breeze or a fond memory, or a warm hug. And who wouldn't want to hug a two-thousand-pound walrus?

Also by Pankaj Mishra

NONFICTION
An End to Suffering

FICTION
The Romantics

TEMPTATIONS OF THE WEST

TEMPTATIONS OF THE WEST

How to Be Modern in India, Pakistan, Tibet, and Beyond

PANKAJ MISHRA

Farrar, Straus and Giroux / New York

Farrar, Straus and Giroux
19 Union Square West, New York 10003

Distributed in Canada by Douglas & McIntyre Ltd.
Printed in the United States of America
First edition, 2006

Some of these essays first appeared in slightly different form in *The New York Review of Books*, *Granta*, *The New York Times Magazine*, and *The Guardian Weekend* magazine.

Grateful acknowledgment is made for permission to reprint an excerpt from "Continuities" from *Middle Earth* by Arvind Krishna Mehrotra, copyright © 1984 by Arvind Krishna Mehrotra. Published in 1984 by Oxford University Press. Reprinted by permission of the author.

Library of Congress Cataloging-in-Publication Data
Mishra, Pankaj.
    Temptations of the West : how to be modern in India, Pakistan, Tibet, and beyond / Pankaj Mishra.— 1st ed.
        p.   cm.
    ISBN-13: 978-0-374-17321-0 (hardcover : alk. paper)
    ISBN-10: 0-374-17321-4 (hardcover : alk. paper)
    1. South Asia—Description and travel. 2. South Asia—Civilization—Western influences. 3. Mishra, Pankaj—Travel—South Asia.   I. Title.

DS337.M58   2006
954.05—dc22

                                                                        2006011987

Designed by Jonathan D. Lippincott

www.fsgbooks.com

10 9 8 7 6 5 4 3 2 1

for Barbara Epstein

Contents

Preface

Over the last five years I have traveled to places as far apart as Buddhist Tibet, Bollywood, and Taliban-ruled Afghanistan. *Temptations of the West* describes these journeys in South and Central Asia, through countries that differ radically from each other in many ways but that seem to face the same dilemma: How do peoples with traditions extending back several millennia modernize themselves?

Recent events have ensured that this is no longer an academic question. Western ideologies, whether of colonialism, communism, or globalization, have confronted the countries I visited—India, Pakistan, Afghanistan, Nepal, and Tibet—with the same challenge: modernize or perish. But the wrenching process of remaking life and society in all their aspects (social, economic, existential) frequently collapses in violence, which affects not just South Asia but also, as the horrific events of 9/11 showed, the apparently remote and self-contained worlds of the West.

Needless to say, the societies I traveled through are too internally diverse to be summed up by broad generalizations of the kind preferred by policymakers and op-ed columnists. These interconnected narratives do not presume to offer solutions to their great problems, nor dwell abstractly on democracy, religion, and terrorism. Rather, they seek to make the reader enter actual experiences: of individuals—Hindus, Muslims, and Buddhists trying to find a way in the modern world—and of the traveler, as, confronted with a bewildering complexity, he moves from ignorance and prejudice to a measure of self-awareness and knowledge.

PROLOGUE

BENARES

Learning to Read

I spent four months in Benares in the winter of 1988. I was twenty years old, with no clear idea of my future, or indeed much of anything else. After three idle, bookish years at a provincial university in a decaying old provincial town, I had developed an aversion to the world of careers and jobs which, having no money, I was destined to join. In Benares, the holiest city of the Hindus, where people come either to ritually dissolve their accumulated "sins" in the Ganges or simply to die and achieve liberation from the cycle of rebirths—in Benares, with a tiny allowance, I sought nothing more than a continuation of the life I had led as an undergraduate.

I lived in the old quarter, in a half-derelict house owned by a Brahmin musician, a tiny, frail, courteous old man. Panditji had long ago cut himself off from the larger world and lay sunk all day long in an opium-induced daze, from which he roused himself punctually at six in the evening to give sitar lessons to German and American students. It was how he maintained his expensive habit and also staved off penury. His estranged, asthmatic wife lived on the floor above his—she claimed to have not gone downstairs for fifteen years—and spent most of her time in a windowless kitchen full of smoke from the dung-paved hearth, conversing in a low voice with her faithful family retainer of over fifty years. The retainer, a small, reticent man in pleated khaki shorts, hinted, in that gloomy setting, at better days in the past, even a kind of feudal grandeur.

The house I lived in, the melancholy presence of Panditji and his wife, were part of the world of old Benares that was still intact in the late eighties and of which the chess games in the alleys, the all-night concerts in temples, the dancing girls at elaborately formal weddings, the gently decadent pleasures of betel leaves and opium formed an essential component. In less than two years most of this solid-seeming world was to vanish into thin air. The old city was to be scarred by a rash of fast-food outlets, video game parlors, and boutiques, the most garish symbols of the entrepreneurial energies unleashed by the liberalization of the Indian economy, which would transform Benares in the way they had already transformed other sleepy small towns across India.

But I didn't know this then, and I did not listen too closely when Panditji's wife reminisced about the Benares she had known as a young woman, when she told me about the time her husband came to her family home as a starving student, when she described the honors bestowed on her father by the maharaja of Benares. I was even less attentive when she complained about her son and his wife, more particularly the latter, who, though Brahmin, had, in her opinion, the greedy, grasping ways of the merchant castes.

I didn't pay much attention to the lives around me. I was especially indifferent to the wide-eyed Europeans drifting about on the old ghats, each attached to an ash-smeared guru. I was deep into my own world, and though I squirmed at the word and the kinds of abject dependence it suggested, I had found my own guru, long dead but, to me, more real than anyone I actually knew that winter I spent slowly making my way through his books.

On an earlier visit to the library at Benares Hindu University, idly browsing through the stacks, I had noticed a book called *The American Earthquake*. I read a few pages at random, standing in a dark corridor between overloaded, dusty shelves. It seemed interesting; I made a mental note to look it up on my next trip to the library. Months passed. By then I had moved to Benares, and one day, while looking for something else in the same section of the stacks, I came across the book again. This time I took it to the reading room. An hour into it, I began to look at the long list under the heading "Other books by Edmund Wilson." Later that afternoon I went back to the shelves, where they all were, dust-laden, termite-infested, but beautifully, miraculously, present: *The Shores of Light, Classics and Commercials, The Bit Between My Teeth, The Wound and the Bow, Europe Without Baedeker, A Window on Russia, A Piece of My Mind . . .*

It was miraculous because this was no ordinary library. Wilson's books weren't easily accessible. I had always lived in small towns where libraries and bookshops were few and far between and did not stock anything except a few standard texts of English literature: Austen, Dickens, Kipling, Thackeray. My semicolonial education had made me spend much of my time on minor Victorian and Edwardian writers. Some diversity was provided by writers in Hindi and the Russians, whom you could buy cheaply at Communist bookstores. As for the rest, I read randomly, whatever I could find, and with the furious intensity of a small-town boy to whom books are the sole means of communicating with, and understanding, the larger world.

I had realized early on that being passionate about literature wasn't enough. You had to be resourceful; you had to be perpetually on the hunt for books. And so I was, at libraries and bookshops, at other people's houses, in letters to relatives in the West, and, most fruitfully, at the local paper recycler, where I once bought a tattered old paperback of Heinrich Mann's *Man of Straw*, which I—such were the gaps in my knowledge—dutifully read, and made notes about, without knowing anything about his more famous and distinguished brother. Among this disconnected reading, I had certain preferences, a few strong likes and dislikes, but they did not add up to coherent standards of judgment. I knew little of the social and historical underpinnings to the books I read; I had only a fleeting sense of the artistry and skill to which certain novels owed their greatness.

I had problems too with those books of Edmund Wilson I had found at the library, some of which I read in part that winter, others from cover to cover. Many of them were collections of reviews of books I could not possibly read at the time, or else they referred to other books I hadn't heard of. Proust, Joyce, Hemingway, Waugh, yes; Malraux and Silone, probably; but where in India could one find John Dos Passos? Wilson's books also assumed a basic knowledge of politics and history I did not have. They were a struggle for me, and the ignorance I felt before them was a secret source of shame, but it was also a better stimulus to the effort his books demanded than mere intellectual curiosity.

I was never to cease feeling this ignorance, but I also had a sense as I groped my way through Wilson's work that my awareness of all these unread books and unknown writers was being filtered through an extraordinarily cohesive sensibility. Over the next few months it became clear to me that his powers of summary and explication were often worth more attention than the books and writers that were his subjects. There was also a certain idea that his lucid prose and confident judgments suggested and that I, at first, found so attractive, the image of a man wholly devoted to reading and thinking and writing. I thought of him at work in his various residences—Provincetown, Talcottville, Cambridge, Wellfleet—and in my imagination these resonant names became attached to a promise of wisdom and serenity.

The library where I found Wilson's books had, along with the university, come out of an old, and now vanished, impulse: the desire among Hindu reformists in the freedom movement to create indigenous centers of education and culture. The fundamental idea was to train young Hindu men for the modern world, and like many other idealisms of the freedom movement, it hadn't survived long in the chaos of independent India, where even the right to education came to be fiercely fought over under the banner of specific castes, religions, regions, and communities.

Sectarian tensions were particularly intense in North India, especially in Uttar Pradesh, the province with the greatest population and second-highest poverty rate in the country, where caste and political rivalries spread to the local universities. The main political parties, eager to enlist the large student vote in their favor, had begun to put money into student union elections. Politically ambitious students would organize themselves by caste: the Brahmin, the Thakur (the so-called warrior caste), the Backward, and the Scheduled (the government's euphemism for former untouchables). The tensions were so great that academic sessions were frequently interrupted by student strikes; arson, kidnapping, and murder among students became common features of campus life.

Miraculously, the library at Benares had remained well stocked. Subscriptions to foreign magazines had been renewed on time; you could find complete volumes of the *TLS*, *Partisan Review*, and *The New York Review of Books* from the 1960s in the stacks. Catalogs of university presses had been dutifully scrutinized by the library staff; the books, as though through some secluded channel untouched by the surrounding disorder, had kept flowing in.

The library was housed in an impressively large building in the style known as Hindu-Saracenic, whose attractive pastiche of Indian and Victorian Gothic architecture had been prompted by the same Indian modernist aspirations that had created the university. But by the late eighties chaos reigned in almost every department. Few books were to be found in their right places; the card catalog was in complete disarray. In the reading room, students of a distinctly criminal appearance smoked foul-smelling cigarettes and noisily played cards. Some of them chose to take their siestas on long desks; bored young women spent hours scratching their initials into tabletops.

It was hardly a congenial place for long hours of reading, but since I wasn't enrolled as a student at the university, I could not take books out of the library. I was, however, allowed to sit in the reading room, and I was there almost every day from the time it opened in the morning. Since I had little money, I walked the four miles to the library from my house. For lunch I had an omelet at a fly-infested stall outside the library and then a glass of sticky-sweet tea which effectively killed all hunger for the next few hours. In the evening I would walk home along the river and sit until after dark on the ghats, among a mixed company of touts and drug pushers; washermen gathering clothes that had rested on the stone steps all afternoon, white and sparkling in the sun; groups of children playing hopscotch on the chalk-marked stone floor; a few late bathers, dressing and undressing under tattered beach umbrellas; and groups of old men, silently gazing at the darkening river.

Many of my days in Benares were spent in this way, and when I think of them, they seem serenely uneventful. But what I remember best now are not so much the clear blue skies and magically still afternoons, glimpsed from my window-side perch at the library, as the factors that constantly threatened to undo that serenity. For a radically different world existed barely a few hundred meters from where I sat reading about Santayana.

The university in those days was the scene of intense battles between students and the police. Anything could provoke them: a student who was not readmitted after being expelled; an exam that a professor refused to postpone. A peculiar frenzy periodically overtook the two sides, whereupon the students would rampage through the campus, smashing furniture and any windowpanes left unbroken from their last eruption of rage. Challenged by the police, they would retreat to the sanctuary of their hostels and fire pistols at the baton-charging constables. In retaliation, the policemen would often invade the hostels, break into locked rooms, drag out their pleading, wailing occupants, and proceed to beat them.

I once saw one of their victims, minutes after the police had left, coughing blood and broken teeth, his clothes torn, the baton marks on his exposed arms rapidly turning blue. Another time I saw a policeman with half of the flesh on his back gouged out by a locally made hand grenade. Anxious colleagues watched helplessly from behind their wire mesh shields as he tottered and collapsed on the ground. Terrified bystanders like myself threw themselves to the ground in a defensive reflex we'd seen in action movies. The grenade thrower—a scrawny boy in a big-collared shirt and tight polyester trousers who, I learned later, had targeted the policeman after being tortured by him in custody— stood watching on the cobblestone road, fascinated by his handiwork.

Such violence, extreme though it seemed, wasn't new to the university, which had long been witness to bloodier battles between the student wings of Communist and Hindu nationalist organizations. These two groups tended to be allied with different ends of the caste system: The lower castes tended to be Communist; the upper castes tended to be Hindu nationalist. But frequently now the violence came for no ideological reason, with no connections to a cause or movement. It erupted spontaneously, fueled only by the sense of despair and hopelessness that permanently hung over North Indian universities in the 1980s, itself part of a larger crisis caused by the collapse of many Indian institutions, the increasingly close alliance between crime and politics, and the growth of state-organized corruption—processes that had accelerated during Mrs. Gandhi's "Emergency" in the mid-seventies.

For students poised to enter this world, the choices were harsh, and it didn't matter what caste you belonged to; poverty was evenly distributed across this region. Most of the people I knew were deeply cynical in their attitude toward their future. You could work toward becoming a member of either the state or national legislature and siphon off government funds earmarked for literacy and population control projects; if nothing worked out, you could aspire, at the other end of the scale, to be a lowly telephone mechanic and make money by selling illegal telephone connections.

Most of the students in this traditionally backward area of India came from feudal or semirural families, and aspired to join the Civil Service, a colonial invention that even in independent India continued to offer the easiest and quickest route to political power and affluence. But there were fewer and fewer recruitments made to the Civil Service from North India, where the decline in standards, as well as the cheap availability, of higher education had made it possible for millions to acquire university degrees while they had less and less prospect of employment. Bribery and nepotism had played a major part in the disbursement of the jobs in the minor government services. Students from the lately impoverished upper castes suffered most in this respect; if poverty wasn't enough, they were further disadvantaged by the large quotas for lower-caste candidates in government jobs.

The quotas, first created by Nehru's government in the early 1950s and meant as a temporary measure, were expanded and used by successive governments as an electoral ploy to attract lower-caste votes. The upper-caste students found themselves making the difficult adjustments to urban life only to confront the prospect of being sent back to the oblivion they had emerged from, and their sense of blocked futures, which they acquired early in their time at the university, was to reach a tragic culmination in 1990 in the spate of self-immolations following the central government's decision to provide even larger quotas in federal jobs for applicants from lower castes.

My own situation was little different from that of the people around me. I had recently spent three years at the nearby provincial university at Allahabad, where I was in even closer, more unsettling proximity to the desperation I saw in Benares. I was upper-caste myself, without family wealth, and roughly in the same position as my father had been in freshly independent India when the land reform act of 1951—another of Nehru's attempts at social equality, it was meant to turn exploited tenants into landholders—reduced his once well-to-do Brahmin family to penury. My mother's family had suffered a similar setback. Like many others in my family who laboriously worked their way into the middle classes, I had to make my own way in the world. Looking back, I can see my compulsive pursuit of books, and the calm and order it suggested, contrasting so jarringly with the rage and desperation around me, as my way of putting off a grimly foreclosed future.

So, during my months in Benares, I was able to live at a slight tangent to the chaos of the university. And I was able to do this, I now see, partly because of Rajesh.

I got to know Rajesh early in my stay at Benares. A tall, wiry, good-looking man in his mid-twenties, he had continued to live in Benares after finishing his studies at the university. He was eccentric and moody. He would start reciting Urdu poetry one moment and then denounce its decadence the next and start enumerating the virtues of the farming life. "All these wine drinkers with broken hearts," he would say. "You can't compare them to simple peasants who do more for humanity." He used to say he would rather be a farmer than join government service and do the bidding of corrupt politicians. On other occasions he would tell me about the good works honest civil servants in India could achieve and how he himself aspired to be one of them. There was also an unexpected mystical side to him. I once saw him standing on the ghats gesturing toward the sandy expanses across the river. "That," he was saying to his companion, a slightly terrified young student, "is *sunyata*, the void. And this"—he pointed at the teeming conglomeration of temples and houses behind us—"is *maya*, illusion. Do you know what our task is? Our task is to live somewhere in between."

Rajesh revered Gandhi and distrusted Nehru, who he said was too "modern" in his outlook, but then he would change his mind and say that Gandhi wasn't "tough" enough. All of these opinions he delivered with a faraway look; they formed part of monologues about the degraded state of contemporary India. "Where are we going?" he would say, dramatically throwing up his hands. "What kind of nation are we becoming?" He loved Faiz, the Pakistani writer whose doom-laden poetry he knew by heart; he was also fond of Wordsworth, whom he had studied as an undergraduate; he showed me a notebook where he had copied down his favorite poems, "The Solitary Reaper" among them.

But I could never get him to talk about them. He did not listen much, and he did not like anyone interrupting his monologues. It wasn't easy to be with him.

He had been at the university for eight years when I met him, and at first he appeared to be another of the countless students who hung around the campus, mechanically accumulating useless degrees, applying for this or that job. I had come to him with an introduction from a mutual friend at my undergraduate university. This friend believed that "studious" people like myself needed powerful "backers" at Benares Hindu University—he used the English words—and that Rajesh was well placed to protect me from local bullies and criminals. Rajesh himself believed so and was more than happy to take me under his wing. "You are here to study," he told me at our first meeting, "and that's what you should do. Let me know if anyone bothers you, and I'll fix the bastard."

Part of his concern for me came from an old, and now slightly melodramatic, reverence for "studious" Brahmins. He was Brahmin himself but considered himself unequal to what he felt to be the proper dignity of his caste. The feeling was widespread in the region, where the traditional dominance of Brahmins was beginning to collapse in the face of a serious political challenge by assertive lower castes. The decline of Brahmin prestige and authority, intimately linked to their diminishing political importance, was symbolized by a famous family of Benares, which was once very close to the Nehru-Gandhi dynasty and had been pushed into irrelevance by the new, militant kind of low-caste politician. The members of the family still wore their caste marks on their foreheads; they still observed fasts, regularly bathed in the Ganges, were chief guests at temples on holy days, and would not accept food from low-caste people. But it was only this excessive concern about their public image, and an overdeveloped sense of uncleanliness and contamination, that remained of their Brahminness. No crowds of job seekers and flunkies gathered at their house anymore; the women in the family walked around the bazaars unescorted and unrecognized; visiting journalists went elsewhere for good copy.

Rajesh felt the general change of status differently. He fasted religiously, went to offer flowers at the temple of Hanuman, the monkey god, every Tuesday. His regard for Faiz and love for Urdu poetry spoke of an older Brahmanical instinct for learning and the arts. But he also gave the impression that none of the old ways or values mattered anymore in a world in which Brahmins were forced to struggle to survive with everyone else. "Yes, I am a Brahmin too," Rajesh would say, and then add, mysteriously, "but I have done things no Brahmin would have ever done."

I remember my first visit to his room, which was in one of the derelict-looking hostels with piles of broken furniture scattered on the front quad. The stairs to his room were splattered with blood-red patterns made by students spitting betel juice. In the assorted shabbiness of his room—light from a naked bulb falling weakly on scabby blue walls, unmade bed, discarded slippers, rickety table, cheap denim jeans hanging limply from a solitary nail in the wall, a bamboo bookstand tottering under the weight of old newspapers—I noticed a jute shoulder bag lying open on the ground, bulging with crude pistols. No attempt had been made to conceal the pistols, which seemed to belong as naturally to the room as the green plastic bucket next to them. Their presence made me nervous; so did the hint of instability given by Rajesh's speech and manner, the long monologues, the unconnected references to Wordsworth, to India. I began to wish I saw less of him.

But it was hard to break off contact, even harder to be indifferent to the innocent friendliness he exuded every time I saw him. He often appeared at the library, "checking up," he said, on whether I was being my studious self or whether I was there to "ogle the girls." I would try to avoid him by disappearing from the reading room at the time he was likely to show up there, but he would then appear at a later hour. He also took a surprising amount of interest in my reading, surprising because although he had done an undergraduate course in English, I rarely saw him reading anything more than the Hindi newspapers scattered around the tea shops on the campus. "Edmund Wilson! Again! Why," he would ask with genuine bemusement, "are you always reading the same man?" He listened patiently while I tried to say a few explanatory words about the particular book or essay he had pointed to. He once caught me reading *To the Finland Station*, and I had to provide a crude summary, in fewer words than used by Wilson, of Trotsky's main ideas. I couldn't, of course, refuse; the thought of Rajesh's instability, the pistols in his room always forced me to summon up a reasonably friendly response. It could be exhausting being with him at times. Why, I would wonder, did he, who seemed to have read little beyond Faiz and the Romantics, want to know so much about people so distant from us, like Trotsky or Bakunin? (More simply, why couldn't he spend his time with other people in the university?)

Rajesh was well known in student circles. There was a special respect for him among other upper-caste students from nearby villages; lonely and vulnerable in what to them was the larger, intimidating world away from home, they saw Rajesh as a sympathetic fellow provincial and older protector. Rajesh fitted the role rather well: He was physically bigger and stronger than most students on the campus; he had a certain reputation—a lot of people seemed to know about the pistols in his room—and it pleased him to be thought of as a godfather-like figure.

A small crowd instantly gathered around whenever I went out with him to a tea stall and eagerly hung on to every word he spoke. He often talked about politics, the latest developments in Delhi, the current gossip about the size of a minister's wealth; he would repeat colorful stories about local politicians, the imaginative ways in which they had conned the World Bank or some other development agency, the bridges that were built only on paper, the roads that existed only in files.

Indeed, I often wondered—although he seemed content simply talking about politics—if he was not planning to be a politician himself; students with a popular mass base in the university who proved themselves capable of organizing strikes and demonstrations were often handpicked by local political bosses to contest elections to the local municipal corporation. Rajesh seemed to know people off campus as well; I once noticed a couple of conspicuously affluent visitors who had driven to see him in a sinister-looking pale green Ambassador with tinted windows.

But I was preoccupied, particularly with Wilson's writings and their maze of cross-references that sent me scurrying from book to book in an effort to plug at least some of what I felt were egregious gaps in my knowledge. One of the books I came across in this way was Flaubert's *Sentimental Education*, which I had read rather indifferently in a Penguin Classics edition sometime back. Wilson's essay on the politics of Flaubert, collected in *The Triple Thinkers*, made me want to reread it. When I did so, I found Flaubert's account of an ambitious provincial's

tryst with metropolitan glamour and disillusion full of the kind of subtle satisfactions that a neurotic adolescent sensibility would be especially susceptible to. I identified with Frédéric Moreau, the protagonist,
with his large, passionate, but imprecise, longings, his indecisiveness,
his aimlessness, his self-contempt. I cannot ever forget the sick feeling
that came over me after I finished the novel late one evening at the library. I was only twenty, and much experience, and many more books,
lay ahead of me. But I couldn't fail to recognize the intimations the
novel gave me of the many stages of drift and futility I was encounter-
ing and was yet to encounter in my own life.

I recommended *Sentimental Education* to Rajesh one evening and
gave him a photocopy of Wilson's essay. I didn't expect him to read all
of it; but he had been curious about Wilson, and I thought the essay
was a good example of his writing. I didn't hear from him for a few
weeks. My life went on as before. I left for the library early in the morning and came back to a house reverberating with the exuberant jan-
gling of sitars, the doleful twang of sarods, the hollow beat of tablas. I
ate every evening with Panditji's wife, sitting cross-legged on the floor in
her dark kitchen, awkwardly inhaling thick smoke from the wood fire,
over which Shyam dextrously juggled hot chapatis from one calloused
palm to another.

Later, back in my room, trying to read in the low-voltage light, I
would hear the bells for evening prayers ring out from the adjacent
temple. I spoke little to the Americans who, after their lessons with Panditji, came up to the roof to smoke opium. I already knew I could not
share my intellectual discoveries with them. They hadn't heard of Edmund Wilson; one of them, a Princeton undergraduate, straining to
recognize the name, thought I meant the biologist E. O. Wilson. The
cultural figures they spoke about, and appeared to miss in the often oppressive alienness of this most ancient of Indian towns, were then unknown to me; it was to take me a few more years to find out who David
Letterman was. But the Americans were, like me, whatever their reasons, refugees from the modern world of work and achievement, explorers of a world that antedated their own, and I was sympathetic to
them.

———

Several weeks after I'd last seen him, Rajesh abruptly reappeared one afternoon at the library. He had been away, he said, on urgent work. Now he was on his way to visit his mother, who lived in a village forty miles west of Benares. Would I accompany him? I thought of making some excuse, but then I realized I needed some diversion, and I said yes. Besides, I was curious about Rajesh's background, of which he had told me nothing until then. I could guess that he wasn't well off, but one could have said the same for most students at the university.

We left one cold foggy morning on the small-gauge, steam-engined train that in those days ran between Benares and Allahabad. A chilly wind, gritty with coal dust, blew in through the iron-barred windows as the train puffed and wheezed through an endless flat plain, stubby fields stretching to tree-blurred horizons, coils of smoke torpid above ragged settlements of mud huts and half-built brick houses. The train was empty, and Rajesh and I stretched out on hard wooden benches, wrapped from head to toe in coarse military blankets, hurriedly sipping the cardamom-scented tea that seemed to turn cold the moment the vendor lifted the kettle off his tiny coal stove.

We got off at a small station populated entirely, it seemed, by mangy dogs. Another half hour tonga ride from there, the horse's hooves clattering loudly against the tarmac road. Mango groves on both sides. Here and there, a few box-shaped houses with large courtyards where men slumbered on string cots; cold-storage warehouses; tiny shuttered shops. At an enclave of mud huts, swarthy blouseless women swept the common yard with brooms made of leafy neem twigs that left the earth raked over with crow's-feet patterns. Finally, at the end of a row of identical roadside buildings, there was Rajesh's own house, brick-walled, one room, poor—but what had I expected?

The door was opened by Rajesh's mother, a tiny, shrunken woman in a widow's white sari. She looked frankly puzzled to see me at first but grew very welcoming when Rajesh introduced me as a friend from the university. After the early-morning light, it was dark and damp inside the high-ceilinged room. There was a solitary window, but it was closed. In one corner, partitioned off by a flimsy handloom sari, was the kitchen, where a few brass utensils dully gleamed in the dark and where Rajesh's mother busied herself with breakfast. In another corner, under a sagging string cot, was a tin trunk, leprous with rust. There were religious calendars in garish colors on the walls: Shiva, Krishna, Hanuman. I recall being unsettled by that bare, lightless room and its extreme poverty, something not immediately apparent in Rajesh's life in Benares.

During the morning Rajesh had become silent. Now he left the room while I sat in a straight-backed wicker chair and talked to his mother, both of us forced to speak very loudly to make ourselves heard above the hissing sounds from the kerosene stove. It wasn't easy to express sympathy in that high-pitched voice, and sympathy was increasingly required of me as she began to tell stories from her past: She had been widowed fifteen years ago, when Rajesh was still a child, and soon afterward her wealthy, feudal in-laws had started to harass her. The house in which she lived with her husband and son was taken away from her, and they refused to give back what little dowry she had brought with her. Her parents were dead, her brothers too poor to support her. There was only Rajesh, who had worked since he was thirteen, first in the maize fields and then at a carpet factory in Benares, where he had gone to evening school and done well enough to enter the university. The years had somehow passed.

But now she was worried. Rajesh, she felt, had reached a dead end. There were no more openings for him. All the jobs were going to low-caste people. And not only did Rajesh have the wrong kind of caste, but he also had no connections anywhere for a government job. She added, with a touch of old Brahmin pride, he had too much self-respect to work for low-caste shopkeepers and businessmen.

How little of Rajesh's past I had known! I knew a bit about those carpet factories; they had been in the papers after some human rights organizations petitioned the courts to prohibit them from using child labor. There had been pictures of large-eyed, frightened-looking children in dungeonlike rooms, framed against their exquisite handiworks. I was shocked to realize that Rajesh had been one of them. The tormenting private memories of childhood that he carried within himself seemed unimaginable.

On the train back to Benares, Rajesh broke his silence to say that he had read *Sentimental Education* and that it was a story he knew well. "*Yeh meri duniya ki kahani hai. Main in logo ko janta hoon,*" he said, in Hindi. "It is the story of my world. I know these people well." He gave me a hard look. "Your hero, Edmund Wilson," he added, in English, "he also knows them."

What did Rajesh, a student in a provincial Indian university in the late 1980s, have in common with Frédéric Moreau or any of the doomed members of his generation in this novel of mid-nineteenth-century Paris? As it happened, I didn't ask him to explain. I had already been made to feel awkward by the unexpected disclosures about his past, and the day had been somewhat exhausting. We talked, desultorily, of other things and parted in Benares.

It was two years later, when I was in Benares again, that I next heard about Rajesh. The man who told me, someone I remembered as one of Rajesh's hangers-on, appeared surprised that I didn't already know that he had been a member of a criminal gang specializing in debt collection on behalf of a group of local moneylenders and businessmen. That explained his mysterious absences from Benares, I thought, as well as the pistols in his room and the sinister-looking Ambassador with tinted windows.

It was, the man said, a good, steady business; once confronted with the possibility of violence, people paid up very quickly, without involving the police. But then Rajesh had graduated to something riskier, and here, although shocked and bewildered by what I had been told, and fully expecting the worst, I could not take it in.

At some stage, the man said, dramatically pausing after every word, Rajesh had turned himself into a contract killer. It was an extremely well-paid profession and a well-connected one. You worked for small-time contractors who in turn worked for wealthy industrialists and also did favors for local political bosses who did not always rely on their own "private armies" (the local term for loyal henchmen) for certain jobs. You got to know everyone well after a few years in the business. You worked for all these important people, yet you were ultimately on your own. The chances of survival weren't very high. Sooner or later the police came to hear of you. Fierce loyalties of caste and clan ensured that every murder would be avenged. It was what would one day happen to

Rajesh, his onetime friend predicted. In a typical ambush of the kind often reported in the local papers, he would be on his motorcycle when four men would surround him at a busy intersection in the old city and shoot him dead. The prurient excitement on the man's face filled me with disgust and anger.

I never did hear what happened to Rajesh. Such stories were in the newspapers every day. But it took me awhile to sort out my confused feelings. I kept seeing Rajesh at that busy crossing, trapped in the dense swarm of scooters, cycle rickshaws, bullock carts, cars, buses, trucks, and bicycles, the four men converging upon him, producing crude pistols from their pockets . . .

Rajesh had bewildered me: his self-consciousness about his Brahmin identity, the pistols in his room, his constant talk of the void. I could now see that he had been struggling to make sense of his life, to connect the disparate elements that existed in it; but so, in a different way, was I.

In 1996 I thought of writing something on Edmund Wilson. I had tried before, in 1995, the year of Wilson's centenary, but what I wrote then seemed to me too much like a reprise of what a lot of other people had already said. I realized, though, that I had been trying to write about him in the way an American or European writer would have. What I had in mind was a straightforward exposition of Wilson's key books; it hadn't occurred to me that a separate narrative probably existed in my private discovery of Wilson's writings in a dusty old library in the ancient town of Benares.

Browsing through old papers in preparation for another attempt, I came across a photocopy of his essay on Flaubert's politics. It looked familiar. Idly flipping through the essay, I reached the pages on *Sentimental Education*, where I saw some passages underlined in red. As I'm not in the habit of marking up a printed text, I wondered who had done this. I read the underlined sentences:

> Frédéric is only the more refined as well as the more incompetent side of the middle-class mediocrity of which the dubious promoter represents the more flashy and active aspect. And so in

the case of the other characters, the journalists and the artists, the members of the various political factions, the remnants of the old nobility, Frédéric finds the same shoddiness and lack of principle which are gradually revealed in himself . . .

On another page the underlined passage read:

Flaubert's novel plants deep in our mind an idea which we never quite get rid of: the suspicion that our middle-class society of manufacturers, businessmen, and bankers, of people who live on or deal in investments, so far from being redeemed by its culture, has ended by cheapening and invalidating all the departments of culture, political, scientific, artistic, and religious, as well as corrupting and weakening the ordinary human relations: love, friendship, and loyalty to cause—till the whole civilization seems to dwindle.

The passage offered a small glimpse of Wilson's way of finding the sources and effects of literature in the overlap between individual states of mind and specific historical realities. But I hadn't noticed this when I discovered the piece. I read it again and thought about the red underlinings. And then, after almost seven years, Rajesh strode back into my consciousness. I remembered the afternoon I had given *Sentimental Education* and Wilson's essay to him; I remembered his words to me on the train, words I dismissed as exaggeration, the determined look on his face as he said, "It is the story of my world. I know these people well. Your hero, Edmund Wilson, he also knows them."

What had he meant by that?

The question did not leave me. And there came a time when I began to think I had understood very little, and misunderstood much, during those months in Benares. I recalled the day I went to visit Rajesh's village, and I at last saw that there had been a purpose behind Rajesh's invitation to his home, his decision to reveal so frankly his life to me. Even the cryptic remarks about *Sentimental Education* and Wilson on the train: He wanted me to know that not only had he read the novel, but he had also drawn, with Wilson's help, his own conclusions from it.

In the hard and mean world he had lived in, first as a child laborer and then as a hired criminal for politicians and businessmen, Rajesh would have come to know well the grimy underside of middle-class society. What became clearer to me now was how quick he had been to recognize that the society Flaubert and Wilson wrote about wasn't much different from the one he inhabited in Benares. "It's the story of my world," he had said. I couldn't see it then, but in Benares I had been among people who, like Frédéric Moreau and his friends, had either disowned or, in many cases, moved away from their provincial origins in order to realize their dreams of success in the bourgeois world. Only a handful of them were able to get anywhere near to realizing their dreams while the rest saw their ambitions dwindle away in successive disappointments over the years. The degradation of bribery, sycophancy, and nepotism that people were forced into in their hunt for jobs was undermining in itself; so pervasive was the corruption around them that neither those who succeeded nor those who failed were able to escape its taint.

The small, unnoticed tragedies of thwarted hopes and ideals Flaubert wrote about in *Sentimental Education* were all around us. And this awareness, which was also mine but which I tried to evade through, ironically, the kind of obsessive reading that had led me to the novel in the first place, had been Rajesh's private key to the book. Thus, where I saw only the reflection of a personal neurosis—the character of Frédéric in particular embodying my sense of inadequacy, my harsh self-image—he had discovered a social and psychological environment that was similar to the one he lived in.

That discovery did honor to both Flaubert and Wilson. The worlds we knew in Benares were many years away from those of the French novelist and the American critic. Yet—and this was a measure of their greatness—they seemed to have had an accurate, if bitter, knowledge of its peculiar human ordeals and futility. It was a knowledge Rajesh himself arrived at by a somewhat different route. "To fully appreciate the book," Wilson had written of *Sentimental Education*, "one must have had time to see something of life." It sounds like a general sort of adage, but Rajesh exemplified its truth even as he moved into another world, taking what in retrospect look like all the wrong turns. Rajesh had known how to connect whatever little he read to the world around himself, much in the same way Wilson had done in his essay and in his other writings, a way that revealed a symbiotic relationship between life and literature that I, despite all my reading, was not fully to grasp until long after I had left Benares and thought again of that time of hopeful, confused striving when I first read Edmund Wilson.

PART ONE

ALLAHABAD

The Nehrus, the Gandhis, and Democracy

1. The Colonial City and the Countryside

In September 2000 India held its third general election in as many years after the coalition government dominated by the Hindu nationalist BJP (Indian People's Party) collapsed in New Delhi. The Hindu nationalists, who had conducted nuclear tests and challenged Pakistan to a final war over Kashmir soon after joining the coalition government in 1998, were expected to strengthen their position and resume their work of turning India into a militant Hindu state. I thought then of returning to Allahabad, the North Indian city where I had lived as an undergraduate student from 1985 to 1988, a time when Hindu nationalism still seemed as marginal in India as it had been for the previous four decades.

Allahabad lies in the heart of the vast North Indian plains, at the confluence of the two sacred rivers of Hinduism, the Ganges and the Yamuna. Flying across the plains on a clear day, you can follow the rivers as they descend from the Himalayas and then meander through great expanses of flat cultivated land, past clusters of ancient cities and towns. Three millennia ago their waters provided the basis for the civilization of the original Aryan settlers of North India. Each winter hundreds of thousands of pilgrims still travel to Allahabad from all across India for a religious fair near the confluence, and every twelve years the Kumbh Mela, the largest human gathering in the world, attracts millions of Hindus to the site.

Yet the place isn't easy to get to. Commercial flights have been discontinued, and during the election period the overnight train from Delhi was overbooked. To get to Allahabad in time for the early campaigning, I had to take the multi-stop flight from Delhi to Benares, along with a tour group of Italians traveling to see the erotic temple sculpture at Khajuraho, and then drive eighty miles east to Allahabad.

The flight is operated by one of India's private airlines. The breakfast was freshly cooked and warm, the toilets were clean and generously supplied with cologne, and the courtesy and efficiency of the staff were like marvels compared with the resolute badness of the state-owned Indian Airlines. Miles out of Delhi, moving deeper into a part of India still untouched by the entrepreneurial energy and foreign investments of recent years, the flight could seem part of the good things contact with the global economy had brought to India: higher standards of health and hygiene; a greater alertness to individual needs.

But an older India of caste and poverty is never far away even on a plane with its Western-style amenities, its atmosphere of international ease and luxury. In Khajuraho, after the package tourists had departed, another kind of people came on board: dark-complexioned, barefoot cleaners with little brushes and rags. They filled the cabin with the smell of sweat and chewed tobacco, and as they went scuttling through the narrow aisles on hands and knees—as if their degradation were required by their low caste—the expression on the face of the pretty short-skirted stewardess, who could have been the glamorous poster girl of a European or an American airline, was one of pure distaste.

The long, bone-rattling drive afterward to Allahabad on potholed roads, through calf-deep floods, past the tin-roofed shacks and rain-battered villages of mud and thatch—the cowering huts, so picturesque from the plane, now appearing frail, in danger of collapsing onto the sodden earth from which they had been so arduously raised, the low-caste women paving tiny courtyards with cow dung, the men spinning rope for the string cots, the sky low and gray over the flat fields and tiny huts and the buffaloes placid in muddy pools—the long drive through a world that belonged to itself as fixedly as it would have two centuries ago was a reminder of how far even the superficially good things of a globalized economy were from this heavily populated and impoverished part of India.

India, with its severe disparities of income, caste, and religion, is split into so many separate worlds. You can live in one without knowing anything about the others, and no world has an obvious past until you make the effort of dredging it up. I didn't find out until later that the region between Allahabad and Benares, familiar to me from my time as an undergraduate student at Allahabad University, hadn't always been so impoverished. In the early years of the nineteenth century, when the British were still more interested in business than empire, the area had been an important trade center for North India, and its merchants and moneylenders had been known for their initiative and energy.

But as always in India, the prosperity so created had been shared out among a very small group of people; it had led to little except the creation of zealously guarded hoards or, occasionally, an opulent mansion in the midst of a teeming bazaar. When trading routes changed and the region lost its importance, the private fortunes quickly dwindled, the mansions fell into ruin and were taken over by squatters. The region was restored to the wretchedness and cruelties that were probably always there under the gloss of temporary affluence.

Affluence is still a rare achievement, but the gloss has got shinier and deeper. At the time of the elections, my hotel in Allahabad was a new white eight-storied building of egregious luxury, built by a local manufacturer of bidis (cheap Indian cigarettes), who had recently begun to dabble in politics. Every effort had been made to make it conform to international specifications. The menu at the coffee shop offered Mexican and Italian food. A Muzak version of "The Sounds of Silence" played in the elevators. When the power supply broke down, as it frequently did in the city, a massive basement generator groaned into life. The corridors were thickly carpeted; the double-glazed windows kept out the loud film music from the small slum just outside the hotel, where a rain-fed gutter overflowed into the tin-roofed shacks and left green stains of slime on the pale earth around them.

The hotel was fated to remain empty—and so it was—most of the time. Its luxury couldn't but seem pointless. It met no local needs; it required no local expertise. In fact, people from as far as South India had to be imported to fill in managerial positions. Its purpose, if you could call it that, seemed to lie in its being an assertion of wealth and power in the midst of general deprivation, quite like the newly built houses with Doric columns and Palladian façades in the area around the hotel.

The solidity of the building, its quiet interiors, the monumental presence of its white façade in the middle of the city—in all its deliberate order and calm, the hotel underlined its separateness from its setting. Its effect was felt most keenly by the menial staff, who traveled each day from their homes in the flood-threatened outskirts of Allahabad and approached their place of work with something like awe. They looked very ill at ease in their green uniforms and were obsequiously polite with guests, calling to mind the Indians who had come to serve in the new city of Allahabad built by the British after the rude shock of the Indian Mutiny of 1857, the city whose simple colonial geography was plain from my sixth-floor hotel room, the railway tracks partitioning the congested "black town," with its minarets and temple domes, from the tree-lined grid of "white town," where for a long period no Indians, apart from servants, could appear in native dress.

Allahabad was Prayag, a small pilgrim center, before the British, in the early nineteenth century, began to use it as a military base, guarding the up-country trade on the river Ganges. When, in 1857, Indian soldiers in British-led armies mutinied, the British struggled to retain their power across most of North India, except in Allahabad, where they were not challenged greatly. They quickly put down the few soldiers who did rebel; they razed to the ground those houses in the old quarter that belonged to rich supporters of the insurrectionists. No stories of unspeakable atrocities against British women and children emerged from Allahabad as they did from Kanpur, just 150 miles away to the north on the Ganges.

Nevertheless, the British wished to make a point. The pacifier of Allahabad was a devout Christian colonel called James Neill, who believed "the word of God gives no authority to the modern tenderness for human life." Under his direction, some six thousand Indians were hanged, shot, or tortured to death, in just a few days.

It was in the months following the pacification that eight villages were confiscated, as a senior official stated, from "dirty Indian niggers" and were turned into the exclusively British enclave of Civil Lines. The great buildings of the city—the Romanesque cathedral, the university tower and dome, the Gothic public library, the Baroque High Court— came up in the decades that followed the suppression of the mutiny, a time of serenity for the British in India, when India officially became part of the empire and the natives remained quiet for the most part.

In Allahabad, the civil and military administration, the hospitals, schools, and the high court produced a small Anglo-Indian society. For these exiled people, the compensations for the city's great heat and isolation were to be had in untroubled leisure, in the clubs, polo grounds, and large bungalows with wide verandas and sprawling lawns where it was common for a family to have fifty to sixty servants. When, in 1887, the young Rudyard Kipling came to work in Allahabad after some exciting years as a journalist in Lahore, he found himself alienated; the "large, well-appointed club, where Poker had just driven out Whist and men gambled seriously, was full of large-bore officials, and of a respectability all new."

When you look now at the buildings of the period after 1857, their playfully diverse architectural styles seem to confirm Kipling's vision of a people savoring their privilege. In their rhetorical magnificence— quite like that of my hotel—they stand apart from, and indeed loom over, everything around them; they suggest a people made absolutely secure by wealth and unchallenged power. At the public library—built as a memorial to the official who dispossessed the "dirty Indian niggers" of Civil Lines—there are relief figures of Indian peasants and potters and silk weavers on carved capitals. The peasants are wiry, obviously well-fed men with turbans; the physical aspects and setting of the potters and silk weavers have been similarly improved. They are unsettling, not least because severe British methods of revenue collection had ravaged the countryside, forcing generations of the rural poor into vicious circles of endless debt and bondage to local landlords and moneylenders. It is hard to imagine that the architect was aware of the crude irony of his representations; more likely that he was indulging a fantasy about the Indian countryside, a romantic idea about peasants created at a safe distance from their actual condition.

The romance had gone, but this distance hadn't really diminished with independence; the administrators and the masses still lived in separate worlds. At the commissioner's office, an old sprucely painted bungalow with trimmed hedges in Civil Lines, a middle-aged woman in a torn white sari held a creased piece of paper and pleaded with attendants wearing red-sashed livery. The widow of one of the laborers killed in a mining accident, she had traveled a long way from her village that morning to beg the commissioner to expedite relief money sanctioned more than two years ago by the government. The audience wasn't granted; the woman was told to take her application to a lower official and not bother the commissioner's office with petty requests.

I accompanied the commissioner and the district police chief on their inspection tour of rural police stations two days before the elections in Allahabad. We traveled in two white Ambassadors with blue sirens and official flags on the bonnet. Villagers turned to look at us warily as we raced through a series of traffic jams on narrow country roads. At the first sign of an approaching bottleneck, the driver put on the siren, and bodyguards cradling AK-47 guns leaned out of the windows, forcing big, overweight trucks off the roads and onto muddy ledges where they stood leaning dangerously.

Policemen everywhere stood to attention and saluted the cars as they went past. At official bungalows with little flower beds and manicured lawns, junior officials vied with each other to open the car doors and escort us to dining tables overloaded with warm snacks. More members of the Civil Service would invariably join us at this point. These were election observers sent to the region from other states, men in their thirties and forties, eager and fluent. A brisk bonhomie would ensue around the dining table as people compared notes on who was posted where and who was about to be promoted. There would be little talk of the election or the police stations we had visited (some of them in total disarray—small dark rooms full of dusty files and broken furniture, smells of urine and alcohol emanating from lockups—easily imagined as local centers of tyranny, settings for the third-degree torture and custodial deaths and rapes you read about in the papers).

At the beginning of the inspection tour, the police chief, who had the reputation, rare in Allahabad, of not soliciting bribes, looked concerned. His English marked him as a man who had entered the Civil Service from a modest small-town background; he couldn't have been unaware of what occurred in the police stations. Yet after the first, where he scolded the paunchy official in charge who had been clumsily making up the number of men arrested and guns seized, he hurried through the rest, with a look of distaste on his face. The commissioner looked restless throughout the tour and found his voice only with the other Civil Service men. He had earlier spoken to me with feeling about the inconveniences of living in the English town of Hull, where he had been sent by the Indian government to undergo some training. He now spoke mournfully—others around the dining table shaking their head sideways in approval—of criminals with hundreds of police cases against them, who had not only joined politics but also become "honorable ministers" and to whom he was required to show proper deference.

Dignity, and how to hold on to it: That was what preoccupied these men, most of whom the Civil Service had rescued from a lower-middle-class shabbiness—the dignity whose emblems included the bungalows, the white cars with sirens, the red-sashed attendants, and the attentive lower officials; the dignity that came out of asserting one's distance from everything tainted by the ordinary misery and degradation of India: the widow outside the commissioner's office, the criminals working as ministers, the corrupted men in the rural police stations.

In the assertion of that distance lay the self-image of the colonial administrators, and over time this has changed as little as the actual hierarchies and structure of the administration itself. Only the gap between rhetoric—more intense in an India with democratic aspirations—and reality has widened. For people in small towns and villages—the majority of India's population—the sources of power and justice are still somewhere in the larger unknown world, and you can spend all your life waiting for them to work in your favor.

Consider this village thirty miles out of Allahabad: a huddle of huts, unpainted brick houses, and narrow mud lanes on a stony slope. My car was the only motorized vehicle on the rutted country road that dusty late afternoon. Its appearance from behind an abrupt bend startled the bullock cart drivers and shepherds and excited fear among the people at this village, standing by the side of the road, holding the little green plastic flags of the Samajwadi (Socialist) Party, waiting for the local candidate, Mr. Reoti Raman Singh, to arrive. They stood stiffly, not daring to come closer, until summoned by the driver, when they moved awkwardly and surrounded the car. Anxious, thin, sun-hardened faces with roughly cut hair, young and old, pressed against the windows; frankly curious eyes quickly took in my camera, diary, pen—glamorous items in this context—and suddenly clouded over with uncertainty. When I asked them about the local issues they wished their member of Parliament to resolve, they shook their heads. One of the best-dressed persons among them, an old man in white kurta and dhoti and thick white mustache, said that there were no problems at all and resumed his scrutiny of my personal effects. It was only when my exasperated driver, a recent migrant to Allahabad from a nearby village, introduced me as a journalist and urged them to tell me the truth that the old man began to speak.

The others prompted him, in shy whispers at first, and then everyone spoke at once. This village was different from those I had already visited that day only in the quality of its deprivation. It was privileged in having a tube well for drinking water, but the nearest hospital was nine miles away, and though the government had installed an electric pole, there had never been any "current." The biggest problem related to the government's primary school; it had been around for several years, but the teacher came only once a week from Allahabad and even then only for a couple of hours or so. There was no way of predicting when he would come, and so the students dressed each morning for school and spent the day waiting for the teacher outside locked doors. That wasn't all. The teacher took all the rice which the government sent for the pupils every year. He had also carved out personal profits from the building of the new one-room school for girls; the foundation was nine inches instead of the usual twenty inches, and the building could collapse any moment.

Earlier that day I had been traveling with Reoti Raman Singh, the candidate for Allahabad's parliamentary constituency from the Samajwadi Party. Fierce monsoon rains had accompanied us en route from Mr. Singh's rambling old mansion in the old quarter of Allahabad to the rural districts. The windshield wipers flailed uselessly; the road was reduced to frothy mud. When the rain stopped, soft parkland rolled out on both sides, the green of the grass, trees, and bushes brilliantly vivid and separate in the gray light of the still-turbulent sky; water gurgled through roadside ditches; and for a moment at least it was possible to take pleasure in the poverty-ravaged landscape, to see pastoral beauty in the young boys and girls herding sheep and buffaloes on grassy slopes.

Mr. Singh was a tall, stooping man; he walked with a slight limp and gave an impression of some deep debility, along with a great kindness. He sat impassive in the front of the Jeep and hardly moved whenever his personal attendant, a thickset man in a safari suit, reached out from the back seat to adjust the silk scarf around his employer's neck. The scarf, stiff with starch, was important. Mr. Singh belonged to an old distinguished feudal family of the region, one that had made its name and wealth in precolonial times, and the external symbols of his prestige had to be maintained. At a railway level crossing, a blind man in wet rags came up to the Jeep and, hopping a bit on his bare, calloused feet, sang a devotional song. Mr. Singh obliged with a generous gift of one hundred rupees, three times the daily wages of a laborer. There was both approval and envy on the faces of the small crowd of onlookers as they watched the rupee note passing from Mr. Singh's attendant to the blind man; Mr. Singh, or "Kunwar Sahib," Prince, as he was called, had done the thing expected of him.

Early that morning at his house in Allahabad, men from nearby villages had sat silently in small dark rooms, tense with the urgency of those matters they waited to lay before Mr. Singh: power and water connections, a clerical job, a property dispute. Their blank faces cracked and betrayed disappointment when Mr. Singh, already running late that morning, was rushed out to the Jeep waiting in the front yard. There were many more supplicants at the villages where he stopped, mostly men from the low Nishad (fishermen) caste, small-limbed and dark and half naked, who ran up to the Jeep, hands folded, heads bowed. Mr. Singh addressed them in the local dialect; his manner was easy yet authoritative. He asked them directly about their problems and was quick to respond. He promised to fire the policeman who had been extorting money from one village; he promised to build a culvert linking another two villages across a canal within a month of his election; at villages requiring water, he promised to have tube wells dug. He reminded them of the electricity and water he had brought to villages in his region. He didn't say that he had done the good work in his official capacity as a member of the state legislature; it was an earlier contract, and not the obligations of elected office, that he was invoking, the contract between the upper-caste wealthy feudal lord and his destitute but loyal subjects. The faces in the crowds looked satisfied; they nodded, childlike, as he spoke, and as he prepared to leave, people lunged forward and tried to reach through the open window to touch his feet. It was as if after the unmet expectations from the flawed institutions of democratic India, after the many disappointments, an uncared-for people had found some security in the still-persisting ideals of noblesse oblige.

Drinking water, police harassment, electricity, schools, and hospitals: These weren't the themes being discussed when I left Delhi, although the media had been as obsessed with the elections as it was with Kashmir, where the Indian Army had fought several bloody battles with Pakistan-backed armed intruders over the summer.

The media grew each year, with new newspapers, magazines, and TV channels appearing almost every week. But only a very small part of what they produced could be called journalism. During the battles in Kashmir, they had assumed the role of cheerleaders and worked up a lot of hysteria among the metropolitan middle classes for whom war and jingoism appeared to clarify, if only momentarily, a self-image that had been blurred by eight years of rapid social and economic liberalization. False stories, disseminated by the Indian Army about the torture of its soldiers by the Pakistanis, were retold endlessly even after it was revealed that they were false. Correspondents in battle fatigues shouted breathless reports into microphones as shells screamed overhead. Stylish young army officers boasted at length about their plans for the Pakistanis. There was little embarrassment when on national TV one of the officers echoed the Pepsi-Cola slogan, *Yeh Dil Maange More* ("This Heart Wants More") and was then killed in battle soon afterward or when in its haste to convert the skirmishes into a splendid little war for itself the government announced on Independence Day that its highest military honor was to go posthumously to a soldier who turned out to be alive in a Delhi army hospital.

And then, as abruptly as it had started, the war was over and forgotten. No one seemed to know how much money had been collected for the families of the 266 dead soldiers; the countless relief funds and benefit concerts and fashion shows became part of yet another Indian scam. Political pundits and analysts replaced military strategists and experts on television and seemed to shuttle endlessly between recording studios, chatting about "swings" and "anti-incumbency factors" and "index of opposition unity." The English-language press was full of opinion polls and analyses, and the suave spokesmen for the two main political parties, the Congress and the Hindu nationalist Bharatiya Janata Party (BJP), exchanged creative insults in daily debates about the foreign origins of Sonia Gandhi, the leader of the Congress, and the alleged failure of the BJP government to act on early intelligence reports about the intruders in Kashmir.

The television experts and newspaper columnists called it an election without issues. But the separation of issues from elections had occurred long before. Elections, held almost yearly, had become a national drama, preceded and followed by even greater dramas of betrayals, defections, buying and selling legislators, no-confidence motions, coalition collapses, new ministries, speculations about who was in and who was out, etc. The drama, created this time by questions like "Is Sonia an agent of the Vatican?" and "Did our soldiers die in vain in Kashmir?," helped suppress the real issues and also brought about a temporary cohesion and passion among a fragmented, apathetic population.

Yet in Allahabad, once known as the most politically minded city in India, even the drama was missing. As late as the 1980s, politicians and lawyers, dressed in contrasting white and black, gathered at the old coffeehouse in the heart of the "white town" every morning and evening to gossip about various political figures and the size of their wealth. But I found the coffeehouse empty. Waiters in scruffy white livery and turbans stood around vacantly under fans hung high from cobwebbed wooden beams on the ceiling, and lizards made drowsy by the moist heat clung unmovingly to the faded painting of Gandhi on the walls, where the bright-blue paint had peeled off, exposing the solid masonry underneath.

One morning I went to Anand Bhavan, the family mansion of the Nehrus. It is only a five-minute walk from the campus of Allahabad University, where I had lived as an undergraduate; strange to think that I hardly ever went there.

Not that there was much to see. On the morning I went, gaudily dressed peasant women and children sat cross-legged in the long arcades, cautiously running their hands over the cool marble floors. Outside, the posters at pavement stalls were all of fleshy-lipped Indian film heroes. The usual election party banners, the tempos with loudspeakers, and the motorcycled boys with party flags and bandannas were hardly visible on the streets. I walked through the wide verandas and balconies and peered into rooms where French meals were once served on Dresden china with Czech glasses and where, in a more political time, Mahatma Gandhi and Jawaharlal Nehru and other great men of the Congress Party discussed ways of liberating India from colonial rule. In a newer building on the large walled compound, I could see yet more peasant women, also in gaudy nylon saris, shuffling shyly through an ill-lit gallery of photographs from hopeful times: Nehru, the first prime minister of independent India, inaugurating dams and factories, what he called "the new temples of India"; Nehru with other celebrities of the postcolonial world, Nasser, Sukarno, Nkrumah; and Nehru's daughter, Indira Gandhi, in an elegant silk sari, hugging Fidel Castro at a summit meeting of nonaligned nations.

In Allahabad, a decaying city whose brief moment of glory belonged to the anticolonial struggle, you couldn't but feel distant from these celebrations of postcolonial nationalism and third world solidarity. It was also hard not to wonder what, if anything, the peasant visitors made of the photographs. Most of them came on day trips from the vast rural region around Allahabad where the young Jawaharlal Nehru had, after his seven years at Harrow and Cambridge, first been exposed to "the degradation and overwhelming poverty of India." Their parents and grandparents were probably among the enthusiastic voters who, after independence, repeatedly elected Nehru to the Indian Parliament from a rural constituency near Allahabad. But they themselves had remained close to destitution.

Things hadn't changed much even for those with privileged access to the owners of Anand Bhavan. In the late 1970s, Dom Moraes, the Indian writer and poet, met an old couple, Becchu and his wife, Sonia, who had worked there for much of the century. Moraes was then researching a semiauthorized biography of Indira Gandhi; the officials in charge of the mansion let him remove the leatherbound books from the shelves and discover Nehru's interest in Balzac, Dickens, Maugham, and Koestler. The same officials, one rainy day at Anand Bhavan, brought Becchu and Sonia to see Moraes and told him that "Becchu was beating Sonia too much. Now he is not beating. Since she is becoming blind, he is taking care."

The two of them sat before Moraes, "dripping and shivering after coming in from the cold." The interview wasn't a success. Moraes got only a blurred picture of the "splendour, hedonism, and ostentation" that had marked life at Anand Bhavan until the early 1920s (when Gandhi, the charismatic new leader of the freedom movement, partly converted the Nehrus to his ascetic and defiantly Indian lifestyle); Becchu, a "skinny old man," kept shouting at his wife in between fits of crying. His "convulsive sobs turned into positive roars of sorrow" when Moraes mentioned Indira Gandhi's defeat in the national elections she had held in 1977, two years after imposing a "state of emergency" on India and suspending civil rights.

Becchu's grief, however, was more personal. During her nine years as prime minister of India, Mrs. Gandhi had promised him a pension; it hadn't been paid, and after her defeat it now looked very unlikely indeed. An unsettled Moraes tried to console the servant with a big tip. Becchu stretched out a "wizened hand" for the rupee notes, but his wife, "blind or not," was quicker. "She whipped the money away and stuffed it in her blouse," and Becchu started to wail.

2. The Dynasty

Nehru was often perceived by foreign visitors as a "lonely Indian aristocrat . . . presiding over his deficient but devoted peasantry." But the description "aristocrat," which Nehru himself encouraged, is too easily achieved in India; you only need to be placed slightly above the general wretchedness.

The Nehrus were Brahmins from Kashmir who in the early eighteenth century became minor courtiers to Mughal emperors in Delhi. After the British destroyed Muslim power in India in the nineteenth century, the Nehrus found roles in the new imperial dispensation. Motilal Nehru, Jawaharlal's father, was trained as a lawyer, and he moved to Allahabad in 1886 to practice in the High Court that the British had established. He first lived in Allahabad's old "native" quarter; a brothel filled with very young Nepalese women now stands on the site of his house. But he outgrew these modest beginnings very quickly, at the same pace, in fact, as Allahabad's importance as an administrative and educational center. There was much money to be made from representing in court the decadent and exuberantly litigious landed gentry of North India, the upstart men rewarded with grants of land by the British for their loyalty during the mutiny of 1857, and soon after buying Anand Bhavan, Motilal acquired liveried servants, horses, an English chauffeur for his imported car, and an Irish tutor for his son and started to order his clothes from Savile Row.

These were also the affectations of the half-literate landlords he represented. In Bengal, where India's first modern culture was almost a century old, these aspirations to respectability would have been met with sarcasm. Rabindranath Tagore and then Nirad Chaudhuri wrote witheringly of the shallow and ostentatious Anglicization of socially ambitious Indians. In feudal North India, which possessed little of the self-confident egalitarian spirit of the Bengal Renaissance, the meeting of East and West usually resulted in tackiness and a crude kind of snobbery: Nehru's younger sister, who was educated by an English governess, looked down upon Nehru's wife, Kamla, mostly because the latter could not speak fluent English.

As his letters to this sister, Vijaylaxmi Pandit, reveal, Nehru was closer to her than to the woman his father had bullied him into marrying; he later gave her glamorous ambassadorial jobs in London, Moscow, and Washington. At a crucial moment in India's transition to independence in 1947, Nehru confided more in Lord Mountbatten, the pompous and incompetent last viceroy of India, than in many of his Indian colleagues, including Gandhi. But then Nehru's greater intimacy with English or Anglicized people, which Gandhi himself remarked upon, was hardly the result of his upbringing in Allahabad.

His intellectual and emotional outlook was formed by his early years in England, by the strain of liberalism in English life, of which the Fabians, whom he admired, were an obvious manifestation. This later made him a hero to Anglicized Indians. But in India he was restless and alienated, with a mystical longing for the Himalayas, and he was actually floundering until he met Gandhi. For it was Gandhi who set Nehru out on the path to individual greatness by first alerting him to his world—the awakening Nehru later elaborated upon in such books as *The Discovery of India*—and then by anointing him, among many deserving aspirants, his political heir.

After independence, India became Nehru's private laboratory for the ideas—a state-controlled economy, industrialization—that he had picked up from his reading and travels. It also forgave mistakes of the kind—his refusal to share power with Muslim leaders made the partition of India inevitable; his complacent belief in pan-Asian solidarity led to India's military humiliation by China in 1962—that would normally be expected to taint any political career.

Other postcolonial leaders were similarly unassailable. But unlike Nasser, Nkrumah, and Sukarno, Nehru was aware of the dangers in his situation. In 1937 the *Modern Review*, a prominent Indian magazine of the time, published the following anonymous analysis of Nehru: "He has all the makings of a dictator in him—vast popularity . . . an intolerance of others and certain contempt for the weak and inefficient . . . His overmastering desire to get things done, to sweep away what he dislikes and build anew, will hardly brook for long the slow process of democracy . . ."

This remarkably acute description of a postcolonial leader in a hurry is more remarkable still when you learn the author was Nehru himself. It was the kind of comment that probably made him appear to his daughter like "a saint who strayed into politics." Certainly, such self-awareness was absent from Indira's own life; the gap between father and daughter was wide. "You are such a stranger to me," Nehru once wrote to her, "and perhaps you do not know much about me."

Indira, in fact, liked to think of herself as a "tough politician," one of her more accurate self-descriptions. Interestingly, very little in Indira's early life hinted at the toughness. Born in 1917, just as the freedom struggle switched into high gear, she grew up in a distracted household. Nehru was usually away, in prison or traveling across India. It was Indira who accompanied her perennially ill mother to various spas and sanatoriums in India and Europe and, in the process, drifted through nine schools in Switzerland, England, and India without distinguishing herself at any of them. Her star fellow pupil at Badminton School in England was the English novelist Iris Murdoch, who later remembered Indira as being "very unhappy, very lonely."

This unsettled upbringing probably only deepened the usual teenage insecurities. She was tall for her age and thin; she had a large nose and skin that she saw as too dark. Mrs. Pandit, who didn't think Nehru's wife was good enough for him, also didn't much rate his daughter, Indira, whom she described as "ugly and stupid," a remark that Indira overheard as an adolescent and took with her into her tormented old age, its wound still unhealed, or so she claimed to a close friend a few months before she was assassinated in 1984.

Indira later tried to inject some excitement and glamour into what had been a dull, anxiety-infested childhood and adolescence. In his biography, Dom Moraes reports her claim that from her house in Allahabad she saw the British police shooting dead Chandrashekhar Azad, an Indian revolutionary. This, though, is quite implausible, given the considerable distance between Anand Bhavan and the park where Azad was killed. And the most convincing rebuttal of her claim that she was ill-treated in a British prison comes from Mrs. Pandit's daughter, Nayantara Sahgal, who, in a shrewd book about her ambitious cousin, excerpted letters written by her mother at the time from the same prison, all of which attest to the kid glove treatment the Nehrus generally got from their British jailers.

"She lives in a world of dreams and vagaries," Nehru had noted when Indira was seventeen years old. "Extraordinarily self-centred . . . remarkably selfish," he wrote to his sister. "She must have depths." Nehru hoped that his daughter would travel and learn languages and then "with this background of mental training and a wider culture discover the fascinating place that is India," just as he himself had. With this in mind, while in prison, Nehru dedicated a book of letters about world history to her; she didn't read it until several years later. After his wife Kamla's death in 1936, he arranged for Indira to study at

Somerville College, Oxford, but she preferred to hang out with some fashionably left-wing Indian friends in London and failed her Latin exams twice.

He was probably most disappointed by his daughter's intention, soon after returning from England in early 1940, to marry one of the hangers-on at Anand Bhavan, a young Parsi man called Feroze Gandhi (no relation to Mahatma). He registered his own protest against the "absurd haste of a marriage" and then brought much pressure to bear upon Indira through his friends and relatives. Mahatma Gandhi, worried that Indira might be getting swept away by her sexual feelings for Feroze, recommended a celibate marriage to her, a proposal Indira responded to with some obvious irritation. Surrounded by powerful men and their bullying advice, she wished to be, for once, her own person, and it is hard not to sympathize with her, even though the marriage was, as everyone expected, a disaster. Feroze was as unformed as she was, and although he eventually became a vigorous parliamentarian, prior to his early death in 1960, Indira remained, much to his resentment, in thrall to her father's immeasurably greater power and style.

Harold Laski, whom Indira met in England, had noted her "timid desire to submerge [her] personality in [her] father's" and warned that "you'll just become an appendage." This was just what she did become in the years after independence: Nehru's companion on his trips abroad, a housekeeper, and the host of official parties at Nehru's house in New Delhi, the quite solemn occasions devoted to classical Indian dance and music, whose Gandhian austerity drove out at least one guest, W. H. Auden, who later complained to Nicolas Nabokov about the alcohol-free evening with the Nehrus.

In one of her letters to Dorothy Norman, a Manhattan socialite whom Indira had befriended during her visit to New York with Nehru in 1949, Indira confessed to not having found her "métier." She also confided to Norman her desire to retire to a small house in England with her two sons, Rajiv and Sanjay. She claimed to have little in common with the Indians she and her father were surrounded by: "They amuse me and they irritate me and sometimes I find myself observing them as if I were not of the same species at all."

Nevertheless, for someone so much at odds with her environment, Indira was quick to accept, and then grow into, the responsibilities thrust upon her by the coarse politicians she complained about, the powerful regional bosses of the Congress who brokered the party's compact with the popular mass base that the freedom movement had created, and who made her, in 1959, the president of the party. Just a few months later the first ominous sign of her authoritarian ways appeared when she persuaded Nehru to dismiss, on spurious grounds of law and order, the Communist government in the South Indian state of Kerala; it was the first democratically elected Communist government anywhere in the world.

The ease and speed of Indira's ascent to the prime minister's office, two years after Nehru's death in 1964, surprised everyone at the time. It looks inevitable in retrospect. In the mid-1960s the Indian economy was crippled with food shortages, and there was much dissatisfaction with the way things had gone since independence.

Successive governments had remained preoccupied with Nehru's ambitious blueprint of an industrial and technical infrastructure for India, a strategy that, while creating thousands of exportable scientists and software engineers, doesn't directly address India's basic problems of poverty, disease, and illiteracy, problems that Indira spoke of constantly but did little to solve. The vast, complicated administrative network the British had set up to retain their hold on India had remained intact, except that the civil bureaucrats, the unaccountable rulers of India during colonial times, had to accommodate for the first time the ambitions of elected politicians.

The state-controlled economy encouraged corruption as much as inefficiency, and the bureaucrats and politicians parceled out its large and varied booty of big public projects, defense contracts, bribes from businessmen, jobs, foreign trips, telephone connections, etc., a serious, steady internal plundering of the overcentralized state's resources that in the early nineties would expose India to the drastic therapies of the IMF and the World Bank. National politics became and, beyond the excitement of new slogans and personalities, had remained a set of transactions, with regional and caste leaders delivering votes to a broad-based national party like the Congress in exchange for a share of the power and resources at the center.

There were regular elections, which, along with freedom of the press, are the major achievements of Indian democracy, and the Congress often lost at the state and local level. But these setbacks did not much weaken the party's stranglehold—quite like that of the PRI in Mexico—over the immensely powerful federal government in Delhi. Its supremacy wasn't successfully challenged by other parties until 1977, after a spell of dictatorship, and then only, as it turned out, for the sake of rewiring the network of patrons and clients the Congress had set up. Not surprisingly, despite universal suffrage, India has been very slow to develop, beyond a small minority privileged by caste, class, and education, a sense of citizenship or an awareness of the individual rights enshrined in the country's radically democratic constitution—hence the Nehrus' own family servant futilely expecting to be favored with a pension that was, after a lifetime of service, his by right.

The democracy Nehru wanted to create had barely thrown up any real challenges or potential political heirs to him. Indira's own long proximity to power had made her ambitious, despite all her fantasies about becoming a London house owner, and as a minister in the cabinet of Nehru's immediate successor, Lal Bahadur Shastri, she quickly showed a talent for the constant petty intriguing of Indian politics. She publicly disparaged the dhoti-clad Shastri, also a native of Allahabad but from a much humbler family. Some Anglicized admirers of Nehru in Delhi, who became Indira's advisers, strengthened her conviction that only someone from the Nehru family could provide enlightened leadership to India. As it happened, after Shastri's unexpected death in 1966, the party bosses found themselves unable to trust each other as supreme leader and ended up elevating a pliant-seeming Indira as the prime minister of India.

Indira quickly outgrew her patrons, however. She was offered a fresh start by the Congress Party's dismal performance in the national elections in 1967; she declared herself a socialist, committed to destroying the sinister influence she claimed big landlords and businessmen had over the Congress and the Indian government. She nationalized banks and insurance companies, stopped all government privileges and payments due to the royal families of India, and announced various programs for eradicating poverty. *Garibi Hatao* ("Remove Poverty") was the obvious but effective slogan she used in the national elections in

1971 to win overwhelming support among traditionally poor low-caste Hindus and Muslims, who, weary of the many middlemen and false promises since independence, saw the daughter of Nehru as their true savior.

Things briefly appeared to be working out for Indira. The introduction, during Nehru's time, of high-yielding crops had made India self-sufficient in food production in the late sixties. Indira encouraged this "Green Revolution" and also made herself popular among the relatively affluent class of cultivators by offering them state-subsidized power, water, and fertilizers. Events outside India also helped Indira to marginalize the Congress power brokers. In 1971, the Pakistani Army responded to the disaffection among Pakistan's eastern Bengali-speaking population with a near genocide.

Millions of Bengali refugees arrived in India subsequently, straining an already shaky economy. Indira prepared India well for the war with Pakistan that began to seem imminent as the Indian Army trained and armed Bengali insurgents; she swiftly secured military and diplomatic support from the Soviet Union after it became clear that Richard Nixon, who suspected her of being an intellectual, would "tilt" toward Pakistan. India eventually fought and won a short war with Pakistan and carved out a new nation. As the liberator of Bangladesh, Indira became, briefly, a universally celebrated figure. No longer the "dumb doll" that a particularly bitter critic of the Nehru dynasty had dubbed her at the beginning of her time as prime minister, instead she embodied Shakti, the Hindu metaphysical concept for female energy and power.

Indira's speeches grew more confident, full of references to her family's prestige and self-sacrificing spirit. She also used the opportunity to banish all remaining and potential rivals within the Congress and to reward her lackeys with important positions in the executive, legislative, and the judiciary. The man she appointed as the president of the Congress Party soon devised the slogan "Indira Is India, and India Indira." The president of India during much of Indira's tenure in the early 1980s was Zail Singh, famous for claiming that at her command he was ready to wield a broom and become a lowly sweeper. But the sycophancy alone wasn't enough; most of the men Indira promoted were also required to put a fixed amount of money into her coffers.

This new ruthless and amoral side of Indira was almost all that India saw of her for the next decade. It bewildered and alienated even the few friends she had made during her insecure early years; the relatively frank letters to Dorothy Norman became dull rituals before ceasing altogether around the time of the Emergency. Indira's later years leave any potential biographer with little else to detail besides the intricacies of Indian politics. Indeed, much of Indira's life seems to show how a not particularly sensitive or intelligent woman was exalted by accident of birth and a callow political culture into the chieftancy of a continent-size nation and how a drab inner life came to be filled with an exaggerated sense of self and mission and an all-consuming quest for personal power.

The autocrat's search for unqualified loyalty usually ends within her own family. Indira's closest colleague in the seventies was her younger son, Sanjay Gandhi; while holding no official position, he had by the time the Emergency was declared in 1975 become the de facto ruler of India. Like many other undereducated scions of third world dynasties, Sanjay had a weakness for cars. In the late sixties he abandoned his apprenticeship at the Rolls-Royce factory in England, where he was regularly arrested for speeding, and came back to India with the ambition to make small cars for Indian consumers. Indira's government awarded his new company a license despite competitive applications from Toyota, Renault, and Citroën. The nationalized banks advanced him generous loans; government officials bullied car dealers into placing large cash orders. No usable cars ever emerged from Sanjay's factory. Nevertheless, banks and industrialists continued to fund his company, and Sanjay diversified into equally bogus "consultancy services" in order to channel the incoming money into his personal accounts.

His little racket was one of the many instances of the crony capitalism that flourished alongside the rhetoric of socialism. Such brazen corruption, which had become commonplace in India by the early seventies, was made still more intolerable for the poor by rising inflation. Successive droughts and an inefficient and venal public distribution system had made food scarce. The Congress started doing badly in local elections. Large-scale protests by students and workers erupted across India in the run-up to the declaration of the Emergency in June 1975. Jayaprakash Narayan, an old Gandhian idealist, emerged from retirement to lead the growing opposition to Indira.

Indira, in turn, denounced the agitation for her removal as part of a broad CIA-backed conspiracy. She had already used the military and the police to crush a Mao-inspired insurgency in Bengal, and when a delayed court judgment invalidated her election to the Indian Parliament and made it imperative that she resign, she decided to do away with the fast-unraveling façade of democracy.

In the anonymous self-analysis he published in 1937, Nehru had seen himself as "too much of an aristocrat for the crudity and vulgarity of fascism." Sanjay Gandhi, an admirer of Ferdinand Marcos and a devoted reader of *Archie* comics, had no such aesthetic inhibitions. On the day before the declaration of the Emergency, he went about cutting off the power supply to newspaper offices in Delhi and drawing up lists of opposition leaders to be arrested. Later Sanjay personally vetted the daily content of the media, which quickly turned to highlighting his speeches and passed over in silence—what V. S. Naipaul described as the "great silence" of the eighteen-month-long Emergency—the detention without trial of more than 110,000 people and the deaths of hundreds of protesters in police shootings all across India.

Lumpen young men gathered around Sanjay. They extorted money from small and big businessmen and apparently also dabbled in murders and kidnappings. But Sanjay had larger aspirations. "I firmly believe," he claimed, "that the best ideology for the people is my ideology." He wanted to "beautify" India's cities, make the country "ultra modern"; he wanted India to be a first world player, not just a backward third world country; and his aggressive nostrums— overpopulation? forcibly sterilize and give the poor vasectomies; ugly cities? bulldoze the slums—had much support among middle-class Indians, who were as impatient as Sanjay with the stubbornly destitute majority of India's population.

With her son unofficially, if fully, in charge, Indira retreated into her own world; the extraordinary self-centeredness Nehru had noticed now kept all reality at bay. "There is no show of force whatsoever anywhere in the country," she stated repeatedly. "My family has been very much maligned," she told a British journalist, "and of course my son is not in politics at all." Nayantara Sahgal attributes the falsehoods to Indira's profound craving to be seen as the truest and most principled leader of the Indian masses. This explains why she expected to win, and therefore held, the national elections in 1977, in which the unprotected poor, who suffered most from the violent evictions and the terroristic "family planning" schemes of the Emergency, voted her out of office.

Difficult times might have then seemed inevitable for Indira. But the coalition of opposition parties began collapsing soon after it ended one-party rule over India. Its leaders, greedy after their long exclusion from the perks of high office, squabbled among themselves. They tried intermittently to arraign Indira for her various excesses during the Emergency, but their clumsiness only made her seem a victim, a role she took to passionately as she toured around the poorer parts of the country, asking for forgiveness and sympathy.

Soon after she was voted back to power in 1980, Sanjay Gandhi died while attempting some stunts in a light airplane above Delhi. The freak accident—"the best thing that could happen to India," as one of Indira's own cousins tactlessly but truthfully remarked—seems to have deepened Indira's delusions. Throughout her remaining four years in office, she traveled, on government helicopters and planes, from one Hindu guru and temple to another, pleading for divine protection from her "enemies"—the CIA, Sikh militants, the leaders of the opposition, and even Sanjay's widow, Maneka—who seemed to her to be everywhere, undermining her, personally, as much as the "national interest."

In 1982, Indira expelled Maneka from the prime ministerial residence in New Delhi; her assistant tried to search Maneka's luggage as she left, and Indira herself tried to hold on to Sanjay's young son, Varun. In Kashmir, in 1984, Indira engineered, through bribes paid to legislators, the collapse of a democratically elected government; it was the first of a series of events that forced Kashmiri Muslims into a full-scale anti-India insurgency in 1990. In Punjab, Sanjay and the Congress Party had promoted an extremist Sikh preacher called Bhindranwale in order to undermine the principal Sikh party, the Akali. In the early eighties Bhindranwale turned against his sponsors and declared war on India. The random killings of Hindus by Bhindranwale's men in Punjab came as an opportunity for Mrs. Gandhi to stoke up a nationwide hysteria about the various threats to India's "unity and integrity."

Much of the media echoed her insinuations about the "antinational" tendencies of the Sikhs and Kashmiri Muslims. I remember from my own small-town childhood the abruptness with which many lower-middle-class Hindus began to distrust and scorn the Sikh neighbors they had previously lived alongside in perfect amity for decades. The Hindu nationalists owe their rapid blood-strewn progress partly to this antiminority frenzy Indira worked up during her last years in office.

In June 1984, Indira ordered the army to force Bhindranwale and other Sikh militants from the Golden Temple in Amritsar. The ill-conceived assault upon the Mecca of Sikhism resulted in the massacre of hundreds of innocent pilgrims as well as the desecration of many sacred sites. Barely four months later, on October 31, 1984, Indira was assassinated by two of her own bodyguards; both men were Sikhs seeking revenge for the brutalities in Amritsar.

But the bigger outrage occurred during the following three days, when mobs led by the Congress "hit men" that Sanjay had once nurtured went around Delhi with electoral rolls that listed Sikh-owned houses. The police stood idly by as over three thousand Sikhs were murdered in Delhi. Altogether five thousand Sikhs were killed across India, and as a whole generation of enraged young Sikhs took up arms against the Indian state, thousands more died in Punjab during the next decade.

I do not want to be remembered for anything," Indira told an interviewer in one of those fits of imperial pique that became more common toward her death. It is not a desire that posterity can honor. The hard-edged realpolitik with which Indira and her son replaced Nehru's impatient but benign patriarchy seems tailor-made for the BJP and its middle-class constituency. In a 2001 poll in *India Today*, India's highest-circulation newsmagazine, a majority of the middle-class respondents made plain their yearning for a "strong leader" like Indira Gandhi.

The fascistic undertones are unsettling. But this is also what Indira helped create: a widely shared mood among the Indian middle class, compounded equally of fear, aggressiveness, contempt, and apathy; a climate of opinion in which India's various encircling cruelties—the uprooting of hundreds of thousands of tribal families by big dam projects, the suicides of hundreds of farmers victimized by the economic policies of the last decade—feel far away, in which the deaths of more than fifty thousand people in Kashmir in the last decade incite little debate beyond the narrow parameters of "national interest," and the pogroms against the minorities can go unpunished, a national mood, Indira's truest legacy, that now seems almost crucial to the building of a new Indian identity, of which Hinduism, nuclear bombs, beauty queens, and information technology tycoons have, in recent years, become essential, if conflicting, components.

3. Bourgeois Anxieties

Most middle-class people I talked to in Allahabad had to think hard when asked about the chances of the four main candidates and were often unable to remember their names; they worried more about the uncollected garbage on the streets, the lack of drainage, the pot-holed roads, the power and water breakdowns. They talked about growing corruption and crime in the city, about the recent murder of a young female doctor, the rise of mafia dons, the deteriorating environment outside their homes, and the general atmosphere of insecurity. They did not think that the elections would make much of a difference. Some of them denounced politicians, described democratic politics as being "ill suited" to India, and wished that the army could take over. They said they lived with large fears about their property, their families, and sometimes their lives.

This subdued fear and foreboding were a curious fate for the middle class, which, created during colonial times, had inherited the British instinct for law and order. After 1859, while the British grew increasingly self-absorbed, a small group of Indians had begun to embrace some of the benefits the British had brought to India while colonizing it. In 1887, the year Kipling arrived in Allahabad, the network of English-style universities was extended to the city. The general British policy was to consolidate their rule over India through exposing an elite class of Indians to European civilization. This elite class of Indians grew fast, each generation building upon the achievement of the preceding one, and for at least six decades after the establishment of the first college in 1873 (where the father of Pandit Nehru was a student) Allahabad was to witness a political and intellectual awakening without precedent or parallel in North India. The Congress Party did not only find a base in the Nehru family mansion but also recruited many important members in the city. There were literary associations and clubs, new magazines and newspapers, libraries and reading rooms.

Few traces of this sudden flowering now survive. It seems more and more like a freakish episode that nationalist passion and the British, relatively benevolent in their last years, had together brought about, something which eventually worked against, but also required, the order and certainties of colonial rule and which couldn't have withstood the pressures of poverty and population arising from even a minimally democratic India.

The scramble for basic livelihood has now undermined colonial institutions built for very different purposes. The most prominent example in Allahabad is the university I went to. It was once known as the Oxford of the East, where much of the intellectual fervor of the colonial period had originated. Soon after independence, it was overwhelmed with students from nearby poverty-stricken areas, who came not for the higher learning the university offered but to improve their prospects for government jobs. However, there weren't that many government jobs available (opportunities in business and private industry had been further limited by Nehru's decision to adopt a socialistic economy for India), and most of these students, adrift after acquiring several useless degrees, became part of the floating reserve army of the unemployed, who ultimately found subsistence in the related vocations of crime and politics.

There had been a police raid on one of the hostels just before I arrived in Allahabad. During my time Hindu Hostel, as it was known, had been much feared for its large population of criminals who had taken refuge there, encouraged by old laws that forbade the police from entering the premises without authorization from the university. Over the years the criminals had driven out most of the students and had come to rely on pure terror to establish their right over the hostel.

When the electricity board cut off the power supply after bills remained unpaid for several years, they went in a mob and burned down the local power station. Power was duly restored, and after a student leader from the hostel arranged for the digging of a tube well on the hostel's grounds, the residents became fully self-sufficient. The hostel was no longer connected to the university, its reputation repulsing even ordinary visitors to the nearby Alfred Park, its very presence suggesting an extreme kind of secession from the city.

Finally, the university administration, headed by a new man, acted. The local police, bolstered by additions from outside the district, surrounded the hostel early one morning. Roads leading to it were sealed off before the police stormed the building and took the residents by surprise. These elaborate preparations were necessary; the residents, armed with crude country pistols and bombs, had thwarted an earlier police attempt to enter the hostel.

The police raid on the hostel didn't excite any fresh hopes for the university or the city. The yellow-painted trucks and dirty canvas tents of the police standing on the hostel grounds were seen as temporary; as soon as the policemen were gone, the criminals were expected to return and throw out any students the university might assign to the hostel in the new academic year.

Middle-class people learned to live with these little setbacks, which they saw as commonplace, secretly hoping that they would move on without being sucked into the violent world around them, something possible at any time, as I myself found out.

After a week of living in an empty hotel in Allahabad, I had become used to its silence and was surprised to be woken up one night by noises coming from next door. I checked the time; it was two in the morning. The man at the reception said he would "do some inquiries"; he never called back. I waited for the noises—mobile phone tinkles, hectic shiftings of furniture, room service orders, hollow television baritones—to cease, but they only grew louder. They went on for about half an hour. I wondered if I should call the reception again or get up and ask the new arrivals to pipe down. In the end, laziness kept me in bed, and at some point I drifted back into sleep.

In the morning, the elevator and lobby were full of young aspiring politicians, recognizable by their white cotton kurta pajamas, mobile phones, and keen-eyed look, three things that often went together as the distinguishing signs of some tainted priesthood. They had come to meet someone—probably, I thought, the film star from Bombay Shatrughan Sinha, who had been campaigning on behalf of the BJP's candidate, and whose arrival in the city prompted several people to phone me, wanting to know if I was Mr. Sinha's secretary.

Silence was restored in the adjacent room the next night, and I didn't think any more of it. Three days later I was introduced to Piyush, who worked as a local correspondent for *The Times of India*. He came up to my room, and the first thing he said was that he had met Raja Bhaiyya at the room adjacent to mine three days before. I was startled. Raja Bhaiyya: I knew the name. One of the feudal lords of the region, he belonged to one of the many landed families whose control, mostly by means of terror, of various small principalities had been tolerated by the British as long as the revenues came in on time and who were now sustained in independent India through electoral politics.

With several cases of murder, kidnapping, extortion, and gunrunning still pending against him, Raja Bhaiyya, like many other scions of pseudoroyal families, had become a politician and secured his victory in elections to the state legislature not by hard-selling good intentions or promises, but by the simple expedient of "booth capturing," whereby armed men took over voting booths, drove away all legitimate voters, and then filled the ballot boxes at their leisure.

Unaffiliated at first, Raja Bhaiyya had joined the Hindu nationalists after they promised to make him a minister in the state government. Soon after assuming power, he arranged for the transfer of a police officer who had shown unusual zeal in pursuing criminal cases against him (it had always been hard to prosecute Raja Bhaiyya, for no one dared take the witness stand against him, and he had secured several acquittals in the courts).

It was then the national press had suddenly taken notice of him. There were accounts of his brutality, a trait he had inherited from his father, who, according to one story, used to feed his opponents to the crocodiles in a nearby lake. The story was probably apocryphal; but the legend had held, and then there were the stories that couldn't be dismissed. Piyush had researched Raja Bhaiyya's criminal background and seen the lake, whose large fish population Raja Bhaiyya claimed as his legitimate source of income. He said that it was good I hadn't gone up to his room that night in my irritated state. Apparently, Raja Bhaiyya didn't take well to criticism. A Muslim shopowner who had spoken against him had recently been hacked to pieces in the middle of a crowded bazaar by one of his henchmen (the murderer was arrested; but as always there were no witnesses, and later I was to see pictures of decayed unclaimed corpses at the police station notice boards in Raja Bhaiyya's region).

Piyush said, "The responsibility of high office has mellowed him only slightly. Perhaps, he now thinks a bit before ordering someone's murder."

Piyush, shy and talkative at the same time, detailed Raja Bhaiyya's excesses with sarcastic energy. But behind his eagerness lay boredom. Later, when the talk turned to his own work as a journalist in Allahabad, he asked me about jobs in the Delhi papers. Researching spectacular crime and corruption, chasing after provincial politicians, interviewing minor celebrities from the metropolises: He had done all this for two years, and he now wished to get out of Allahabad.

I recognized that urge. It was what I had myself felt, as a student in Allahabad, when the stories of Raja Bhaiyya, and people like him, weighed upon me oppressively, and I longed constantly for a life beyond them.

That life lay for most people in the British-created refuge from the threatening chaos of India, Civil Lines, whose prestige and glamour after independence were to grow in Allahabad and in hundreds of other towns and small cities across British-ruled India, all with their own Civil Lines. For hundreds of thousands of educated Indians who had just emerged from a background of poverty, a job with the colonial bureaucracy, kept more or less intact after independence, was the chief way to get to Civil Lines. Once there, you inherited the lifestyles of the British almost instinctively. Eighty-five years after Kipling, Arvind Krishna Mehrotra, one of India's finest poets in English, remembered his childhood in the Civil Lines of the 1950s, Indians by then fully installed in the bungalows vacated by the British, and found that same faux colonial world of clubs and new respectability that Kipling wrote about:

At seven-thirty we are sent home
From the Cosmopolitan Club
My father says, "No bid,"
My mother forgets her hand
In a deck of cards.
I sit on the railing till midnight,
Above a worn sign
That advertises a dentist.

I go to sleep after I hear him
Snore like a school bell.
I am standing alone in a back alley
And a face I can never recollect is removing
The hubcaps of our dull brown Ford.
The first words I mumble are the names of roads,
Thornhill, Hastings, Lytton . . .

Although the roads, Mehrotra writes, were later renamed after Hindu nationalists or provincial leaders, the old life of Civil Lines went on for a while. But there had to come a time when it felt the weight of the anarchic world just outside. When I visited Allahabad, a different and ominous resident had just begun to appear in Civil Lines. It was the wife of a judge at the Allahabad High Court who spoke of this to me one evening at her bungalow, her tone alternating between impatience and sudden gloom. There was no power, and we sat, perspiring, in her candlelit living room, surrounded by framed pictures of her children, one of whom had just got married in Boston, while two servants outside on the dark veranda carefully wiped golf clubs. One bungalow away, a local mafia don had forced out the original landowners and started building a commercial complex called Mak Tower. The building was only four stories high; to the judge's wife the word "tower" was a menacing sign of the man's vanity and ambition, a menace she felt extended to the whole of Civil Lines. She said, "There is no opposition from the residents, who in any case fear the mafia man and what he might do to them."

I had met the man she mentioned. His name was Atiq Ahmed. He was a Muslim politician who had just resigned from the Samajwadi

Party over its failure to back Sonia Gandhi in her attempts to form a coalition government after the BJP government's collapse, and he lived in the warren of narrow lanes, with overhanging two- or three-story houses and small shops, which made up the old quarter across the tracks from Civil Lines. It had rained heavily on the evening I went with a friend to see him. A stench from uncollected mounds of garbage hung in the humid air; the unlit road was all large water-filled craters, treacherous and almost impossible to negotiate in the dark. Mr. Ahmed had famously shot his greatest rival in one of the more public squares in the old city. By living where he did, he had made it difficult for his own would-be murderer to reach his house. The walled compound was patrolled by armed men and ferocious-looking Dobermans, and packed with gleaming new Toyotas and Hondas and Tata Sumo jeeps. Tall, stocky men walked around the veranda of the house, speaking into mobile phones; a row of sofas with frayed blue-satin upholstery lined the wall, several rooms beyond which probably were—though hard to imagine in this rough masculine atmosphere—the living quarters for women.

Mr. Ahmed's thick curling mustache, his burly frame and brisk waddle suggested a brute panache. But he dressed simply in a white kurta pajama, a long scarf wound around his head, Bedouin-style, and he received us in a small bare room, where a singlet hung limply from the lone hook on the yellow walls and a wrinkled sheet with a faded red-roses print covered the bed in one corner, under a glossy calendar picture of Mecca at night.

Ostentation in general wasn't Mr. Ahmed's style. His power seemed to partly lie in remaining, or at least appearing to be, a man of the people, someone who had begun his career by stealing tar from road construction sites, had become a contractor for the railways, successfully contested the elections to the state legislature, and then, after a series of strategic murders of potential rivals, had emerged as the unchallenged authority in a part of the old quarter populated largely by poor Muslims, thin, gaunt, angular-featured men in prayer caps who stood idle before lightless shops and gazed warily at the passing cars.

For local politicians in need of Muslim votes, Mr. Ahmed was the person to talk to, and the phone rang constantly, with callers from Benares, Mirzapur, Pratapgarh, and Fatehpur entreating him to visit these neighboring constituencies and work his special persuasive magic on the Muslim voters, who formed up to 20 percent of the electorate of the region. Mr. Ahmed usually pleaded busyness, uncancelable engagements. He was gruffly matter-of-fact; while I was with him, he received many telephone calls informing him that an associate of his had been shot, and after ascertaining that the man was still alive and arranging for him to be taken to a "nursing home," Mr. Ahmed became increasingly brusque in his replies. Putting the phone down, he would assume a friendly demeanor, and with the graciousness that is the politician's acquired skill, he would urge us to take more pistachios from the bowl on the table before us.

In between phone rings, he talked, seriously and engagingly; he spoke like the man who had moved on, after the petty crimes and murders, to a higher idea of himself. He worried about the Brahmin vote bank in Allahabad. He feared that most of it would go to BJP's Brahmin candidate, the incumbent Mr. Joshi, even though the Congress had also put up a Brahmin candidate. He thought the Brahmins weren't ready to accept Sonia Gandhi's leadership. He worried, too, about the "fascist" tactics of the BJP. The Hindu nationalists had no respect for democracy, he said. They had staffed the district administration with their upper-caste sympathizers—this was something I heard often—and were going to rig the elections in their favor.

It wasn't just his expressed concern for democracy that made judgment on Mr. Ahmed difficult. In his area, almost a ghetto with its boxed houses and cramped lanes and restricted lives, among a minority made insecure and fearful by the rise of the Hindu nationalists, Mr. Ahmed with his wealth and political power offered certain guarantees to otherwise unprotected peoples. His power, though often asserted in violent and arbitrary ways, kept at bay the violence and arbitrariness of other men in other ghettos: the Raja Bhaiyyas, the Hindu nationalists, the corrupt policemen.

Now he was extending his suzerainty to the city across the tracks, and he made the inhabitants of Civil Lines nervous. The judge's wife spoke to me of the general turning away from the city, a retreat that appeared more extensive than that of the British after the shock of the mutiny in 1857, but without the power and security of the latter. "People living here in Civil Lines," she said, "long stopped taking any kind of interest or pleasure in their city; they want to have as little to do with it as possible. They send their children out of the city for studies; sometimes they too move out."

4. The Reclaiming of India

The middle class, which had depended for a long time on its close affiliations with the executive and legislative branches of the administration and on its class loyalties, now weakened at a time when every man was for himself, the middle class in small towns and cities sees itself as besieged. In this you could detect the beginning of the end of an India that thought itself safe in the cocoon of colonial privilege, an India that with all its inherited advantages had failed to create a democratic and egalitarian society and was instead forced to accommodate people like Mr. Ahmed.

It could all seem fated from the time, soon after independence, when the new bourgeois self-confidence that had once contributed to the making of modern India decayed into a desire for colonial forms of self-assertion and authority: the high-placed job with the government, the big bungalow, the graveled driveway, the servants in the kitchen, the uniformed sentinel at the gate. Many more Indians seek to enter that world. The reclaiming of India by Indians, the logical result of independence from colonial rule, often appears to have only just begun.

This process is inevitably hardest and longest for people whom the caste system and poverty had previously kept in darkness. Ram Dular Singh Patel, the candidate in Allahabad of the Bahujan Samaj Party, which claimed to represent the interests of the Dalits (the all-inclusive term for all formerly untouchable and oppressed castes), thought politics could short-circuit the process. Dalits form roughly 20 percent of India's population. By using their vote effectively, they could be a force for instability, and instability was good, Mr. Patel said, looking searchingly at me, since "it confuses and bewilders Brahmanical forces and hastens their breakup."

The leaders of Mr. Patel's party had been known to begin their press conferences by asking all Brahmin journalists to leave. It was a kind of reverse humiliation, a small retribution for centuries of oppression, and my initial nervousness about contacting Mr. Patel had grown after he failed to return my calls. I had then gone to his house early one morning with the hope that he would be more receptive to a visitor at home. He lived in Allahapur, a residential area built on sloping ground near the Ganges, where the broad, straight streets of Civil Lines suddenly shrink and turn into a maze of narrow, often unpaved lanes with potholes and open gutters and piles of filth. When I was there last, the houses were no more than two or three square or rectangular boxes of brick and cement stacked on top of or next to each other. They formed unbroken walls on both sides of the lane, their façades moldy and grimy after three months of monsoon rains; some of these were boardinghouses and lodges where many students from the region around Allahabad live. The lanes were choked with cows and pigs, which seemed unusually big in that constricted space, and street vendors selling vegetables and fruits and fried snacks in open stalls, but a steady stream of rickshaws, scooters, and motorcycles still managed to wend past them. Before a hand pump, a man furiously soaped his swarthy torso, as two men waited behind him, brushing their teeth. A tangle of electric cables hung loosely and dangerously from electric poles at every corner, illegal power connections you could acquire by bribing the local electricity staff.

Mr. Patel's house, a white two-storied building, was separated from the main lane by a stretch of bare ground that heavy rains had scored into a miniature mountain valley of gullies and mounds. My shoes left a trail of mud as I walked up a staircase at the back of the house to one of these rooms, where bleary-eyed young men in undervests and pajamas sat cross-legged under fast-spinning fans. There was no furniture apart from a wooden cot and an old sofa with its straw stuffing exposed; some rumpled and frayed sari-like sheets on the rough floor indicated the place where the men slept. The walls were bare except for a poster with the words "God loves you" and a garish oil painting in garish colors of Dr. B. R. Ambedkar, Gandhi's rival and the original leader of the Dalits.

The men in the room, dark and thin and subdued-looking, shot quick glances at my clothes and shoes, and it occurred to me that I was the only fully dressed person there. One of the men introduced himself, ordered tea, and then informed Mr. Patel, dressing for the day in an inner room, of my arrival. The man's name was Sandip. A thick beard covered his round, rather jovial face. His undervest had tiny holes in it, but the upright way in which he sat suggested authority. He told me, speaking with the practiced fluency of a public speaker, that the other young men, most of them Dalits, were student volunteers for Mr. Patel's campaign. Some of them were from villages outside Allahabad; others lived nearby, in the dingy boardinghouses I had just passed.

They stared at me as Sandip spoke, still sitting where I had surprised them, and I wondered if, after the first burst of caste loyalty and enthusiams that had taken them to Mr. Patel's home, they had found themselves at a loose end, unsure of what they were supposed to do.

Mr. Patel soon appeared. He was tall and lean, with thick hair and pencil-thin mustache, and a mole in the middle of his forehead that looked incongruously like the caste mark of the devout Brahmin; in his crisp white kurta and dhoti he stood out in the bare room full of shabbily dressed students, who, passive until this point, immediately clustered around him. He was at first surprised, and then pleased, to see me; it turned out that there hadn't been any press coverage so far of his campaign. But he didn't have much time; he was on his way to address meetings in the rural areas south of the Yamuna River. The leaders of his party were soon arriving in Allahabad to lend support to his campaign, and they were arriving in a helicopter. Mr. Patel himself planned to travel in the helicopter with them, the resonant fact for him; he kept repeating it, to the extent that it seemed that the helicopter had become, like the expulsion of Brahmins from press conferences, another small way of experiencing a long-denied power.

The students looked impressed, and after his first moment of surprise, Mr. Patel spoke to me slightly mockingly, dismissing my questions in his slow, deliberate voice, inviting smiles from the students, who watched his face intently.

The real issue in this election, Mr. Patel said, wasn't one that anyone outside his party had taken up. It was this: How can Dalits live in India with dignity and self-respect and receive equal opportunities in education and employment? Fifty years after independence most Dalits were victims of the worst kind of exploitation: They were worked into the ground and underpaid; in villages they were not allowed to draw water from the communal well; they were killed at random, and their wives and daughters raped. There was only one way of stopping all that: by welding the Dalits into a solid political unit. Mr. Patel clenched and unclenched his fist to illustrate his point. It was an unsettling gesture after the softness of his voice. The combined strength of the Dalits, Mr. Patel continued, would then hold the balance of power against "Brahmanical forces," who after all were just 20 percent of the population as opposed to 20 percent Dalits, 30 percent other Backward castes, and 15 percent Muslims and other minorities.

And then after this swift reckoning Mr. Patel left, quickly pattering down the stairs, a small retinue of party men with flags and banners running to keep pace with him. The students dispersed and became idle again. Sandip, who had been standing next to Mr. Patel, suddenly laughed embarrassedly and said that he himself was a "student leader," the first Dalit to have won an election to his college's student union, which the upper castes had previously monopolized. His ambition now—and here Sandip's voice suddenly became full of passion—was to help elect Mr. Patel as the first Dalit member of Parliament from Allahabad, where duplicitous Brahmins from various political parties had managed to fool the Dalit masses with false promises for over fifty years.

Later that afternoon, I was at a tea shack in Civil Lines when a Tata Sumo jeep flying the BJP flag—saffron-colored, with a lotus in the middle—stopped before it. Two students emerged, identically plump in tight jeans and T-shirts with mobile phones strapped to their trouser belts. The jeep was new, with plastic covers still draped across the seats. It was probably a temporary gift, along with the mobile phones, from the party. It emerged that the students had been going from door to door in the middle-class parts of the city, campaigning for Dr. Murli Manohar Joshi, the BJP's Brahmin candidate for Allahabad. Despite this, the two saw themselves not as active politicians but as members of the Sangh Parivar, the family of both extreme and moderate Hindu nationalist groups, which, since they do not take part in electoral politics, are free to make unpopular gestures of Hindu assertion, such as the recent attacks on Christians across India that the BJP's sister outfit, the Bajrang Dal, organized.

They were trying, they said, to present the issues before the people, such as whether India was to be ruled once again by a foreigner, an "agent of the Vatican" (the Italian-born Sonia Gandhi); whether India was to defeat attempts by Islamic fundamentalists to destroy it; whether India was to regain its past glory as a strong, self-sufficient Hindu nation.

They looked confused when I asked them how the BJP proposed to achieve the last-mentioned aim. One of them began to say something about India's nuclear tests and then stopped. When I asked them about the Dalits and Mr. Patel, they were scornful. They said that the politics of hate and animosity Mr. Patel and his party practiced would weaken Hinduism and India. The Dalits were welcome to join the mainstream of Hindu society, but their current demands for more reservations in government jobs was going to lead to civil war. As it was—and here they became agitated—India faced all kinds of challenges from abroad. Did I know that Osama bin Laden had issued a call for jihad against India? The pope already had a dangerous agent in India, Sonia Gandhi. And now America had declared war through its missionaries, who were bribing innocent Hindus to convert to Christianity. Had I heard about the beating up of the missionaries last winter in Allahabad? They knew the man responsible for it. It was the right thing to do; it had sent a clear message to America: that Hindu India would fiercely rebuff any attempts to undermine it.

Raised from ordinariness by the elections, and given a slightly glamorous identity by the jeep and mobile phones, the students hadn't really bothered to think through their rhetoric. They found it easier to work with a sense of the enemy: bin Laden, Sonia, the pope. I hadn't asked, but I knew they were Brahmins; their political affiliations and opinions were enough of a hint. Most of the educated upper castes were with the BJP; the rest of the parties fought over the Backward caste and Dalit and Muslim votes in the intensely competitive politics based on group identity that had emerged in India after the politically torpid years under the Congress.

Just fifteen years ago I couldn't have encountered people like Sandip or the BJP's supporters; the Dalit students wouldn't have been clustering reverently around Mr. Patel. The Congress then had a brute majority in the Parliament. For much of the time since independence, it had managed to keep the lid on most of the bewildering social and political contradictions of India; it had appeared to address all the different claims made by rich and poor, Hindu and Muslim, Brahmin and Dalit, North Indian and South Indian.

This elastic appeal was the party's legacy, along with its nationwide organization, and its association with the great names of Gandhi and Nehru. It had been sustained as much by the glamour of its dynasty as it had by the ineptitude of opposition parties or by the monopoly it came to have over the institutions of the colonial state, the system of rewards and punishments it created within the civil bureaucracy and the newly opened state-controlled industries. The Congress's unchallenged dominance had made for a simple political and intellectual life in the country. Academics and journalists looked for shelter in the great network of state patronage created by the Congress. Small talk and gossip crowded out political discussion in the newspapers. It was rare for the politicians and journalists who used to cluster at the old coffeehouse in Allahabad to do more than speculate about who was in or out of favor with the big bosses of the Congress.

In the end the Congress had been undermined by its own inner complexity. The peace it maintained between antagonistic groups began to crumble, and this was as much due to an ossified leadership as to the fact that individuals as well as special interest caste and regional groupings had become more conscious of what was owed to them, the self-awareness that the stability of colonial and then Congress rule—a sterile stability with no end but itself—had managed to suppress for the most part. Provincial party bosses challenged the leadership and were, in turn, themselves challenged by newly emergent activists from below. India had now reverted to being a nation with many minorities, each with its own grievances.

The Congress, weighed down with self-serving coteries and lobbyists and dulled by its years in power, had been late to wake up to the fact that it could no longer meet the conflicting needs of Brahmins and Dalits, rich and poor, Hindu and Muslim. It tried to appease everyone and sought renewal through the few surviving members of the Nehru-Gandhi dynasty.

Some measure of the Congress's confusion was revealed by an election meeting at the university student union. It was to be addressed by Rita Bahuguna, the Congress's candidate from Allahabad. She had been elected mayor of Allahabad three years ago, but this wasn't going to help her defeat Mr. Joshi, the BJP MP. She was blamed for the deteriorating civic condition in the city, but she was, in effect, powerless since the municipal corporation spent most of the little money it had on staff salaries. The hall was packed, a mixed crowd of students and teachers perspiring under slow fans. Mrs. Bahuguna was late, and a series of student leaders appeared on the platform, assured the audience of her imminent arrival, and then proceeded to harangue those waiting. Their oratorical style was fierce; broad speakers squatting under tall portraits of freedom fighters boomed and clanged as the students clasped the microphone close to their faces and shouted into it at the very tops of their voices. The passion in these leaders, who looked so much like other students, thin-limbed, dressed in ill-fitting shirts and pants and plastic sandals, was oddly disturbing. One by one they came and after expressing their frenzy retired sheepishly to the side of the platform, where they sat half listening to other speeches, their sweat-glistening faces blank.

They spoke of many things: the BJP's failure in Kashmir, the arrogance of Mr. Joshi, the sitting MP from Allahabad, whose commando bodyguards had physically evicted from Mr. Joshi's house the father of a man who had been drowned in a boat accident. But they never strayed far from their chief target: the police and university administration that had "conspired" to force students out of their hostel.

The speeches stopped as more leaders arrived: not students, but middle-aged men, large paunches showing under loose white kurta pajamas, many-ringed fingers clutching mobile phones. These were the local Congress's senior people. Small garlands of stringy sunflowers and roses mysteriously appeared in the hands of the student leaders as they lined up to greet the newcomers.

A tall, long-faced man with gold-rimmed glasses hung around his neck received the most garlands, all of which he immediately took off and handed to his pretty young daughter. He didn't look like a politician, and in fact he was a former admiral of the Indian Navy; his arrival in the city had been reported in the morning papers. He had been recently sacked by the BJP government for not very clear reasons, and he had subsequently taken to touring the country on behalf of the Congress, denouncing the government, particularly the defense minister, who was responsible for sacking him.

Cut off from the easeful life of high office and navy clubs, the man appeared to be struggling to know his new audiences. Hailed by the preceding speaker as a national hero, he started off his speech with an exhortation to the students to emulate Stanford University.

This provoked no titters, just puzzlement; few students in that hall would have even heard of Stanford. His daughter looked anxious, but he improved as he went on, his sentences composed of as many English words as Hindi, as he spoke about the fascist tactics of the Hindu nationalists, their attempt in particular to "saffronize" (saffron, the Hindu color) the armed forces. Then, while discussing parallels in Nazi history, he asked the students if they had read the chapter entitled "Triumph and Consolidation" in William L. Shirer's history of the Third Reich. The students, now massed around the doors, looked on mystified.

Rita Bahuguna finally arrived. Fresh garlands appeared—perhaps the same ones, I couldn't tell—as the town leaders queued up before Mrs. Bahuguna. In the new hierarchy that sprang up, the student leaders had to vacate their places, and even the admiral was ignored for a while.

Mrs. Bahuguna, sitting in her blue sari among burly white-clad men on the platform, was small and frail. A few rose petals clung to her hair when she rose to give a strangely brusque speech. She didn't need to establish her "credentials" (she used the English word) before students, she said. She was their teacher after all (even though she was the elected mayor of Allahabad, Mrs. Bahuguna still taught medieval Indian history at the university). She said she knew all about her problems, none of which had been solved by Mr. Joshi, also a former teacher, of physics, at the university. She ended by denouncing the police raid on the hostel and promised to ensure, if elected, a safe environment for students inside the university.

The crowd had grown suddenly quiet. The police action had been popular with the students. Vinod, a young man sitting next to me, had smiled wryly when the student leaders spoke, in loud, sentimental tones, of the poverty of parents who sent their children to the university in the hope they would pass the Civil Service exams and help them in their old age. Vinod himself was one of the countless students from poor families at the university preparing for the Civil Service exams, and fortunate enough to live in a bare, tiny hostel room, much like the one I had once lived in, where thick books on general knowledge and Indian economy stood in a tall pile on the solitary table, next to a rusty hot plate on which he made tea and warmed omelets brought from a stall outside the hostel gates. But he approved of the police operation, and so did, he said, most of the students, who couldn't find cheap accommodation anywhere outside the hostels. He said that Mrs. Bahuguna had been wrongly advised by the city leaders, several of whom were close to the criminals residing at Hindu Hostel. It was an-other instance of the Congress's protecting only its own interests and being out of touch with general feeling; it was now going to cost them votes among the students.

Vinod felt that Mrs. Bahuguna, who was the daughter of an influen-tial Brahmin politician in the city, should have known better. She had come late to politics herself, several years after the death of her father, but she hadn't played her moves too badly until that point (although she lost the first parliamentary election she contested, from a neighbor-ing constituency; she had opposed the Congress on that instance, mocking it for choosing Sonia Gandhi, a foreign woman, as its presi-dent. A few weeks before the present elections, she had managed to get Sonia Gandhi's backing for the contest in Allahabad).

The Congress leaders in Delhi had chosen Mrs. Bahuguna for her father's name, a Brahmin name that it expected would put a dent in the Brahmin support for the BJP, while attracting Muslims, among whom her father had been popular. She already had some support among the small group, not more than 2 percent, of the electorate, liberal, edu-cated people in the city—teachers, lawyers, journalists—who, though not always political, felt comfortable with her, saw her as a bulwark against the Hindu nationalists. The student union hall she spoke from was full of teachers from the university, many of them women in stylish saris. The next morning at her house, there were more women, door-to-door campaigners wearing fresh lipstick and smelling of deodorant. Some were part of a study group called Chetna (Consciousness) and also ran a private organization called Sahyog (Assistance), which supervised shelters for bonded child laborers and battered women.

There was much that was admirable about these women. It was they who seemed to affirm a sense of a shared society otherwise absent in small cities like Allahabad. But generating middle-class support within the city wasn't going to be enough to elect Mrs. Bahuguna. I accompanied her to the villages south of the Yamuna River, where she had to work hard to win the Dalit and Muslim votes for the Congress. Driving out of Allahabad, the city rapidly receding after the bridge over the swollen and muddy Yamuna, she seemed a bit out of her element. She held the end of her sari over her nose to block the diesel fumes from passing trucks and tractors, as she talked to me of the conferences she had attended in European and American cities as mayor of Allahabad.

At the small roadside settlements of half-built brick houses and shops we passed, men holding Congress flags ran up to her. These were local party workers, who were to "deliver" their villages' uncommitted voters, mostly illiterate, to the Congress. Important men, many of them old enough to have known her father, they would have been paid the small price for this support: employment for their sons or brothers, the expediting of housing and agricultural loans after the election.

A heavily built man with a Hindu, stereotypically sagelike white beard and long hair sat behind Mrs. Bahuguna in her large new Jeep. Dal Bahadur, the Congress candidate from Allahabad in the previous election, prompted her as soon as he saw the party workers. He knew all their names; he knew the caste they belonged to and introduced them to Mrs. Bahuguna with gruff familiarity. She exhorted them to work harder for her victory, her bookish Hindi strikingly different from the dialect Dal Bahadur spoke. She turned back, slightly flushed, and then, as the Jeep moved on, she returned to chatting with me. "I had a good time in New York," she told me at the gas station where we had stopped to refuel, and then suddenly started to wave at someone behind me. I turned to find a couple of slightly amused petrol station attendants. "Will you remember me on election day?" she shouted at them. There was a fluency to her speech and an ability to change register that she couldn't have acquired during her long career as an academic. It matched the sudden silences in the Jeep, and it seemed as if coming late to politics, she had been surprised by the inherited politician's skills rising to the surface, as if she had only recently tapped into some new elastic part of herself.

But her family background had also burdened her with a sense of entitlement. This was what made her so abrupt with the students; this was what that afternoon made her work her way through a series of poor low-caste villages, offering little more than her father's faded good works and the talismanic name of the Nehrus and Gandhis.

At one of the roadside settlements, a small crowd was waiting under a string of paper Congress flags hung between two mango trees. Mrs. Bahuguna mounted a wooden cot that served as a platform and gave a speech that was barely audible. She spoke of Sonia Gandhi's bereavement and the sacrifices of the Nehru-Gandhi family. The crowd watched her, not hearing much, but still agog. Many of them had walked a long way through the surrounding fields to see her. They were like the people Sonia Gandhi and the then prime minister Vajpayee would address in Allahabad a few days later. The celebrity speakers were hardly visible to a majority of the audience, and the speeches were all lost in the bewildering echoes from loudspeakers, but it was the seeing that seemed important, the contact with the powerful and privileged.

I saw a number of light-eyed boys with sharp features in the crowd; it turned out that they belonged to a Muslim community of horse riders from Rajasthan that had migrated to this part of India two generations ago. This community of three thousand lived in the mud huts lining the road; most were unemployed and survived by skinning cows killed in road accidents. Nearly all were illiterate. An old Hindu man from the adjacent tea shack, himself only slightly better off, was sympathetic to their plight. He told me, *"Yeh bilkul zero hain.* These people are completely zero." Some of the boys came over as he talked and stared at me, frank appraisal on their raw young faces. They nodded with unexpected vehemence when the man said that it was a school, above all, they wanted their member of Parliament to provide.

A few miles ahead—open fields of wheat and rice on both sides, an occasional hut in the distance—a freshly painted signboard announced a girls' school. I saw a small shack with just one long room, dark, the mud walls without windows, the only light coming from between the stacked bundles of straw on the roof. The roof would have leaked during the finest drizzle, and the ground around the jute mat where the children would have sat was damp. There were simple sums scrawled on the blackboard on one of the walls.

A couple of young men appeared as I stood there. They were the two teachers; they cycled in from nearby villages every morning and then cycled on to a local college, where they studied for postgraduate degrees and also "prepared" for the Civil Service. They were paid a monthly salary of four hundred rupees by the school's owner, a local contractor for gravel, for whom the school was only one business among many.

At the talk of teachers' salaries, Mrs. Bahuguna's secretary, a plump, friendly young man with glasses, who had followed me into the room, perked up. He had been traveling in my car after the Jeep had filled up with local Congress leaders, and a little while before he had been explaining to me why Mrs. Bahuguna would win. There was no question about the areas we were traveling through; her father had done so much work here, they all remembered him. Teachers all across the state (and there were sixty thousand in Allahabad constituency alone), he said, were going to vote against the BJP and for the Congress. They had been on a strike protesting their low salaries, but the BJP-run government had done nothing. And now a senior leader of the teachers' association had been murdered in Lucknow. (I had seen the newspaper reports that morning. A week later there was a report of a police "encounter" in which the alleged killer of the leader had been shot dead, "police encounter" being the all-Indian words for summary execution. A journalist from *The Times of India* arrived to see the bullet-riddled body lying next to a police inspector who was still on the wireless to his headquarters, shouting excitedly, for the official record, about bullets flying everywhere. There were allegations from the teachers' association that the police had murdered the so-called killer of their leader in order to quickly close the case before the complicity of the BJP government could surface.)

By the afternoon dark clouds had gathered in the big sky as we drove along a muddy river, more cars now following Mrs. Bahuguna's Jeep on the narrow road. For the next many miles, it rained, a fierce, blinding rain, from which cyclists and bullock cart drivers sheltered in wet, cowering groups under massive mango trees or under the leaking corrugated iron roofs of tea shacks and paan stalls. The windows began to fog up; the cars, jolted from side to side by large potholes, proceeded warily. Barefoot children in rags, their wet hair plastered to their skulls, ran after the bouncing rocking cars and pounced upon the propaganda leaflets thrown from their windows.

There was no welcoming party at the next riverside village, and no one seemed to know much about the place, except Dal Bahadur, the sagelike man, who now disappeared, leaving the rest of the party standing on a rain-soaked knoll.

I followed him on the muddy lane squelchy with rainwater and sheep and cow droppings. In front yards messy with straw and dung, women sifting wheat stopped to stare at me, their pink and purple saris bright against the pale mud-yellow of the houses. Naked children with distended bellies shrank to the one side as I passed them. An old man slumped on a string cot gestured at me from inside his hut, and when I went in, he wanted to know if I was from the government.

It was cool and fragrant inside the hut, the smell of cow dung almost turned into something heady and intoxicating by the rain. Two boys in their early teens came in: both thin, with sticklike legs, their large eyes glowering in the dark room. Their father was a rice farmer and fisherman, like most people in the village. Rice and fish was what they ate, the food cooked on the chulha fire in a little alcove before the room, cakes of cow dung stacked to one side of it. They had never been to school, and they had no other clothes than what they wore, clothes their father had bought from the nearby bazaar two years ago. The oversized polyester pants and shirts torn at the armpits and around the collar were adequate for ten months of the year, and when winter arrived, they tied straw to the insides of the shirts.

It took the boys some time for them to get used to my presence, and even then they spoke with difficulty; they did not understand the simplest words, the sparse vocabulary reflecting the bareness of the room that, apart from the string cot, had no furniture or personal possessions, words and things both absent and making for a kind of all-enveloping vacancy.

Back where the cars had stopped, Dal Bahadur had emerged with a few old women timidly trailing behind him. They stood speechless, their wizened, toothless faces half hidden by sari veils pulled down to nose level, as Mrs. Bahuguna asked them about their "problems." Still, they said nothing, and so Mrs. Bahuguna began to describe Sonia Gandhi's presidency of the Congress and how women were best placed to understand other women's problems. They looked on, puzzlement appearing in eyes that held great anxiety and patience. And now an embarrassed Dal Bahadur prompted them, in his gruff voice, "Don't you know who this is? Don't you remember how her father once distributed lai chana?"

Lai chana! The puffed rice and chick peas that were the poor man's snack, stuffed in rusty tin containers in the gloomy one-room shops in shanty markets we had passed. It was hard not to feel the pathos of the situation. Decades after it had been made, the old women were being asked to remember a meaningless offering from a long-dead politician, in a village which near-total destitution had taken beyond the simple deprivation of the rural poor elsewhere, beyond lack of water, electricity, primary schools, and hospitals to the earliest, most elemental form of human community, where the outside world intruded only in the form of election-time visitors and the propaganda leaflets the ragged children had pounced upon.

The more you examine the reclaiming of India by Indians, the more uneven the whole process looks. It is never very clear who is reclaiming what. Mr. Patel, the candidate of the Bahujan Samaj Party, had presented himself as a Dalit to me. I had been nervous about going to his house and possibly facing expulsion. I had been relieved to find him a friendly figure, eager for attention from the press. It now turned out that he wasn't a Dalit at all. He was a Kurmi, which—so important these differences—made him a member of a technically "Backward" caste, much better placed, socially and financially, than the Dalits.

Accordingly, Mr. Patel also turned out to be the owner of a large agricultural estate outside Allahabad. He also was a very recent member of the Dalit party whose strategy for instability he had explained to me, the party whose leaders in their few months in power in the state of Uttar Pradesh had emptied the state exchequer and had created little empires for themselves in addition to building grandiose monuments to Dalit leaders.

Mr. Patel had joined the party just a few weeks before the elections. It was Sandip, himself a Kurmi, who told me this, a trifle sheepishly. We were driving south of Allahabad, into the poor districts of Meja and Karchana, where there was a large Dalit population. Mr. Patel sat in the front seat and was unusually quiet. Party flags fluttered from on top of houses and shops. Few of them were of Mr. Patel's party. At places where meetings had been arranged, and microphones and platform set up, hardly anyone, apart from a couple of party workers, waited to greet him, and Mr. Patel had to move on without giving his speech.

It was in the embarrassing silences that descended inside the Jeep after every aborted meeting that Sandip started talking about his own family. Proudly, he told me about the number of relatives he had in the state and central Civil Services. "Why did you join politics then?" I asked. He immediately said, "I wanted to explore other options." There was no irony; he spoke in earnest. Later, attempting clarification, he added: "It is not enough for Dalits to join the Civil Service. They have to enter the arena of politics and take on the Brahmanical forces there. It is Dalit assertion that will expose the BJP's self-serving rhetoric about the terrorism and the threats to India's integrity."

Brahmanical forces, Dalit assertion, India's integrity—the words stood for certain recognizable realities. But it was possible to see too much in them and to forget the simple intentions of the politicians using them, people who weren't always sure what they meant and who, despite the difference in rhetoric, spoke for themselves alone and in the end were fighting for the same things. Misused by politicians, the words had acquired the neutrality of mathematical figures; you could fit them anywhere in the hectic accounting of electoral politics, which in a socially and economically restricted society had become an increasingly attractive means for upward mobility.

To the mass of peasantry and workers, and the middle class of lawyers, doctors, engineers, bureaucrats, teachers, and businessmen, a new class of professional politicians was steadily added since 1947. Thousands of men have emerged from amongst the general mass of deprived people and taken important positions within central and state legislatures. These are men with no special training or skills, sometimes not even those of basic literacy and oratory. A large number of them are criminals. Few of them offer anything apart from their caste and religious identity. Most of them are content to plunder the state's resources and sometimes share the loot with members of their family or caste group. They all seek the power that in societies degraded by colonialism often comes without a redeeming idea of what it is to be used for, the kind of power that, in most cases, amounts to little more than an opportunity to rise above the rest of the population and savor the richness of the world: junkets to New York for Mrs. Bahuguna, helicopter rides for Mr. Patel, free railway passes and gas connections and "commando" bodyguards and chauffeur-driven cars and crowds of supplicants outside one's door.

Behind the rhetoric of caste and religious redemption, the defections and betrayals, the collapse of governments and fresh elections, the constant intrigues in Delhi and state capitals, behind all the endless drama of politics in India, there lies the fear these men exalted above their station feel: that at any moment the richness of the world might be withdrawn and they might be returned to the small house in the dingy lane, the meanness and insignificance from which the profession of politics had rescued them.

With this fear often comes a contempt for the electorate, an impatience with the process of appeasing and wooing people you have left behind. The people, in turn, aren't slow in developing their own contempt for the upstarts among them. A lot of people in Allahabad claimed to have known Mr. Joshi, the incumbent MP for Allahabad, during the time when he lived in a two-room house, dressed in khaki shorts, and hitched rides on scooter pillions to the university where he taught—unmemorably, people said—physics. But Mr. Joshi, living now in a well-marbled house, traveling in a bulletproof Ambassador with tinted windows, and accompanied by ferocious-looking commandos in black and with carbines and AK-47 guns framing his small white dhoti-clad figure, the commandos not really required except as badges of status—there was no danger to Mr. Joshi's life, at least in his own town—Mr. Joshi, beginning to appear now in the society columns of the Delhi papers, had managed to place himself well above small-town envy and resentment.

The reference to Mr. Joshi's humble past was usually followed by some example of his newfound arrogance, which was in fact the irritable manner of a man prevented from rising even higher. For over a decade he had been considered the third most important leader of the

BJP, and during his tenure as minister for human resources and development, he had tried but failed to improve that seemingly perennial third-placeness. He had sought to impose a new educational curriculum that drastically revised Indian history as a continuous battle against idol-breaking Muslims but was stopped by his own prime minister. He had come up with a new slogan for the economic nationalists within the BJP: "Computer Chips, Not Potato Chips." He had played up his reputation as a man of science among the urban middle classes. Among rural Brahmins, he did not fail to mention his campaign against cow slaughter. "Hindu civilization," he lectured me, "couldn't have existed without cows, without their milk, curd, manure. They are at the basis of our national identity."

But it was a different basis for national identity, nuclear bombs, that he spoke of to the small crowd of peasants and menial workers outside a small technical institute in Allahabad three days before polling day. He had arrived four hours late, and until then most people, many of whom had been paid to attend, had just stood there, wearing bright orange BJP visors, punished by the harsh sun, among mounds of garbage and black rain-dried filth from overflowing gutters and piles of junked rusty machinery. The tone was set by the first speakers, local politicians, who scrambled to touch his feet, tore garlands out of the full arms of a boy wearing a grimy sleeveless singlet and draped them around Mr. Joshi's neck, before applying a few more layers to the vermilion caste marks on his forehead. In a long, rambling speech, one reported a conversation with a visiting "lady" from Paris; she had exclaimed at the mention of Allahabad: "Isn't that where the great son of India Mr. Joshi lives?" Mr. Joshi, sitting hunched on the floor, marigold petals sticking to his well-oiled hair, his legs dangling from the stage, looked impatient as speaker after speaker went on in this vein. When his turn came, he started by mentioning the great boost given to India's prestige by the nuclear tests and added that the disapproval of the international community could not deter India. "How many bombs should we build?" he asked the audience in the interactive style I was told he had developed after being criticized for his uninspiring oratory. A few feeble voices went up. "Twenty!" "Fifty!" "A thousand!" Mr. Joshi nodded at the last figure. He mentioned the battles in Kashmir. He said he had told Pakistan, "If you provoke us one more time, we'll smash you to pieces."

There was a smattering of applause from among the harried perspiring faces in the crowd. He mentioned the water sports complex he was planning to build on the Ganges. He boasted of how he had got rid of all the "Communists" working in the government-funded Indian Council for Historical Research.

And then he was through, and quick to leave, a small, brisk figure walking in the narrow corridor the commandos created for him by pushing and shoving blindly at the pressing crowds, back to the white Ambassador, where he was once again inscrutable behind tinted glass windows as the cars raced off, sirens blaring hysterically, past the auto repair shops and tea shacks and the bewildered men in rags squatting on ground turned into black paste by diesel oil and rainwater.

Mr. Joshi's next stop that day was a new mansion of gray marble and fake Spanish tiles in a high-walled compound several miles out of Allahabad. It was where the Jaiswals, a merchant caste, had arranged an election meeting. Paunchy men in baseball caps, dark glasses, broad-band gold watches and rings and chains sat on plastic chairs before a stage where the banner proclaimed: ALL FELLOW CASTE-BROTHERS ARE WELCOME. This was Mr. Joshi's constituency, upper-caste men with money, part of the strong network of Hindu nationalist sympathizers and volunteers, whose complaints about his aloofness and arrogance had grown louder as the elections approached. He had no choice but to sit through the banal comedy of speeches and introductions and garlandings that began all over again.

Almost all of the speakers spoke of how the Jaiswals through their success as shopkeepers had forced the rest of Hindu society to treat them with respect. But they had been deprived of affirmative action in government jobs, a great injustice, which they expected Mr. Joshi to rectify as "honorable minister" in the new government. Mr. Joshi sat on the edge of the stage, his legs dangling, as they had at the previous meeting, looking impatient. In his speech he dealt with this request in the same way he had dealt with a similar request a few days earlier at another upper-caste conclave, where speaker after speaker had spoken of their exploitation by the Brahmins as well as, astoundingly, by the Dalits; he promised to give the matter his "most sympathetic consideration."

There was a swimming pool lunch afterward. Mr. Joshi sat in the middle of the table and ate fast from his leaf plate. One of the more persistent speakers, a plump safari-suited man, the owner of the mansion, sat next to him and kept shouting at the serving boys to refill Mr. Joshi's plate. Mr. Joshi had to keep waving the boys dressed in red livery and rubber flip-flops away as they hovered over his shoulders with glinting steel bowls of dal and kheer.

His lunch finished, Mr. Joshi looked ready to leave. But various people approached him and whispered in his ear; he nodded and nodded. The commandos ate in another corner of the pool; they looked surprisingly relaxed. One rinsed his oily fingers in the swimming pool. There were others who had done so, but it was the commando the safarisuited owner saw, and he wrenched away from Mr. Joshi's conversation, his face suddenly filled with horror.

It rained early in the morning on polling day. But the voting booths in the city, set up in schools and colleges and small parks, remained empty long into the afternoon. An unusually low 30 percent of the electorate had bothered to show up until four in the afternoon, an hour before voting officially ended. Bored policemen played cards, their truncheons and rifles resting on the ground, and polling agents from the contesting parties sat looking morose behind small children's desks as a thin trickle of voters shuffled through the voting procedures, past the polling officials stern behind rough wooden tables piled with voting lists. The streets in the old quarter were deserted, and in the strangely unrestricted vistas, the old houses of the rich merchants and traders— often built adventurously, with art deco and Mughal and Rajput motifs—looked worn down by time, heat, rain, as well as the constant friction of passing tongas, scooters, rickshaws, cars, and motorcycles, of the yells of the fruit-vegetable vendors and haggling housewives and the music blaring from tiny electronic shops.

Shutters covered all the one-room shops. I went to see the brothel standing on the site of the oldest ancestral home of the Nehrus. Young girls from Nepal, wearing white saris, fresh jasmine in their hair and thick lipstick on their small mouths, sat gossiping in small cool dark rooms facing an empty lane.

The only noticeable crowd was in the Muslim quarters. The vote here was going in the Congress's favor. It was what Mr. Ahmed had asked of his fellow Muslims, and the burka-clad women walked silently to the booths in small, determined groups. But they weren't the only reason that the polling agents of the BJP looked nervous. Most of the Hindu middle class on which the BJP had depended in past elections had decided to stay away, and this was a setback to Mr. Joshi's chances. There weren't even enough people to cast fake votes, an easier process this time because of the introduction of electronic machines.

Early expectations of Mr. Joshi's defeat after the low turnout were canceled later on polling day when the fabled network of the Hindu nationalists went into action, and the voting percentages rose abruptly to 45 and sometimes 50 percent. An election agent for the BJP, a head-master of a local school, told Piyush, the journalist from *The Times of India*, with anxious satisfaction how he had to bring in students from his own school and persuade the local polling official to let them cast fifteen to twenty votes each in Mr. Joshi's favor. (The Socialist Party candidate, Reoti Raman Singh, organized a sit-down protest outside the district collectorate against the rigging, which was allegedly widespread, but it was too late.)

At a polling booth a few miles out of Allahabad, there had been a fight among party workers from the BJP and Samajwadi (Socialist) Party. A new Tata Sumo jeep stood on the road, its windshield and win-dows broken, its tires slashed. A small crowd of local villagers stood still around it, as though wondering at the swift destruction of something so apparently solid and expensive. A few miles away, in a shantytown, one of the victims, beaten with iron rods, was in a half-built hospital. His bed had no sheets, only a torn mattress with its straw stuffing exposed, and he lay, moaning softly, not in one of the empty rooms but in the dusty corridor, blood-soaked bandages around his head and ribs, blood transfusion tubes attached to his thin arm, surrounded by white-clad BJP men busily summoning press photographers on their mobile phones.

But away from the main roads, and deeper into the countryside, the polling was uneventful, and the turnout was up to 60 and 70 percent. There were no surprises. Most people affirmed their caste solidarities, and the undecided or the weak and ignorant followed decrees issued by the local chieftains. An old man walking to the polling booth, his peasant face creased and wrinkled, said he had been ordered by the government to vote for the BJP. There were others who weren't quite sure whom they were voting for; most recognized the parties only by their symbols: bicycle, lotus, the palm of hand. But there were crowds everywhere—even at a primary school where you had to wade through knee-deep rainwater in the front yard to get to the voting booth—and they brought a holiday atmosphere to the proceedings.

The huts looked freshly cleaned and paved with dung. The women had put on their most colorful saris; the men had well-oiled mustaches and turbans and starched kurtas. At village after village that afternoon, people waited patiently in long queues, under the harsh monsoon sun, the normally impassive faces brimming with excitement—these images stereotypical of Indian elections and democracy, which ignored so much of what was not seen, the caste consolidations, the regimented votes, the feudal decrees, the ignorance and brutality. And yet it was hard not to feel the strength of the hopes and desires of the people lining up to vote, hard not to see poignance in the care and devotion they brought to their only and very limited intervention in the unknown outside world, hard not to be moved by the eagerness with which they embraced their chance to alter the world that wielded such arbitrary power over their lives.

The monsoons had retreated by the time the votes were counted, almost three weeks after polling day. The counting took place in a sprawling Mandi, a local trade center, six miles outside Allahabad. Police Jeeps and trucks choked the broken lanes between large halls beneath corrugated iron roofs where thousands of men sat before a chaos of paper and big gray metal trunks, while echoing loudspeakers announced the results after each round of counting.

Mr. Joshi was expectedly well ahead of the rest. Mr. Singh, solidly supported by the rural poor, was coming in at second place, and Mrs. Bahuguna, despite the Muslim and liberal votes in her favor, was placed third.

Mr. Patel of the Dalit party was a distant fourth. I ran into him at one of the counting sites. He had reasons for his poor performance—the Brahmanical parties had bribed voters with cheap country liquor, and Brahmanical forces in the district administration had subverted democracy—and he was serene in his expectation of defeat. His party was doing well in the rest of the state; it would have enough seats in the Parliament to play its desired role of destabilizer. Mr. Patel himself had done his share of destabilizing in Allahabad: He had taken away Backward caste and Dalit votes from the Congress and Socialist Parties, thus making it easier for the BJP, with just 34 percent of the votes, to win.

But didn't that help the Brahmanical BJP? I asked. Yes, he said, but it was important for the BJP to be in power; it was the political force most likely to cause instability and disorder in the country, which was the long-term plan of his party and Dalits in general.

There were other long-term plans being put into action in the hall where Mr. Joshi sat watching the national results come in on TV, the air thick with the excited voices of the analysts and pundits in Delhi studios. The BJP and its allies were going to win a safe majority in the Parliament. The district officials, who sat at a formal distance from Mr. Joshi, and who had previously appeared to me to be under some slight pressure because of the rigging accusations, now looked more relieved with every passing moment. They were solicitous toward Mr. Joshi, who was certain to be a minister again in the new government; they were quick to leave their sofas and red-sashed attendants as he summoned them with the crook of his finger; standing half bent before him, they gave him the latest news about the increasing margin of his victory.

Wearing a blue embroidered silk scarf, his Brahmanical topknot well oiled, Mr. Joshi watched, with the restless air of a man being left out of big things, the interviews with senior politicians in Delhi studios. When a phone call came from the local radio station, he expressed, with a solemn expression, measured tone, and well-rehearsed words, his utter lack of surprise at having won.

Later that evening—the results declared, the shops in the city again open, Civil Lines once more bustling with shoppers and promenaders, the elections almost forgotten—I saw his victory procession. The sirens could be heard in the far distance; people stopped to stare as the first Ambassadors came into view, moving fast and recklessly on the narrow road crammed with rickshaws and cars and scooters and motorcycles. There was a continuous hooting of horns from the vehicles in the motorcade. Commandos in black, AK-47 muzzles poking out of open windows, shouted abuses at rickshawallahs slowing down their progress, and the startled and frightened men thrust their thin, naked legs at the pedals and slid timidly out of the way. Jeep after Jeep full of slogan-shouting young men in saffron shawls went past before Mr. Joshi's bulletproof Ambassador appeared, piles of rose garlands draped around the crazily revolving blue light. Surprisingly, at this moment of public celebration Mr. Joshi hadn't put himself on show but sat partly hidden behind tinted windows, remote in his soundless cabin from the frenzied sloganeering, safe from the clouds of dust launched by his swift-moving motorcade. Behind his blank face he showed relief, the relief of the man finally allowed, after a brief scare, to continue a private journey that had already taken him from the scooter pillion to a bulletproof Ambassador.

AYODHYA

The Modernity of Hinduism

1. History as Myth

Ayodhya is the city of Rama, the most virtuous and austere of Hindu gods. Traveling to it in January 2002 from Benares, across a wintry North Indian landscape of mustard-bright fields, hectic roadside bazaars, and lonely columns of smoke, I felt myself moving between two very different Hindu myths, or visions of life. Shiva, the god of perpetual destruction and creation, rules Benares, where temple compounds secrete Internet cafés and children fly kites next to open funeral pyres by the river. But the city's aggressive affluence and chaos seem far away in Ayodhya, which is small and drab, its alleys full of the dust of the surrounding flat fields. The peasants with unwieldy bundles under their arms brought to mind the pilgrims of medieval Indian miniature painting, and sitting by the Saryu River at dusk, watching the devout tenderly set afloat tiny earthen lamps in the slow-moving water, I felt the endurance and continuity of Hindu India.

After that vision of eternal Hinduism, the numerous mosques and Moghul buildings in Ayodhya came as a surprise. Most of them are in ruins, especially the older ones built during the sixteenth and seventeenth centuries, when Ayodhya was the administrative center of a major province of the Moghul empire, Awadh. All but two were destroyed as recently as December 6, 1992, the day, epochal now in India's history, on which a crowd led by politicians from the Hindu nationalist BJP demolished the mosque they claimed the sixteenth-century Moghul emperor Babur had built, as an act of contempt, on the site of the god Ram's birthplace.

None of the mosques is likely to be repaired anytime soon; the Muslim presence in the town seems at an end for the first time in eight centuries. This was the impression I got even in January 2002, a month before anti-Muslim rage exploded in the western Indian state of Gujarat, at Digambar Akhara, the large, straw-littered compound of the militant sadhu sect presided over by Ramchandra Paramhans. In 1949, Paramhans initiated the legal battle to reclaim Babur's mosque, or the Babri Masjid, for the Hindu community; in December 1992 he exuberantly directed the demolition squad.

The sect, Paramhans told me, was established four centuries ago to fight the Muslim invaders who had ravaged India since the tenth century AD and erected mosques over temples in the holy cities of Ayodhya, Benares, and Mathura. The sadhus had been involved, he added, in the seventy-six wars for possession of the site of the mosque in Ayodhya, in which more than two hundred thousand Hindus had been martyred.

Two bodyguards nervously watched my face as Paramhans described this history. More armed men stood over the thin-bricked wall of the compound. The security seemed excessive in what was an exclusively Hindu environment. But as Paramhans explained, caressing the tufts of white hair on the tip of his nose, the previous year, he had been attacked by homemade bombs delivered by what he called "Muslim terrorists."

Paramhans, who died in 2004 at the age of ninety-three, headed the trust in charge of building the temple, which the leaders of the BJP had vowed to build on the site of Babur's mosque. When I spoke to Paramhans in late January 2002, he expected up to a million Hindu volunteers to reach Ayodhya by March 15, defying a Supreme Court ban on construction at the site of the mosque, and to present another fait accompli to the world in the form of a half-built temple.

Thousands of Hindu activists from across India traveled to Ayodhya through the first few weeks of February. Many of them were from the prosperous state of Gujarat, whose entrepreneurial Hindus, often found living in Europe and the United States, have formed a loyal constituency of the Hindu nationalists since the 1980s. On February 27, some of these activists were returning on the train from Ayodhya when a crowd of Muslims attacked and set fire to two of the cars just outside the town of Godhra in Gujarat. Fifty-eight Hindus, many of them women and children, were burned alive.

Murderous crowds of Hindu nationalists seeking to avenge the attack in Godhra rampaged across Gujarat for the next few weeks. Wearing the saffron scarves and khaki shorts of Hindu nationalists, they were often armed with swords, trishuls (tridents), sophisticated explosives, and gas cylinders. They had the addresses of various Muslim families and businesses, which they attacked systematically. The police did nothing to stop them and even led the charge against Muslims. A BJP minister sat in police control rooms while pleas for assistance from Muslims were routinely disregarded. Hindu-owned newspapers printed fabricated stories about Muslim atrocities and incited Hindus to avenge the killings of Hindu pilgrims.

In the end, more than two thousand people, mostly Muslims, were killed. About 230 mosques and shrines, including a five-hundred-year-old mosque, were razed to the ground, some replaced with Hindu temples. Close to one hundred thousand Muslims found themselves in relief camps. Corpses filled mass gravesites; they often arrived there mangled beyond recognition, with fetuses missing from the bellies of pregnant women that had been cut open.

The chief minister of Gujarat, a young up-and-coming leader of the Hindu nationalists called Narendra Modi, quoted Isaac Newton to explain the killings of Muslims. "Every action," he said, "has an equal and opposite reaction." The Indian prime minister at the time, Atal Bihari Vajpayee, who visited the site of the massacres a whole month after they began, expressed shame and lamented that India's image had been spoiled. "What face will I now show to the world?" he said, referring to his forthcoming trip to Singapore. Later, at a BJP meeting, he rejected demands from the opposition and the press for Modi's sacking and proposed early elections in Gujarat. In a public speech, he seemed to blame Muslims. "Wherever they are," he said, "they don't want to live in peace." He added, referring to Muslims and Christians, "We have allowed them to do their prayers and follow their religion. No one should teach us about secularism." A resolution passed by the RSS (Rashtriya Swayamsevak Sangh—National Volunteers Organization), the parent group of Hindu nationalists, from which have emerged almost all the leaders of the BJP, the VHP (Vishwa Hindu Parishad), and the Bajrang Dal, and whose mission is to create a Hindu state, described the retaliatory killings as "spontaneous," stating, "The entire Hindu society had reacted," and even making the following declaration: "Let Muslims understand," the RSS said, "that their real safety lies in the goodwill of the majority." Both Vajpayee and his senior-most colleague, L. K. Advani, are members of the RSS, which was involved in the assassination of Mahatma Gandhi in 1948.

In Ayodhya in January, Paramhans had told me, "Before we take on Pakistani terrorists," he said, "we have to take care of the offsprings Babur left behind in India; these one hundred thirty million Muslims of India have to be shown their place." This message seems to have been taken to heart in Gujarat, where the Hindu nationalists displayed a high degree of administrative efficiency in the killing of Muslims. In Gujarat's cities, middle-class Hindu men drove up in new Japanese cars, the emblems of India's globalized economy, to cart off the loot from Muslim shops and businesses.

The rich young Hindus in Benetton T-shirts and Nike sneakers appeared unlikely combatants in what Paramhans told me was a *dharma yudh*, a holy war, against the traitorous 12 percent of India's population. Both wealth and education separated them from the unemployed, listless small-town Hindus I met in Ayodhya, one of whom was a local convener of the Bajrang Dal (Hanuman's Army), the storm troopers of the Hindu nationalists, which has been implicated in several incidents of violence against Christians and Muslims across India, including the 1998 murder of a Australian missionary in the eastern state of Orissa. In response to a question about Muslims, he dramatically unsheathed his knife and invited me to feel the sharpness of the triple-edged blade, in the form of the trident of the Hindu god Shiva.

But despite their differences, the rich and unemployed Hindus shared a particular worldview. This was outlined most clearly for me, during my travels across North India in early 2002, by students at Saraswati Shishu Mandir, a primary school in Benares, one of the fifteen thousand such institutions run by the RSS. The themes of the morning assembly I attended were manliness and patriotism. In the gloomy hall, portraits of the more militant of Hindu freedom fighters mingled with such signboarded exhortations as GIVE ME BLOOD AND I'LL GIVE YOU FREEDOM, INDIA IS A HINDU NATION, and SAY WITH PRIDE

THAT YOU ARE A HINDU. For over an hour, boys and girls in matching uniforms of white and blue, marching up and down in front of a stage where a plaster of paris statue of Mother India stood on a map of South Asia, chanted speeches and songs about the perfidy of Pakistan, of Muslim invaders, and of the gloriousness of India's past.

This message clearly resonates at a level of caste and class privilege, flourishing in a society where deprivation always lies close at hand. But the school and most of its pupils and the surrounding area were firmly middle-class; just beyond the gates, banners advertising computer courses hung from electric poles bristling with illegal connections. The out-of-work upper-caste advertising executive I met at my hotel in Benares seemed to be speaking of his own insecurities when he suddenly said, after some wistful talk of the latest iMac, "Man, I am scared of these mozzies. We are a secular modern nation, but we let them run these madrassas, we let them breed like rabbits, and one day they are going to outstrip the Hindu population, and will they then treat us as well as we treat them?'

The Muslims of course have a different view of how they have been treated in secular, modern India. In Madanpura, Benares's Muslim locality, a few minutes' walk from Gyanvapi, one of two Moghul mosques the Hindu nationalists have threatened to destroy, I met Najam, a scholar of Urdu and Persian literatures. He is in his early thirties and grew up with some of the worst anti-Muslim violence of postindependence India. In the slaughter in Benares in 1992, he saw Hindu policemen beat his doctor to death with rifle butts.

"I don't think the Muslims are angry anymore," he said. "There is no point. The people who demolished the mosque at Ayodhya are now senior ministers in Delhi. We know we will always be suspected of disloyalty no matter what we say or do. Our madrassas will always be seen as producing fanatics and terrorists. We know we are helpless; there is no one ready to listen to us, and so we keep silent. We expect nothing from the government and political parties. We now depend on the goodwill of the Hindus we live with, and all that we hope for is survival, with a little bit of dignity."

Hindu devotees throng the famous Viswanath Temple in Benares all day long, but few, if any, Muslims dare to negotiate their way through the scores of armed policemen and sandbagged positions to offer namaz at the adjacent Gyanvapi Mosque. It is not easy for an out-sider to enter the Indian Muslim's sense of isolation. There was cer-tainly little in my own background that could have prepared me to understand the complicated history behind it. As Brahmins with little money, we perceived Muslims as another threat to our aspirations to se-curity and dignity. My sisters attended an RSS-run primary school where pupils were encouraged to disfigure the sketches of Muslim rulers in their history textbooks. At the English medium school I went to, we were taught to think of ourselves as secular and modern citizens of India and view religion as something one outgrows.

In the 1970s and 1980s, when I heard about Hindu-Muslim riots or the insurgencies in Punjab and Kashmir, it seemed to me that religion was the cause of most conflict and violence in India. The word used in the newspapers and in academic analyses was "communalism," the an-tithesis of the secularism advocated by the founding fathers of India, Gandhi and Nehru, and also the antithesis of Hinduism itself, which was held to be innately tolerant and secular.

Living in Benares in the late eighties, I was unaware that this ancient Hindu city was also holy for Muslims, unaware too of the seventeenth-century Sufi shrine just behind the tea shack where I often spent my mornings. It was one of many in the city, which both Hindus and Muslims visited, part of the flowering of Sufi culture in medieval North India. It was only in 2002, after talking to Najam, the young Per-sian scholar I met in Benares, that I discovered that one of the great Shia philosophers of Persia had sought refuge at the court of a Hindu ruler of Benares in the eighteenth century. And it was only after return-ing from my most recent trip to Ayodhya that I read that Rama's pri-macy in this pilgrimage center was a recent event, that Ayodhya was for much of the medieval period the home of the much older and presti-gious sects of Shaivites, or Shiva worshipers (Rama is only one of the many incarnations of Vishnu, one of the gods in the Hindu trinity, in which Shiva is the most important); many of the temples and sects cur-rently devoted to Rama actually emerged under the patronage of the Shia Muslims who had begun to rule Awadh in the early eighteenth century.

Ramchandra Paramhans in Ayodhya had been quick to offer me a history full of temple-destroying Muslims and brave Hindu nationalists.

Yet Paramhans's own militant sect had originally been formed to fight
not Muslims but Shiva-worshiping Hindus, and it had been favored in
this long and bloody conflict by the Muslim nawabs, who later gave
generous grants of land to the victorious devotees of Rama. The nawabs, whose administration and army were staffed by Hindus, kept a
careful distance from Hindu-Muslim conflicts. One of the first such
conflicts in Ayodhya occurred in 1855, when some Muslims accused
Hindus of illegally constructing a temple over a mosque, and militant
Hindu sadhus (mendicants) massacred seventy-five Muslims. The then
nawab of Awadh, Wajid Ali Shah, a distinguished poet and composer,
refused to support the Muslim claim on the building, explaining:

> *We are devoted to love; do not know of religion.*
> *So what if it is Kaaba or a house of idols?*

Wajid Ali Shah, denounced as effeminate and inept and deposed a
year later by British imperialists, was the last great exponent of the Indo-
Persian culture that emerged in Awadh toward the end of the Moghul
empire, when India was one of the greatest centers of the Islamic world,
along with the Ottoman and the Safavid empires. Islam in India lost
some of its Arabian and Persian distinctiveness, blended with older cultures, but its legacy is still preserved amid the squalor of a hundred
small Indian towns, in the grace and elegance of Najam's Urdu, in the
numerous songs and dances that accompany festivals and marriages, in
the subtle cuisines of North India, and the fineness of the silk saris of
Benares, but one could think of it, as I did, as something just there,
without a history or tradition. The Indo-Islamic inheritance has formed
very little part of, and is increasingly an embarrassment to, the idea of
India that has been maintained by the modernizing Hindu elite over
the last fifty years.

That idea first emerged in the early nineteenth century, as the
British consolidated their hold over India and found new allies
among upper-caste Hindus. In India, as elsewhere in their empire, the
British had largely supplanted, and encountered stiff resistance from,
Muslim rulers. Accordingly, the British tended to demonize Muslims as

fanatics and tyrants and presented their conquest of India as at least partly a humanitarian intervention on behalf of the once-great Hindu nation that had been oppressed for centuries by Muslim despots and condemned to backwardness.

Most of these early British views of India were useful fictions at best since the Turks, Afghans, Central Asians, and Persians who together with upper-caste Hindu elites had ruled a variety of Indian states for over eight centuries were rather more than plunderers and zealots. The bewildering diversity of people that inhabited India before the arrival of the Muslims in the eleventh century hardly formed a community, much less a nation, and the word "Hinduism" barely hinted at the almost infinite number of folk and elite cultures, religious sects, and philosophical traditions found in India.

But these novel British ideas were received well by educated upper-caste Hindus who had previously worked with Muslim rulers and then begun to see opportunities in the new imperial order. British discoveries of India's classical sculpture, painting, and literature had given them a fresh invigorating sense of the pre-Islamic past of India. They found flattering and useful those British Orientalist notions of India that identified Brahmanical scriptures and principles of tolerance as the core of Hinduism. In this view, such practices as widow burning became proof of the degradation Hinduism had suffered during Muslim rule, and the cruelties of caste became an unfortunate consequence of Muslim tyranny.

A wide range of Hindu thinkers, social reformers, and politicians followed the British in dismissing the centuries of Muslim domination as a time of darkness and upholding imperial rule with all its social reforms and scientific advances as preparation for self-rule. Some denounced British imperialism as exploitative, but even they welcomed its redeeming modernity and, above all, the European idea of the nation—a cohesive community with a common history, culture, values, and sense of purpose—which for many other colonized peoples appeared a way of duplicating the success of the powerful, all-conquering West.

Muslim leaders, on the other hand, were slow to participate in the civilizing mission of imperialism; they saw little place for themselves in the idea of the nation as espoused by the Hindu elite. British imperialists followed their own strategies of divide and rule; the decision to partition Bengal in 1905 and to have separate electorates for Muslims further reinforced the sense among many upwardly mobile Indians that they belonged to distinct communities defined exclusively by religion.

It is true that Gandhi and Nehru worked hard to attract low-caste Hindus and Muslims; they wanted to give a mass base and wider legitimacy to the political demands for self-rule that intensified in the early twentieth century under the leadership of the Congress Party. But Gandhi's use of popular Hindu symbols, which made him a mahatma among Hindu masses, caused many Muslims to distrust him. Also, many Congress leaders shared the views not of Gandhi or of the poet Rabindranath Tagore, who criticized Western-style nationalism, but of such upper-caste ideologues as Veer Savarkar and Guru Golwalkar, the spiritual and ideological parents of Hindu nationalists of today.

2. The Rashtriya Swayamsevak Sangh: Indian-Style Fascism

On the evening of January 30, 1948, five months after the independence and partition of India, Mahatma Gandhi was walking to a prayer meeting in the grounds of his temporary home in New Delhi when he was shot three times in the chest and abdomen. Gandhi was then seventy-nine years old and a forlorn figure. He had been unable to prevent, and so was widely blamed by many Hindus for, the bloody creation of Pakistan as a separate homeland for Indian Muslims. The violent uprooting of millions of Hindus and Muslims across the hastily drawn borders of India and Pakistan had tainted the freedom from colonial rule that he had been so arduously working toward. When the bullets from an automatic pistol hit his frail body at point-blank range, he collapsed and died instantly. His assassin made no attempt to escape and even, as he would later claim, shouted for the police.

Millions of shocked Indians waited anxiously for further news that night, fearing unspeakable violence if Gandhi's murderer proved to be a Muslim. There was much relief, and also some puzzlement, the next morning when the assassin was revealed as Nathuram Godse, a Hindu Brahmin from western India, a region relatively untouched by the murderous passions of the partition.

Born in a lower-middle-class family, Godse began his career in 1932 as a Hindu activist with the RSS, which had been founded by a Brahmin doctor called Hegdewar in the central Indian city of Nagpur seven years previously. The RSS was, and remains, dedicated to establishing a Hindu nation by uniting Hindus from all castes and sects and by forcing Muslims, Christians, and other Indian minorities to embrace Hindu culture. Godse received both physical and ideological training from members of the RSS and absorbed their ideas about the greatness of pre-Islamic India and the havoc wrought upon Hindus by eight centuries of Muslim invasions and tyranny.

During his trial, Godse made a long and eloquent speech in English explaining his background and motives. He claimed that Gandhi's "constant and consistent pandering to the Muslims," whom he described variously as fanatical, violent, and antinational, had left him with no choice. He blamed Gandhi for the "vivisection of the country—our motherland" and denounced the latter's insistence upon nonviolence, saying that it was "absurd to expect [four hundred million] people to regulate their lives on such a lofty plane." He claimed it was the terrorist methods of Hindu and Sikh freedom fighters, not Gandhi's nonviolence, that had forced the British to leave India, and hoped that with Gandhi dead, "Indian politics would surely be practical, able to retaliate," and the nation, he claimed, "would be saved from the inroads of Pakistan."

Godse requested that the judge at his trial show him no mercy, and he did not appeal against the death sentence passed on him. He went to the gallows in November 1949 shouting such slogans as "Long Live the Undivided India" and singing paeans to the "Living Motherland, the Land of the Hindus." The Indian government under Pandit Nehru banned the RSS a few days after Gandhi's murder and arrested thousands of its members. The ban was lifted a year later, after the RSS agreed to have a written constitution and confine itself to "cultural" activities, a promise it quickly broke.

Not much is known about the RSS in the West, although both the former prime minister Atal Bihari Vajpayee and his deputy, L. K. Advani, belong to it and have never repudiated its militant ideology, the ideology of Hindu nationalism that seeks aggressively to "Hinduize" South Asia and has often threatened to plunge the region, which has the largest Muslim population in the world and two nuclear-armed nations, into catastrophic war.

After September 11, 2001, the Hindu nationalists presented themselves to the West as reliable allies in the fight against Muslim fundamentalists. But in India their resemblance to the European fascist movements of the 1930s has been clear for a long time. In his manifesto *We, or Our Nationhood Defined* (1938), Guru Golwalkar, director of the RSS from 1940 to 1973, during which time both Mr. Vajpayee and Mr. Advani joined the organization and rose to become senior leaders of its political wing, said that the Nazis had manifested "race pride at its highest" by purging Germany of the Jews. According to Golwalkar, India was Hindustan, a land of Hindus where Jews and Parsis could only ever be "guests," and to which Muslims and Christians came as "invaders." Golwalkar was clear about what he expected from both the guests and the invaders:

> The foreign races in Hindustan must either adopt the Hindu culture and language, must learn to respect and hold in reverence Hindu religion, must entertain no idea but those of the glorification of the Hindu race and culture, i.e. of the Hindu nation and must lose their separate existence to merge in the Hindu race, or may stay in the country, wholly subordinated to the Hindu nation, claiming nothing, deserving no privileges, far less any preferential treatment—not even citizen's rights. There is, at least should be, no other course for them to adopt.

Golwalkar and his disciples in the RSS and Congress saw India as the sacred indigenous nation of Hindus which had been divided and emasculated by Muslim invaders, and which could be revived only by uniting India's diverse population, recovering ancient Hindu traditions, and weeding out corrupting influences from Central Asia and Arabia. This meant forcing Indian Muslims to give up their allegiance to such alien lands and faiths as Mecca and Islam and embrace the so-called Hindu ethos, or Hindutva, of India, an ethos that was, ironically, imagined into being with the help of British Orientalist discoveries of India's past.

By the 1940s the feudal and professional Muslim elite of India had grown extremely wary of the Hindu nationalist strain within the Congress. After many failed attempts at political rapprochement, this elite finally arrived at the demand for a separate homeland for Indian Muslims. The demand expressed the Muslim fear of being reduced to a perpetual minority in a Hindu majority state and was, initially, a desire for a more federal polity for postcolonial India. But the leaders of the Congress chose to partition the Muslim-majority provinces in the west and east rather than share the centralized power of the colonial state that was their great inheritance from the British.

This led to the violent transfer of millions of Hindus, Sikhs, and Muslims across hastily drawn artificial borders. The massacres, rapes, and kidnappings further hardened sectarian feelings; the RSS, which was temporarily banned after Gandhi's assassination, found its most dedicated volunteers among middle-class Hindu refugees from Pakistan, such as the former home minister, Lal Krishna Advani, who was born in Muslim-dominated Karachi and joined the RSS as early as 1942. The RSS floated a new party, the Jana Sangh, later to become the BJP, which entered electoral politics in independent India in 1951 with the renewed promise of a Hindu nation; although it worked for much of the next three decades in the gigantic shadow of the Congress Party, its sudden popularity in the 1980s now seems part of the great disaster of partition, which locked the new nation-states of India and Pakistan into stances of mutual hostility.

In Pakistan, a shared faith failed to reconfigure the diverse regional and linguistic communities into a new nation. This was proved when the Bengali-speaking population of East Pakistan seceded, with Indian help, to form the new state of Bangladesh in 1971. Muslims in India continue to lack effective spokespersons, despite, or perhaps because of, the tokenist presence of Muslims at the highest levels of the government. Politically, they are significant only during elections, when they form a solid vote bank for those Hindu politicians promising to protect them against discrimination and violence. Their representation in government jobs has steadily declined.

Secularism, the separation of religion from politics, was always going to be difficult to impose upon a country where religion has long shaped political and cultural identities. But it was the only useful basis on which the centralized government in Delhi could, in the name of modernity and progress, establish its authority over a poor and chaotically fractious country. However, when Sikh and Muslim minorities in the states of Punjab and Kashmir challenged the great arbitrary power of the Indian government, Nehru's heirs, his daughter, Indira, and grandson Rajiv, were quick to discard even the rhetoric of secularism and to turn Hindu majoritarianism into the official ideology of the Congress-run central Indian government.

The uprisings in Punjab, and then Kashmir, were portrayed by the Indian government and the middle-class media as fundamentalist and terrorist assaults on secular democracy. In fact, although tainted by association with Pakistan and religious fanaticism, the Sikhs and Kashmiri Muslims expressed a long-simmering discontent with an antifederalist state in Delhi, a state that had retained most of the power of the old colonial regime and often wielded it more brutally than the British ever had. The uprisings were part of a larger crisis, one that has occurred elsewhere in postcolonial nations, the failure of a corrupt and self-serving political and bureaucratic elite to ensure social and economic justice for those it had claimed to represent in its anticolonial battles.

By the 1980s, when the Hindu nationalists abruptly rose to prominence, the Congress had disillusioned lower-caste Hindus and looked incapable of preserving even the interests of its upper-caste Hindu constituency. It kept raising the bogey of national unity and external enemies. But the disturbances in the border states of Kashmir and Punjab only gave more substance to the Hindu nationalist allegation that the Congress with its "pseudosecularism" had turned India into a "soft state," where Kashmiri Muslims could blithely conspire with Pakistan against Mother India.

It was in the 1980s, with the Congress rapidly declining and the pseudosocialist economy close to bankruptcy, that the Hindu nationalists saw a chance to find new voters among upper-caste Hindus. Like the National Socialists in Germany in the early 1930s, they offered not so much clear economic policies as fantasies of national rebirth and power. In 1984 the VHP announced a national campaign to rebuild the grand temple at Ayodhya; the mosque the first Moghul emperor, Babur, had erected was, they said, a symbol of national shame; removing it and rebuilding the temple were a matter of national honor.

Both history and archaeology were travestied in this account of the fall and rise of the eternal Hindu nation. There is no evidence that Babur had ever been to Ayodhya or that this restless, melancholic conqueror from Samarkand, a connoisseur of architecture, could have built an ugly mosque over an existing Rama temple. Rama himself isn't known to recorded history; the cult of Rama worship arrived in North India as late as the tenth century AD, and no persuasive evidence exists for the Rama temple that apparently once stood on the site of the mosque.

But the myths were useful in reinforcing the narrative of Muslim cruelty and contempt. At first, they found their keenest audience among wealthy expatriate Hindus in the U.K. and the United States, who generously bankrolled a movement that in upholding a strong self-assertive Hinduism seemed to allay their sense of inferiority induced by Western images of India as a miserably poor country. In India the anxieties that persuaded many upper-caste Hindus to support the BJP were much deeper. In 1990 the government in Delhi, then headed by defectors from the Congress Party, decided to implement a long-standing proposal to reserve government jobs for poor "Backward-caste" Hindus. Upper-caste Hindus were enraged at this attack on their privilege. The BJP saw the plan for affirmative action as potentially destructive of its old goal of persuading lower-caste groups to accept a paternalistic upper-caste leadership as part of presenting a united Hindu front against Muslims.

Later that year the leader of the BJP, L. K. Advani, decided to lead a ritual procession on a faux chariot—actually a Chevrolet—from Gujarat to Ayodhya, where he intended to start the construction of the Rama temple. Appropriately, he set out from the temple in Somnath, Gujarat, which, looted by a Turk conqueror in the eleventh century AD, was lavishly rebuilt in the early 1950s by devout Hindu leaders of the Congress Party. This wasn't just playacting, however; more than five hundred people, most of them Muslims, were killed in the rioting that accompanied Advani's progress across India. Hindu policemen were indifferent and sometimes even participated in the violence. When I was in Benares recently, a friend casually pointed out a distant relative of his walking down the street. He was a retired police officer who liked to boast of how he had shot and killed fourteen Muslims during a riot in the city of Meerut.

It is strange to look back now and recall just two decades ago the temple-mosque controversy was hardly heard of outside Ayodhya. Local Hindus first staked a claim on the mosque in the mid-nineteenth century, and British officials allowed them to worship on a platform just outside the building. In 1949, two years after independence, a Hindu civil servant working together with local abbots surreptitiously placed idols of Rama inside the mosque. The story that Lord Rama himself had installed them there quickly spread. The local Muslims protested. Prime Minister Nehru sensed that nothing less than India's secular identity was threatened. He ordered the mosque to be locked and sacked the district official, who promptly joined the Hindu nationalists.

The idols, however, were not removed, and Muslims gradually gave up offering namaz at the mosque. During the three decades that followed, the courts were clogged with cases concerning Hindu and Muslim claims on the site. In 1984 the VHP began a campaign for the unlocking of the mosque. In 1986 a local judge allowed the Hindus to worship inside the building. A year later Muslims held their largest protest demonstration since independence in Delhi.

Until 1984, however, Babur's mosque remained relatively unknown outside of a small circle of litigious, property-hungry abbots in Ayodhya. Religion was a fiercely competitive business in Ayodhya. The local abbots fought hard for their share of donations from millions of poor pilgrims, and, more recently, wealthy Indians in the United States and the U.K., and they were notorious for murder and pillage; the attack on Ramchandra Paramhans that he blamed on Muslim terrorists was probably the work of rival abbots. But as the movement for the temple intensified, entrepreneurs of religiosity such as Paramhans were repackaged by Hindu nationalist politicians as sages and saints and turned into national celebrities. Rama himself suddenly evolved from the benign, almost feminine, calendar art divinity of my childhood to the vengeful Rambo of Hindu nationalist posters.

The myths multiplied in October 1990, when Advani's Chevrolet-chariot procession was stopped and police in Ayodhya fired upon a crowd of Hindus attempting to assault the mosque. The largest-circulation Hindi paper in North India, *Dainik Jagran*, spoke of "indiscriminate police firing" and "hundreds of dead devotees" and then reduced the death toll the next day to thirty-two. The rumors and exaggerations, part of a slick propaganda campaign, helped the BJP win the elections in four North Indian states in 1991. The mosque seemed doomed. When on December 6, 1992, a crowd of mostly upper-caste Hindus, equipped with shovels, crowbars, pickaxes, and sometimes just their bare hands, demolished Babur's mosque, the police simply watched from a distance.

Uma Bharti, one of the more vocal of Hindu nationalist politicians, cheer-led the crowd, shouting, "Give one more push and break the Babri Masjid." The president of the VHP announced the dawn of a "Hindu rebellion," while a leader of the BJP said for "those who want to see the flag of Pakistan flutter over Kashmir, the process of showing them their right place has begun."

That evening the crowd rampaged through Ayodhya, killing and burning thirteen Muslims, some of whom were children, and destroying scores of mosques, shrines, and Muslim-owned shops and houses. Protests and riots then erupted across India. Altogether two thousand people, mostly Muslims, were killed. Three months after the massacres, Muslim gangsters in Bombay retaliated with bomb attacks that killed more than three hundred civilians.

In Delhi, the elderly Congress prime minister, Narasimha Rao, napped through the demolition. The next day he dismissed the BJP governments, banned the RSS and its sister organizations, and promised to rebuild the mosque. The leaders of the BJP tried to distance themselves from the demolition, saying that it was a spontaneous act of frustration, provoked by the anti-Hindu policies of the government. However, the Central Bureau of Investigation (CBI) concluded that such senior leaders of the BJP as L. K. Advani, subsequently home minister of India, had planned the demolition well in advance. As for the anti-Muslim violence, Advani claimed in an article in *The Times of In-*

dia that it would not have taken place had Muslims identified themselves with Hindutva, the same sentiment echoed after the riots in Gujarat.

Six years after the demolition, the BJP, benefiting from India's "first past the post" electoral system, became the dominant party in the ruling National Democratic Alliance (NDA) in Delhi. Despite its being forced to share power with more secular parties, the BJP's ideological fervor seemed undiminished, if ultimately unfulfilled. Certainly, the Hindu nationalists have tried hard to whip up Hindu passions. In early 1998, during their first few months in power, they conducted nuclear tests, explicitly aiming them against Pakistan, which responded with its own tests. The VHP and Bajrang Dal distributed radioactive earth from the nuclear test site as sacred offerings; they were also responsible for an unprecedented series of mob attacks on Christians across India. About half of these occurred in Gujarat, but Advani claimed that there was "no law and order problem in Gujarat" and at a meeting of Hindu nationalists shared the dais with the new chief of the RSS, K. S. Sudarshan. The latter spoke of "an epic war between Hindus and anti-Hindus," asked Christians and Muslims to return to their "Hindu roots," and also attacked secular intellectuals as "that class of bastards which tries to implant an alien culture in their land."

A clearer sense of the worldview RSS members subscribe to from childhood can be had from a long discourse K. S. Sudarshan, the present supreme director of the RSS and a regular adviser to Mr. Vajpayee and Mr. Advani, delivered to RSS members in 1999. In this speech, later published in Hindi with the title of *Ek Aur Mahabharata* ("One More Mahabharata"), Sudarshan claimed that a new epic war would shortly commence between the demonic and divine powers that apparently forever contended for supremacy in the world. Sudarshan identified the United States as the biggest example of the "rise of inhumanity" in the contemporary world. As he described it, violence was endemic in America, where the institution of the family lay shattered and where "all the tender feelings of man" had died. Referring to the Monica Lewinsky affair, he asked, "What can you say about a nation whose president itself is so crazed with lust?" He claimed that India exercised the "greatest terror" over America, primarily because Indians were extremely intelligent and talented. He had touched on this theme in his praise of India's nuclear tests in 1998, when he said that "our history has proved that we are a heroic, intelligent race capable of becoming world leaders but the one deficiency that we had was of weapons, good weapons." America, he said, was trying to subjugate India through its multinationals. Sudarshan ended his speech by denouncing the international conspiracy hatched against India by the United States alongside the World Trade Organization, the pope, and Sonia Gandhi, a conspiracy he predicted would result in a "final victory" of Hindu nationalism.

This mishmash of anti-American rhetoric, paranoia, moral arrogance, and ill-digested history brings to mind the rants of Osama bin Laden. But the comparison with Al Qaeda or other radical Islamists does not go very far. The RSS doesn't reject so much as seek an alternative route to Western modernity. In fact, much like the Japanese nationalists of the 1930s, the RSS upholds modern science and technology as the essential way to national strength; four out of the five supreme directors of the RSS so far have held college degrees in medicine, nuclear physics, biology, chemistry, and engineering. Suffering from an inferiority complex vis-à-vis the modern West, Hindu nationalists are obsessed with beating the West at its own game.

During the six years the BJP held power in New Delhi, the RSS members I met exulted in private conversation about their well-placed colleagues in the Indian government. But the RSS does not aim at capturing state power alone. As M. G. Vaidya, the RSS's official spokesman, an elderly man wearing a dandyish silk scarf and a rakishly tilted black cap, told me in his Delhi office in September 2002, "Forming a state without building and unifying a nation doesn't work. Look at the Soviet Union. The Communists had power, but the nation was not with them, and they collapsed."

Golwalkar had hoped to reorganize India into a microcosm of the RSS, achieving the "perfectly organized state of society wherein each individual has been moulded into a model of ideal Hindu manhood and made into a living limb of the corporate personality of society."

Some part of this vision also motivated my father and uncles, who, like hundreds of thousands of Brahmin men in the 1940s, became active members of the RSS; a couple of my uncles were in prison briefly after Gandhi's murder. These young, educated Brahmins were anxious about how they would fare as a somewhat privileged minority in independent democratic India. The ideal Hindu manhood proposed by the RSS—to be both a Hindu man and to mold your world according to your image—was irresistible to them. The vision did require them to subjugate their will and intellect to a larger cause. But this was and is considered so even now by some a small price to pay for security and identity in a poor, chaotic country.

The RSS's large-scale schemes of molding individuals seem closer to the engineering of human souls that Stalin and Hitler attempted in their different ways. They mark the RSS as "totalitarian." Anxieties about the fascistic outlook and makeup of the RSS are not allayed by its strongly hierarchical and centralized organization, in which the word of the supreme director is final and the members have little say in the shaping of policy.

There is also its reputation as a secretive, extraconstitutional force, which does not provide details about the size and spread of its membership. "The RSS is not interested in publicity," I was told by the brusque young man in charge of the RSS's media office in Delhi. Mr. Sudarshan declined my request for an interview; neither did he reply to a letter seeking clarifications on some of his assertions. The deputy prime minister, L. K. Advani, also declined to be interviewed on his connection with the RSS, which he joined in 1942, as a young student in what is now the Pakistani city of Karachi. Other members of the RSS bluntly refused to talk to someone they described as an "anti-Hindu" writer. The few members I did manage to talk to suddenly became elusive after the first meeting.

"The Hindu nationalists are cautious at present, especially with the foreign press," a senior Indian journalist told me. "Their fascistic nature has been obscured so far in the West by the fact that India is a democracy, has regular elections, and has a potentially large consumer market. They have managed to speak with two voices, one for foreign consumption and the other for local. But they know that religious extremists are under closer scrutiny worldwide after 9/11, and they know that they don't look too good after the killings of two thousand Muslims in Gujarat."

Tarun Vijay, the youngish editor of the RSS Hindi weekly *Panchajanya*, who was represented to me by Delhi journalists as the "modern face of Hindu nationalism," was, he confessed to me, "wary." He said he was "very skeptical" about foreign media and "left-wing Indians and secularists." "Westerners don't understand," he said, "that the RSS is a patriotic organization working for the welfare of all Indians." Mr. Vijay's own career seems to prove this. Born in 1956 to a middle-class family in North India, Mr. Vijay was educated eclectically at schools run by Gandhians and American Presbyterians. But he was impressed most by the "selflessness" and "patriotism" of the RSS members he met as a young man. They inspired him to leave home and work in western India, protecting tribal peoples from exploitation and discrimination. They had even helped arrange his marriage.

When I met him, Mr. Vijay had been working on *Panchajanya*, a magazine with a circulation of ninety thousand, for over a decade. The magazine's first editor, in the late forties, was Vajpayee; the dusty walls of Vijay's office are covered with large enlargements of Vajpayee's old editorials demanding that the Indian government take an aggressive line with Pakistan over Kashmir. During that time, the Hindu nationalists became the most powerful political group in India, and Mr. Vijay was considered to have contributed to their success. The English-language newsmagazine *Outlook* described him as one of the closest confidants of Deputy Prime Minister Advani. He would show up frequently on STAR TV, India's most prominent news channel. For some time he appeared to be destined for even higher things—a ministerial or advisory position with the federal government, an ambassador's job. But when we met, his suave manner often broke to reveal impatience and restlessness.

"I was educated at a Christian school," he said. "Some of my best friends are Muslims. My wife wears jeans, and she wears her hair short; we eat meat at Muslim homes; we go to church on Christmas Day. There are reasonable people among Muslims, but they are afraid to speak out their minds. We are trying to have a dialogue with them. We are trying to talk with Christians also. After all, Jesus Christ is my greatest hero. But the left-wing and secular people are always portraying us as anti-Muslim and anti-Christian fanatics."

An Indian journalist who reported regularly on the RSS later explained Mr. Vijay's defensiveness as that of an ambitious man who recognizes the extreme aspects of Hindu nationalism as a disadvantage in the modern world. The journalist thought I should meet Uma Bharti, probably the most famous woman among the Hindu nationalists and one of the senior leaders accused of demolishing the mosque in Ayodhya in 1992.

Power and responsibility—she was now the federal minister for sports and youth affairs—seemed to have tempered her nationalist zeal. I met her at her office, where her ocher robes—ocher, the Hindu color of renunciation—stood out brilliantly against the bare blue-painted walls, and the bureaucrats running around in Western-style trousers and shirts seemed the employees of a spiritual self-help corporation. Ms. Bharti, then forty-two years old, and a self-declared sanyasin, someone who has renounced the world for the sake of spiritual wisdom, started her life in a poor low-caste village in Central India. A decade ago her tales of Muslim cruelty toward Hindus sent her vast audiences into a frenzy. But in her conversation with me, Ms. Bharti seemed keen to distance herself from Hindu nationalism. In fact, her aides granted me an interview on the condition that I would question her only about her work among underprivileged Indians.

She brushed aside a question about the killings in Gujarat and instead told me that she had not forgotten what it meant to be poor, low-caste, and a woman in a small village in the middle of nowhere. She was very young when her father, a Communist activist fighting against local landlords, died. Her mother worked as a menial laborer in order to support her family. She was four when she saw her house burned down and the family cattle destroyed by a vengeful landlord in her village. It was then she began to memorize the Hindu epics, mostly by listening to other people recite them. Devout Hindus invited her to their homes for religious discourses. She acquired a reputation as a divinely inspired speaker. Later, local leaders of the VHP saw her potential and turned her into a performer before the large, intense Hindu audiences clamoring for a Rama temple.

It was a sense of injustice—why were Hindus not allowed to worship where Lord Rama was born?—that had provoked her into joining the campaign for the Rama temple in Ayodhya. But, she said, she now derived her "ultimate satisfaction" from attacking poverty and social injustice. She felt herself inspired by not just Hanuman, the Hindu monkey god, and Shivaji, the seventeenth-century militant Hindu chieftain, but also Che Guevara, the Latin American revolutionary. For her religious past that she now wished to outgrow, Ms. Bharti had a simple explanation. She wanted to fight injustice, she had wanted power, and "religion seemed the only way to have it."

3. Engineering Souls

After a few days in Delhi, I traveled to the Central Indian city of Nagpur, where the RSS was established in 1925. At first, Nagpur seems an unlikely birthplace for the RSS. Its grand colonial buildings and broad avenues confirm its reputation as an educational and administrative center. Its new shopping complexes and residential high-rises speak of the affluence the city has known since the Indian economy was liberalized in the early 1990s. Nagpur has few Muslims, and its largest community consists of Dalits, who have traditionally shied away from the RSS, which they consider, not unfairly, as dominated by, and serving the interests of, Brahmins. It was in Nagpur in 1956 that Dr. B. R. Ambedkar, the Dalit leader who was a disciple of the American philosopher John Dewey and who drafted the Indian constitution, led a mass conversion of low-caste Hindus to Buddhism in protest against the inequities of Brahminical Hinduism.

I went to see Shyam Pandharipande, who belongs to an old Brahmin family and now edits Nagpur's only monthly feature magazine in English. Mr. Pandharipande's father was an early member of the RSS, and so was Mr. Pandharipande himself, before his disillusionment with Hindu nationalist ideology led him toward Gandhi-inspired environmental organizations. His long experience of the RSS seems to have given him an acute insight into its workings. He told me that when Dr. Hegdewar, a native of Nagpur, set up the RSS in 1925, his first recruits were all very young Brahmin men from educated middle-class families.

He persuaded some of these Brahmins to travel to many different parts of India and set up RSS branches there. It was these missionaries who first brought most of the current leaders of the BJP—Vajpayee and Advani—into the RSS. The RSS really began, Mr. Pandharipande said, as a rearguard action by privileged and insecure Brahmins who felt that they would have little place in a new democratic India where low-caste Hindus would grow assertive and demand their rights.

In 1926 the first shakha (assembly) was held in an open ground. Young RSS members, dressed in khaki shorts, white shirts, and black caps, did military-style drills, played traditional Indian team games, learned to use the lathi (a thick bamboo stick), and were intellectually indoctrinated with ideas about Muslim invaders and the need for Hindu unity. In 2000 the RSS celebrated its seventy-fifth birthday with a giant shakha at its Nagpur headquarters of sixty thousand uniformed men and boys.

The shakha quickly became the most important ritual in the life of an RSS member; it was also a recruiting ground for new members, mostly boys, attracted by the idea of open-air games. One evening, a couple of months ago, I went looking for a shakha in Nagpur. I was accompanied by Devendra, a young advertising executive in his mid-twenties. He told me that he had attended RSS shakhas as a child much in love with the outdoors, but then, like most people of his generation, he had grown bored of the Indian games. He had wanted to play tennis, but the RSS men disapproved of Western sports.

We drove through a sudden monsoon shower. The streets were empty; so were the small parks within middle-class localities where the shakhas were usually held. We were about to give up when unexpectedly we found a crowd of middle-aged men in a leaky damp-stained room at the corner of one of the larger parks.

These were mostly retired Brahmin professionals, engineers, doctors, civil servants, the kind of middle-class people that had always formed the backbone of the RSS. They sat in neat rows on the damp cement floor, many of them dressed in the RSS uniform. Before them, on a small stage, were framed photographs of the RSS's founder Dr. Hegdewar—his mustache in the photo almost as thick as the marigold garland that framed his face—and of the densely bearded Guru Golwalkar, Hegdewar's successor. An ocher flag hung listlessly over the photographs.

We had arrived during a *baudhik*, an intellectual session. A thin man in a black cap gave a long, rambling speech, the principal, and perhaps overplayed, themes of which were the perfidy of Muslims, the cunning of Christian missionaries, and the need for Hindu unity. The elderly audience, which had listened to the same speech many times before, was attentive. As he spoke, blank white envelopes were passed around the assembled crowd, to be filled with rupee notes. When the talk ended, we walked in a brisk queue toward the stage, taking it in turns to pick up rose petals from an urn on the floor and throw them in the general direction of Dr. Hegdewar's photograph, before dropping the envelopes in a little bag and walking back to our seats. The RSS prayer—"Salutations to thee, O loving Motherland"—and some slogans—"Victory to Mother India!"—concluded the shakha.

I had been, I later discovered, to the annual ceremony called Guru Dakshina ("Offering to the Guru"), where RSS members express their dedication to the aims of the organizations in the form of a cash donation. The ceremony was repeated at roughly forty-five thousand shakhas the RSS now holds across India and also, as reported by newspapers the next day, at the home of a senior minister in New Delhi, where Mr. Vajpayee and Mr. Advani joined other RSS members in affirming their allegiance to the elite order of Hindu nationalism.

The superior organization of the RSS, which until recently reached up to the highest levels of the Indian government, is its strength in a chaotic country like India. Its members run not just the biggest political party in India but also educational institutions, trade unions, literary societies, and religious sects; they work to indoctrinate tribals and low-caste groups as well as affluent Indians living in the West. It is through what Guru Golwalkar called the "untiring, silent endeavor of hundreds and thousands of dedicated missionaries" that the RSS hopes to create a Hindu nation.

The scale and diversity of this essentially evangelical effort are remarkable. I was startled when Tarun Vijay triumphantly showed me his magazine's headline about the patenting of cow urine in the United States. Western science, he said, had validated an ancient Hindu belief in the holiness of the cow; it was another proof of how the holistic Hindu way of life anticipated and indeed was superior to the discoveries of modern science, economics, ecology, and sociology. The cow had reemerged as the key to self-sufficient, ecologically sustainable living.

This was more than rhetoric. Forty miles outside of Nagpur, at a clearing in a teak forest, I came across an RSS-run laboratory devoted to showcasing the multifarious benefits of cow urine. The supervisor, a middle-aged RSS member called Chandrashekhar Kundle, told me that this was a favorite project of Ashok Singhal, the president of the RSS affiliate VHP. Most of the cows were out grazing in the forest, but there were a few frightened-looking calves in a large shed, "rescued" recently, Mr. Kundle said, from some nearby Muslim butchers. In one room, its whitewashed walls spattered with saffron-hued posters of Lord Rama, devout young Hindus with vermilion marks on their forehead stood before test tubes and beakers full of cow urine; they were distilling the holy liquid, it turned out, to get rid of the foul-smelling ammonia and make it more palatable. In another room, tribal women in garishly colored saris sat on the floor, before a small hill of white powder—dental powder, Mr. Kundle explained, made from cow urine.

The nearest, and probably unwilling, consumers of the dental powder and other products made from cow urine were the poor tribal students in the RSS-funded primary school next to the lab. In gloomily dark rooms, where students both studied and slept, and where their frayed laundry hung from the iron bars of the windows, there were gleamingly clean portraits of militant Hindu freedom fighters. We sat in the small office of the headmaster, a thin, excitable young man wearing polyester trousers. It was market day in the nearby town, and from the window, above which hung a large fantastical map of undivided India, I could see tribal women who had walked from their homes and now sat on the porch examining the sores and callouses on their bare feet, waiting to meet their children during recess.

The principal explained to me how Joshi-ji, the RSS member in charge of the education department in the federal government, was making sure new history textbooks carried the important message of Hindu pride and Muslim cruelty to every school and child in the country. Meanwhile, the principal had his work cut out. His task was to make the students aware of the glorious Hindu culture from which tribal living had sundered them; he expected them to go home and educate their parents and relatives and alert them to the dangers of Christian missionaries, who were disturbingly active in the tribal areas that the students came from. The message of the RSS, the principal said, was egalitarian and modern; it believed in raising low-caste people and tribals to a higher level of culture.

To prove this, he offered to summon a student, his brightest, and ask him to recite the Gayatri mantra, an invocation from Sanskrit scriptures, which for centuries only Brahmins could recite without fear of punishment. A boy in his early teens and wearing a vermilion mark on his forehead arrived. The headmaster looked on approvingly as the boy gave Mr. Kundle the RSS salute by placing his right arm parallel to the ground and close to his chest but grew nervous as he proceeded to stumble and bluff his way through the mantra.

John Dayal, the vice president of the All India Catholic Union, told me that the RSS has spent millions of dollars in trying to convert tribal people to Hindu nationalism. Dayal, who monitors the missionary activities of the RSS very closely, claimed that in just over eighteen months the RSS distributed 350,000 trishuls, or tridents, in three contiguous tribal districts in Central India.

Dr. B. L. Bhole, a political scientist I met at Nagpur University, saw a Brahminical ploy in these attempts. He told me that the RSS had tried to turn not just Gandhi but also Dr. Ambedkar, the greatest leader of the Dalits, into a Hindu nationalist icon. K. S. Sudarshan, the current supreme director of the RSS, had recently garlanded the statue of Dr. Ambedkar at the park in Nagpur where the latter rejected Hinduism and converted to Buddhism in 1956. Dr. Bhole thought this outrageous. He had joined local Dalit activists and intellectuals in ritually "purifying" the statue after Sudarshan's visit.

Dr. Bhole said, "The RSS can't attract young middle-class people anymore, so they hope for better luck among the poorest, socially disadvantaged people. But the basic values the RSS promotes among low-caste people and tribals are drawn from the high Sanskritic culture of Hinduism, which considers the cow as holy et cetera and which seeks to maintain a social hierarchy with Brahmins at the very top. The united Hindu nation they keep talking about is one where basically low-caste Hindus and Muslims and Christians and other communities don't complain much while accepting the dominance of a Brahmin minority. But the problem for the RSS is that most of the low-caste Hindus and tribals don't want to learn any Brahmin mantras. They form an increasingly independent political group within India today; they no longer want any kind of Brahmin paternalist leadership. Even such low-caste leaders of the BJP as Uma Bharti want to focus on tangible rights for their community; they won't be fobbed off with nationalist ideology. Their assertiveness is really the greatest achievement of democratic politics in India, which has so far been dominated by upper-caste Hindus."

Dr. Bhole said, "The RSS has been most successful in Gujarat, where low-caste Hindus and tribals were indoctrinated at the kind of schools you went to; they were in the mobs led by upper-caste Hindu nationalists that attacked Muslims and Christians. But the RSS still doesn't have much support among low-caste people outside Gujarat. For the RSS, this is a serious setback, and the only thing they can do to increase their mass base is keep stoking anti-Muslim and anti-Christian passions and hope they can get enough Hindus, both upper-caste and low-caste, behind them."

The consistent demonizing of Muslims and Christians by Hindu nationalists may seem gratuitous—Christians in India are a tiny and scattered minority, and the Muslims are too poor, disorganized, and fearful to pose any kind of threat to Hindus—but it is indispensable to the project of a Hindu nation. Hindu nationalists have always sought to redefine Hindu identity in opposition to a supposedly threatening "other." They hope to unite Hindu society by constantly invoking such real and imagined threats as are posed by the evangelical Christians and militant Muslims.

Visiting villages and towns across North India in the last few years, I found Muslims full of anxiety about their fate in India. They spoke to me of an insidious and regular violence, of the frequent threats and beatings they received from local Hindu politicians and policemen.

At one mosque in the countryside near Ayodhya, a young man broke into a conversation about police harassment and loudly asserted that Muslims would not suffer injustice anymore, and they would retaliate. His elders shouted him down. An argument broke out—the young as usual accusing the old of suppressing the truth—and then a mullah gently led me out of the madrassa with one arm around my shoulders, assuring me that the Muslims were loyal to India, their homeland, where they had long lived in peace with their Hindu brothers.

Professor Saghir Ahmad Ansari, a Muslim social activist in Nagpur, told me that the Muslims he knew feel "that the Hindu nationalists, who were implacably opposed to their existence in India, now controlled everything, the government, our rights, our future." He said he worried about the Muslim response to Gujarat. "When the government itself supervises the killing of two thousand Muslims, when Hindu mobs rape Muslim girls with impunity and force one hundred thousand Muslims into refugee camps, you can't hope that the victims won't dream of revenge. I fear," he said, "although I don't like saying or thinking about this, that the ideology of jihad and terrorist violence would find new takers among the one hundred thirty million Muslims of India. This will greatly please the Islamic fundamentalists of Pakistan and Afghanistan who are presently very downcast after the defeat of the Taliban and Al Qaeda."

Mr. Ansari's fears about vengeful Muslims were proved right a month after I spoke to him. In September 2002, Muslim terrorists from Pakistan murdered thirty-five Hindus at the famous Akshardham Temple in Gujarat in ostensible retaliation for the mass killings of Muslims in the state earlier that year. It was the biggest attack by Muslim terrorists anywhere outside the Indian state of Kashmir, and the Hindu rage it provoked further insured the victory of Hindu nationalist hard-liners in elections held in Gujarat in December 2002.

In August 2003, two bomb explosions in Bombay killed more than fifty people, the sixth and most lethal in a recent series of similar blasts across the city. Soon after visiting the site, L. K. Advani, the then deputy prime minister, blamed terrorists based in Pakistan. This was to be expected. Hindu nationalists routinely describe India as besieged by Muslim terrorists backed by or based in Pakistan, especially in the disputed valley of Kashmir. This time, however, Mr. Advani's accusation was qualified swiftly by the Bombay police. It revealed that the four persons arrested in connection with the attacks were Indian Muslims, part of a new group called the Gujarat Muslim Revenge Force. They may have received logistical support from a Pakistani militant outfit with links to Al Qaeda, but they were Indian citizens.

The radical Islamist movements that spread quickly in the last decade in Pakistan, Bangladesh, and Afghanistan had until now left largely untouched India's 140 million Muslims. Indian Muslims stayed away from the anti-India insurgency of their culturally distinct coreligionists in Kashmir. More remarkably, no Indian Muslim in the past seems to have heeded the many pied pipers of jihad in Afghanistan and Pakistan who lured Muslims from all parts of the world and who managed to delude even a non-Muslim from California.

It may be that most Indian Muslims were and are too poor and depressed to join radical causes elsewhere. It is also true that they have an advantage denied to most Muslims in the world: They can participate in regular elections and, since they constitute 13 to 14 percent of India's population, choose their representatives, if not rulers.

But this faith in democracy, which Indian Muslims have long expressed by voting tactically in large numbers, has been tested repeatedly in recent years. In 1996 an inquiry identified some of the Hindu police officers and politicians responsible for the killings of over a thousand Muslims in Bombay in 1992 and 1993. To date no one has been tried and convicted. The perpetrators of the very public massacres in Gujarat are mostly known, but they are unlikely to face justice.

So the surprising issue, perhaps, is not that militant groups with international connections, such as the Gujarat Muslim Revenge Force, are emerging in India, but rather that it has taken them this long to do so. The members of such organizations are educated, with degrees in business management, forensic science, chemical and aeronautical engineering. They have been radicalized in a geopolitical environment that has never been more highly fraught for the Muslim community at large. While the rage and resentment of these educated Muslims may have purely Indian origins—in Gujarat or Bombay—these emotions are also inspired by international events—the wars in Afghanistan and Iraq, the car bombs in Bali, Casablanca, Riyadh, and Baghdad—that probably still seem remote to an older, impoverished generation of Indian Muslims.

The growth of religious militancy in South Asia is likely to enthuse many Hindus. As they see it, Gujarat proved to be a successful "laboratory" of Hindu nationalism, in which carefully stoked anti-Muslim sentiments eventually brought about a pogrom, and a Muslim backlash seemed to lead to even greater Hindu "unity."

The victory of the BJP in Gujarat indicated that this plan was going well. It hinted that well-to-do Indians were likely to support the Hindu nationalists, even the extremists among them, as long as they continued to liberalize the Indian economy and help create a consumer revolution. But neither the BJP nor their supporters had reckoned with the larger, neglected majority of India's population, which expressed its skepticism about Hindu unity by voting out the BJP in the general elections in May 2004.

Opinion pollsters, political pundits, and journalists had predicted an easy victory for the ruling NDA (National Democratic Alliance), the coalition of BJP and its allies, which claimed in its advertising campaign to have created an "India Shining" in the previous six years. But it was the opposition Congress that emerged as the single largest party in the 545-seat Indian Parliament. These results surprised most middle-class Indians, for it was during the BJP's six years in power that India's urban prosperity achieved by the economic reforms initiated in 1991 became most visible. The BJP had supported the reforms, which benefited greatly those who were best placed to take advantage of new opportunities in business and trade and the economy's fast-growing service sector (information technology, jobs offshored by Europe and America), the educated middle class, the BJP's primary constituency, which, despite growing fast in recent years, still makes up less than 20 percent of India's population.

The reforms also attracted a generation of rich Indians who live in the United States and the U.K. and were eager for cultural and economic links with their ancestral land, a desire that turned nonresident Indians into the BJP's most devoted followers and sponsors and helped the BJP itself evolve rapidly, despite its Hindu nationalism, into a keen advocate of economic globalization. During its six years in power, new freeways, shopping malls, brand-name boutiques, Starbucks-style coffee bars, and restaurants with exotic cuisine and London prices transformed the cities of Bangalore, Hyderabad, Delhi, Chennai, and Bombay. Newfound wealth created a heady mood among the middle class, what the leaders of the BJP called the "feel-good factor" (so important that in March 2004 the BJP was initially reluctant to send the Indian cricket team to Pakistan out of the fear that it might lose and make the cricket-obsessed nationalist middle class feel not so good anymore).

Most English-language newspapers began to print entire daily supplements in order to cover film premieres, fashion shows, champagne-tasting sessions in five-star hotels, and the lifestyles of beauty pageant winners, models, Bollywood actors, and other celebrities. The general air of celebration overwhelmed many formerly left-wing intellectuals, academics, and journalists. Convinced that the BJP would be in power for many years, they aligned themselves openly with the party and lobbied for political and diplomatic posts. Some of the most influential TV news channels, newspapers, and magazines, including *India Today*, once India's best newsmagazine, were content to become an echo chamber for the BJP's views.

Not surprisingly, the BJP, and its supporters and advisers in the media, couldn't see beyond the "India Shining" of the Hindu middle class and turn their attention to the 70 percent of Indians living in the countryside. They barely noticed the Indians who live in slums or in equally degrading conditions in the big cities, the fact that while high-tech hospitals in the big cities cater to rich Indians and foreigners, or medical tourists, public health facilities in small towns and villages decline rapidly; that communicable diseases such as malaria, dengue, and encephalitis have revived; that half of all Indian children are undernourished and more than half a million of them die each year from diarrhea; that an estimated five million Indians are infected with HIV/AIDS.

A powerful ideology often shaped the reforms the BJP espoused: that the free market can usurp the role of the state. This meant that government often withdrew from precisely those areas where its presence was indispensable. Though India had more than sufficient food grains in stock, the government's failure to distribute it effectively led in recent years to an unprecedented rise in the number of drought-affected villagers starving to death in many of the most populous states.

In this new India, preoccupied with life-or-death economic issues, the temple in Ayodhya may appear a dead issue, but it stands ready to be ignited by the BJP as it struggles to broaden its constituency beyond the affluent middle class. You reach Ramjanmabhoomi (Rama's birthplace), as it is now called, through a maze of narrow, barricaded paths.

Armed men loom up abruptly with metal detectors and perform brisk body searches. These are members of the Provincial Armed Constabulary (PAC), which is notorious for its pogroms of Muslims in North Indian towns, and they are particularly on the lookout for cameras. Pictures of the site have not been allowed by the government for the last decade.

A canvas canopy protects the platform built over the rubble of the mosque, on which stand the idols draped in garlands and sequined cloth. A priest in a silk kurta and with caste marks on his forehead sits below the platform briskly dispensing prasad (tiny sugary balls) and squirreling away the soiled and wrinkled rupee notes tentatively offered by peasant pilgrims.

As I groped for some small change one afternoon in February 2003, a PAC inspector wandered over, asked me if I was a journalist from Delhi, and attempted a little history. He told me that Lord Rama had placed the idols inside the mosque in 1949; it was his wish that a temple be built on his birthplace. My companion, a resident of Benares, challenged this, saying that the idols had been placed there by a district official. The inspector did not defend his story; he only smiled and replied that this proved that the official was a true Hindu.

Many such true Hindus looked the other way while the temple was prefabricated in Ayodhya and other cities across India. In a vast shed a short distance from the Ramjanmabhoomi lie stacks of carved stone pillars. Here you can buy promotional literature—*The Blood-soaked History of Ayodhya* and *Ayodhya: An Answer to Terrorism and Fundamentalism* are the best-selling titles—and also admire the miniature glass-cased model of the temple. The labor is cheap—two pounds a day for craftsmen—but the temple, whose architect previously designed the Swaminarayan Temple at Neasden, seems to have come out of a garish fantasy of marble and gold.

Local abbots are impatient with the slow pace of the construction; it is easy to see why. The offerings at the temple are likely to run into millions of dollars annually. Much money has already arrived from generous donors in India and abroad. No one knows where most of it has gone; rumors point to the opulent new buildings in Ayodhya and elsewhere.

As for the mosque, which appears now in memory as a melancholy symbol of a besieged secularism, there seems little hope it will ever be rebuilt. It has fallen victim not just to the ideologues but to less perceptible changes in India's general mood in the last decade. The talk of poverty and social justice; the official culture of frugality; the appeal, however rhetorical, to traditions of tolerance and dialogue—all these seem to belong to the past, to the early decades of idealism. A decade of proglobalization policies has created a new aggressive middle class, whose concerns dominate public life in India. This class is growing; the current numbers are between 150 and 200 million. There are also millions of rich Indians living outside India. In America, they constitute the richest minority. It is these affluent, upper-caste Indians in India and abroad who largely bankrolled the rise to power of Hindu nationalists. In the global context, middle-class Hindus are no less ambitious than those who in the Roman Empire embraced Christianity and made it an effective mechanism with which to secure worldly power. Hinduism in the hands of these Indians has never looked more like the Christianity and Islam of popes and mullahs and less like the multiplicity of unselfconsciously tolerant faiths it still is for most Indians.

It was this modernized Hinduism that Gujarat in 2002 provided a glimpse of, as Benetton-clad young Hindus carted off the loot of digital cameras and DVD players in their new Japanese cars. It is this Hinduism that Ayodhya presents both a miniature image and a sinister portent of, with its syncretic past now irrevocably falsified, its mosques destroyed, its minorities suppressed, an Ayodhya where well-placed local abbots helped by elected politicians wait for new lucrative connections to the global economy and prove, along with much else, the profound modernity of religious nationalism.

BOLLYWOOD

India Shining

In Bombay in December 2003 I met Mahesh Bhatt, one of India's most famous and successful filmmakers. He told me, "Bollywood is part of what our culture has become. We are lying to ourselves all the time."

It wasn't what I expected to hear from Mahesh when I e-mailed him from London, explaining that I wanted to explore the world of Bombay films, or Bollywood, and requesting an interview. I had seen and liked some of his forty-odd films, the autobiographical ones about his illegitimate birth, his unhappy childhood with his Muslim mother, and his extramarital affair with a mentally ill actress that had made his reputation in the 1980s. Though he had stopped directing films five years back, he still wrote screenplays and supervised his daughter's and brother's production companies. He had published a book about his philosopher friend U. G. Krishnamurti. He made documentaries but was also increasingly known for his denunciations in the press and on television of Hindu nationalists, sexual puritans, and U.S. foreign policy.

I saw him often on television, where he was a striking figure in his loose black shirt, which set off the white hair remaining on his shiny pate. I had once seen him shout during a debate with a Hindu nationalist leader, "I insist on my right to watch pornography." "Mark my words," he said on another occasion, "Hindu fundamentalism will destroy this nation." More recently, he had turned down an invitation to a breakfast prayer meeting at the White House and described George W. Bush as the "worst villain in the world."

Drama was clearly important to Mahesh. "My God died young," he told me, and then went on to describe how he, angered by a God who kept apart his Muslim mother and Hindu Brahmin father, had one day immersed his small statue of Ganesha in the Arabian Sea off Bombay. When I first met him in Bombay, on the sets of *Murder*, a film he had written for his brother, he had just returned from his first visit to Pakistan. It had been, he said, a profound emotional experience. He had felt his buried Muslim self come alive in Pakistan. The visit had also stirred up memories of his long-suffering Muslim mother.

Though only fifty-five years old, he remembered his life as a long journey with clear-cut stages. In his twenties he had taken a lot of LSD and gone "shopping in the spiritual supermarket." In his thirties, when he finally made it as a filmmaker, he had come to know a "great inner emptiness," feeling only sadness as his fax machine spun out box-office figures from across India. It was in Los Angeles, the "capital of materialism," that he had decided to renounce the "pursuit of success." He had rejected his onetime guru, Osho Rajneesh, by flushing his rosary beads down the toilet. He spoke with passion and conviction, and I didn't feel I could ask him if the water pressure in his Bombay toilet had been strong enough to flush away the beads.

His outspoken views had made him unpopular in Bollywood. "He is a self-publicist," one film journalist told me. "Ask him why he helps his brother and daughter make B-grade films. Or why he rips off Hollywood plots for his scripts."

But Mahesh was frank about his own work. "I have made a lot of trashy films. Recycling old formulas, which is what Bollywood does most of the time. I guess one has to keep working." He said he regarded filmmaking without illusions, as a business like any other. "Don't wait for the ideal offer; there is no such thing," he told a young actor, a part-time model with a gym-toned body who had come to seek his advice. "What will you do at home anyway, apart from bodybuilding?"

After the actor left, he turned back to me. "These young people probably want to hear something else. They come to me, they think I am in the business, doing a lot of work, and will encourage them. But I can't. I can't make Bollywood bigger than it is."

He said that his own films, even those that had made him rich and famous, had left him "deeply unfulfilled." He added, "But I know that there is no fulfillment awaiting me anywhere. My friend U. G. Krishnamurti says that there is no other reality apart from the one you live with every day."

There seemed something too neat and packaged about Mahesh's self-awareness. But while in Bombay, I found myself traveling often to his office in the suburb of Juhu. I walked straight past the reception to his small room, where I usually found him lying on a long sofa, under a broad window with a view of shanties cowering under grimy buildings. Two mobile phones rested on his ample stomach. One of them rang more often than the other, but Mahesh picked up both at the sound and then, raising his neck from the sofa, squinted at their screens for what seemed a long time before deciding to answer.

He was brusque on the phone, except to his wife and daughter. "Who is this?" he would often ask, and then start repeating, "Bye, bye, bye," in rapid succession before ending the conversation. The door opened to admit Nirmal, his personal attendant, with tea and coffee, or some of the young, trendy people working at the office. Occasionally there would be someone Mahesh had arranged to see: a Pakistani actress hoping to work in Bollywood; a Parsi musician and ballet dancer wishing to try her hand at films; a tall, arrogant-looking actor wearing a Superman T-shirt, who, I learned, was the grandson of a notorious Bombay politician and had acted in *Murder*. Soni, Mahesh's wife, came once; a petite, shy woman, she had acted in many art house films in the eighties and was now trying to direct a film.

The door opened less often for the aspiring actors, directors, musicians, distributors, and publicists who waited at the reception, hoping to waylay Mahesh or his brother, Mukesh. They grew animated as Mahesh emerged from his room. A couple of them often trailed him, with pleading voices, all the way to the building's compound and spoke rapidly and uninterruptedly until he got into his car.

There were more young men at the gate to the walled compound. I saw them every day, chatting with the *chowkidar* (watchman) and the drivers of the cars parked inside, breaking off only to gaze expectantly inside cars going into the compound. Mohammed, the driver of my hired car, said that they were "aspirers" who had traveled to Bombay from various parts of India, hoping for a "break" in Bollywood. They were often found outside producers' offices, waiting to catch the attention of the important or powerful people there.

This was how most people tried to gain a foothold in what was a very crowded and self-contained world. India produces more films annually than any country—up to a thousand in several Indian languages, made in Bombay as well as Madras, Hyderabad, Trivandrum, and Calcutta. Bombay, or Bollywood, is the biggest and best known of the Indian film industries and has the biggest audience. Releasing up to two hundred films a year, it faces little competition from Hollywood, which has never garnered more than 6 percent of the market in India.

In 1896, the Lumière brothers brought moving images to India, shortly after introducing them to Europe. The first Indian feature film was released in 1913 in Bombay. By the 1930s a film industry of sorts was in place in Bombay, with studios and independent production companies and stars and films that borrowed or adopted narrative styles as varied as village folk theater, Victorian fiction, the *Ramayana* and the *Mahabharata*, and Hollywood comedies and melodramas.

The film industries in India now employ up to six million people, mostly on a contractual basis. There are twelve thousand cinema theaters in India with an average capacity of seven hundred seats, priced anywhere between thirty cents and three dollars. Since the finance for films comes from outside the legal economy, no one knows what the actual turnover of Bollywood, or of any other film industry in India, is. Films are often made for less than a million dollars, although some of Bollywood's recent films have cost as much as thirty million dollars, much of the money spent on music composers, shooting stints in Europe and America, and the stars, who are now more powerful than anyone else in the business.

Not surprisingly, most of the aspirers wanted to be stars, not technicians. Occasionally, one of them succeeded and gave fresh currency to the dream of success. Mallika, a young actress I met at Mahesh's office, was an aspirer when two years ago she left her conservative family in a small town near Delhi in order to seek a career in Bollywood. Long queues of "gorgeous women," she said, preceded her at every producer's office she went to. After a few modeling assignments and casting couch offers, she had finally found some "decent work." But then her father ostracized her after her first film, in which she kissed the male lead seventeen times—a record of sorts in prudish Bollywood.

Mallika thought that he was unlikely to respond well to her next film, *Murder*, in which she had played an adulterous wife.

She said, "The film is very bold, although I hate the word. People abuse it so much in Bollywood, which is full of dishonest tight-asses. How long are they going to show sex by bringing two flowers together on the screen? India has the second-largest population in the world. Do they think it came about by bringing flowers together?"

I met Mallika at the end of what had been a long day of shooting for her. But she came into Mahesh's office looking very excited, wearing a small white T-shirt and low-slung blue jeans over very high heels. A preview, or what she called promo, of *Murder* had just begun to appear on many of India's film-based television channels.

I had seen an unedited version of this promo at Mahesh's office earlier that afternoon, accompanied by a film "broker." A rapid succession of scenes shot in India and Thailand showed Mallika being undressed by invisible hands, making love, and walking provocatively on a beach, the camera firmly focused on her hips. The broker had pronounced the film "very bold." It was likely to get an Adults certificate from the censor board. But this did not much bother the distributors, who were convinced that *Murder* was going to be a "big hit."

Mallika said, "I have been getting lots of SMS about the promo. It is very hot. Lots of skin show. But you tell me. You must have seen lots of films in London; what's so bold about showing a housewife feeling passionate and saying she wants to make love? What is a bored housewife to do when she is feeling horny?"

Mallika told me that filmmakers from South India constantly approached her, wishing to cast her in soft porn films. They appalled and depressed her, as did most filmmakers in Bollywood. She really wanted to work abroad, in Europe or America, where "real" films were made. She spoke of the work of Pedro Almodóvar and Roberto Rodríguez.

As she spoke, she kept brushing back thick, wavy hair from her full-lipped, oval face. On that Sunday evening, Mahesh's office was deserted, with only a *chowkidar* waiting four floors down along with Mohammed, the driver of my hired car. Mallika and I sat on a sofa, separated by a few inches, the narrow space into which she suddenly dropped, while still speaking of Almodóvar, two glossy photos.

They were publicity stills from *Murder* and showed her pouting in a bikini and sarong. When Mallika asked me if I had seen the promo for *Murder*, I had lied, mostly because I couldn't work up a response. But now the photos lay on the sofa, and as I looked at them, I felt Mallika's eyes on my lowered face.

She said, "I want you to look at them. I want you to tell me if men are going to drool over me or not in this film. I want you to give me an honest opinion."

English in India can be a deceptive medium. Even when the language is used well, as it is by an elite minority among the country's two hundred million–strong middle class, the undertones can be confusing. Moods and gestures are hard to figure out. Irony and humor are often perceived but rarely intended.

"You should meet Mallika," Mahesh had said. "She is the next sex bomb of Bollywood. It would be an interesting story for you." Mahesh had many such stories for me. But although grateful, I wasn't always sure what *he* made of them or what his true relationship with Bollywood was.

One evening, as we were leaving his office, Mahesh paused before entering his car and gestured to one of the young "aspirers" standing near the gate to the compound.

The man Mahesh had signaled to was a tall, rather handsome man wearing a black bandanna. As he walked toward us, his broad shoulders stooped, until he stood half bowed in a silent *namaste* before Mahesh.

Mahesh said, "This is Pritam. He has been coming to my office every day for eight years now, hoping to get a role in my films. I have often offered him money for the return fare to his town in Bengal, but he has always refused. Would you like to talk to him?"

I felt Pritam lift his head slightly to look at me. I felt a small crowd at the gate watching us. I nodded.

Mahesh told Pritam while slowly getting into his car, "OK. Be here at two-thirty tomorrow."

Driving back to my hotel, Mohammed was frantic with curiosity. He knew about Pritam, who was apparently famous in these parts. He had indeed been coming to the office for eight years but had not managed to speak to Mahesh sahib for the last three. And he had never gone up to his office. Was he now finally being given a "break"?

I said I didn't know. When I arrived at the office the next day—late, around four—Pritam was standing with the drivers. As my car slid past the gate, his face appeared in the window. Half bent, he accompanied the car until it stopped and then held my door open. I saw his beseeching eyes and the sweat patches on his ironed blue shirt. I said I was sorry to be late. He didn't seem to understand. I said that I was sure Mahesh would call for him soon.

Upstairs, Mahesh was lying on his sofa, bubbling with news. He got up as I came through the door. He said he was traveling to Delhi the next day to see Sonia Gandhi, the Italian-born leader of both the Congress Party and the opposition in the Indian Parliament. Some Muslim theologians had arranged the meeting. They felt that Mahesh was best placed to convey their frustration with the Congress's failure to fight the anti-Muslim program of the Hindu nationalist government.

Mahesh said, "It is a sad reflection on our politics that they can't find anyone to approach except Mahesh Bhatt." He showed me a folder of photographs sent to him from the western Indian state of Gujarat. The pictures were of Muslims attacked, some by Hindu policemen, in recent months: close-ups of bloody wounds on skulls, backs, and legs or of shattered car windshields, television sets, and dressing table mirrors. Each photo had the date and time of the attack written on the back. The accompanying letter from a Muslim described how his daughter had been "beaten like a dog."

We talked about politics for a while. Mahesh's mobile phones kept ringing. A journalist wanted Mahesh's opinion on the Oscars. "To hell with the Oscars," Mahesh said, "I am not interested in it. Bye, bye, bye." Another journalist asked about the film Mahesh planned to make about the real-life con man caught conspiring with the police commissioner of Bombay. His daughter called. Her first film was due for release. Mahesh said that she was very nervous about it.

Nirmal brought us fresh coffee in styrofoam cups. A publicist from Lucknow arrived. "An important man," Mahesh explained. He was there to talk about Mahesh's upcoming visit to North India.

Around five or so Mahesh told Nirmal to summon Pritam.

Mahesh said, "He told me once that he had committed a murder—his uncle, I think. I think he wanted to impress me. I want to ask him about that."

When Pritam came through the door, his face glistening with sweat, Mahesh said, pointing to the bathroom behind him, "Go and wash your face."

Water dripped from his face and onto his shirt when he came out. Mahesh said, "Sit down."

He looked awkward on the small, high-backed chair, his long legs jutting out.

Mahesh gestured toward me. "He is a writer, wanting to know about Bollywood. What can you tell him?"

This was how Mahesh introduced me to actors, producers, distributors, and others in the film industry, often exhorting them to take me behind the "glossy surface" of Bollywood and reveal its "harder reality."

As it turned out, Pritam couldn't tell me much about Bollywood, partly because he had spent eight years hoping that Mahesh would introduce him to it. He hadn't gone to any other filmmaker, convinced that Mahesh would give him his "break."

"Why do you think that?" Mahesh asked.

Pritam smiled uncertainly and said in slow but precise English, "Because I know that in my heart, sir. I know that you will take me to the summit of success. I have believed this for the last eight years, and I will believe this for the rest of my life."

Mahesh said, in Hindi, "But why did you tell me that you had killed your uncle?"

Pritam wiped his mouth and leaned forward on his chair. "It is true, sir. I wanted to tell you that I can be very serious about anything, even murder. I only have to put my mind to it."

He described how he had been provoked into murdering his uncle. He seemed to have worked on the story, which came out smoothly. His father had died when he was very young. Soon afterward, his uncles had appropriated his mother's land and house. One of Pritam's uncles had been particularly vicious. Pritam had seen him repeatedly assault his mother. At seventeen, he had first thought of murdering him. He spent a year planning the murder before finally stabbing the uncle in question. As part of his meticulous preparation, he had left no clues for the police; they were still baffled by the murder.

His mother, Pritam said, was a *devi*, a goddess. He couldn't bear anyone being cruel to her and wanted above all to look after her.

Mahesh said, "In that case, what are you doing in Bollywood? You have come to the wrong place. You come to Mahesh Bhatt thinking he will make you a star. Mahesh Bhatt is telling you that you are chasing illusions, that you should go home and look after your mother. Do you want money for the train fare?"

Pritam shook his head. "I want you to give me a chance, sir. I won't go home without having worked with you."

Someone opened the door to announce that the publicist from Lucknow was leaving. Mahesh said to me in English, "Why don't you talk to Pritam while I meet the publicist in my brother's room?"

Without Mahesh in the room, Pritam relaxed. I wanted to know where and how he had lived in Bombay for the last eight years. He replied, looking distracted, slightly puzzled perhaps by the bareness of the room he had long wanted to enter, that he lived like an ascetic, did not drink or smoke, and ate very little. He stole whatever money he needed.

How? I asked. But Mahesh returned to his room just then, and Pritam produced a letter in Bengali from his mother, evidence, he said, of his mother's good heart.

Mahesh asked him to translate it aloud.

"My dear son," Pritam began slowly, his eyes darting from Mahesh's face to mine, "I have not heard from you for a long time and you have not sent me any money. I don't worry much, because I know that your faith in Mahesh sahib will be rewarded one day . . ."

The letter spoke of her continued suffering at the hands of her greedy relatives. When it ended, Pritam looked up hopefully at Mahesh. One of Mahesh's phones rang just then. He picked both up and, while squinting at them, said to Pritam, "I think you should go home and help her."

Pritam stayed on for a few more minutes, drinking tea, surveying the room, while Mahesh spoke on the phone. I was relieved when Mahesh told him as he left that he would "try him out before the camera." Outside, Pritam immediately conveyed the news to the crowd of chauffeurs and aspirers. Mohammed was very pleased on his behalf; it was the kind of break he hoped for himself.

I wondered later if Pritam had written the letter himself, just as he had made up the story about the murder, in order to impress Mahesh. In its extreme, raw emotions, his story sounded too much like a Bollywood film.

I didn't suggest this to Mahesh, however. I wanted Pritam to have his "break." Also, I knew a little about Mahesh's background, and he seemed unlikely to doubt a story just because it was too melodramatic. His own father, also a famous producer and director in his time, had lived with his Hindu wife while maintaining a Muslim mistress, Mahesh's mother, in another part of Bombay. He came irregularly to his second home, and didn't stay long. As a child Mahesh had spent many hours waiting for his father and then, when he did not turn up, consoling his mother.

Mahesh said, "My mother loved him intensely until her death. I always remained slightly in awe of this aloof man who would come and go away, and who had such a hold over my mother. When she died a few years back, he came to our house chanting Hindu scriptures and holding *gangajal* [Ganges water]. He saw my mother's corpse and said, 'Put some *sindoor* [vermilion, the cherished symbol of matrimony for Hindu women] in her hair. She was always asking me, "Put some *sindoor* in my hair." I want this done now.'"

The extent of Mahesh's father's love for his mistress was made clear, Mahesh explained, when his father himself died. "I used to ask my mother, 'Where will his corpse go?' As it turned out, he had left explicit wishes that he be cremated in our part of town. My mother's sisters knew what this meant. He was publicly acknowledging his devotion to the woman who loved him. My aunts showed up at the cremation. I saw them whispering and stealing a fistful of ashes. I asked them what they had done with the ashes. They said they had sprinkled them over my mother's grave. They were wishing for some kind of union. Critics accused me of melodrama when I put some of my background in my film *Zakhm*. I felt with that gesture that I had made my peace with him. This is what melodrama does; it reconciles people. This is what the best Bollywood films achieve."

My own memory of Bollywood films was different. As a child in small railway towns, and then as an undergraduate in Allahabad, I had watched them frequently. For weeks I would gaze longingly at the posters suspended atop electricity poles, or draped on the sides of the tonga that clattered down dusty, narrow streets with understocked shops and faded signboards, the driver announcing, through a megaphone, the latest arrival at the local cinema.

I was particularly struck by the posters of new films. They often featured men gnashing their teeth and pointing outsized guns at each other against a backdrop of exploding skyscrapers and women showing bare arms and, sometimes more daringly, legs. My parents did not allow me to watch these films, claiming that they were too violent. They spoke fondly of the tragic or flamboyantly romantic male actors of a previous era—Dilip Kumar, Raj Kapoor, Guru Dutt, Dev Anand. They happily let me go to films from the 1950s and 1960s, some of which enjoyed reruns in small-town cinemas, and whose mostly melancholy songs, leaking out of a hundred transistors in our railway colony, filled the long afternoons of my childhood.

But I wasn't much interested in the stories, where love, timidly expressed, was usually thwarted, worldly success proved an illusion, and whose songs rendered sweet the cruelest disappointment. Like many young men in India—and, unknown to me, also in Africa and the Middle East—I was fascinated by Amitabh Bachchan, although I watched most of his films after I left home and was pursuing an undergraduate degree in Allahabad.

Bachchan, a gawkily tall actor with a baritone voice, often played the role of the poor, resentful young man pitted against venal politicians, businessmen, and policemen; women, apart from tearful mothers, played minor roles in his films and were often treated ungallantly. There was little in Bachchan's own background that hinted at political discontent. Before seeking a career in films in Bombay, he had held a well-paid *boxwallah*'s job in Calcutta. His father, a distinguished poet in Hindi, had friends among the Nehrus and the Gandhis. But on-screen Bachchan was the "angry young man," and he spoke directly to an audience that was no longer moved by the gentle self-pity of the actors that my parents liked.

For many Indians, there was much to be angry about in the 1970s and 1980s. Freedom from British rule in 1947, and the proclamations of socialism and democracy, seemed to have benefited only a small minority of the country's population, mostly politicians, big businessmen, and civil servants, people who plundered the state-controlled economy and protected their power and privilege almost as fiercely as the British had once dealt with challenges from the natives.

Bachchan first became famous around 1975, the year that Indira Gandhi responded to a mass political movement protesting against corruption and inflation by suspending India's democratic constitution and imprisoning many people opposed to her. In several of his films, Bachchan expressed the cynicism and despair that were particularly acute among unemployed lower-middle-class men in small towns. He usually sought to avenge himself on an unjust society. Pure exhilaration rippled across the always frankly expressive cinema audience when, after successive humiliations, he finally exploded into violence.

This was an especially gratifying moment in Allahabad. For some years before I arrived, the university, once known as the Oxford of the East, had been a setting for battles between unemployed, and probably unemployable, young men seeking to make a career in state- or national-level politics. Crude bombs and guns often went off in the middle of the campus. People like myself, who were there to acquire a degree and then apply for a job with the government, felt small and anxious and scared most of the time.

Bachchan empowered us briefly. I remember watching one of his films in Allahabad: how the audience roared its approval as he, playing a chief minister, first eloquently denounced his cabinet and then machine-gunned all its members.

A more intractable world began just outside the cinema, where the police constables waved their iron-tipped lathis and exacted bribes from rickshaw drivers and street-side vendors. Corrupt men ruled here through a long, invisible hierarchy—the money passed all the way to the police officers at the top—and the best way to deal with them was to join them. But to spend three hours in the cinema—on the bare wooden seats, amid the peanut shells on the floor, the cigarette and bidi smoke languidly rising through the rays from the projector—was to partially fulfill all the fantasies the posters had nurtured. It was to shed, however briefly, our deprivations and to embrace the heady conviction that if the world failed to yield its richness—sex, wealth, power—it would be severely punished.

As it turned out, I rarely went to the cinema after I left Allahabad and moved to Delhi. The older I got, the more Bollywood films began to seem long and unreal. Occasionally, late at night in Indian hotel rooms, I would come across previews of Bollywood's offerings on television. A few glimpses of songs and dances in Swiss meadows, or at opulent weddings, Muslim terrorists in Kashmir and Pakistani villains plotting against India, and plump action heroes saving their motherland, and I felt I'd had enough.

I couldn't enter these films as unselfconsciously as I had before. Yet neither was I distant enough from them to enjoy them as kitsch. And there were always enough unread books on the shelves staring plaintively at me.

It was years later, while spending part of my time in London, that I became interested again in Bollywood films. Popular among a younger generation of British Asians, they were shown frequently on television. In the late nineties, new Bollywood films had begun to appear in the U.K. box-office charts. Academics published monographs on them, arguing for their sociological import and neglected artistic quality. In 1999, Amitabh Bachchan, his name still unknown to most people in Europe and America, was elected ahead of Laurence Olivier as the "Star of the Millennium" in a BBC online poll.

Articles and profiles of Bollywood stars appeared in even the mainstream English newspapers following the success of the West End musical *Bombay Dreams*, which Andrew Lloyd Webber produced in collaboration with A. R. Rahman, a Bollywood composer. These articles usually portrayed Bollywood films as an exotic, somewhat amusing novelty. They rarely tried to explain why these films had been popular in many places—the former Soviet Union, Eastern Europe, the Middle East, China, and the Far East—where Hollywood had little or no influence or how they had penetrated countries with such strong indigenous cultures as Egypt and Indonesia.

After many years, I saw a new Hindi film in London. *Kal Ho Naa Ho* ("Tomorrow May Never Come"), better known as *KHNH*, was a worldwide hit, especially popular among South Asians in Britain and America. Its male lead was Shah Rukh Khan, one of three superstar Khans who are apparently as bankable in Bollywood as Tom Cruise and Tom Hanks in Hollywood. Part of a new "youth movement," its producers had turned their back on the formulaic films made throughout the eighties and early nineties—sterile years, I had read, for Bollywood and very different from the current climate since, according to various Web sites and magazines I looked up, there were now in Bollywood people with the talent and the courage to be *hat ke* (literally "different from"). *KHNH*, for instance, was *hat ke*. So was its young director, Karan Johar. The *hat ke* generation was bringing about as much of a revolution in Bollywood as young filmmakers, inspired by European cinema, had briefly achieved in Hollywood in the late sixties and seventies. They were the counterculture, connecting to a new, sophisticated audience.

*K*HNH was unlike any Bollywood film I had ever seen, mostly because it was set entirely in New York City and its characters were almost all Indian-Americans. But it also featured many songs, and its plot traced a romantic triangle much used in Bollywood. A woman meets two boys, loves one, and is loved hopelessly by the other. Together they sing and dance for a bit, along with a gregarious cast of brothers, sisters, parents, grandmothers, and grandfathers, before the young man she fancies is revealed to be fatally ill. Many tears later (the film is more than three hours long), he dies, but only after bravely

singing and dancing through the lavish wedding of his heartbroken survivors.

The next day I looked up DVDs of Johar's previous two films, both
of which had been equally successful among middle-class and expatriate Indians. Their titles also beginning with the letter *k*, they were
known as *KKHH* and *KKKG* respectively. They were set in London and
in an India greatly resembling a cross between England and America.
KKKG was, the subtitle claimed, "all about loving your parents." The
parents in this instance headed a corporate family that lived in an
English-style country house and traveled in helicopters. Their son lived
in London—not in any of the modest suburbs where most of the Indian
immigrant communities live but in posh Hampstead—and he drove a
red Ferrari.

Johar's other film, *KKHH*, was partly set in a college modeled on
Riverdale, the American high school depicted in *Archie* comics, and
the main characters based on the high-spirited teenagers Archie, Veron-
ica, and Betty. They played basketball instead of cricket and eventually
secured highly paid jobs in an India made up almost entirely of equally
affluent and charming relatives.

I saw other new films. I read books and fanzines and online interviews
with Bollywood stars. In December, I finally traveled to Bombay,
where I met Karan Johar. "My films reflect," he told me, "my own reality. I love my parents, they love me. No matter where we are in the
world, we are Indians and at home. I write out of my experience."

Johar was upbeat about Bollywood, which he said was entering another era of filmmaking. Another young filmmaker, Ram Gopal Varma,
much praised for his films about the Bombay mafia, said, "There is no
point in patting ourselves on our backs. Our best films are not much
better than an average film from Hollywood. I feel we have much more
to learn from even B-grade Hollywood films. I have learned a lot from
The Exorcist."

Was this true? I couldn't tell. In Bombay, I became more aware that
Bollywood was a world unto itself, in which the criteria normally used
for judging films and their makers were only partly valid.

"Pictures," F. Scott Fitzgerald once wrote, "have a private grammar, like politics or automobile production or society." Fitzgerald thought that people merely watching and commenting on films could not understand how Hollywood studios actually worked, the peculiar pressures they brought to bear upon screenwriters, directors, and actors. Bollywood too seems to have its own peculiar grammar. The songwriter, or lyricist, music composer, dance director, and costume designer are frequently more crucial to a film's success than the script, which is often improvised on the sets.

Bollywood's economic workings are more mysterious. It still exists in what was known as the informal and high-risk sector of the Indian economy. Banks rarely invest in Bollywood, where moneylenders are rampant, demanding up to 35 percent interest. The big corporate houses seem no less keen to stay away from filmmaking. A senior executive with the Tatas, one of India's prominent business families, told me, "We went into Bollywood, made one film, lost a lot of money, and got out of it very fast," adding that "the place works in ways we couldn't begin to explain to our shareholders."

Since only six or seven of the two hundred films made each year earn a profit, the industry has generated little capital of its own. The great studios of the early years of the industry are now defunct. It is outsiders—regular moneylenders, small and big businessmen, real estate people, and, sometimes, mafia dons—who continue to finance new films, and their turnover, given the losses, is rapid. Their motives are mixed: sex, glamour, money laundering, and, more optimistically, profit. They rarely have much to do with the desire to make original, or even competent, films.

Sometimes, shooting schedules drag on for years as the producer struggles to make interest payments to his various creditors. The delays are often caused by actors working in several films at once. The actual process of filmmaking seems equally arduous. For instance, actors record their dialogue not during but after the shooting, which can cause their voices to seem out of sync with their facial expressions, thus heightening the impression of artificiality. It is rare that an actor working without a proper script turns in a good performance.

In any case, not much by way of acting—as distinct from dancing and fight stunts—seems required of Bollywood stars in the films they choose to work in. Even in real life, they tend to act out fantasies nearly as extreme as those they help create on-screen. The most famous of them was recently caught hunting deer and gunrunning. A few months before I arrived in Bombay, Salman Khan, one of the three superstar Khans, had run over and killed or wounded four men sleeping on a pavement while speeding late at night in his Land Cruiser. Mohammed pointed out the spot of the accident to me every time we passed it and repeated his account of how Khan had managed to bribe the witnesses to change their accounts of the event.

Bachchan, whom I had once idolized, seemed disappointingly unaware of what he represented to millions of Indians or what he could do with his enormous influence. In interviews he deflected questions about his political friends and spoke instead of his new intimacy with his son, Abhishek; he said he talked to him every day about girls, and they exchanged dirty jokes. In recent years he had lost millions of pounds in ill-advised business ventures, including the Miss World Contest. Helped by politicians and businessmen, with whom he was photographed frequently, and the popular Indian version of *Who Wants to Be a Millionaire*, which he had anchored, he had recently managed to emerge from debt; he returned to making mediocre but well-paying films.

It wasn't easy, as I had discovered in London, to sit through most of Bachchan's films again. I found I preferred the older films my parents had admired, the films about love and loss, in which male as well as female characters faced adversity with strength and dignity and did not confuse revenge with justice. I liked too the more contemporary films made by Mahesh Bhatt, Gulzar, and Ram Gopal Varma. I did not like remembering the self that had once been stirred by Bachchan's films, by their visions of private, bloody revenge.

I was not surprised to learn that these films had been made during a particularly low moment in Bollywood's history. Watching them again made me think that a small-town audience of today was probably better served by new films with multisyllable titles, even if it felt bemused by their pseudo-Indian setting and characters and their detachment from issues of poverty and corruption.

But as I learned quickly in Bombay, the small-town audiences with their cut-price tickets and long queues of eager, young fans don't matter as much as they used to. The rapid spread of television in the late eighties and early nineties forced many cinemas to close down. The big profits now came from the multiple cinema complexes, or multiplexes, of the big cities, such as Delhi, Bombay, Madras, Calcutta, Hyderabad, Pune, and Bangalore, and what was known as the "NRI (nonresident Indian) circuit."

Karan Johar was one of the shrewd auteurs making films for the growing upper middle class of the larger Indian cities as well as for the millions of Indians living in England and America, the Indians who, according to Shah Rukh Khan, "seem to like love stories, pretty things, yellow flowers, high-speed action, women in saris, opulence." Excited by the success in 2002 of a film called *Lagaan*, nominated for the best foreign film category at the Oscars, many people in Bollywood are aiming even higher, at Hollywood, the American and the British market. But even those who scoff at such ambitions, arguing correctly that most Americans are likely to find Bollywood wholly alienating, have little time for audiences outside the big cities.

"Frankly, I couldn't give a fuck for the villages," Ram Gopal Varma was quoted as saying in *Time*. When we met, he denied having said this but then went on to stress that he was content to make small-budget films for educated people in the cities. Sitting serenely in his office high above Nariman Point, miles away from the dusty northern suburbs of Bombay, where most film people live and work, Pritish Nandy, once a poet and journalist and now a film producer, told me, "I don't want to make films for people I don't know." Karan Johar, made defensive by my suggestion that his films spoke primarily to affluent Indians, asserted, "No one now can make a film for an all-Indian audience."

People still try, however. *LOC Kargil*, the biggest film of the winter of 2003, was defiantly non–*hat ke*, a throwback to such big-budget multistarrers as *Sholay*, the all-time Indian hit. Four hours long, it features almost all of Bollywood's established and rising stars, including Amitabh Bachchan's son, Abhishek. Its success seemingly assured, it deals with an event that has aroused much passion in India, the deaths of over five hundred soldiers in the summer of 1999 during the desperate Indian effort to regain the hills in Indian-held Kashmir, seized by a group of Pakistan-backed Muslim militants.

The day before the film was released across India, I went to a preview with Khalid Mohammed. I first met him when he was a writer with *The Times of India*, famous for his slash-and-burn reviews of Hindi films. He still reviews new releases scathingly in the evening daily *Midday*. But he offends more people in the industry now that he is a filmmaker himself. "He should make up his mind about what he wants to be," one director had complained to me.

I liked Khalid. He seemed a solitary man in the bare, curtained-off rooms of his apartment, where he had lived with his grandmother and where he had written scripts for films about his Muslim family: the mother who, abandoned by her Pakistani husband, married a Hindu prince from Rajasthan, only to die with him shortly thereafter in a plane crash; the aunt who shuttled for years between India and Pakistan, wanted in neither country. Mohammed was especially happy to drive me to Khalid's home. He and his family had seen twice Khalid's film about the survivors of the anti-Muslim pogrom in Bombay in the early nineties.

When I met Khalid in Bombay in late 2003, his new film had just been released. It was unlike anything he had done, a drama, inspired by Ingmar Bergman's *Autumn Sonata*, about mothers and daughters. Mostly panned by other reviewers, it had disappeared from most cinemas and was playing at a resoundingly empty thousand-seater in Bombay. A friend of Khalid's told me, "He was lucky to make the film he wanted—even very distinguished filmmakers can't get sponsors for their projects—but now he has blown his chance."

Khalid felt the failure keenly. "I am reeling," he said, only half-jokingly, on the phone. He blamed the distributors. It was a "multiplex film," but they had released it in the big halls. He was writing a novel about Iranian restaurant owners in Bombay and updating his coffee table biography of Amitabh Bachchan.

We drove to the preview of *LOC Kargil* in Film City, a few miles out of Bombay. Khalid said that the Bachchans were anxious about their son's career. It was Jaya, Amitabh Bachchan's wife, who had arranged the preview.

I had heard about other anxious parents in Bollywood. Many of the new actors had little to recommend them apart from their famous film families; to the "aspirers" they appeared to be blocking their way. Mallika had complained, "Abhishek Bachchan has had *fifteen* flops, but he still gets great offers."

Abhishek wasn't present at the preview, but the audience, arriving in new, imported cars, mostly constituted his friends in the industry. A few minutes into the screening, it became clear that the film wasn't going to boost young Bachchan's, or anyone else's, career. Although, in reality, the United States government had forced the Pakistani government to withdraw the armed infiltrators from Indian-held Kashmir, Hindu nationalists in India had claimed a military victory over what they described as a perfidious enemy. *LOC Kargil* attempted to elaborate this myth and to justify and commemorate the martyrdom of Indian soldiers.

For the first hour, the soldiers tearfully took leave of their wives, lovers, sisters, and mothers. Thrown into battle, they uttered invocations to the goddess Durga as they clambered up steep, stony hillsides. They sang patriotic songs as they died and shouted crude profanities as they plunged their bayonets into the hapless Pakistanis. I left the hall after three hours of this and paced the deserted foyer until with a final patriotic song the film ended, and all the chauffeurs standing at the back emerged and hurried to their cars.

In the car on the way back to Bombay, Khalid's mobile phone rang continuously. There had been other previews across the city. The reviewer of *Midday*'s rival, *The Afternoon Dispatch & Courier*, rang to say that the film was "major trauma." Karan Johar called to say he was watching and hating it. Someone from the preview said that he had seen Abhishek's mother, Jaya, weeping copiously as the flag-draped coffins of Indian soldiers appeared on the screen. Khalid himself was cautious, wondering only if the film had come at the wrong moment. Relations between India and Pakistan had dramatically improved. There was talk of the Indian cricket team's traveling to Pakistan for a series of matches. But no one could tell how the audience might react.

Khalid was more severe in his review three days later. Titled "Out of Control," it described the film as a "four-hour plus bullet-o-rama." It mocked the film's "umpteen flashbacks to the beauteous, tearful and suffering fiancées and wives waiting back home." Then, in a more serious tone, it deplored the "disturbing religio-political sub-text" and the fact that none of the principal actors portrayed an Indian soldier from the Muslim community.

When I returned to Bombay after seven weeks, the Indian cricket tour to Pakistan had been announced. The verdict on *LOC Kargil* was also in. The Indian Army had gone out of its way to help its director, J. P. Dutta, who had already made a successful war film. Hindu nationalist leaders had organized special screenings in Delhi and exempted film exhibitors from sales tax. But they had not managed to save the film from sinking rapidly at the box office.

Its failure did not seem to have affected Abhishek's career very much, however. I saw him at a dinner party at the JW Marriott Hotel, a favorite haunt of young Bollywood stars. Almost as tall as his father, but with a fuller face and smile, he sat surrounded by his friends, young directors, writers, and actresses, and entertained them with an account of his visit to a film festival in Morocco. He recounted a long story about the Irish actor Colin Farrell and his desperate and unsuccessful pursuit of a Bollywood starlet at the festival.

Khalid was among the guests seated farther away from Abhishek and exempt from joining in the slightly forced laughter. He said he still felt hurt by the failure of his recent film. He had abandoned his novel. A producer had given him money to write and direct a thriller set in London. If all went well, he would start shooting later in the year. He wanted to wipe out the "stigma of a flop."

This stigma of failure seemed to weigh slightly more heavily on J. P. Dutta, the maker of *LOC Kargil*. He seemed surprised when I rang him from Mahesh's office and told him that I would like to meet him. "Can you come right now?" he asked.

Mahesh said, "He is probably surprised anyone wants to see him." Mahesh had told me earlier that his daughter's film had done badly. "She is now learning what failure means, especially in the film industry, where only success counts. She is entering the real world."

Sitting in his office—all sleek white marble and black leather swivel chairs and statues of Ganesha—J. P. Dutta seemed disinclined to enter the real world. A small man wearing a gray beard and thick silver chain around his neck, he spoke in monosyllables until I asked him why *KHNH* had succeeded and *LOC Kargil* hadn't.

It was an unfair question, but it set him off. He spoke at length, interrupting his monologue with short, bitter laughs.

"I will tell you. Because we are not making films anymore. We are marketing them. Please understand what I am saying. People are making films for the metros [metropolitan cities] and claiming that they are hits. But India is not confined to the metros. Our cinema must come out of Indian culture. The films of the fifties and sixties were also city-based. But people outside cities identified with them. It is because they had meaning and depth. What has happened now? Our values have degenerated. The idealism of independence is gone. We are not reflecting our times. Where is the human angle in our cinema? I knew I was not making a commercial film with *LOC Kargil*. It was a tribute to our soldiers who risk their lives to defend their nation. My brother was an air force officer who died in a MiG-21 crash. I know what my film means to our nation's soldiers. I was not concerned whether it sinks or swims with the general public. But you know it is doing great business outside the metros. There are big queues outside the cinemas in UP and Orissa . . ."

They all say that," Tishu said when I reported Dutta's remarks to him, "particularly the old, feudal-style filmmakers who feel left behind by the new kids on the block. But he has a point about the new films lacking roots in India."

I had known Tishu when he was a student at the university in Allahabad. In Bombay last winter, I sought him out after discovering a film about student politics in Allahabad that he had written and directed. The film's characters and settings conveyed accurately the violence and cynicism through which most people at the university picked their way. Its lively dialogue employed well the Hindi dialect of the region. It seemed to me more like a *hat ke* film than any I had previously seen.

But it also had songs and dances, which disrupted the narrative and its carefully built up mood and rendered a good film more or less unwatchable for an audience outside India.

Tishu didn't disagree with me. He simply said he couldn't have raised the money for a film without songs. It had been hard enough anyway to make something that reflected the world he lived in. He had "struggled" for ten years in Bombay, writing scripts or working as assistant director for very little money, before he could dream of making his own film. The student leaders in Allahabad had protested against their depiction in the film. The university authorities had accused him of showing the university in a "bad light" and had canceled his permission for shooting on the campus. Then the producers had delayed distributing the film for more than a year.

Things had worked out in the end. The film had made a profit; it had also got good reviews. Tishu had just finished shooting his second film about drugs and foreign tourists in Manali and was already planning his third venture.

However, despite his success, he wasn't happy in Bombay. It was expensive to live in; the weather was oppressive, the work hard; he hadn't had a vacation with his family for over fourteen years. Worse, he couldn't escape the sense of being only slightly better than the mediocre people around him.

He knew how his work compared to the contemporary cinema of England, France, or even Iran and Egypt. A friend of his, an established writer-director, claimed to be successful only because Bollywood had never had a George Cukor.

Bollywood is in a crisis, financially as well as intellectually. The overwhelming majority of the films failed at the box office, partly because the people making these films did not know India outside of Bombay. They barely knew anything about the experiences of ordinary people in Bombay. The audience couldn't be fooled forever. After all, it now had satellite television, other modes of fantasy to choose from. Not surprisingly, Bollywood had lost much of its traditional audience in not just India but also places like China, North Africa, and the Middle East.

There were young, talented people around, but it was absurd to think of them as forming a counterculture as yet. For there were still relatively few opportunities for them to flower. The money went to established names working with old formulas, and the lessons of their repeated failure were not learned. There were more expensive miscalculations like *LOC Kargil* on the way and more talentless sons and daughters of rich people waiting in the wings.

It isn't just outsiders like Tishu who chafe at the inadequacies of Bollywood. One evening in Bombay, I went to see Shashi Kapoor, a member of Bollywood's first film dynasty and one of the few Indian actors known internationally, primarily for his roles in such films as *Shakespeare Wallah, Heat and Dust*, and *My Beautiful Laundrette*. Unhappy with his work in Bollywood—there was no film of his, he said, he felt proud of—Kapoor had set up his own production company in the 1970s and made a series of much-admired films, including the award-winning *36 Chowringhee Lane*. But the "financial news" remained bad—there were no audiences for the films in India—and, in the early nineties, Kapoor had found himself in the courts with his creditors. He said, "The same people who used to call me the Messiah of Good Films sued me for very small amounts."

"Shashi," Mahesh had told me, "has seen the dark side of the industry." But Shashi appeared content to be out of the business. "I was a failure; I knew I couldn't make money, and I decided to leave. I am sixty-six years old. I have had a good life. Why complain?"

The younger filmmakers trying to work their way out of the mainstream didn't, and perhaps couldn't, share Kapoor's equanimity. Aditya Bhattacharya, the grandson of Bimal Roy, the greatest filmmaker of Bollywood's golden era, had recently returned to India after several years in Italy, attracted by the news that things were changing in Bollywood. He had then discovered that they were not changing fast enough for him. Some weeks before we met in the new Taj hotel in the suburb of Bandra he had published a letter in *Midday* to the creator of *Boom*, the biggest flop of the season. "What happened to the story, bro?" he had written. "Things like script, editing, storytelling, the movie? What was this magnum-pocus about? What exactly did you want to share?"

When I saw Aditya, he was full of rage at the people who had financed the film. "This clever boy arrives in Bombay," he said, "talking of what he had done in London and New York. They give him seventeen crores [two and one-half million pounds] to play with; he signs up Amitabh Bachchan and other big stars and then produces a turkey.

"I saw the script. It had disaster written all over it. But people here didn't have a clue. Most actors and actresses don't know how to assess a script. They are happier if someone narrates them the story. No wonder, they still don't work with scripts and improvise the dialogue on the sets."

We left the hotel and walked down the promenade beside the sea. It was very late, but a few families still lingered around the peanut and popcorn stalls. Aditya pointed out to me the bungalows of Bollywood's famous stars. He then suddenly began to denounce them.

They did nothing, he said, when their own city burned during the anti-Muslim pogroms in 1993 and instead prostrated themselves before Bal Thackeray, the chief of the Shiv Sena, the Hindu extremist organization, which then ran the city's government. He spoke of the stars' close friendship with the mafia and their hypocritical refusal to support Bharat Shah, a popular financier arrested for his alleged links to the mafia. Bollywood celebrities, he said, still lined up to appease Bal Thackeray, whose daughter-in-law had become a powerful fixer in the industry.

"No one," Aditya said, "should be fooled by the success of films like *KHNH*. It is like the big party the feudal landlord throws before he goes bankrupt. People might make a little money by promoting the regressive values of these confused Indians living abroad. They are like salesmen who have persuaded people to buy a defective lighter. But sooner or later people are going to realize that the lighter doesn't work, and they need a better one."

Aditya went on to describe the growing financial nexus between politicians, film stars, and the mafia. He spoke of the illegal and illogical ways in which films were financed. There were probably personal reasons for his bitterness; he had financed his own new film with difficulty. But I saw little reason to dispute his account.

In London, I had gone to see *KHNH* with Sally Potter, a British filmmaker known for her experimental style. She gasped when after two very long hours the intermission sign came up. But she appeared to be enjoying the film, especially the songs, which effortlessly appropriated and mixed the rhythms of disco, rap, and gospel. When I saw her a few days later, she said that she wanted to explore the musical form in her next project. It was capable of speaking a universal emotional language that was no longer possible for cinema in its more rational European or American forms.

This seems right, and probably explains why Bollywood films managed to reach a very large and diverse audience in the third world. With their songs and dances and their unabashed love of glamour and escapism, they offer to Western audiences what Hollywood films have rarely attempted since the end of the 1950s and the beginning of the counterculture. Their formulaic plots seem refreshingly artless to people who have grown weary of the irony, cynicism, and pessimism of European and American films. This partly explains the success in Britain and America of the musical *Bombay Dreams* and, to a lesser extent, the Bollywood-influenced *Moulin Rouge*.

But—and I didn't tell Sally Potter this—*KHNH* baffled me. For a *hat ke* film, it barely acknowledged the peculiar dilemmas of people living between cultures, a theme that gives much literary fiction about Indian-Americans its emotional richness. And *KHNH* was, as I discovered, typical of many new Bollywood films set abroad or in a purely notional India. Their character seems to be fazed by neither Indian tradition nor Western modernity, neither home nor abroad. In *KKHH*, a miniskirted Indian student from London breaks into a devotional song after being taunted for her lack of cultural roots by the other students at the *Archie* comics school. In *KKKG*, an Indian child manages to get all the white British people present at her school in Hampstead to sing the Indian national anthem.

These films seem to me to use a different idiom from the one that once gave Bollywood a devoted following in underdeveloped countries. It was in Bombay that I began to understand something of their emotional language. I began to see that they were rooted in something after all and that their amiable visions of a world that existed for Indians to painlessly inhabit, and perhaps, dominate, had a potentially vast audience.

"I write out of my experience," Karan Johar had told me. This experience seemed limited; like many young *hat ke* filmmakers, Johar was, I discovered, the son of a rich producer. But it was more widely shared than I had imagined.

After ten years of economic liberalization, a small but growing number of Indians live as well as middle-class Europeans and Americans. During this time, many Indians in Britain and America have begun to see their ancestral country as an investment opportunity and a cultural resource. These rich but insecure Indians have bankrolled generously the Hindu nationalists' rise to power and now support the assertion of Indian military and economic power. They also form the newest and most lucrative market for Bollywood films.

"India is shining," the Hindu nationalist government claimed in a series of poster and newspaper advertisements in late 2003. The prime minister and his deputy repeatedly cited the growing prominence of Indians around the world and asserted that twenty-first century was going to be the "Indian Century." Many of the new Bollywood films increasingly came out of, and stroked, the same Indian fantasy of wealth, political power, and cultural confidence.

The fantasy isn't without basis. The gap between the two hundred million–strong middle class and the other eight hundred million Indians has widened, but the consumer economy has grown steadily, along with India's foreign exchange reserves. And so in Bombay, the stylish hoardings for *KHNH*, the baby-faced actors on it dressed as if for a wedding, seemed rightly indistinguishable from the "India Shining" ads— the government's pictures of happy-looking Hindus, Muslims, and Sikhs—as well as the giant posters of Amitabh Bachchan and other Bollywood superstars cheerfully promoting Swedish cell phones, Swiss watches, and American colas.

Film posters in my childhood hadn't been so slick. Nor were the government's ads for family planning, *Hum Do, Hamare Do* ("Two of Us, Two We Have"). The austere culture of underdevelopment those badly painted images spoke of now exists out of sight, in the villages and towns, where the country's poor majority still live or in the slums, almost entirely concealed by giant hoardings along many Bombay streets.

Cable television channels as well as the new pages in the English-language newspapers report on fashion designers, models, former and current Miss Worlds, theme parties, new clubs, and champagne-tasting sessions. They appear to take their cues from upper-middle-class Indians wishing to, as the Hindu nationalists claimed, "feel good." And Bollywood films set in the West or a Westernized, unrecognizable India seem to have become yet another echo chamber of upwardly mobile Indians.

In Bombay, I often found myself gazing at the many pictures of Bachchan in a gray beard and smart Western suit looming over the stagnant traffic. The angry young man of the seventies seemed as iconic as ever in the ad where he said, with a reassuring smile, "Don't worry, be happy."

Mahesh told me, "People attribute greatness to Bachchan. They have a statue of him at Madame Tussaud's. But I find him an empty figure. There is not much there. Many people feel this. But no one wants to say this in public. It is part of what our culture has become."

He added, "We are lying to ourselves all the time."

This was what he had written about in *The Times of India* that morning. His friend Vijay Anand, who made many of the acclaimed films of the sixties, had died the previous day. Mahesh wrote that he had been "revolted" to see the news of a distinguished filmmaker's death conveyed by ticker at the bottom of the screen on television while a reporter breathlessly described how the crockery for a leading actress's wedding was being imported all the way from Paris. He had accused the media of "trying to create a world in which we hope to eliminate life's most unbearable features and replace them with those which conform with our own wishes."

I had grown used to these pronouncements from Mahesh. They appeared in *The Times of India* on an almost daily basis, usually sharing the page with reports of opulent weddings and wild parties. I often agreed with them. But their frequency and intensity made me wonder.

I met many people in Bollywood who doubted Mahesh's intentions and described him as a publicity seeker. He also had many admirers. The actors he has worked with spoke well of him. Tishu had said, "That man has talent. He is connected with an emotional reality outside Bombay. This is rare in a place where people lose sense of who they are and what they can do after just a little bit of success. That is why these people from small towns flock to him."

I still wasn't sure. Had Mahesh been sincere when he told Pritam that he would like to try him out? At his office, Pritam still tried to catch my eye anytime my car passed him. Mohammed asked me almost continuously if anything had happened. When I asked Mahesh, he said that he was waiting for his brother's next film to move ahead.

I have never identified with Bollywood," Mahesh had told me. And now he was, he claimed, looking at life beyond it. He couldn't see himself in politics, which had turned into a circus; he mocked the reports and photographs in the newspaper of film stars joining the BJP or Congress. He said, "But I do want to speak for the Muslims in this country. Two thousand Muslims were killed in Bombay in 1992 and '93, and now two thousand of them have been killed in Gujarat. But no one gets punished; the killers are free and flourishing. I fear we are breeding a generation of terrorists."

His meeting with Sonia Gandhi had gone well. He had spoken frankly, telling her of the desperation of Muslims in Gujarat. She had listened carefully and thanked him afterward.

There had been a moment of uncertainty when the Muslim theologians accompanying him had asked him to button up his shirt at his chest. He said he had complied, but only after some hesitation. He didn't want to defer to politicians. There were enough film people already doing that.

The day before I left Bombay, the newspapers there were full of reports of a row at an awards ceremony in Dubai, one of Bollywood's versions of the Oscars, between the reigning superstar, Shah Rukh Khan, and Amar Singh, the powerful politician accompanying Amitabh Bachchan. Apparently, Singh had shouted at the businessmen organizers of the event after discovering that they had placed Bachchan and him in the eleventh row. It was an insult, he said, to the great artist who ought to have been in the front row. Shah Rukh Khan had intervened on the organizers' behalf, and there had been enough angry words for journalists to feast on.

Asked to comment by *The Times of India*, Mahesh attacked Amar

Singh. "When will our power-drunk politicians realize that with power comes responsibility?" he wrote. "What was the need to use brute force in a matter as trivial as seat arrangement?" He also criticized Bachchan: "No one in the world can insult you without your permission."

Two days later I was in the Simla hills, preparing to leave for London, when Mahesh rang me from Lucknow. "You missed the excitement," he said. "My piece created an uproar. I have just had the wife of a senior police officer on the phone. She told me that I should get out of Lucknow. It is Amar Singh's territory, and he was out to get me."

Mahesh said, "I am staying where I am. I am not scared of Amar Singh."

Apparently, the businessman organizer who had stood up to Amar Singh had lost a contract worth twelve million pounds in India. Feeling himself under intense pressure, Shah Rukh Khan had apologized to Singh. But his pride had been hurt, and he was reconsidering his position. He had sent a text message to Mahesh, saluting his courage and honesty.

Mahesh said, "Such is the inner rot of Bollywood."

In London, I read of a dispute between Mahesh and Mallika. The latter had not only refused to do a nude scene in *Murder* but had also rejected the option of a body double. Mahesh had been quoted as saying, "My only grouse is that she agreed to the nude scene in the first place. She remains a small town girl with a conservative heart. What is the point of pretending otherwise?"

But when I rang Mallika from London, two day before *Murder* was due to be released, she had forgotten about the nude scene. She had apparently forgotten too her wish to work abroad.

She said she was flooded with new offers. "The initial reports of *Murder* are just great," she told me. "The distributors are over the moon. The producer is receiving 'overflow checks . . .' "

"What are those?" I asked.

"I don't know. Probably, something good. But you must be here to see it. The movie has created a big hoopla, you know. It is everywhere; the promos were a sensation; the TV channels, the press, everyone is talking about it . . ."

She faltered briefly when I asked why this was so. "Oh, you know . . ." she began. "It is probably because of the skin show, the promos, lots of hot shots, bold scenes, adultery . . .

"But you know," she added, "there is so much more to the film. Lots of women trapped in loveless marriages will identify with my character.

"Anyway, it is a great feeling to have the film rising from my shoulders," she said. "You know, I am much sought after. Interview after interview. The BBC just called from London. By the way, can you get a magazine called *Man's World* in London? I am on the cover. They say I have 'the hottest body on the planet.' "

She gave a short, nervous laugh. "They can't think beyond this, but I guess it is their problem, not mine."

Murder opened on April 2. In his review for *Midday*, Khalid denounced the film for its "voyeuristic flashes of semi-nudity and obscenity," mocked Mallika for her "motor mouth and cheesy posters," and accused Mahesh of hypocrisy. But the opening box-office collections were as good as Mallika had predicted, and within days, *Murder* had become the first successful Bollywood film of 2004.

In London I read a report about Mahesh and Mallika's visiting a Delhi cinema where *Murder* was being shown. "I come here to titillate you," Mahesh was quoted as telling a rapturous audience. Mallika told a journalist that her father wasn't happy with the film and her mother couldn't get a ticket. She blew kisses at the audience and said, "I have worked like a Viagra when the market was so down." The report said Mahesh and Mallika were planning to work together on another film.

On my last day in Bombay, I had seen Pritam standing in the small crowd outside Mahesh's office. In early April, I called Mohammed from London and asked him to find out what, if anything, had happened. Mohammed reported that Pritam was still where I had last seen him. He had hoped to get his break in May, when work began on Mahesh's brother's next film, but he was less sure now. I wondered if I should ring Mahesh. And then I thought that he had been right all along: I thought that Pritam should go home.

PART TWO

PART TWO

KASHMIR

The Cost of Nationalism

1. The Killings in Chitisinghpura

On the evening of March 20, 2000, Nanak Singh was chatting with some friends and relatives near his house in Chitisinghpura, a remote Sikh-dominated village in the Himalayan valley of Kashmir. Most of the locals were hung over, having spent the previous days celebrating Holi, the Hindu festival of color, which the Sikhs also observe. Singh, who works for the animal husbandry department of the India-backed government in Kashmir, wasn't particularly suspicious when about seventeen armed men in combat fatigues showed up and ordered the men out of their houses, telling them to stand before the *gurdwara* (the Sikh prayer site), with their identity cards.

Singh assumed, like many other Sikhs, that the men were from the army; people in villages all across the valley were accustomed to being searched and interrogated by Indian security forces. The four million Muslims of Kashmir live precariously between the eternally warring countries of India and Pakistan. Nanak Singh, however, is, along with most other residents of Chitisinghpura, a Sikh, and thus a tiny minority of Sikhs in Kashmir, just over 2 percent of the population, have enjoyed a tentative immunity throughout the ten years of violence, an immunity that neither the local Hindus, most of whom have migrated to India, nor the Muslims, always suspect in the eyes of Indian security forces, have had. If you were a Sikh and worked for the government, as many of the Sikhs in Chitisinghpura did, such checking was a formality. Nevertheless, there were a few Sikhs who had premonitions and hid themselves in their houses.

It was dark, and Singh couldn't really see the faces of the men, although they spoke both Punjabi and Urdu, the languages of North India and Pakistan, as they used flashlights to check the identity cards of the nineteen Sikhs standing and squatting before the walls of the *gurdwara*.

The checking done, the soldiers stepped back a few inches from the lineup. A moment passed; there was a single shot, and suddenly they raised their guns—AK-56s or AK-47s—and began firing blindly at the Sikhs.

Singh felt the entire row of Sikhs crumple with brief cries of pain and fell immediately to the muddy ground himself, dragged down by the weight of the dying man beside him. He assumed that he had been hit and found it strange that he felt no pain. In fact, by collapsing so early to the ground, he had missed a bullet.

Half buried by a bloodied corpse, Singh heard the armed men move away with quick steps to the other side of the village. Minutes later he heard more gunfire.

Soon after that the men were back; they seemed to be in a hurry. Singh heard their leader instruct the men to quickly put a bullet into each of the nineteen Sikhs lying there, all of whom except for him, Singh believed, were already dead.

Not daring to breathe, Singh dimly perceived a tall figure loom over him in the dark and raise his gun. He heard the shot; he felt the bullet penetrate his left thigh, felt the first warm sensation of pain, and then the man moved away.

As it turned out, Nanak Singh's luck lasted; he is the only survivor of the village massacre in which thirty-five Sikhs died.

Since 1990 thousands of Muslim guerrillas have been waging a war against the Indian presence in Kashmir, a war in which more than fifty thousand people—civilians, guerrillas, Indian soldiers, and policemen—have died, a war that came after four decades of Kashmiri resentment of Indian rule. The guerrillas are supported by Islamic fundamentalists in Pakistan, who wish to see Kashmir incorporated into the latter as part of a larger Islamized state. Pakistan, which was carved out of Hindu-majority India during the violent and confused partition of 1947 as a separate homeland for Indian Muslims, has never stopped claiming the Muslim-dominated valley for itself. India has fought two wars over Kashmir with Pakistan, in 1948 and 1965, and came very close to a nuclear war in both 1990 and 2002. The Indian government sees the Pakistani support of the guerrillas as a "proxy war" and has deployed up to half a million soldiers to suppress the insurgency.

But the Sikhs have remained neutral, and over the last ten years guerrillas as well as soldiers from the Indian Army camps frequently visited Chitisinghpura, their usual aggressiveness and tension defused by the isolation and serenity of the pastoral setting—the houses with thatch and corrugated iron roofs and vegetable gardens and the brisk stream and the melancholy willows and the forest of chenar, walnut, and almond, and the high mountains looming above the village—which even today make the great turmoil of the valley seem far away. The guerrillas, some of whom were from Pakistan and Afghanistan, used to play cricket with the children; they often asked for wheat and rice (Chitisinghpura is relatively prosperous, with revenues from apple and rice farms and transport businesses). The Indian Army, which routinely patrolled the village, knew about the guerrillas' visits from some of the concerned villagers but was strangely indifferent.

On the evening of the massacre of the Sikhs, a patrol party from Rashtriya Rifles (one of the Indian Army's units in Kashmir) was less than a mile away from the village; the men heard the gunshots but, for reasons still unclear, did not bother investigating. Forty-five minutes after the sound of gunfire had stopped, the first Sikh ventured out of his house and found the corpses of his friends and relatives. Then came a terrifying five-mile walk through pitch-black darkness to reach the closest police station; given the circumstances, the Sikhs thought it safer to not seek help from the army camp although it was much closer to the village. The police arrived seven hours after the killings.

I heard the news from Abbas early next morning. He is a Muslim, the Srinagar correspondent of an Indian newspaper. The dignity and solidity of his bearing—the tall, well-built frame, the elegantly cut Kashmiri jackets he wears—made him reassuring to be with in the city where everyone—the tense crowds in the streets, the jumpy soldiers in their bunkers, and the passionate Muslims speaking of the atrocities of Indian rule in bare dark rooms—seemed on edge. A mutual acquaintance had asked Abbas to help me out during my stay in Srinagar, and he had done so dutifully, but not without a certain wariness that I put down to some slight resentment; I wasn't the first or last of the inexperienced, and possibly biased, journalists from India he had been asked to assist.

His voice on the phone was calm. In the days I had spent in Srinagar, relatively and unsettlingly quiet days, the news of sporadic custodial killings, land mine blasts, and gun battles between Indian security forces and guerrillas coming in from other places in the valley, I had often heard him say, "If you live here, you have to be prepared for anything. Anything can happen anytime in Kashmir." His words with their tinge of melodrama had made me wonder if he saw a certain glamour in his job, the dangerous nature of the world he worked and lived in, like the reticent taxi driver, quick to point me toward the vegetable market where seventeen Muslim civilians had been blown to bits by a bomb explosion a few days before in one of the random incidents of violence in the valley.

But now something even bigger had happened, and Abbas was as serene as always. He had no details yet, but he thought we should leave immediately for the village. When he arrived a half hour later at my hotel with two other Kashmiri journalists, his mood was light. The atmosphere inside the battered Ambassador was already one of good-humored banter, and the jokes and repartee in Kashmiri, which I couldn't follow, got louder after each encounter with the frankly contemptuous Indian soldiers at roadblocks, who poked AK-56 muzzles through hastily rolled-down windows, demanded identity cards, and wanted to know where we were going and why.

In villages alongside the road men in blue and black cloaklike pherans stood in worried little circles and glanced nervously, out of the corners of their eyes, at the cars racing past. In the rice and saffron fields, stubbly and glittering with frost, soldiers stood with their backs to the road, light machine guns slung over their shoulders. Outlined against the blue, misty mountains in the distance, they were like hunters from a nineteenth-century sketch.

At the village itself, where there was nothing they could do, they looked more casual, the elite commandos almost dandyish in their black headdresses and bulletproof overalls, sheepishly standing where a group of angry Sikhs had barred their way to the village. There were tiny shards of glass on the ground; some car windows had already been smashed by the Sikhs, and a photographer roughed up, his camera lens broken. The soldiers had watched it all and done nothing; they now quietly watched the Sikhs rage at senior officers from the army and police who had begun to arrive, their cars disgorging more and more men in fatigues.

The Sikhs were mostly survivors from the night before, mostly middle-aged men, who had stayed in their homes when the armed men came. Others were from nearby villages who had been in Chitisinghpura since dawn. But many of the Sikhs standing before the policemen now had already assumed that the killers were Muslim guerrillas. They were shouting, beating their chests, feeding upon each other's energy. The army and police officers heard them expressionlessly. "Give us guns, and then we'll deal with these Muslims," one man with a long gray beard kept shouting. "They know what we did with them in 1947. We are not cowards like the Kashmiri Hindus! Do they think they can throw us out of Kashmir? We'll show them!" and then, spittle growing at the corner of his mouth, he added, "This is a country we have ruled." The historical reference—to the early nineteenth century, when Sikh governors sent out by the king of Punjab had ravaged the valley and tormented the Muslims—made the Kashmiri Muslim policeman before him flinch.

More journalists and government people arrived. The Sikhs wouldn't let anyone past and continued to curse and lament. Behind them, a frightful clamor, like that of a thousand crows, arose from the top of the hill where the bigger *gurdwara* was situated. It was the sound of the weeping and wailing women, and it seemed to bewilder the roosters in the village, which were to go on dementedly for several hours after dawn, their exultant cries hanging discordantly above the village amid the grief and despair of the women.

Throughout the long drive to the village, I had been dreading the moment when I would encounter the dead men, but when I entered the courtyard of the *gurdwara* where the bodies had been placed on the ground, my first impression, after the early-morning mistiness of the

Kashmir valley, the mud-colored villages and pheran-draped men, was incongruously of color, the reds and yellows and purples of turbans and scarves and shawls and blankets. There was a crush of people inside the courtyard, Sikh men and women everywhere shouting, gesticulating, crying, wailing. I had been standing for some time, unable to move or speak, when I felt a hand on my shoulder. It was a boy, not more than ten years old, his hazel eyes under the crimson headcloth full of curiosity. "Are from the media?" he asked, and when I nodded, he said, "They shot a sixteen-year-old boy." He pointed toward one of the bodies. I hadn't wanted to look at any of the faces of the dead men; his words jolted me into doing so. The face had gone white, the flesh tight on the bones, and skull-like hollows had begun to deepen on his cheeks and around his eyes. His middle-aged mother sat beside him, a jade green shawl draped around her head; she would have been grieving all night, and in between lifting her arms and beating her chest, the tears running down her face in an unbroken stream, she forced out a tiny yawn.

Photographers and TV cameramen were already climbing the trees and the walls of the courtyard for a better view. I saw relatives gathered around a young girl in a red long skirt, talking to her in loud voices, shaking her shoulders, pointing to the dead father lying before her, but the stony expression on her face did not break, the eyes remained glassy, she hadn't cried at all, someone standing behind me said, and she needed to if she wasn't to go insane with grief.

When I walked over to the other side of the village, where another sixteen men had been similarly lined up and fired upon at close range, the bodies were still being transported to the *gurdwara* in improvised stretchers. There was a delay when a young widow sitting on the muddy ground would not let go of her dead husband. She clasped his head tightly in her lap until relatives prized her hands away and held her arms. Struggling to break free, she screamed as the men quickly carted away the corpse. Her stringy hair was loose, her pale wrists streaked with blood where the glass of her shattered bangles had bitten into her flesh, and her screams were loud in this densely forested side of the village, the ground covered with straw and houses roofed with thatch; the big turbaned men collecting the corpses and the overwrought widow seemed to belong to a scene of medieval cruelty.

———

I spoke to a few elderly Sikhs standing near a tea shack. Some of them were away when the killers arrived, others had stayed put in their homes, and after the first few awful hours of confronting what had happened their emotions had been dulled. They didn't want to speculate about the identity of the killers. They kept saying, "It was too dark; you couldn't see anyone." I noticed a wariness; their response to the journalists present seemed to suggest what I had heard before from other unprotected people in India: "You'll come and go, but we have to live here, with the consequences of what we say to you."

But there were some Sikhs who seemed convinced that the Muslim guerrillas were the killers, and they were the most aggressive and outspoken, raising slogans against Pakistan and Muslims, vowing revenge ("Blood for Blood"). They surrounded the very senior bureaucrats as they arrived at the courtyard and demanded arms to protect themselves against the Muslims. In one of the groups under attack I recognized the inspector general of police, a Kashmiri Hindu; just a few days earlier, I had seen him in his overheated walnut-paneled office, boasting on the telephone about the number of guerrillas killed that day. He looked anxious and lonely now, as the Sikhs confronted him.

They were especially rough with the commissioner of Srinagar, one of the few Kashmiri Muslim officers of the Indian Administrative Service in the valley; he was shouted down as he tried to speak. It was a senior Hindu army officer who saved him from unceremonious expulsion from the village—and a previous high-level Muslim visitor had indeed been thrown out—by joining the Sikhs in their slogan shouting, slogans that asserted the military traditions of the Sikh faith, that came from the time of the persecution of the Sikhs and Hindus at the hands of Muslim invaders and conquerors.

The Sikhs appeared to demand a swift and brutal response. And so when the crowd of villagers, growing in numbers as the news spread across the valley, each new arrival bringing his own outrage, abused and drove out the first VIP, a senior state minister, stoned his car, shattered his windshield; when his bodyguards let loose a few rounds into the air from their AK-47s and there was temporary panic because some people thought that the guerrillas had attacked; when men began sprinting all across the forest outside the village, and the commandos threw themselves on the damp ground and prepared to shoot, the little commotion assuaged the growing need for drama, and suddenly there was relief all around, and the commandos appeared less dandyish and more sheepish when they got up with muddy stains on their bulletproof overalls.

But something suspect lay in that need for drama, which, in the few hours it took to broadcast the TV images of the widows, was to be amplified all across India. There had been a small war in Kashmir in the summer of 1999, when Pakistan-backed infiltrators, many of them regular Pakistan Army recruits, occupied high mountain positions past the border. Hundreds of Indian soldiers had died while trying to dislodge them, and the media, slicker but also much more coarse after ten years of economic liberalization, had brought about a general intoxication with war in millions of middle-class Indian homes. Opinion polls in English-language newspapers had shown much of the middle class demanding an all-out invasion of Pakistan; letters in the popular press had even called for a nuclear bombardment of Pakistan. The media themselves had joined in the frenzy, young awkwardly helmeted reporters shouting into microphones over the noise of artillery fire, "You have got to be here to know what it is like."

And that need for drama, for swift, brutal responses to brutality, wasn't going to be appeased by Bill Clinton's condemnation of the massacre. When I left the village and returned to Srinagar later that day, the groups of worried Muslims I had passed in the morning had been broken up. They were already in roped-off enclosures, squatting on the ground while soldiers searched their houses. Buses were being stopped, their passengers lined up and interrogated by the side of the road; a multitude of localized crackdowns was taking place in the region.

Retribution was the theme of the slogans the Sikhs had shouted. It was what motivated the policemen, and the great need for some kind of retaliation would partly shape the events of the next few days.

It had begun that very morning, even as I stood there among the corpses and the wailing women. A minute's walk from the *gurdwara*, away from the Sikh-dominated part of the village, an official from the Special Operations Group (this is one of the draconian Indian security agencies set up to suppress the insurgency, and it is dominated by Sikhs) had arrived at the house of Sonaullah Wagay, one of the few Muslims living in Chitisinghpura.

Wagay is less well off than the Sikhs; he is a peasant who makes some money on the side by selling milk from his cow, and he would have been bemused when the Hindu subinspector, arriving in a Jeep and abruptly barging in, told him that the police were looking to recruit some local young men. Wagay told him that his youngest son is—strangely for a Kashmiri Muslim—a soldier in the Indian Army, but that the eldest one is deranged, and the middle one, Mohammed Yaqub Wagay, has been unemployed since finishing school and spends his time leading the prayers at the local mosque—he was being considered as an imam—and playing cricket with the children in the village.

It was Yaqub who had tried to prevent Wagay from rushing to the Sikh side of the village after the killings. Yaqub had returned from his evening prayers and was sitting on the timber logs outside the house, chatting with four friends, including a Sikh, when they heard the rattle of automatic guns. All five immediately ran to their homes and locked themselves in.

When they mustered up the courage to emerge some time later, they were warned by Sikh neighbors returning from the sites that they might be attacked by angry Sikhs and that it might be better to stay inside their homes, and that's where Wagay and his sons spent the long, tense night, until the arrival of the police in the morning.

After the first confusing lie about recruiting local youth into the police, the SOG subinspector didn't waste time in getting down to business. He asked for the middle son, Yaqub Wagay. When the diminutive and very frightened Yaqub arrived, the subinspector gently caught hold of his arm and then ushered him toward the waiting Jeep. "Don't make a noise," he told Yaqub's maternal uncle, a retired soldier. "We have to talk to him." And then he was off.

"We have to talk to him": That line has been heard in thousands of Muslim homes in the past decade. Young men suspected of being guerrillas have been taken away by Indian security men and returned if not as corpses, then badly mutilated, the torture marks still visible in places where hot iron rods have been applied. The chances of a man's returning unviolated from interrogation and third-degree torture were greater if you knew someone in the civil administration or the many Indian military organizations. But you had to get in your application very fast, and Wagay, though relatively well connected, was under no illusions about what could happen to his son. He simply ran from his house, past the rice fields, the minesweepers in the rice fields "sanitizing" the road for the VIPs descending upon the Sikh village, past the carloads of Sikhs and journalists and army officers hurtling down the broken dusty road, to the police station in the nearby town of Mattan.

There he pleaded that his son had nothing to do with the guerrillas and that the Muslim families living in the region had a very good record; none of the young men had ever gone to Pakistan or Afghanistan for training in light weapons, none of them were jihadis, and indeed several of them like his son, and Yaqub's maternal uncle, had been in the Indian Army. The police, some of whose members were Kashmiri Muslims and sympathetic to Wagay, registered his FIR (first information report), but there was little else they could do; they had no influence over the Special Operations Group, which had its own murky ways of functioning. All Wagay could do was hope for the best.

Two days later I was watching the premier Indian TV news channel at my hotel in Srinagar, the capital of India-ruled Kashmir. I had been thinking about the killings in Chitisinghpura. The question of why the guerrillas would kill Sikhs, who had never previously been targeted, and then invite international censure kept troubling me. But the news on TV didn't seem to offer any answers. It was full of Bill Clinton's state visit to India—the first by an American president in more than two decades—which had begun hours after the killings in Chitisinghpura; his condemnation of the massacre and well-planned tributes to Indian democracy had been met with great enthusiasm and gratitude among the up-and-coming middle class, which, like many third world middle classes, is fiercely nationalistic but at the same time craves approval from the West.

The killings of the Sikhs overshadowed everything Clinton said about Kashmir and Pakistan. Interestingly, the correspondents of the two major TV channels from New Delhi had arrived a day before the massacre in Kashmir in expectation of a major incident. But it was the potential shifts in the American position on Kashmir that occupied the media; the mysterious circumstances of the killings were hardly mentioned. There appeared to be little mystery at all: India's national security adviser had already blamed the massacre on Hizbul Mujahideen and Lashkar-e-Toiba, the two major Pakistan-based guerrilla outfits. L. K. Advani, the Indian home minister and a hard-line member of the BJP government in Delhi, had spoken of a deliberate policy of "ethnic cleansing" pursued by Muslim guerrillas, and that had more or less settled the matter. No one took any notice of the strident denials from Pakistan-based guerrilla organizations that are normally very eager to claim credit for any spectacular act of violence in the valley.

Clinton was traveling to Pakistan after his stay in India, and Indian pundits on television speculated endlessly about whether he would come down hard on Pakistan's new military ruler for his country's support of the Muslim guerrillas in Kashmir and whether the State Department would be repulsed enough by the killings into declaring Pakistan a "terrorist state." But the Americans themselves seemed to have some doubts: journalists from *The Washington Post* and *The New York Times* among other major American media covering Clinton's visit, had been skeptical of the Indian version. There seemed little reason for the guerrillas to kill Sikhs just before Clinton's visit, an act that would inevitably lead to international outrage and thus discredit their cause.

It was what intrigued me about Chitisinghpura, and so when the "Breaking News" caption appeared on the edge of the screen, and the home secretary himself appeared to make a statement about the Sikh killings, I was both surprised and curious. Clinton was still in India at that time, and the home secretary had some of the breathless eagerness of the Indian reporters covering the president's visit. The Indian security forces, he announced in a jubilant tone, had made a "major breakthrough." They had arrested a native of Chitisinghpura village called Yaqub Wagay, who had provided valuable information about the Muslim guerrillas responsible for the killings, and "follow-up action" was expected at any time.

It was around this time, two days after the killings, that Muslim men started disappearing from the villages around Chitisinghpura. At least three of the disappearances followed the same pattern: A red Maruti van with civilian number plates arrived in a village, and armed men suddenly emerged from it to grab an individual, usually tall and well built.

The small, cramped van was used to abduct Bashir Ahmed and his friend Mohammed Yusuf Malik, sheep and cattle traders in a village called Hallan. The same red Maruti was spotted waiting on the lonely willow-lined stretch of road outside the walled compound of Zahoor Ahmad Dalal's house in a suburb of Anantnag, the second-largest town in the valley, minutes before Dalal stepped out to go to the mosque for evening prayers on March 24.

Dalal, twenty-nine years old, slightly plump with flushed red cheeks, had done very well with the small cloth-retailing shop he suddenly inherited when his father died on a pilgrimage to Mecca in 1984. Business hadn't been easy in the last ten years of endless curfews and regular strikes, but Dalal had not only survived but actually flourished. Inside his large compound, he had built several warehouses, planted rosebushes, dug a fishpond, and very recently built a new house adjacent to the old one where his widowed mother lived. His sister's marriage—always an onerous task in subcontinental families—was happily arranged in Anantnag. He regularly made the long journey to Delhi to order fresh stock; his warm, ebullient manner had earned him many friends in the valley, including the Indian paramilitary men who sat in the bunker near his house.

The visit to the mosque was part of a routine, and he dressed casually for it: nylon slippers and track suit bottoms under a checked shirt and maroon wool jumper. When he didn't return home that evening in time for dinner, his mother and uncle thought that he might have gone to visit one of his many friends in the area.

They began to worry later that evening, after the friends and relatives they contacted said they hadn't seen Dalal. On the morning of March 25 Dalal's uncle, Nissar, went to the local police station. The inspector there suggested that they might want to wait before registering a first information report. Anantnag is the stronghold of "renegade militants" called Ikhwanis, former guerrillas who after being captured or surrendering worked for the Indian Army and who often kidnapped and killed for money. It was likely that they had seen the affluent and unprotected Dalal as a good source of easy money. The police inspector was being pragmatic; why register an FIR and endanger Dalal's life when fifty thousand rupees as ransom might bring him back unharmed?

Dalal's uncle heeded the advice and immediately went to the headquarters of the Ikhwanis, a minifortress in the heart of the old town, and then to the headquarters of the Special Task Force, an Indian antiinsurgency organization that was known to hire the "renegade militants." No one at these places had either seen or heard of Dalal. At the police headquarters, the superintendent of police, a reputedly ruthless man named Khan, was not present. His superior officer told Dalal's uncle that if the Indian Army had kidnapped his nephew, there was nothing anyone could do and sent him away. At five o'clock in the evening, Nissar returned to the police headquarters and was informed that the superintendent was busy, along with units from the Special Task Force and the SOG, busy supervising an "encounter" with guerrillas in a village called Panchalthan, thirty kilometers from Anantnag, and that there might be some news of Dalal's whereabouts when they returned.

The morning of March 26 brought the news of the deaths of five of the seventeen men allegedly responsible for the Sikh killings. I saw the news in curfew-bound Jammu, where angry Sikhs had been rioting for three days. For a brief moment Chitisinghpura was back on the front pages of the Indian papers. There had been a four-hour-long "encounter" between the guerrillas and the police and army in Panchalthan on the early morning of March 25, a few hours after the disappearance of Dalal. The army spokesman said that all five men were "foreign mercenaries," belonging to Pakistan-based Islamic terrorist outfits; the most important piece of evidence they presented was the army fatigues the five men were dressed in, the uniform the original killers of the Sikhs had been wearing. The police issued a separate statement in which Yaqub Wagay was mentioned as having provided the information that led the police and the army to the hideout of the mercenaries, a hutlike shelter for shepherds on top of a steep hill that had been shelled with mortars during the encounter. Later in the evening the police released three black-and-white photographs of three of the five dead men. The bodies were "roasted and disfigured beyond recognition," reported *The Kashmir Times*, but the army fatigues were unmistakable, looking almost brand-new.

Dalal's uncle met Khan and the men from the Special Task Force when they returned from Panchalthan. They hadn't seen Dalal. By now Nissar was beginning to panic; on the previous day he had heard about the disappearance of Ahmed and Malik, the sheep and cattle traders from Hallan, a little before the time Dalal left his house to go to the mosque, and he had heard about the red Maruti van.

Two days later he ran into a group of Gujars from the villages around Anantnag. Two of their friends, both called Juma Khan, had gone missing. The Gujars weren't involved in any guerrilla activity but still faced much harassment by Indian security men since their long beards, hooked noses, and tall frames made them look like Afghans. They told Nissar that they had gone in a procession to the government's local headquarters in Anantnag to lodge a complaint about the missing men they suspected had been abducted by the police or SOG.

Before the day was through, and purely by chance again, Dalal's uncle encountered another Gujar, this time from Panchalthan; he had a disturbing story to tell about the "encounter" that had kept Khan, the notorious police officer, from his desk for so long the previous day.

Panchalthan lies at the base of the thick hilly forests that line the valley of Kashmir on its southeastern side. Some miles south is the region of Doda, where some of the most vicious battles between the guerrillas and Indian Army have been fought. Hardly a day goes by without either of the two combatants lapsing into massacres or rape or arson or torture, and the knowledge weighs heavily on those traveling through the heavily militarized and isolated area around Panchalthan.

The road is unpaved, and its perennially dug-up appearance made me worry about the possibility of land mines placed by guerrillas to ambush the military convoys that regularly make their way to the ordnance depot near Panchalthan. The day before I visited in late May, the ordnance depot had been attacked with rocket grenades, and the resulting tension was palpable. Women in long black veils walked quickly, as if seized by silent panic. In bazaars along the road, sullen men lurked in dark, bare shops. Tense pedestrians avoided all conversation, never forming groups, eyes always averted from the army men in the make-shift bunkers at every street crossing and bend in the road.

The closer we got to Panchalthan, farther from the nearest town, past the hostile army men at checkpoints, who pretended not to under-stand why we were going to Panchalthan and insisted on searching the car, one hand wrapped around the triggers of their guns, the greater my fear. And it was shared by the Kashmiri driver and journalist I was trav-eling with. Far too many journalists investigating strange events in remote parts of Kashmir had been killed.

But the villages along the broad valley seemed peaceful; a few hay-topped houses spread across shimmering fields, where women in color-ful head scarves sang traditional songs as they planted the paddy and then, as dusk fell, sat cross-legged upon little Kashmiri rugs to sip salty tea from samovars.

A hill, uncultivated for the most part and rising almost vertically from the base of the valley, looms over the village. On the top—known to the villagers as Zountengri ("Hilltop of the Moon")—are two wood and mud huts used as shelters by Gujar shepherds from the village. The land slopes down steeply from here to the valley; as a military position, it is close to invincible. Nevertheless, it was here, according to both the army and the police, that the five "foreign mercenaries" were trapped and killed and vast quantities of arms and ammunition discovered in an operation that lasted four hours, and from which soldiers and police emerged unscathed.

In a previous "encounter," not far from Panchalthan, the army had bullied the villagers into acting as human shields as they attacked a guerrilla hideout; in remote places on the valley, you did what the men with guns instructed. But on this more recent occasion the villagers weren't asked for their help.

In the early hours of the morning of March 25 they had been woken by the noise of gunfire. It went on for some time, and then, abruptly, there were some big bangs, mortar shelling. When the firing stopped, it was light, and some of the villagers ventured outside their homes. They saw four soldiers dragging large kerosene canisters up the hill. As the villagers watched, two of the soldiers stopped and partially emptied their canisters before trudging on.

A few minutes later the villagers saw smoke arise into the misty morning air; they heard the sound of crackling wood. Not long afterward the army men summoned the elders of the village. Although scores of men from the army and the Special Operations Group stood idly by, the commanding officer asked the villagers to remove the bodies of the "mercenaries" from the smoldering huts.

The men went in to find five completely charred and disfigured bodies dressed in army fatigues on the ground. All of the dead men looked as if they had been tall and well built, quite like the guerrillas from Afghanistan and Pakistan the villagers had seen before. They noticed that one of the bodies was headless; they saw a tree trunk and two logs of wood soaked in blood. Then, as the soldiers watched impatiently, the villagers carried out the bodies and, after the briefest of religious ceremonies, buried them in separate graves around the hill.

The Gujar shepherd from Panchalthan whom Dalal's uncle met up with was one of the men who had helped bury the bodies. And after the man finished telling his story, Dalal's uncle pulled out, very tentatively, a photo of his nephew he had been carrying everywhere with him. He asked the Gujar if any of the men he helped bury resembled the man in the picture. The Gujar stared hard at the creased photo of Dalal, and then abruptly started to weep.

A fter the army and policemen left in a convoy from Panchalthan that morning of the "encounter," the villagers returned to the huts on Zountengri and found a pit full of fast-burning clothes and shoes. They quickly put out the fire and retrieved whatever they could. It was among these scorched scraps that Dalal's relatives found the maroon jumper and checked shirt he had been wearing when he left his house for his evening *namaz* three days before.

That evening the family formally went into mourning. There was no point in investigating the identity of the killers, or the circumstances of the killing; they were only likely to bring more trouble upon themselves. Sympathetic Kashmiri Muslim officials at Anantnag provided the family with facts—the red Maruti was one of the many "seized vehicles" kept at Anantnag police station and had been signed out on March 24 for "operational purposes" by a Sikh officer of the SOG—but didn't encourage them to follow it up. Instead the family's efforts were now aimed at retrieving Dalal's body from the remote grave at Panchalthan and giving him a proper Islamic burial.

This wouldn't be accomplished for nearly two weeks, however, and would never have happened at all had the Gujars not initiated, in a bold pursuit of justice, unusual for Kashmir, yet another series of horrific events.

In the same pit of half-burned belongings, a Gujar called Rafiq, the son of one of the two missing Gujars, had discovered his father's identity card, ring, shreds of clothes, and shoes. He had been looking for his father for some days, and it was purely by chance that he thought of coming to Panchalthan. His discovery had been the first sign that the five dead men had been civilians, among the seventeen who had disappeared after the killings in Chitisinghpura.

For the next few days, the Gujars, always close-knit as a community, walked fifteen miles each day to the government's district headquarters in Anantnag to appeal for the bodies' exhumation. At first, the government officials kept stonewalling them: The relevant officer isn't present; he is very busy. But on March 31, the Gujars managed to extract an order from the chief judicial magistrate for a public exhumation of the bodies. It was a major victory. Tens of thousands of Muslims had been killed by Indian security forces in Kashmir in the previous decade, but there had rarely been a postmortem or exhumation.

That wasn't the end if it, however. The army controlled the road to Panchalthan and refused to let anyone through. The civilian administration in Anantnag, too scared to take on the army, was still waiting to know if the Gujars would be allowed to pass when the villages near Panchalthan were visited by kinds of terror, armed men from the SOG who beat up the Gujars and threatened to kill them if they went ahead with their attempts to exhume the bodies.

The Gujars, buoyed by their victory in obtaining the exhuming order, decided to protest the harassment by the SOG. They began the long walk to Anantnag on the afternoon of April 3. The procession included relatives of the two killed Gujars, Rafiq walking in the front, and other sympathetic villagers. The news of the killings in Panchalthan had gone around, as had the unexpected news of the Gujars' exhumation order, and the crowd swelled and swelled after each village.

By then numbering five thousand, the procession crossed three army checkpoints without much trouble. But at a little village called Brakpora, at a little dirt road crossing hemmed in by shacks selling grocery, men from the SOG were waiting for them.

Rafiq, the first man to establish a connection between the half-burned personal effects at Panchalthan with the five missing men, was one of the first to be shot. In the end, nine men died in the firing, so ferocious that the doctors in the local hospital removed twenty bullets from the groin of one corpse.

The unprovoked firing made the national news—in the usual vague terms: "Eight people killed in police firing"—but the army still would not allow the civilian officials to enter Panchalthan. Finally, on April 6 and 7, the bodies were exhumed and, though badly defaced, were identified by relatives of the five men. The first grave revealed a chopped-off nose and chin of a Gujar who was found buried in a separate grave. Dalal's face had been partly gouged away; he had no bullet marks on him; he may have been burned alive. The last body was headless—the head couldn't be found—but the relatives identified him by his trousers, which he still wore under the army fatigues.

The government officials at first refused to part with the bodies and then relented after demanding that the relatives perform the burials secretly that same night. The government made few other concessions to outraged public opinion. Khan, the police officer who had jointly led the operation with an army brigadier, was suspended from active duty, but he was reinstated very soon afterward and then awarded a president's medal for courage displayed in an earlier operation. Other officials were merely transferred out of Anantnag.

Accusations were formally lodged against the SOG men who had fired on the Gujar demonstrators. On April 11, the government announced a special investigation into the Panchalthan killings. But the government refused to charge anyone with murder until DNA samples taken from the dead men were matched with those of their supposed relatives.

The DNA tests seem subsequently to have been forgotten until March 2002, when *The Times of India*, India's leading newspaper, revealed their results. Apparently, the results had been officially sent to Kashmir the year before by a laboratory in Hyderabad but were suppressed by the local government because they exposed a clumsy attempt by Indian officials to fudge the samples taken from the relatives of the five murdered men.

The turnover of atrocities in Kashmir is so high, and the situation in general so murky, that it is hard to get to the truth. Few people in India even talk of Chitisinghpura anymore. And the forgetfulness and murkiness will remain. Such killings are soon supplanted by something bigger; there is the usual exchange of allegations between India and Pakistan, the usual outrage and condemnation around the world, and no more than a few people know what is really going on.

The government remained steadily indifferent to the several requests from human rights organizations and Indian political parties for an independent probe into the massacres of the Sikhs. In the Indian Parliament, the Union law minister asked members from opposition parties to drop their demand for an inquiry into the recent killings since it only helped Pakistan "point accusing fingers at India." A spokesman for the BJP exhorted members of Parliament to instead "concentrate on exposing the evil designs of Pakistan."

The truth about the killing of the Sikhs has yet to be discovered. There has been no official inquiry, despite requests from human rights organizations and political parties, and there are new facts, apart from the clumsy and brutal attempt to blame it on "foreign mercenaries," which cast a considerable shadow on the Indian version of events.

Five years later not a single person or group has been plausibly held responsible for the killings, and the Pakistan-based guerrilla outfits have continued to deny their involvement. Within a few days after the massacre, most of the Sikhs I had seen so vehemently blaming, without much evidence, the Muslim guerrillas, and who had then gone on to do the same on national and international TV, had left Kashmir with their families. Those Sikhs who stayed on in Chitisinghpura are even more reluctant to talk to journalists. Some complain privately about the special favors bestowed by the government upon a few chosen men: large sums of money given as "compensation," jobs for the unemployed, special recruitment into the police.

But the appeasement hasn't prevented many Sikhs outside the village from expressing their doubts; the killings in Chitisinghpura, many of them believe, were organized by Indian intelligence agencies to influence Clinton, and the Western journalists covering his visit, into taking a tougher line toward Pakistan.

Yaqub Wagay, arrested soon after the Sikh killings, was brutally interrogated by the SOG and made to sign false confessions. A senior government official admitted to me that he was innocent, and in fact he was released on bail in the Chitisinghpura case, before being rearrested, farcically, in connection with the Panchalthan case, on the basis of the evidence allegedly supplied by him about the five "foreign mercenaries." He is now out of prison.

For those who live in Kashmir, the expectations of justice, rarely fulfilled in the Indian subcontinent, are more than optimistic; they belong to fantasy. It makes it all the more difficult for the victims to bear their human losses. At Dalal's house, the once carefully tended plants and hedges were already running wild just a few weeks after his murder, the fish in the pond were mostly dead, and a few men sat slumped on the floor in a bare hall under the Islamic calendar of mourning. His mother, persuaded by her male relatives to emerge from the dark room where she had taken to since her son's death, broke down as soon as she noticed the photos of Dalal I had been studying. The pictures showed a young man in dark glasses and trendy clothes, a happy, contented man, someone who had managed to find, amid the relentless violence of the insurgency, a new style and identity for himself, and when Dalal's mother, still crying, while her mother, Dalal's grandmother, sat beside her, quietly wiping her tears with the frayed end of her head scarf, asked what was the point of talking to the press, of speaking about her son to me—he was gone and wouldn't come back; the people who had killed him were too powerful—it was hard not to feel pierced by the truth of what she was saying, hard not to be moved by her grief and the pain, amid the great human waste of Kashmir, of her helplessness.

More than fifty thousand people—and these are conservative figures—have been killed, maimed, or disappeared in the last ten years. The Indian Army and police have lost a few thousand men but have killed many more Muslim guerrillas and civilians. There is hardly a family among the four million–strong Muslim population of the valley which hasn't been affected. Abbas said, while we discussed possible stories I could cover, "You must do widows and orphans." I had foolishly asked, "Where can I find them?" Abbas had let the remark go; he simply said, "Anywhere." And it was true; widows and orphans were as ubiquitous as graveyards and ruins in the valley.

After each of my travels around the city and the valley I came back to the hotel room, relieved that the day's work was over and that I could retreat for some hours at least from the world around me, from the stories—of torture (one hospital alone witnessed 250 cases of death by acute renal failure, caused by putting human bodies under heavy rollers in the army's interrogation centers called Papa 1 and Papa 2), of summary executions, rapes, kidnappings, and arson—stories that emerged unprompted in the most casual of conversations with Kashmiris and that formed the grisly background to life in the valley.

The oldest among Kashmiris often claim that there is nothing new about their condition, that they have been slaves of foreign rulers since the sixteenth century, when the Moghul emperor Akbar annexed Kashmir and appointed a local governor to rule the state. In the chaos of post-Moghul India, the old empire rapidly disintegrating, Afghani and Sikh invaders plundered Kashmir at will. The peasantry was taxed and taxed into utter wretchedness; the cultural and intellectual life, which under indigenous rulers had produced some of the greatest poetry, music, and philosophy in the subcontinent, dried up. Barbaric rules were imposed in the early nineteenth century: a Sikh who killed a Muslim native of Kashmir was fined nothing more than two rupees. Victor Jacquemont, a botanist and friend of Stendhal's who came to the valley in 1831, thought that "nowhere else in India were the masses as poor and denuded as they were in Kashmir."

But this background of constant suffering could remain invisible to the casual visitor; the physical beauty of the place, enhanced by the valley's isolation from the rest of the world, and more tempting for foreign adventurers, is still, even after these last ten years of violence, overwhelming. All through my stay, memories of previous trips kept bubbling up, visits made in less troubled times, just before the insurgency began in 1990, that first visit which for me—as for anyone who had never been away from the hot, dusty Indian plains—was the first exhilarating revelation of beauty.

I hadn't then really noticed the Kashmiris. They did appear very different with their pale, long-nosed faces, their pherans, their strange language, so unlike any Indian language. They also seemed oddly self-possessed. But in the enchanting new world that had opened before me—the big deep blue skies and the tiny boats becalmed in vast lakes, the cool trout streams and the stately forests of chenar and poplar, the red-cheeked children at roadside hamlets and in apple orchards, the cows and sheep grazing on wide meadows, and, always in the valley, the surrounding mountains—in so private an experience of beauty it was hard to acknowledge the inhabitants of the valley, hard to acknowledge the more prosaic facts of their existence: the dependence upon India, the lack of local industry, the growing number of unemployed educated youth.

Then, as the years passed, the news from Kashmir took its place with the other news—equally bad, of murders and destruction—from Punjab and the northeast, the distant struggles that were, ultimately, marginal to one's own life in a very large and deprived country where almost everyone is struggling. In any event, I found I couldn't always get the necessary information about Kashmir. There were some good books published by small imprints, but you had to search hard for them. To read what was reported in the press was to be told that Pakistan had fomented trouble in Kashmir, and the Indian Army was taking care of it. It was to understand that there really wasn't a problem except one of law and order, which the relevant military and paramilitary organizations would soon deal with. The missing physical details had to be imagined; and they turned out to be much grimmer than what I once could have thought of.

Srinagar's big hotel with its vast lawns and bare trees overlooking the lake was empty, but the staff still felt obliged to work themselves up each morning, like the Indian papers, into cheerful falsehoods: "Everything is fine today, sir, there is no problem at all, there is as much violence here as in any Indian city."

In their softly lit, carpet-muffled offices, trays of tea and biscuits regularly brought in by uniformed servants, Indian officials presented statistics about the number of guerrillas killed, guns, rocket launchers, and grenades seized. In a gloomy room, the furnishings dark with grime, piles of unread newspapers in one corner, a member of the Kashmir Bar Association presented me with some counterstatistics about the number of Muslims killed (eighty thousand in his estimation), tortured, raped, or gone missing.

The day before I arrived, a senior guerrilla from one of the pro-Pakistan outfits had been shot dead. But weariness—there had been too many killings of that sort—and the fear of being fired upon by the Indian police or Army kept public mourners in their homes; the streets remained clear of the thousands of grieving men that had once taken the corpses of "martyrs" to the graveyards scattered everywhere in the city, often adjacent to destroyed houses, a sudden swarm of green headstones and irises in the dusty broken streets.

The festival of Eid came and went, but the shops still closed early, the tense busyness abruptly giving way to silence and darkness, and each evening, in little stockades beside the roads, sheep with purple paint on their backs restlessly awaited slaughter. The long boulevard along the lake, filled in my memory with vacationers, remained deserted and dusty, the hotels on the boulevard serving as barracks for paramilitary soldiers. The houseboats cowered under the snowcapped mountains to the north, the jaunty names on their gables—*Miss England*, *Manhattan Adventure*—as gaudily ironical as the "Bright Career Institute" sighted in an alley full of spectacularly ruined houses, heaps of bricks that had already been plundered for wood. Filth lay in small mounds everywhere in the alleys and bazaars of the gray old city—the stronghold of the pro-Pakistan guerrillas—where Indian soldiers stood alert in their improvised bunkers at every bend and corner, the bunkers seeming like some kind of trap, sandbag walls roofed with corrugated iron and blue weather-beaten tarpaulin, light machine gun muzzles pointing out from small squarish holes between the sandbags, behind which you occasionally saw the frightened eyes in dark faces, the help-lessness of soldiers in this hostile setting, hundreds of miles away from home, somehow made more poignant by the "Happy Eid" messages painted in Urdu on little cardboards stuck to the sandbags. And every-where on the narrow broken roads you saw, and hastily stepped aside to make way for, big machine gun–topped trucks in fast-moving convoys of three or four, often flying the defiant banners—INDIA IS GREAT—of a besieged army.

The military controlled the roads, but the pro-Pakistan guerrillas were still at large in the countryside, the forests and hollows, the hills and flatlands of the valley. The myths once attached to them had been embellished; they now came out of nowhere—detonated a land mine, ambushed a convoy, fired and threw hand grenades at street pa-trols—and then vanished once more. The soldiers and the policemen emerged from the shock and blood to rage against whomever they could. The victims were often civilians, who just happened to be around when the guerrillas struck. Whole towns and villages had been laid waste in this way: shops and bazaars burned, houses razed, people shot at random.

This was how Jalaluddin's photocopy shop at Pattan, a small town a few miles north of Srinagar, came to be destroyed. The guerrillas had come early in the morning, shot one policeman on the main street, and then disappeared. The police came looking for the guerrillas and ac-cused the Muslim shopkeepers of helping them escape. Then, before the shopkeepers could put down their shutters and escape, more police-men arrived, this time with cans of petrol. Jalaluddin's shop was the first to be set alight possibly because it was very new; he had only recently brought the Xerox machine and Honda generator from Delhi, in a long and difficult journey, during which he'd had to bribe his way out of more than one roadblock.

The fire quickly spread to the adjacent shops, one in the ramshackle row of single rooms lining the highway, footwear and grocery stores, computer and typing institutes, shaky in structure, quick to combust with their wooden frames. The smell of burned wood was still in the air when I visited Pattan two days later.

"If you live in Kashmir, you have to be prepared for anything," Abbas had said, and Jalaluddin, and other young men, had already moved beyond rage, hoping now to receive compensation from the government for the destruction of their property, large enough to enable them to rebuild their shops. The men—well educated and articulate, and handsome, with sharp features and artlessly staring eyes in the Kashmiri manner—were matter-of-fact about the lack of options. There were no jobs to be had if you couldn't afford large bribes to government officials: fifty thousand rupees to secure fourth-class employment as a chaprasi (servant) in a despised administration that then exposed you and your family to the fury of the guerrillas.

An old man, short and squat, with dull, bloodshot eyes in a round, puffy face, came and stood behind Jalaluddin as he spoke. The owner of a house that the fire had consumed, he had been lucky to get out with his wife, five daughters, and two grandsons, and it was his story that the young men began to tell me: the cousin who been killed in an "encounter," the son, a banana seller in the bazaar, whom the police had kidnapped and then returned on a ransom payment of five thousand rupees.

The young men insisted on showing me the extent of the destruction. The photocopy shop had been completely gutted, the wooden beams charred and swollen into a kind of delicate filigree. The cream-colored Xerox machine lay on the floor, the shiniest and most expensive thing in the shop, and it was with lingering solicitude that Jalaluddin turned it over and around to reveal the shattered glass and blackened underside.

One of the walls had collapsed, exposing the derelict shell, greater when seen from above, of the adjacent burned house, where a garish poster of a Swiss chalet remained on one of the bare walls, the broad-brushed sentiment on it still legible: "A smile works magic like the sun and makes things bright for everyone."

The Muslim middle class in the valley still largely consists of people connected to the government as elected or nonelected officials, and during the insurgency it hadn't stopped carving out private profits from public works; if anything, the violence and instability, the constant destruction and rebuilding had offered more opportunities of raiding the state exchequer. Jammu, the Hindu-majority city outside the valley, was full of newly built mansions of senior ministers and bureaucrats; in remote villages in the valley, corruption finding its own level everywhere, the massive new houses of local petty officials stood apart from the enclosing shabbiness.

Twenty miles south of Srinagar, past steep slopes and startlingly panoramic views of the pear and apple orchards and rice fields and the tall mountains on the horizon, lies the hillside town of Charar-e-Sharif. It was here that the shrine of Kashmir's fifteenth-century patron saint, Sheikh Nuruddin, stood, until 1995, when it was torched and destroyed during fighting between the Indian Army and guerrillas. Kashmiris, both Hindu and Muslim, grieved at its loss. In Kashmir, Islam had escaped the taint it acquired elsewhere in the subcontinent from forced conversions and temple destroying during the several centuries of invasions and conquests by Muslims from Arabia and Central Asia. It had come to the valley in the fourteenth century by way of Central Asian and Persian missionaries and, blending well with earlier Hindu and Buddhist cultures, had taken on a uniquely Kashmiri character; it was to become known not for invaders but for the great Sufi saints whom both Hindus and Muslims revered. Sheikh Nuruddin was one of the earliest and greatest of these saints.

It wasn't clear who started the fire, the guerrillas, some of whom were from Pakistan, who, contemptuous of the pacificism of Sufi Islam, had turned the shrine into a bunker, or the Indian Army, which had laid a siege around the shrine. But the destruction was international news, and for some months various Kashmiri political and religious outfits as well as the government repeatedly promised to rebuild the shrine.

Five years later Charar-e-Sharif and its inhabitants appeared overtaken by events in the valley. The rebuilding amounted to an ungainly corrugated iron roof over unpainted walls in the middle of a slushy field. A lot of money had been collected from shocked devotees, the government had pitched in, but little work was done, the funds disappearing, as with all delayed reconstruction projects, into many pockets.

The part of the town that had been destroyed and partly rebuilt was still a mess of rubble and open gutters and uncollected rubbish. A few new houses and shops had come up: small, bare, windowless rooms, often with plastic sheets as doors, where ancient men sat embroidering wicker baskets for kangris (little earthenware pots with charcoal embers that Kashmiris keep under their pherans), their thin legs drawn up against the wall, a hookah quietly smoldering beside them.

Word of my presence in the town had quickly spread. The car, the notebook, and the camera had their own associations here, and as I prepared to leave, about forty men appeared before the tiny stationery store where I been talking to some schoolchildren (there are about twenty schools in the thinly populated region). The men had walked four miles from their village, across the hilly countryside, after hearing that an official-seeming person was in town. The pipes in their area had burst, and there had been no water for eight days. They had trudged to the assistant engineer's office but found it locked; they had gone to the local police station but hadn't been allowed a hearing; they were now melting the snow in the gullies for water, but there wasn't much snow left. Raggedly dressed, large holes gaping from their pherans, their thickly bearded faces white with dust, they seemed to have emerged out of a scene of eighteenth- or nineteenth-century wretchedness, the kind that made Victor Jacquemont conclude that nowhere in India were the masses as poor and denuded as in Kashmir.

The continuing backwardness of Kashmir, its failure, or inability, to join the modern world and find new identities for itself: This was what the commissioner of Srinagar, an official of the central Indian government, had spoken to me about at his house; so too, although less directly, Abbas, who had told me on the very first day I met him that his ancestors had come to Kashmir from Samarkand in Central Asia.

Their connection to the Islamic world outside India was often exaggerated by leaders of Indian Muslims in the nineteenth and twentieth centuries; it was one way of holding on to an idea of personal and collective worth amid the general degradation of the Muslim community under colonialism. What struck me, however, was that Abbas, whose work as a correspondent for a major Indian newspaper gave him status, even prestige in Kashmir, still needed to make the claim. But it was really an idea of dignity and selfhood that he was affirming, an idea that could take on a special urgency among such thoroughly trampled-upon people as the Kashmiris.

The troubles began, Kashmiris say, with foreign rule. After the Moghuls, Afghans, and Sikhs, the valley fell in the mid-nineteenth century to a petty Hindu feudal chief who had helped the British defeat the Sikhs. The British ceded the entire state—the valley together with Hindu-majority Jammu and Buddhist-dominated Ladakh and the northwestern parts that later were to come under Pakistani rule—to the chief for a meager sum of seven and one-half million rupees. The sale is still a source of rage and shame for Kashmiris.

Things didn't improve much under the new Hindu rulers. In 1877 a famine killed two-thirds of the population. Thousands of underfed, underclothed Muslims died while carrying rations on their backs for troops in remote Himalayan outposts. Muslims were rarely given jobs; the administration was staffed overwhelmingly by the small minority of Hindus (about 4 percent of the population in the valley). The maharaja and his Hindu courtiers built up fabulous private fortunes. Even prostitutes paid one hundred rupees as tax to the maharaja; Muslims who were found slaughtering cows were banished to the remote Andaman Islands in the Indian Ocean.

The son of the last Hindu maharaja of the state, Karan Singh, records a Buddha-like epiphany in his autobiography. Born at the Hôtel Martinez in Cannes, an entire floor of which had been taken over by his father, he spent his childhood in Kashmir more or less free of contact with Muslims and poverty. His father, Hari Singh, was fond of shooting and hunting and racing, also, it is said, of London prostitutes. Life in his palace was an endless search for entertainment. As Karan Singh writes, "We spent hours working up lists for lunch and dinner parties, seating plans and menus." Once his father asked a friend to take Singh around the city and show him the kingdom he would one day inherit. The friend drove him to the Muslim-majority areas and pointed at the dilapidated buildings and shabbily dressed men on the streets, and said, "These are your people." Karan Singh was astonished.

The more astonishing thing about this event is its date, in the 1930s. Barely ten years later India was free of both colonial rule and the maharajas. The Muslim elite of India were to demand and receive a separate homeland in the form of Pakistan, and the maharaja of Kashmir, faced with a choice between joining India or Pakistan, would reluctantly accede to India, which had adopted a secular, democratic, and egalitarian constitution, giving Indians a new idea of themselves, of their past and potential.

But such was the course of Indian history until then that it was mostly Hindus who took up these opportunities, who saw in modern education and the modern world the possibilities of personal and communal development. The Muslims of India, whose political power had been comprehensively destroyed by the British and many of whose leaders remained trapped by fantasies of recapturing their old glory in India, took some time before even attempting to catch up with the Hindus.

In all this time, the Muslims of Kashmir, cut off from larger events and trends in British-ruled India, and held down by the tiny Hindu minority of rulers and administrators, were barely able to move at all. Illiteracy and poverty were widespread; political opposition to the Hindu maharaja was met with brutality. As in India, a few educated Muslims were left to carry the burden of their country's humiliation and backwardness.

2. The Politics of Secularism

It is no coincidence that the person who articulated best the fears and frustrations of all Indian Muslims was a Kashmiri, Mohammad Iqbal, one of the most important Muslim philosophical thinkers of modern times. Iqbal was born in 1877 in what is now Pakistan to an illiterate family of shawl peddlers and tailors. His parents managed to send him to school and college, where he did very well. He was already famous for his poetry when he went to Cambridge in the early years of the twentieth century to study philosophy.

Iqbal followed many other Indians in being deeply impressed by European progress in the nineteenth century; the idea of individual struggle and fulfillment, and the related idea of the individual's responsibilities to society and the nation, could not but come as a revelation to people from listless subject communities. Iqbal came to admire Nietzsche. The idea of the Superman, of self-creation and self-assertion, spoke to him in the powerful way it always has to people from colonized countries. But he was also disturbed by racism and hypercompetitiveness, and while in Europe, struggling with the complex mix of admiration, fear, and insecurity the place aroused, he became even more aware of his Muslim identity. The history of Islam acquired new meanings for him; a passing glimpse from a ship of Sicily, the setting of one of Islam's greatest triumphs in Europe, could make him weep.

He came back to India convinced, like many Indians before him, that the progress of his community lay not in imitating Europe but in reforming and reviving the religion he had been born into. To this end, he began to exalt masculine vigor and the great Islamic past in his writings. He became a determined critic of Sufism, of the mystical and folk traditions within Islam that, advocating the rejection of the ego and the self, had found such a hospitable home in his ancestral Kashmir. He saw these traditions as emasculating Muslims, rendering them inadequate before the outstanding tasks demanded of the self and of the larger Islamic community.

Iqbal's ideas about Islam in India had to have political ramifications. Politics itself at that time of colonial oppression was primarily a quest for dignity, an assertion of identity first and then only secondarily an attempt at creating new institutions. As such, it could not be separated from religion, from the larger sense of a shared culture and past which was the beginning of the political sense for all deprived and subjugated peoples. If, as Iqbal believed, Islam was weakened by incorporating the local traditions of Hinduism, then its original purity under the democracy established by the first four caliphs could never be recovered within an India dominated by Hindus. True Islam, as Iqbal conceived, could be reinstated only if Indian Muslims formed a separate nation. The idea which Iqbal put forward at an important political meeting of Muslims in 1930 was the beginning of the two-nation theory, which, seventeen years later, worked itself out in the partition of India and the creation of Pakistan.

For most Hindus in India, Iqbal is the misguided instigator of the movement for Pakistan. I hadn't really thought of him in connection with Kashmir until I met Dr. Mohammad Ishaq Khan in Srinagar, the Kashmiri capital, in March 2000. Dr. Khan teaches medieval history at Kashmir University in Srinagar and has done pioneering work on Islam's acculturation in the Hindu-Buddhist environment of Kashmir. He is a small, round-faced man, gentle in demeanor; he speaks slowly, as if unaccustomed to talking about his work, but in clear qualified sentences that indicate a quietly active mind. During the past decade, the years of the insurgency, when the university ceased to function, he has produced his best work, a book on the spiritual dimensions of Islam that stresses the contemplative aspects of the faith over the ideological ones.

In one of the Kashmiri newspapers I read during a recent visit to Kashmir—pages that were full of bad news but always offering something lively in their editorial pages—I read Dr. Khan's account of his visit to Pakistan. He had met many Kashmiris settled there, but he had stayed away from the awkward subject of politics altogether. When asked why he and other Muslim intellectuals in Kashmir weren't involved in the anti-India insurgency, he had thought of the Persian Sufi Rumi's words: "The intellect is destroyed by partial reason." Nevertheless, he did visit Iqbal's tomb in Lahore, and in a striking passage he describes how overwhelmed he was with emotion as he approached the tomb: "I couldn't control myself. Tears started pouring from my eyes."

Dr. Khan's allegiance was to the Sufi tradition of Kashmir, which Iqbal had rejected. His suspicion of Islam as ideology had only grown after the violence and suffering caused by the insurgency, which one of his own students had joined, someone whom Dr. Khan remembered as denouncing, in the way Iqbal once had, Sufi Islam for turning the Kashmiris into apathetic slaves of Hindu India. The student had gone to Pakistan for training in the military camps and risen high within the leading pro-Pakistan guerrilla group, Hizbul Mujahideen, before being killed in Srinagar in 1999.

Iqbal's personal response to Europe and Islam and the melancholy beauty of his poetry had been reduced in the end to simple ideologies that had sent thousands of other young men to an early death. Nevertheless, the idea of Iqbal as the man who had brought a hope of redemption to the Muslims of the subcontinent survived and—this is what struck me—still had the power, many decades later, of moving even someone like Dr. Khan, committed to the intellectual life, to tears.

It was somewhat easier after that to imagine the impact Iqbal had on millions of Muslims across India with his poetry and philosophy, something comparable to Gandhi's influence on the Hindus, and it was somewhat easier to enter the Indian Muslim's sense of dispossession and understand how much the charisma and persuasive power of men like Iqbal derive from the raw, unformed nature of their community.

For Kashmiris the person who came to embody their fate a generation after Iqbal was Sheikh Abdullah, once hailed as the Lion of Kashmir, who for more than half a century since the early 1930s remained the most popular leader of Kashmiri Muslims. His funeral in 1982 was attended by hundreds of thousands of mourners. But eight years later his grave was desecrated, a moment that marks not only the beginning of the insurgency but also the decline of the politics of personality in South Asia.

Abdullah's early mentor was Iqbal, whom he had met in 1924 in Lahore, when Iqbal was at the height of his fame. Iqbal had first visited Kashmir, the land of his ancestors, three years before and had come away distressed by the condition of the Muslims. "In the bitter chill of winter shivers his naked body," he wrote, "whose skill wraps the rich in royal shawls." He had joined the Muslim-owned newspapers of Lahore in highlighting the fate of the Kashmiri Muslims under Hindu rule: how though they formed 96 percent of the population the rate of literacy among them was only 0.8 percent.

Iqbal was sympathetic to Abdullah, who, like himself, came from a family of poor shawl sellers and was one of the few Kashmiri Muslims who had managed to educate themselves up to the point where they found their way blocked by discrimination on grounds of religion; under the maharaja, only Hindus, who were a mere 4 percent of the population, were allowed to aspire to higher education and better jobs. Consequently, Abdullah had to leave Kashmir for Aligarh, near Delhi, where the first college providing Western-style education exclusively to Muslims had been set up in 1875. On his return to Kashmir in 1930, he joined a small group of graduate students from Aligarh who called themselves the Reading Room Party.

Barely a year later, Kashmir witnessed the first major disturbance in response to the autocratic rule of the maharaja. A Muslim called Abdul

Qadir, who was working as a butler for a European resident, was arrested for giving a seditious speech. Crowds who came to protest at the prison gates were arrested; more protests followed, and at one point the police fired on the demonstrators. Twenty-one people died. Then the procession carrying the bodies for burial became unruly, and Hindu-owned shops along the route to the graveyard were looted.

The maharaja's Hindu army cracked down brutally on Muslim dissenters. Abdullah spent a year in prison with other members of the Reading Room Party. When he was released in 1932, he announced the formation of the Muslim Conference; it was the first organized opposition to the regime of the maharaja in Kashmir. There was a special edge to Abdullah's relationship with the maharaja. No two men could have been more dissimilar: the horse-racing maharaja, with a weakness for fraudulent Hindu holy men, and the devout Muslim and brilliant manipulator of the masses. In his opposition to the maharaja, Abdullah found himself supported by leaders of the Indian nationalist movement against colonial rule, particularly Pandit Nehru, who under Gandhi's patronage had become the unchallenged leader of the Congress Party. The friendship between Abdullah and Nehru grew fast.

There was a special reason for that friendship. Nehru's Brahmin ancestors came from Kashmir and had moved just a few decades before his birth in 1889 to Delhi and Allahabad, where they became one of the first families of modern India. There was always an air of the solitary visionary about Nehru. He was sent to Harrow and Cambridge by his Anglophilic father. He was much influenced by European ideas of socialism and nationalism. His discovery of India came later and made all the more valuable for him the discovery of his roots in Kashmir, the ancestral connection deepened by the pantheistic feeling he, a man who disdained organized religion, had for the Himalayas.

Iqbal once said that though his body was confined to India, his soul existed in Kashmir. Nehru came close to making the same claim in his various scattered writings on Kashmir. He'd visited the state as a young trekker and was enraptured. In *The Continent of Circe*, Nirad Chaudhuri wrote of the Hindu sense of loss associated with the Himalayas: the cold regions the Aryan settlers of North India had come from, the longing expressed by Nehru himself when he wrote in his autobiography, "And I dream of the day when I shall wander about the Himalayas." In official and personal correspondence, Nehru kept coming back to what he himself described as his "partiality for Kashmir."

That partiality took several forms and was to shape Indian attitudes toward Kashmir well after his death. By the time he met and befriended Abdullah in the mid-1930s, Nehru had already begun shape his blueprint for an independent India. In Abdullah, he saw someone who shared his conviction that the old social and economic order of India, represented by the maharajas and big landlords, had to be destroyed through land reforms and centralized economic planning. Abdullah was receptive to Nehru's advocacy of secularism; it was under the latter's persuasion that Abdullah changed the name of the Muslim Conference to the National Conference and acquired a greater following among the small minority of Hindus in the Kashmir valley, as well as among the Hindu majority in Jammu, the southern part of the state. Though distrustful of Abdullah, they found reassuring his growing proximity to Indian nationalist leaders.

As the creation of Pakistan became a certainty, much to the heartbreak of Gandhi and others who had wanted a united India, Nehru was increasingly determined that Kashmir and its Muslim majority should be part of the India he had envisaged and so painstakingly worked toward, an India that was committed to democracy, secularism, and socialism. He was convinced that the idea of a separate nation for the Muslims—the two-nation theory first proposed by Iqbal and embraced by the feudal Muslim elite of North India—was a mistake; he didn't think it could solve the problem of the Muslim community, the problem he defined as social and economic backwardness. He thought the landlords and mullahs who had kept the Muslim masses away from the benefits of education would merely consolidate their power in a new state.

Abdullah's own view of the demand for Pakistan was more qualified and less emotional. He felt, as he confessed in his autobiography, a subconscious sympathy for it; he saw it as a Muslim reaction against Hindu sectarianism, which he believed, despite his personal regard for Gandhi and Nehru, the Congress Party insidiously practiced. Indeed, he thought he could discern strains of Hindu revivalism in Nehru's sentimental attachment to Kashmir.

He could also see that Kashmir's Muslim-majority population and geographical location made for a natural affinity with the new state of Pakistan being carved out from the western, as well as eastern, parts of British India. At the same time, he felt himself out of sympathy with the men leading the agitation for Pakistan, particularly Mohammad Ali Jinnah, the pork-eating barrister from Bombay, who did not disguise his contempt for the Kashmiris and yet assumed that the state with its Muslim majority had no option but to join the new homeland for Indian Muslims. Abdullah also feared that the poor Muslims of Kashmir would get a bad deal in the feudal setup of Pakistan. So it was that in the years leading up to the partition of India Abdullah came to think of independence and democracy as the best option for Kashmir.

The same idea, without, of course, the democracy bit, had struck the maharaja, who, as the time of British withdrawal from India came nearer, was faced, as the ruler of the largest of the 562 states under British paramountcy, with a choice between India and Pakistan.

The maharaja's autocratic ways continued as local opposition to him intensified. In 1946 he put Abdullah and other members of the National Conference in prison for running a highly popular "Quit Kashmir" campaign against him. Nehru's support for Abdullah had already alienated the maharaja from the Indian leadership; Gandhi's questions over the legitimacy of his rule, which had its dubious origin in a sale deed in 1846 between the maharaja's ancestors and the British, made him more receptive to emissaries from Pakistan, who began to visit him with greater frequency. The partition of India was three months old, and he was still talking with both Indian and Pakistan representatives, hoping to buy time and preserve his regime, when a quick series of events forced him to act.

Violence and rioting during partition had affected the southern part of the maharaja's state, where Sikh refugees from Pakistan joined Hindu nationalists and members of the maharaja's police in attacking Muslims. Tens of thousands of Muslims were killed. Many more Muslims fled to Pakistan, where the news of their suffering provoked the always very volatile Muslim tribesmen of the northwestern provinces on the Pakistan border into declaring jihad against the maharaja. In one of the impetuous and confused actions that inaugurated and forever marked the Pakistani position on Kashmir, a few officers of the Pakistani Army provided a ragtag group of jihad-minded tribals with arms and helped them across the border into Kashmir, at the same time as the Pakistani government was still trying to convince the maharaja to hand over Kashmir to Pakistan.

The maharaja's army was no match for the energetic tribal forces, which advanced swiftly through the northwest parts of Kashmir; an older generation of Kashmiris still remembers the killings and looting and rapes that they committed on their way to Srinagar. The maharaja panicked as they came closer and closer. His son, Karan Singh, describes in his autobiography the moment when the lights went out in the palace—the invaders had destroyed the power station—and the noise of howling jackals suddenly sliced through the darkness and silence. The maharaja appealed to the Indian government for military assistance, but the legalistic response from Delhi was that the Indian Army could enter Kashmir only after the state had formally acceded to India. There was no longer any choice for the maharaja. As the tribal army drew nearer to Srinagar, he fled the city for the Hindu-dominated city of Jammu, where he went to bed after instructing his aide-de-camp to shoot him in his sleep if the Indian government's representative didn't turn up with the instrument of accession. He never returned to Kashmir and died in far-off Bombay in 1962.

The Indian Army finally arrived in Srinagar in late October 1947, and its offensive against the invaders became a full-fledged war with Pakistan that lasted more than a year. A cease-fire was eventually declared under the auspices of the UN on January 1, 1949, by which time the Indian Army had driven the invaders out of the valley. However, the northwestern part of the princely state, which is different, culturally and socially, from the Kashmir valley and closer to the Muslim Punjab, remained under Pakistani control, and, though named Azad (Free) Kashmir, is effectively as much a part of Pakistan as the valley is of India.

It was Sheikh Abdullah, released from prison just three weeks before the invasion, who had organized the defense of Srinagar. The National Conference came out in support of the Indian Army. Abdullah not only endorsed the accession to India but also generated popular Kashmiri support for it, which wasn't hard since the atrocities committed by the tribal army had put fear of Pakistan in the Kashmiris, and this fear took a long time to fade.

In retrospect, the tribal invasion seems to have spoiled everything. Certainly, the issue of Kashmir acquired a degree of complication from which it never recovered. Nehru took the dispute to the UN on January 1, 1948, and offered to hold a plebiscite under international auspices to confirm the accession to India. This sounds generous given that Nehru already had physical control of the valley. But Nehru also wanted the legitimacy of popular support for Indian rule over Kashmir. He was confident that with Sheikh Abdullah on his side, India would win a plebiscite in Kashmir.

As things turned out, the Indian offer of a plebiscite under the supervision of the UN was never redeemed. There was no withdrawal of the Indian and Pakistan armies from Kashmir, which had to be achieved before the plebiscite could take place, and the issue got bogged down in various legalities as the years passed. Pakistan remained in occupation of one-third of the state and denounced the accession to India as fraudulent since in its view the maharaja had surrendered all authority by fleeing Srinagar after the Muslims rebelled. The Indians kept dismissing the claim and saying that Pakistan had acted illegally by invading the state and frequently raised the rhetorical ante, as they still do, by stating that the only unresolved issue for India concerned the return of Pakistan-occupied territories.

Positions hardened on both sides as the cold war reached the subcontinent. The State Department under John Foster Dulles always suspected Nehru of being soft on communism and was openly contemptuous of his nonaligned position. The United States drew closer to Pakistan, which it included, in the mid-1950s, in such military treaties as CENTO and SEATO. This further stiffened Nehru's position on Kashmir; there was no more talk of a plebiscite. The Soviet Union under Khrushchev became a consistent supporter of Nehru's line, which became the official Indian line, that Kashmir was an integral part of India and thus not subject to any international arbitration. The cease-fire line between India and Pakistan in Kashmir, called the Line of Control (LOC), became a de facto international border.

This would have been the end of the dispute, the status quo accepted by all parties as an unalterable reality. Certainly, in those early years, the populations in both Indian- and Pakistani-held Kashmir seemed resigned to being where they were. Sheikh Abdullah was now in charge, and almost the first thing he did as prime minister of Kashmir from 1948 to 1953 was to initiate a series of ambitious land reforms whereby ownership of lands in excess of twelve and a half acres was abolished. In effect, this meant taking land away from the Hindu landlords and distributing it among poor Muslim tenants. It was a mini-revolution, and it assured Abdullah the gratitude and support of two generations of Kashmiri Muslims.

Less than four decades later, however, Kashmiris were to take up arms for the first time in their long history; India was to face a popular insurgency in Kashmir and come close to nuclear war with Pakistan. The grave of Sheikh Abdullah, eight years after his crowded funeral, would require around-the-clock protection from vandals.

Jinnah's demand for Pakistan had innocuous beginnings. From the desire for a guarantee of Muslim rights in a Hindu-majority India, it developed into a demand for a confederation of India where Muslims would not have minority status but would share power with Hindus. However, the Hindu leaders of the Congress Party, so close to achieving real political power for the first time, were in no mood to share it.

The clumsily partitioned provinces toward the eastern and the western borders of India weren't what Jinnah had asked for—there were almost as many Muslims in India as in the new state of Pakistan—but it was all the Congress was prepared to part with. In the end, with the British impatient to depart and hustling everyone else, it was the Congress that was eager to settle for partition in order to consolidate its hold on the much bigger Hindu-majority provinces and the institutions of the colonial state—the army, the bureaucracy, and the police—that were its great inheritance from the British.

Among the people who took a harder line as a result of the demand for partition was Nehru, who, over most of a lifetime spent fighting the British, had never accepted the idea of Pakistan and held on to the idea of a united multicultural India. The bloodshed that accompanied the partition came as a bigger blow to him; he was now more convinced than ever of the need to have, in the colonial way, a strong central government for India, with as little autonomy as possible for the diverse communities that constituted it. He regarded all regional assertiveness—and there was much of that across India in the fifties—with suspicion. National unity, along with secularism, became his mantra, which was taken up by almost all political parties and echoed by the colonial bureaucracy that was keen on holding on to its own power.

It was hard, nevertheless, to keep down sectarian demands in a country as diverse as India, where independence had released a new longing for self-expression, where millions of previously disfranchised people could find a political voice only through the community they were born to. A lesser leader would have proved disastrous here. Nehru dealt astutely with the demands for a linguistic reorganization of India, which in the South Indian state of Tamil Nadu, for example, had developed into a movement for outright secession. He used a carrot-and-stick policy—a mix of limited democracy and state repression—to pacify various regional groups and keep them within India.

But his own emotional connection with Kashmir made him wield a big stick there with Sheikh Abdullah, who, soon after becoming prime minister, had come up against the problems of running a large multi-ethnic, multireligious state, problems not unlike those Nehru himself faced, but which Abdullah was much less equipped to deal with. He was primarily the leader of the Muslims of the Kashmir valley, who represented the majority of the state's population, 53 percent. But there were also the influential Hindu majority in Jammu to the south, who resented Abdullah's radical politics, and the Buddhists of Ladakh, who were worried about the power of the valley's Muslims.

As usually happens, the lack of a political alternative turned Abdullah into an authoritarian ruler. Impressed by the Soviet model, he made the party inseparable from the administration, and as the aggrieved tone of his letters to Nehru shows, he interpreted all opposition to him as an attempt to undermine his personal authority and, by extension, the right of the Kashmiri Muslims to run the state after centuries of foreign rule.

In the early 1950s, when the Hindu nationalists in Jammu, the forebears of the BJP, organized the dispossessed landlords and followers of the sulking maharaja into a movement for greater integration with India, Abdullah became more insecure. He had bargained hard with the Indian government to preserve the state from excessive interference by New Delhi; Kashmir, he argued, needed special guarantees for the protection of its autonomy. He now revived his idea of an independent Kashmir, bringing it up with, among other visiting diplomats, Adlai Stevenson in 1953.

This was disturbing news for Nehru. He felt Abdullah moving away from him and toward a course of action that was likely to end in the loss of Kashmir and India's secular credentials. He was quick to act: Abdullah was dismissed in 1953 and put in prison, where he stayed, initially without trial, for all but four months of the next eleven years.

This sounds rather unbecoming of Nehru, who by then was known internationally as a statesman. But national unity had become his obsession. He had praised Abdullah's land reforms; he had ensured there was no viable opposition to Abdullah; he had offered personal friendship to him. But now Abdullah was working against the "national interest." The support and dismissal of Abdullah were consistent with Nehru's belief that politics in Kashmir revolved around personalities. As he had told an activist who was arguing for a democratic alternative to Abdullah, there was "no material for democracy in Kashmir."

The other side, then, of Nehru's enchantment with Kashmir was a fear of losing control, a possessiveness that he gradually transformed into a national imperative; Kashmir, he began to argue, couldn't be separated from India without exposing the Muslims in the rest of India to retaliation from Hindu fanatics. You still hear a version of this idea in liberal circles in India today: that communal riots of the same scale and intensity as those during the partition of India are around the corner if Kashmir is allowed to break away.

And then, in 1953, an old protégé of Abdullah's named Bakshi Ghulam Mohammed took over as prime minister of Kashmir and did everything Nehru wanted to constitutionally integrate Kashmir into India. Promises of autonomy made earlier to Abdullah were canceled, and fear of violence came to dictate Indian policy. Bakshi Ghulam Mohammed was himself sidelined after serving ten years as the India-approved prime minister of Kashmir and was imprisoned in 1965, when he sought to undermine an India-backed chief minister. Kashmir

without Sheikh Abdullah reverted to what it had been for centuries under Moghul rule, a dependency, its fate controlled by a distant great
power whose representatives could do what they wished as long as
no one rocked the boat. Its political life, which had really only begun
with Abdullah, came to be dominated by small men with small aims
of personal empowerment and enrichment, by constant intrigues and
betrayals.

Elections, held periodically in order to demonstrate before the
world the democratic nature of the Delhi-imposed regime, were farcically rigged. The nomination papers of opposition parties would be
rejected or their candidates beaten up and arrested; the National
Conference won most elections unopposed. A concerned Nehru had to
tell Mohammed that it might look better if he were to lose a few elections to a few "bona-fide opponents." The central government poured
money into the state for development and education, and for a handful
of Kashmiris at least, the stakes for holding on to power went higher. A
new elite of politicians and bureaucrats emerged from the culture of
corruption that grew around the administration.

As in the history of any dependency and its court politics, what you
come to miss in accounts of Kashmir is a sense of the people, the
way life went on in the villages and towns. One of the images that
springs to mind is of the corrupt government official in his large house,
his sons studying in the best colleges of India. The other image is of the
peasant in his rice field and mud hut, living as depressed a life as he
was when, in 1831, the French botanist Victor Jacquemont visited
the region.

However, the image alters as you read about the rise in literacy levels today. In all likelihood, today the peasant's son has gone to school—
one of hundreds opened by the Indian government—or even to the
new university or the medical and engineering colleges. The peasant
himself hasn't done badly with his apple orchards; horticulture still
forms the mainstay of the economy.

In less than two decades, then, the peasant's son has become ready
for a job but then finds that his options are very limited. Modern education has taken him away from a life in the rice fields or the apple or-

chards, but there is no local industry in the valley. The only jobs are to be had with the government, and here he finds himself excluded by the culture of bribery and nepotism. In India, he finds himself a foreigner, likely to be discriminated against on grounds of religion; it is not easy for a Muslim to find a job or rent a house in a Hindu-dominated region.

It was this sense of a blocked future that educated Kashmiris came to have, along with the realization, hammered into them by repeatedly rigged elections, of their political impotence, that eventually led to the insurgency in the early 1990s.

In 1975, out of jail and once again chief minister of the state, Abdullah entered into an arrangement with the Indian government whereby he promised to give up the demand for self-determination in exchange for becoming what other men before him had been, a satrap of the Indian state in Kashmir.

The downside to the total investment of faith invited by charismatic individuals like Iqbal, Abdullah, even Nehru is that in the absence of institutions, the welfare of a country comes to depend on a few favored ideas and, more dangerously, on personal temperament. The success or failure of individuals has consequences, sometimes damaging, for many future generations. With Iqbal, the danger always was that his followers would go for the simplest and most emotional of the ideas he was trying out in his mind, and after the first flurry of land reforms, Abdullah wasn't able to offer anything more to Kashmiris than his formidable rhetoric and the glamorous myth of the prisoner of conscience.

A few months before he died, Abdullah, in the style of third world dynasts, anointed as his successor his son, a U.K.-based doctor. Farooq Abdullah, inexperienced but enthusiastic, had barely begun when he clashed with Indira Gandhi, who had by then evolved her own authoritarian style. In 1975 she brought her father's anxiety about national unity to a new hysterical pitch as she arrested opposition leaders for being "antinational" and suspended fundamental rights.

In Kashmir, Mrs. Gandhi found herself thwarted by Farooq Abdullah, who refused her offer of an election alliance between her party, the Congress, and the National Conference. Abdullah's victory in the elections of 1983, and subsequent hobnobbing with other politicians opposed to her, made Mrs. Gandhi determined to get rid of him. Her tactics resembled those of the colonial state, something the British had employed to great effect: encouraging religious sectarianism in order to downplay regional disaffection with the central government. In Punjab, she had built up Bhindranwale, an illiterate Sikh preacher, as a counterweight to the province's anti-Congress government; the preacher subsequently turned into a murderous demagogue and declared war on India. Undeterred by the setback in Punjab, she set to work on building up an atmosphere of Hindu jingoism over the issue of Kashmir.

A few stray anti-India demonstrations and violent incidents were held up as evidence of Farooq Abdullah's unreliability. The Indian press, which for decades had faithfully followed the government line on Kashmir, went along with Mrs. Gandhi. Not that the Hindu middle classes needed much persuasion. By then Nehruvian nationalism had begun to degenerate into Hindu nationalism, into a search for external and internal enemies, the enemies who, when they were not the CIA or Pakistan, invariably belonged to the minority community, whether Sikh, as in the case of Punjab, or Muslim. The mass murder arranged by Congress leaders of three thousand Sikhs in Delhi after Mrs. Gandhi's assassination in 1984 came out of that frenzy of Hindu xenophobia Mrs. Gandhi had herself encouraged.

Abdullah's elected government was illegally dismissed in 1984 by Jagmohan, a governor specially appointed by Mrs. Gandhi after she had transferred the previous governor, who had refused to act against Abdullah, out of Kashmir. The new government, made up of defectors from Farooq Abdullah's party, the National Conference, had to impose a curfew for seventy-two out of its first ninety days in office in order to keep down public agitation against it. Then, in early 1986, Jagmohan dismissed the government and took charge.

During his tenure as governor of the state of Jammu and Kashmir in the eighties and then again in the early nineties, Jagmohan did more than anyone else to provoke insurgency in the state. He came to be known as a pro-Hindu bureaucrat during Mrs. Gandhi's Emergency, when he sent bulldozers into Muslim slum colonies in Delhi as part of an attempted "beautification" of the city. In Kashmir, an isolated state with a docile population always seeming ready to be trampled upon, he was no more subtle.

He saw the distinct cultural identity of Kashmir as something that had to be undermined before the state could join what in India is referred to, without irony, as the "national mainstream." With this all-subsuming idea in mind, he sought to impose a peculiarly Hindu modernity on the state, where the unrestricted sale of alcohol was permitted but Muslims were forbidden to slaughter sheep on a Hindu festival day, a pointless law since no prohibitions on meat exist for Kashmiri Hindus. The number of Muslims being recruited in government service went down. The Hindu nationalists were known to admire the resettlement policies followed by the Israeli government in the occupied territories in the 1970s, and Jagmohan may have been inspired by them in encouraging non-Muslims to work in Kashmir.

The backlash was not long in coming; what a colonized people fear most is the possibility of being swallowed up by the dominant alien culture in their midst, which is why the British had left the great religions of the subcontinent and their many subcultures more or less untouched. As in Algeria, Iran, and Egypt, anxiety about modernization, cultural influences from elsewhere, and rampant unemployment turned, because of Jagmohan, into an anxiety about religion, the notion that not only Muslims but Islam itself was in danger, the same fear that had led many Indian Muslims in the mid-1940s to suddenly embrace, after years of relative indifference toward it, the idea of Pakistan.

The popularity of Islamist parties grew throughout the 1980s, helped by the growth of madrassas, the privately owned theology schools which were often run by Muslims from Assam in eastern India, over a thousand miles away, after mass killings of Muslims in the early eighties had forced their migration to Kashmir. These Muslims from outside Kashmir brought their own fundamentalist variety of Islam to the valley: The clerics suddenly wanted to impose new prohibitions restricting women's rights; they wished to ban Bombay films and beauty parlors.

The Islamist parties came together to fight the elections of 1987, in which Abdullah teamed up with the Congress. Just three years after being thrown out by the Congress, Farooq Abdullah decided he couldn't do anything in Kashmir without the support of the ruling party. But his power-sharing arrangement with the Congress was seen as another humiliation for Kashmir. To no one's surprise, he won the elections, and Kashmiris still talk about the active rigging that went on by Indian election officials. Opposition candidates comfortably in the lead suddenly found themselves defeated; candidates and polling agents were beaten up and tortured. Syed Salahuddin, the current leader of Hizbul Mujahideen, the leading Pakistan-based guerrilla outfit, was imprisoned after almost winning the vote in his constituency.

"There is no material there for democracy." The expressed contempt of Nehru's statement, amplified over time, began to affect a new generation of Kashmiris, the educated sons of peasants and artisans already reduced to futile resentment by corruption and unemployment. It was also around this time that the first groups of young Kashmiri men, most of them highly skilled, some even with engineering degrees, and almost all of them jobless, stole across the open border into Pakistan.

The young men were received by middle-level army officers in Pakistan and set up with salaries and private housing. They were trained in the use of light weapons for some months; many of them were asked to return to the valley and bring back more young men. Other recruits smuggled arms and ammunition into the valley. Slowly the traffic across the border grew; in less than three years thousands of young Kashmiri men had ventured across the border, where they formed the first guerrilla groups that declared war on India in 1990.

Pakistan was a natural ally of disaffected Kashmiris. It had tried to liberate Kashmir by force twice by sending in armed infiltrators—first in 1948 and then in 1965—and on both occasions had failed to muster enough support among the local population, which, though not entirely happy with Indian rule, remained wary of Pakistan. But the fast-growing disillusionment with Indian rule through the 1980s made many Kashmiris look toward Pakistan for assistance; it was the only country in the world that consistently affirmed, at least rhetorically, the Kashmiri "right to self-determination."

For the Pakistani Army officers who received the Kashmiris, the creation and support of the guerrilla groups required no expertise; they had done similar things, on a much larger scale, for the mujahideen fighting the Soviet Army in Afghanistan. Most of the officers worked for the Inter-Services Intelligence. Set up to coordinate the war effort in Afghanistan, the ISI had close links with the CIA and had come to play a considerable extraconstitutional role in Pakistan.

The army's control of Pakistan had not weakened since the last months of 1947, when the war with India over Kashmir transformed the new country, lacking the administrative center or the infrastructure of the former colonial government, into a national security state, with over 70 percent of the national budget being spent on defense. Islam turned out to be a weak nation-building glue in Pakistan. The feudal and professional Muslim elite's fear of being overwhelmed by Hindu India mutated into an anxiety about the assertion of ethnic identities in Sind, Baluchistan, and East Pakistan. The need to pacify ethnic minorities while affirming the power of the central government—a tricky maneuver that in the stronger and more democratic state of India had ended up promoting political life—only further expanded the role of the army and the bureaucracy in Pakistan.

In 1979, when the Soviet Union invaded Afghanistan, Pakistan was thirty-two years old and still without a coherent political life. Just eight years before, it had suffered the traumatic secession of East Pakistan with its large Bengali Muslim population, which became, with India's assistance, Bangladesh. What remained was ruled despotically by an army general, Zia-ul-Haq, who had just hanged his former prime minister, Zulfikar Ali Bhutto, and the primitive economy with a tiny manufacturing base was propped up by export of cheap labor to the Middle East.

The CIA found Pakistan a ready host for its proxy war against the Soviet Union. Billions of dollars' worth of arms and ammunition arrived in Pakistan over the next ten years, transforming the social and political landscape of the entire region while creating a strong Islamic fundamentalist movement all around the world.

The arms went to the mujahideen fighting the Soviet Army, and their sale in the black market was also used to finance an illegal drug trade, a disastrous link that eventually resulted in, apart from cheap heroin on the streets of New York, an estimated five million heroin addicts in Pakistan. The army was brought into the civil administration, and organizations like the ISI acquired their currently limitless and sinister power during this time.

Most damagingly, Zia-ul-Haq revived the idea of an Islamic society in order to postpone the transition to civilian rule he had promised soon after his coup against Bhutto. The state funds available to Islamic organizations went into raising armed outfits that attacked Muslim minorities such as the Shiites and the Ahmediyas, and violent conflict within rival Islamic groups broke out in many parts of the country.

Of the three million Afghans who came as refugees to Pakistan, many went to the province of Sind, where local opposition to their presence developed into a particularly savage civil war in Karachi, the largest city. Hundreds of thousands of Afghan refugees were given food, shelter, and elementary Islamic instruction at madrassas run by an Islamic organization close to the Pakistani Army and sponsored by Saudi Arabia. It was the students at these madrassas who, assisted by Pakistan, went on to form the extremist Taliban.

The Soviet retreat from Afghanistan in 1989 was claimed as a victory by the fundamentalists. The fantasy of a new extensive jihad, such as the one in the seventh and eighth centuries that had established Islam as a world religion, attracted thousands of Muslims to Pakistan, from countries including Egypt, Algeria, Yemen, and Sudan. This globalized jihad, which began as a CIA-initiated move to unite all Muslims against godless communism, found new promoters after 1989, such as Osama bin Laden, whose network of Muslim militants now spans the world. Many of the Muslims initially trained in Afghanistan became leading activists within Islamic fundamentalist movements in Egypt, Algeria, and the Central Asian republics.

About a hundred thousand unemployed men from Pakistan fought the jihad in Afghanistan; a few thousand among them went on to fight in Kashmir. The Pakistani Army itself was infiltrated by Islamic fundamentalists, and the possibility of these fundamentalists seizing political power in a nuclear-armed Pakistan is ever present. Among other equally ruinous aftereffects of the American-Pakistani adventure in Afghanistan, the generous American and Saudi Arabian support for the mujahideen in Afghanistan created and enriched a powerful lobby composed of army officers, smugglers, and drug barons, whose particular, often conflicting needs have shaped Pakistan's domestic and foreign policies and usually work against Pakistan's own larger interests.

Jihad alone brought about a degree of consensus among Pakistan's corrupt ruling elite, holy war having been the very profitable raison d'être of many of them. When American interest in Afghanistan dwindled in the early 1990s, the ISI turned its attention to the long-standing

dispute over Kashmir, which had always aroused much patriotic sentiment within Pakistan. Throughout the 1990s the uprising against Indian rule in Kashmir and the hectic mobilization by the ISI for a fresh
jihad against India proved especially handy as distractions from the
widespread social and economic breakdowns within Pakistan.

India was always the significant enemy. The war with India over
Bangladesh in 1971 had ended with utter humiliation for the Pakistani
Army, with ninety thousand of its soldiers taken prisoner, and revenge
motivated many ISI officers as much as the need to keep invoking jihad. One reason why American arms and money for the mujahideen in
Afghanistan were so eagerly accepted by Zia-ul-Haq was that they
seemed to give Pakistan a "strategic depth" in any potential conflict
with India over Kashmir. In the mid-1990s the government of Pakistan
risked international isolation in supporting the Taliban, partly because
the latter provided facilities in Afghanistan for the training of Muslims
committed to the jihad in Kashmir.

The war in Afghanistan thus brought Pakistan to an unexpected fulfillment of its original mission; instead of becoming the pure homeland
of Muslims, it became the capital of a global movement for jihad, a
holy war against infidels, who seemed to be everywhere. It wasn't what
Iqbal, insecure after his time in the West, thrown back to regretting the
dead glory of Islam in Europe, could have imagined when he first proposed a democratic society of believers. And it wasn't what the Kashmiris, accustomed to a more benign version of Islam, could have
imagined when they turned spontaneously to Pakistan for assistance in
their struggle against India.

The first murders, kidnappings, and bombings by Pakistan-backed
guerrillas began in Kashmir in 1989, while Farooq Abdullah was still
heading a civilian government. Later that year the daughter of the
home minister in the federal government in Delhi, a native of Kashmir,
was taken hostage and then released in exchange for five guerrillas.
Large crowds welcomed the released men on the streets of Srinagar.
They were fired upon by Indian police; five men died. There were
more protests, bigger and bigger demonstrations; hundreds of thousands of men and women filled the streets of Srinagar, shouting,
"*Azadi, Azadi*" ("Freedom, Freedom"). People still speak of the strange
energy in the air at the time. Everyone shared the heady expectation
that freedom was just around the corner, and news of the Soviet with-

drawal from Afghanistan and television images of the fall of the Berlin Wall and the great demonstrations of Eastern Europe only deepened the delusion.

It was then, early in 1990, that the Indian government again appointed Jagmohan as governor; he arrived with a sense of mission whose fanaticism approached that of the Islamic guerrillas. Farooq Abdullah resigned, leaving Kashmir without an elected leader. A series of ruthless actions quickly followed. Hundreds of young men suspected of being guerrillas were taken away from their homes, tortured, and sometimes killed. Unprovoked attacks on demonstrators alone cost hundreds of lives—thanks to jumpy soldiers far from home, given a simple idea of the enemy, and licensed to kill. Thousands of Indian soldiers were brought into the valley—their current number is between three and four hundred thousand—while foreign journalists were expelled and local journalists found themselves confined to their houses.

A range of severe laws were introduced, not that many were needed, since all safeguards for civil liberties had completely collapsed by then. You could be picked up anywhere, interrogated, or killed, and no one would ever come to know what happened. The Kashmiri-American poet Agha Shahid Ali quotes a doctor who attended to a sixteen-year-old boy released from one of the interrogation centers: "Did anything in his lines of Fate reveal that the webs of his hands would be cut with a knife?"

By the time Jagmohan was replaced, after six months as governor, the entire Muslim population of the valley had revolted against Indian rule. The local police had mutinied; the legal system staffed by Kashmiris was close to collapse; more than a hundred thousand Hindus had fled while the hospitals were flooded with tortured and maimed young men; and thousands more were missing, presumed dead, or in Pakistan.

3. The Unending War

The unprovoked firings on unarmed demonstrators by the Indian police and army—a recurring, if little-reported, event in Kashmir over the next few years—alienated even pro-India Kashmiris. Coming after the corruption and arbitrariness of Indian rule in the previous four decades, they created a vast number of humiliated men in Kashmir, people likely to be attracted to the upsurge of nihilistic energy in Afghanistan and Pakistan. So intent were the Kashmiris upon fighting for independence that their cultural and political differences with the Pakistanis became relatively unimportant. The first men who went over to Pakistan were still thinking of an independent and secular Kashmir. But as the movement grew and the ISI found increasing numbers of Kashmiris willing to fight for integration into Pakistan, the country stopped bankrolling those secular Kashmiri guerrillas who were seeking independence. They were betrayed to Indian intelligence agencies, and many of them also killed, by the more militant pro-Pakistan guerrillas. These new insurgents were seen as hard-line Islamic terrorists, especially after they kidnapped and killed Hindus and, later, European and American tourists in Kashmir. Among Kashmiri Muslims, who belong to the peaceable Sufi tradition of Islam, they came to be feared for their fanaticism, which often erupted into violence against women and other unprotected civilians.

Kashmiris, who had expected as much international support as had been given to the East Germans and the Czechs when they filled the streets in late 1989, were surprised by the cautious pro-India policies followed by the European Union and America. But diplomats and policy makers in the West had their reasons to be worried. In 1994, as the Taliban achieved major victories in Afghanistan, the network of radical Islamists began to spread. Islamic fundamentalist outfits in Pakistan became stronger; so did the ISI, which played a large role in shaping Pakistan's domestic and foreign policies. As the Taliban began consolidating its position in Afghanistan, the ISI and the fundamentalists began to export jihad to Kashmir, where guerrilla groups were brought together by the ISI in an umbrella organization called the United Jihad Council. The guerrillas, once raw young Kashmiris, were trained in the use of light weapons in Afghanistan and Pakistan and then sent back to wage war on India. The traffic across the border grew very busy. Even now almost every Kashmiri Muslim you meet has friends or acquaintances who went to Pakistan. However, the Pakistani involvement in Kashmir reached a new pitch when, in the summer of 1999, Kashmiri guerrillas along with Pakistani soldiers were discovered to have occupied strategic Himalayan heights in India-held Kargil.

There were other, larger reasons behind the insurgency in Kashmir, which lay in changes in India. In addition to the shift in Indian politics throughout the 1970s, there was a later cultural shift in the early 1990s, when India's nominally socialist, protectionist economy was opened up to foreign investment, giving rise to a new middle class of people in business and the professions. As with most new middle classes its members were eager to hold on to what they had recently acquired, and their politics were on the whole conservative. Many of them felt India's stability should be ensured by brute force, if necessary, in places like Kashmir and the northeastern states, since stability was essential for business, both locally and internationally. This was an attitude most strongly articulated by the Hindu nationalist party, the BJP, which the middle class helped elect to power in 1998.

Under the Hindu nationalists, India's economy was further globalized, creating a small elite of business tycoons and reanimating the cultural and emotional links many affluent Indian-Americans had with their home country. The BJP attempted to give India, and this global Hindu middle class, a greater international presence by conducting nuclear tests and lobbying for a permanent seat in the Security Council of the United Nations. The government's obsession with India's unity and its deep suspicion of internal and external enemies moved beyond the nationalism of the Congress Party. As the party in power, the BJP had more opportunity to enforce its nineteenth-century idea of nationhood: one people, one culture, one language.

The BJP had kept up a steady rhetoric on Kashmir throughout most of the nineties, before they came to power, even as a harsh crackdown in the state went on. India, they said, had become a "soft" state, easily bullied by its neighbors and secessionists; they spoke of a "proactive" policy and "hot pursuit" of terrorists across the border into Pakistan. In 1999 the battles with Pakistan-backed infiltrators in Kashmir broke out, the first in India to be fought before TV cameras, and suddenly many in the middle class adopted the BJP's extreme rhetoric about the "Kashmir problem."

During the long years of rule from Delhi, most middle-class Indians had been generally indifferent to local politics in Kashmir; for the more affluent, the valley itself was a holiday destination, cherished for sentimental reasons. However, with Pakistan seen increasingly as an ever more implacable enemy, renewed patriotic sentiment and the televised demands for an end to Pakistani support for the guerrillas affected the Indian Army. A friend back from the front told me of a Pakistani soldier in Kargil whose arms had been cut off and who, as he bled to death, kept pleading futilely with indifferent Indian soldiers to take his money out of his pocket and send it to his children and aging mother in Pakistan.

As the Indian Army announced one improbable victory after another, TV reporters and newspaper journalists emerged as cheerleaders, and then, in July 1999, when, under American pressure on Pakistan, the infiltrators withdrew from the strategic heights, the media led the country in celebrating what the Hindu nationalist government described as Pakistan's military and diplomatic defeat.

If the battles in Kashmir hardened public opinion in India, the well-reported arrests of Muslims, allegedly terrorist agents of the ISI, in various parts of India further fed Hindu suspicions about Muslims in general, and Kashmiri Muslims in particular.

According to popular Hindu sentiment about the Kashmir problem, human rights violations by the military could be means of reasserting Indian authority over the state. In the southern Hindu-majority city of Jammu, in the plains, I met a leader of the BJP, Mr. Khajuria, one of the up-and-coming men within his party. Supplicants—job seekers, men with big shiny boxes of sweets to offer Khajuria—thronged outside his flat, often spilling into the living room, furnished with the regulation green carpet of government offices and sofas upholstered in dark blue velvet, with model airplanes on display in the glass cabinet, below large framed pictures of stern-looking BJP ideologues. Khajuria, a small, round man with a big wart on the bridge of his nose, would gently scold the waiting group as he pushed his way through: "Can't you see I am doing an interview?"

He had been a leader of the student wing of the BJP at Jammu University and still had the sweetly ingratiating manner of the ineffectual student politician. I could have predicted before the meeting most of what he said: India was facing "total war" with Pakistan, which could be ended only by invading and conquering Pakistan; the ISI was encouraging Indian Muslims to increase their population in India through hectic breeding; and Muslims were at best unreliable.

But I was still taken aback when eager to make an impression, and bolder now in his remarks, he said that Kashmiri Muslims only understood the language of the *danda*, the policeman's baton. That was the lesson of the maharaja's rule. "Give the security forces a free hand," he said, "and the Kashmir problem would be solved in two weeks."

The Kashmiri Muslim politician Mirwaiz Omar Farooq told me that the Hindu nationalists were determined to hold on to the valley but had little interest in the Kashmiris and knew very little about their long history and culture. Still in his early thirties, Farooq is the youngest of the leading separatist politicians in the Muslim-dominated valley. Most of his colleagues were in prison in the western Indian state of Rajasthan when I saw him in June 2000; he himself was under house arrest, and while we talked, policemen outside were asserting their presence by checking all incoming cars for bombs. On the clean-cut lawns where the trimmed tall hedges looked, distractingly, like giant hand grenades, a small group of men waited for an audience. Though much older, they were reverential toward Farooq, who was also the religious head of old Srinagar, a position previously occupied by his father, an opponent of the pro-India chief minister Sheikh Abdullah, until his assassination in 1990.

At the age of eighteen, Farooq had become the leader of the coalition of parties fighting for liberation from Indian rule; the news, I remember, was greeted with derision in India, as a sign of Kashmir's political immaturity. But people grow up fast in adverse times, and Farooq spoke with the subtlety and skill of an older, more experienced politician.

He was among the majority of Kashmiris, he said, who thought the insurgency had failed, and not only that: It had also undermined an ancient and gentle culture by introducing it to the dangerous cult of the gun. The only hope lay in a dialogue between India and Pakistan that would involve representatives of Kashmir. Although he opposed Indian rule in Kashmir and worried about the hardening of attitudes in India, he was also concerned about the rise of fundamentalist Islam in Kashmir. There was no alternative to a secular democratic state and rapid economic progress. It was Nehru's vision for India all over again, although ironically, in Kashmir, that vision had been dissolved by the same Indian state that was entrusted with the great power to realize it.

Still, the Kashmiris themselves are quick to embrace the modern world whenever the opportunity comes their way. Movement and growth are visible even after more than a decade of damage. Education suffered most in ten years of endless curfews and strikes, and yet even so, one of the most popular small businesses in the valley remains the primary English medium school or coaching institute. A small room and a graduate are all that is initially needed. You are assured of customers, parents who can't afford anything better but are anxious for their children to make their way into the larger world of jobs and professional careers, their anxiety so great and widespread that even the madrassas, the schools run by the fundamentalist Jamaat-i-Islami that moderate Muslims often send their children to, have had to secularize their syllabus.

At the time when political activity was restricted by the insurgency, Omar Farooq accumulated degrees in computer science and political science. When I first met him in 2000, he was studying for an M.Phil. degree in Islamic studies. In the market in Pattan, a few miles north of Srinagar, regularly destroyed and rebuilt after each battle between the police and guerrillas, I found two "computer institutes," tiny rooms really, with a computer in each, full of restless young men—restless because there was no power and they paid by the hour to become familiar with Windows software. At Kashmir University in Srinagar, its vast green campus bordering a lake and monitored by snowcapped mountains, the lines of students for enrollment in the new semester are very long. Students with guns ruled the campus not so long ago. The university, set up in 1948 and already in 1988 known as one of the best universities in India, effectively ceased to function in the nineties. Most of the Kashmiri Hindus on the faculty left. The anomie and corruption elsewhere had infected the university; there was mass cheating, and as a result, the amount of students passing their exams was an unusually high 90.5 percent. The lowest point was reached in 1992, when the university awarded degrees without holding examinations.

But the India-backed drive to restore peace to the state after the elections in 1996 benefited those in education. During the brief respite, the faculty was restaffed with more Kashmiri Muslims occupying senior teaching positions. Seminars and conferences were held again. The percentage of students passing their exams returned to normal. Some of the Muslim students who had been attending colleges and universities in India also returned, after being continually harassed by the police; the university set up new departments of biotechnology and geology for them.

For more than a century after 1846, when the British left, the Kashmiri Hindus had dominated the Muslim-majority population of the valley. Then the land reforms of Sheikh Abdullah, introduced during his time as the India-backed leader of Kashmir from 1948 to 1953, and the spread of free primary education created a new class of ambitious Kashmiri Muslims. However, no new institutions were provided to accommodate these Muslims, and existing facilities were monopolized by the minority of Hindus who ran the schools and colleges and had a disproportionate presence in the state's administration.

At first, the abrupt departure of the Hindus after the insurgency began in 1990 was felt as a blow. Over time the space vacated by them has been filled. Alongside the insurgency and the bloodletting, a new generation of Kashmiri Muslims has emerged to take their positions in the bureaucracy, the universities, and the media, and it is hard not to be impressed by this new middle-class intelligentsia, by the journalists, academics, and politicians in the valley, people like Abbas, my Muslim guide in Kashmir; Dr. Khan, the thoughtful scholar whom I had met in Srinagar; and Omar Farooq himself. They make it possible to believe that along with immeasurable suffering and pain, Kashmir has acquired a new political and intellectual life; that as had taken place once in India, the struggle for greater liberty has turned out to be a rite of passage, an awakening that owes as much to modern education as to the still-strong Sufi Islamic traditions of tolerance and civility.

Pakistan, busy exporting jihad everywhere even as it slowly imploded, couldn't have been expected to be responsive to that awakening; the section in northwest Kashmir which it continues to hold is the most underdeveloped part of the country, and Pakistan has done little for it. India is the bigger, economically stronger, more democratic country that can accommodate Kashmir, make it part of its overall growth. But the gap between India and Kashmir has grown even wider in the last decade.

———

The government keeps inviting the separatists to renounce violence and engage in dialogue; army and police officers speak routinely of "winning back the hearts and minds of the Kashmiris." But this isn't going to be achieved simply by sending Kashmiri schoolchildren on tours of India, one of the Indian government's populist measures, which, as one army officer told me, would not only appease the new generation of Kashmiris but would make them realize what a big and powerful country India is. That is a message that has already been conveyed by hundreds of thousands of Indian troops in Kashmir—the various army and paramilitary groups, some of whose more protected members, more than ten years after the insurgency began, have done well for themselves.

In Srinagar in March 2000, I met Mehbooba Mufti, the daughter of a senior pro-India Kashmiri politician, who was then one of the brave people who traveled around the valley investigating the excesses of both the security forces and the guerrillas. When I saw her, she had just returned from visiting the border with Pakistan near the distant north of the valley. The area was known for timber smuggling, and three timber smugglers, caught while murdering some villagers, had fingered the commanding officer of the local army unit as their protector. That wasn't all. The fabled beauty of the women in the area invited trouble from the Indian soldiers stationed there. There had been accounts of prostitution and rape in the past and, just a few months ago, an incident with a commanding officer who wanted to marry one of the seven daughters of a peasant. The woman was already married, and so was the army officer. The peasant father, who refused to sanction the relationship, was taken away; pieces of his body were later returned in a sack to the village. The army claimed that the man knew of a guerrilla hideout and was leading an army patrol to it when he stepped on a mine.

There were similar stories everywhere—stories either left unreported in the Indian press or deemed too dangerous to investigate, since what was at stake was the "national interest." It was the excuse the India-backed chief minister of Kashmir, Farooq Abdullah, had himself used in 1999 in the state legislature when asked by Yusuf Tarigami, the lone Communist in the state legislature, to reveal the killers of fifteen Muslim villagers in Jammu. It was also, Mr. Tarigami told me, why there was going to be no independent investigation into the killing of the Sikhs at Chitisinghpura, despite repeated requests by human rights organizations.

One of these organizations, Amnesty International, identified Indian intelligence agents and "renegade militants," whose patrons are the Indian Army, alongside armed opposition groups on its list of those likely to be responsible for the killings. These "renegade militants," so called after the army began to recruit captured or "reformed" guerrillas for operations where the costs in human lives and the army's reputation were likely to be too great for the army to use its own men, are the most dreaded group in the valley, more feared than the jihadi guerrillas, more than the army and police officials in remote areas or the jumpy soldiers in their bunkers.

In the early years of the conflict, 1994 to 1996, these renegades had proved very handy: They helped the army rebuild its intelligence network in the valley and also assisted in tracking down and killing hundreds of guerrillas trained in Pakistan and Afghanistan. They proved less effective against the fidayeen, the new "suicidal" guerrillas, often Pakistani citizens, who had started arriving in the valley in larger numbers after the battles of 1999; in fact, many renegades had been murdered by the fidayeen. Nevertheless, they still threatened, and sometimes killed, the families of guerrillas living in the valley or those journalists and human rights activists who were seen as too eager to report the excesses committed by the army. In return, the army and the civil administration looked the other way when the renegades kidnapped and killed for money. A senior government official spoke of them to me as Frankenstein's monsters; the renegades were, he said, the most visible and hated symbol of Indian rule over the valley, and it wasn't going to be easy to tame them.

At Anantnag, the town thirty-five miles south of Srinagar, I tried to see the local "commander" of the renegades. But he was away in Delhi, an unexpected sign of his status with the Indian government; the renegades had recently helped set up the BJP office in Anantnag. A polite policeman directed me to the home of another commander in the same protected compound. Parts of the house looked relatively old, and the rest was under construction, the money for it coming, it seemed, in installments. When finished, it was going to be a huge house, its size and the high walls topped with glass shards making it look like something from an affluent Delhi suburb.

A young, good-looking man in kurta pajamas came out after much apprehensive peeking through the holes in the heavy iron gate. It transpired he was the brother of the commander, Rashid; Rashid himself was at his headquarters a couple of miles away, and the brother drove me there.

The headquarters was a large building that had been vacated by a Kashmiri Hindu family. It had been transformed into a minifortress, with boarded-up windows and a tall corrugated iron gate, behind which, in the courtyard, young men stood dramatically poised with light machine guns to repulse any attack. There were good reasons for their defensiveness. One of the commanders of the renegades had been shot dead a week before in a crowded bazaar, and some months ago the improvised explosive device hidden in an auto rickshaw and intended for the renegades had turned the house ten meters away into a huge mound of rubble.

Rashid was waiting outside the gate, and to see his bodyguards, teenage boys with oversized guns, was to feel the fear and uncertainty their presence brought to the neighborhood, to the tense men in the little meat shops and bakeries lining the alley. As for Rashid himself, his lean, wiry frame, sharp features, and thick mustache, his thick gold ring and blue jeans gave him a Bombay movie star glamour and an impression of brute power until the moment he spoke. Then the quivering jaw and broken syllables betrayed his jitteriness, the jitteriness, I thought, of the doomed man; it made him an attentive host and keen talker. He saw me as taking back an important message to the Indian government conveying his anger at what he perceived as India's disregard for the renegades, the poverty and isolation to which they had been reduced, the temptation they felt to go back to Pakistan, and he shouted at the bodyguards when they showed up with lukewarm tea.

It was hard to get him to talk about the things I was interested in, which he mentioned indifferently when pressed: the bachelor's degree in science from the local college, the lack of work, the journey to Pakistan with no clear motivation with twenty-eight other men, the training in light weapons in Pakistan and Afghanistan for eleven months, then the return to the valley as a guerrilla, the sudden disillusionment with the armed movement for independence, and the recruitment by the army. He was frankly puzzled when I asked him to expand on little details in his narrative, about the camp commander in Pakistan named after Aurangzeb, the last great Moghul emperor and persecutor of Hindus; the deception in Pakistan where he'd had to present himself as a fundamentalist pro-Pakistan Muslim in order to receive his training and small salary. But he elaborated at some length about his local patron, a brigadier in the Indian Army.

The brigadier had asked him to lead an antiguerrilla operation very recently, and he had obliged by killing the two guerrillas who had infiltrated an army camp. Here Rashid pointed at the thin, unshaven middle-aged man in grimy kurta pajamas I had assumed was a supplicant awaiting his turn; he was the one who had covered Rashid as he stormed, guns blazing, the little room where the guerrillas were holed up, the one who shot a dying man to prevent him from reaching for a hand grenade. This thin, unshaven man, Rashid said, had been rewarded by having a police report lodged against him for "asking" a rich merchant in the town for some money. But what, after all, could he do with the little money he was given by the government?

It was at this moment that something hit the high corrugated iron roof sloping into the courtyard; at the deep, heavy sound, everyone — Rashid, I, the three boys with guns — froze for an agonizing second. It was several minutes after the scruffy cork cricket ball had pattered off the roof into the open drain around the courtyard that I heard my heart pounding wildly.

Rashid's face had gone white, and the shame of that inadvertent confession of fear was, I think, what made him grow wild when I asked him about the fidayeen, the suicidal guerrillas. He and his men were the true fidayeen, he shouted, people who were being martyred for being faithful to India. Then he added that he was ready to take on the fidayeen anytime. All he needed was a "free hand."

A "free hand": I heard those words very often in the valley, and it spoke, as nothing else did, of the breakdown of communications, the end of dialogue, and the unthinking preference for violence and terror. Rashid was bemused when I asked him to explain what he meant by a "free hand," because he had already done so, at least indirectly. He had made it clear, without saying so explicitly, that the government, and busybodies from the press and human rights groups, should turn the other way while the families of the guerrillas were harassed, and suspected informers were tortured, and civilians mistreated.

R ashid's idea of a "free hand" wasn't very different from that of the government. The words were part of the accepted vocabulary, more potent than the previous talk of "proactive policy," which really meant pursuing guerrillas across the border into the training camps, easy to fantasize about in Delhi but impossible to achieve without starting, as almost happened in 1990, a war with Pakistan. The borrowed phrase "ethnic cleansing" was even less effective. After each killing of Hindus, it was said that the guerrillas were engaged in "ethnic cleansing," but ethnically, the Sikhs and Hindus were no different from the Muslims of the valley. In the end, the few attempts at subtle rhetoric always collapsed into crudely aggressive demands for a "free hand."

The "free hand" means that the cycle of retribution will continue for a much longer time. In Pattan, outside Srinagar, just a few days after I left, the local police station was attacked with grenades and rockets. In response, the frustrated policemen looted and burned down the entire market. I didn't go back; I didn't feel I could face the helpless shopkeepers I had met on my previous visit. I went instead to Jammu, the city of the plains, where, far away from the new mansions of the politicians and bureaucrats, thousands of Hindu refugees from Kashmir now live.

I t was in early 1990, during Jagmohan's few months as India's appointed governor in Kashmir—and with, some say, his active encouragement—that most of the 140,000-strong community of Kashmiri Hindus left the valley. Jagmohan had originally been made governor in 1984, appointed by Mrs. Gandhi in order to dismiss Kashmir's elected government; he had served for five turbulent years, during which his aggressively pro-Hindu policies further alienated Muslims in the state from India. His limited comprehension of the insurgency, as simply a limited law-and-order problem which could be contained fast, is apparent in his memoir about his time as governor of Kashmir. Many Kashmiris believe that he wanted the Hindus safely out of the way while he dealt with the Muslim guerrillas.

The Hindus had formed a kind of elite in the valley and made their presence felt in the bureaucracy, both there and in Delhi, where government policy on Kashmir often came to be dictated by the fears and concerns of this tiny minority. Their connections with India and their relative affluence made them highly visible targets during the first few months of the insurgency in 1990; several government officials were assassinated by pro-Pakistan Muslim guerrillas who also committed random atrocities against Hindu civilians: rapes, murders, kidnappings.

Approximately 130,000 Kashmiri Hindus left the valley within two months of the insurgency beginning; few have been able to return. The ordeal of displacement was less difficult for the professional elite of doctors, engineers, and academics, who, on leaving the valley, renewed their links with the outside world; they now form a distinct diaspora within India and in the U.K. and America, where large numbers have settled.

It has been the less well-off Hindus in the countryside who have suffered the most. A few miles out of Jammu, on a stony, treeless plain, you suddenly come across hundreds of one-room tenements where thousands of Kashmiri Hindus have been living for the last ten years, waiting, without much hope, for things to improve. It was early spring in the valley and still cold when I visited the camps, but around Jammu the temperatures had begun to rise, and the sun felt more severe on the rocky exposed ground. The tar that held together the thermocoal roof of the igloo-shaped tenements had already begun to melt, and more tar was hard to find; you had to bribe the roadworks laborers.

This wasn't the only thing that worried Gautam, the Hindu I met in one of the camps. In 1990, he had left his apple orchards near Baramulla in the north of the valley with just sixty-five rupees in his pocket. There had been no water for eight days, and the plastic buckets used for storage had begun to run dry.

Gautam sat behind a window with iron bars, half slumped on the single wooden cot in his half-sleeved vest and pajamas. The smell of burned onion came from the tiny room where all five members of his family slept. The walls were bare except for a calendar with pictures of

Rama and Sita; there were a few steel utensils on the shelf over a rusty gas cylinder; a small television sat on a rickety stool. Outside, in the cramped little courtyard edged with an open drain, a mangy dog slumbered in the shade of the overburdened clothesline, and the tin doors of the public latrines were cut so low that you could see the blank face of the person squatting over the hole in the floor.

I wasn't invited in. Gautam, when he relaxed more with me, said bitterly, "We are like a zoo; people come to watch and then go away." He felt betrayed by Jagmohan and the other politicians, especially the Hindu nationalists, who had held up the community as victims of Muslim guerrillas in order to secure Hindu votes but then done very little to resettle them, find jobs for the adults or schools for the young. Gautam had been back to the valley just once; he had been persuaded to do so by his Muslim neighbor who personally came to the refugee camp to escort him back to his village. The warmth between the Hindu and Muslim communities of the valley—so alike in many ways for the outsider, so hard to tell apart—had remained intact and had acquired a kind of poignancy after such a long separation.

But when Gautam returned, he found his house had been plundered; children were playing cricket in his apple orchard, where the trees had been cut down for firewood. Then he was kept awake by fear on his first night, by the sound of gunfire, a sound his Muslim neighbors had gotten used to. In the morning he had heard the news of the deaths of five Indian soldiers in the gun battle with guerrillas. Enraged soldiers were expected any minute to launch a "crackdown." Gautam followed the young men of the village and took the first bus out.

He hadn't gone back again; he didn't know if he could. His son, fourteen years old now, had very few memories of Kashmir, had grown up in a different world, with a sense of injustice and the rage of the young. Gautam often had to stop him from denouncing Muslims and Islam.

I didn't see the boy; he was at school. There was a picture of him in a small plastic frame; with large serious eyes in his pale Kashmiri face, he reminded me of the Muslim boy I had met some days before at a graveyard in Srinagar.

It was my first day in Srinagar. A famous guerrilla had been killed by the army the day before, but there had been no public mourning. At the Idgah cemetery for "martyrs," placed at the edge of a vast, bald field

scarred with muddy puddles and full of signboards with exhortations—
"Lest you forget that they gave their today for our tomorrow"—there
was one fresh grave but, again, no mourners. The grave was of a young
man who had been taken from his home by the police for interrogation. A very old man sat nearby with a teenage boy in large thick-framed
glasses, both hunched over a *kangri*. The boy, Jamal, took me around,
stepping agilely across the graves, his dark eyes somber behind his
glasses.

The earliest graves in that Srinagar cemetery had claimed the most
reverence and space; they were set in large plots, adorned with bead
necklaces and plastic garlands. But as the numbers had begun to rise,
and the graves had been set closer together, the headstone engravings
acquired a uniformity of message and style; the green-painted word
"martyr" occurred in all of them.

The boy pointed out the new grave, the earth still moist under the
wrinkled plastic sheet; it had no headstone yet, but a narrow, freshly
dug bed of yellow irises ran around the perimeter. Irises were, Jamal
said, the flowers used to honor the Muslim dead in Kashmir.

He couldn't have been more than five years old when the insurgency began, but he knew the names of all the "martyrs." There were
some in his own family: his elder brother, who had been killed two
years ago, soon after he returned from Pakistan; his father, who had
died of his injuries after being tortured with hot iron rods. Jamal had
dropped out of school and now came to sit in the graveyard each
evening. I asked him why, and he said, his large eyes earnest, that he
wanted to be close to the martyrs; they had died a holy death in the
cause of jihad and were now in paradise. Later he said that his mother
was worried about his visits to the cemetery; she had been going to various shrines and making him wear amulets to prevent him from becoming a "militant" like his brother.

He wanted to know what Indians in India thought of their army
killing the Kashmiris, and it was the guilt brought on by this question
that made me stay longer with Jamal. Windows opened in the rain-
dampened houses overlooking the graveyard, and curious faces appeared in them, watching me talk to him. The day, already gray, began
to die quickly. The taxi driver grew nervous; the area was the stronghold
of the pro-Pakistan guerrillas.

When I left, the image I carried with me was of the young boy and

the old man sitting against the dirty, overcast sky, the mist-hazy mountains, and the flat, puddle-stained field; it added to the desolation of
those first few days in Srinagar, which, although the terrible scenes of
the massacre were yet to come, had already begun to contaminate my
early memories of Kashmir, of the landscape that had once been a revelation of beauty.

On one of my last days in Srinagar, one of the many days of protest
strikes, enforced by the guerrillas, the city surreally deserted in the middle of the long, sunny afternoon, I went back to the graveyard. There
were more graves, and, with spring finally resurgent in the valley after
many cold days, the irises were in full bloom. But Jamal was gone. The
old man sat all alone in the middle of the graveyard and didn't know
where Jamal was. He hadn't been to the graveyard in several days, but
his mother had come looking for him.

It was some weeks after I left Kashmir that I read a newspaper account of a teenage boy who had driven a car full of explosives into the
army cantonment in Srinagar; it was the first suicide bombing in the
valley. The boy went to a local school, and neither of his parents had
known about his connections with the jihadi outfits. It couldn't have
been Jamal, who had only one parent, but it was while reading about
this boy that I thought of Jamal again. I remembered the wide, serious
eyes; I remembered his talk of martyrdom and paradise and death.

The cycle of violence and destruction has been swift and severe in
Kashmir; the insurgency has poisoned and destroyed many lives.
Yet the insurgents' political cause remains as lonely and hopeless as before. Independence, which a majority of Kashmiris seem to want, and
integration with Pakistan, which for many Kashmiris is the second-best
option after independence, are not possibilities that any Indian government can ever consider without immediately losing the support of the
Hindu middle classes. The European Union and the United States are
unlikely to risk antagonizing India, with its lucrative markets and resources and the trappings of a democracy, by taking up the Kashmiri
cause.

It seems unfair that all Kashmiris can hope for at present is a change
in Indian attitudes, a bit more breathing space, a bit less heavy-

handedness; that the tens of thousands of victims of the decade-long violence will have to wait much longer for even some partial justice.

But then you can't hope for much justice in the subcontinent, where fulfillment comes to very few among the needy and restless millions, and where aspiration itself can feel like a luxury. In Kashmir, isolated and oppressed and then dragged into the larger world of competing men and nations and murderous ideologies, more people have been confronted with this awareness in the last ten years than in all of its tormented modern history.

There will always be young men like Jamal who attempt to dissolve the pain of that awareness in the nihilism of jihadi martyrdom. At the same time, there are many more Kashmiris who wish to make their peace with that pain, who are wearied by the bloodletting and resigned to their lack of options, and who now want the relative stability of the time before the insurgency to return, even if it involves living with the humiliation of continued Indian rule over the valley, the same private, uneasy accommodations with the world that keep the deprived millions elsewhere in the subcontinent from exploding into rage and destruction.

PAKISTAN

Jihad Globalized

Peshawar is a mess. And during my stay there in January 2001, when the smog above the city trapped the acrid smoke from the burning tires that the Afghan refugees huddled around for warmth, and Pakistani traffic policemen wearing new-looking gas masks flailed helplessly in the slow swirl of donkey carts, trucks, auto rickshaws, and cars, I began to wonder, somewhat resentfully, if the romance of Peshawar had been an invention of jaded adventurers from the West, of the eager-faced white men and women you could still see walking in the narrow alleys of the old quarters, visitors in the first flush of their enchantment with the Orient, for whom all those aggressively encroaching shanty colonies and the precariously defended middle-class suburbs, all the Afghan beggar children with startlingly green eyes, and the heroin addicts slumped on broken pavements could fade easily into the general quaintness of the East.

Fifteen years ago Peshawar had glamour. The Soviet Army was in Afghanistan, just forty miles away, propping up a Communist government; and Peshawar was the frontline city for the jihad against Soviet communism that the United States and its allies were sponsoring. Spies from the CIA, KGB, Mossad, and ISI worked the streets and refugee camps where more than one million Afghans lived. The local papers were full of cryptic paragraphs about assassinations and bomb explosions. Margaret Thatcher, George H. W. Bush, Kirk Douglas, and Princess Anne, among other celebrities, showed up to raise the spirits of the anti-Communist Afghan mujahideen. European and American journalists crowded into Dean's Hotel, waiting to be smuggled into the battlefield by their favorite "muj." At Lala's Grill, local fixers cadged kebabs from backpackers looking for the frisson of holy war and gossiped about the number of heroin laboratories near the Khyber Pass. You might even have come across rich Saudis like Osama bin Laden, busy enlisting Arab mercenaries into the jihad.

In early 2001 these excitements had died away, except among nostalgic middle-aged local journalists, whom the proxy war had temporarily rescued from ill-paid obscurity. Dean's Hotel had closed down a few months before my visit. Lala's Grill had acquired the dark-windowed façade of an Indian-Pakistani dive with pretensions, and although a sign asking visitors not to bring in their guns still stood by the main entrance to the Pearl Continental Hotel, the bright cloth banner outside advertised cooking classes for "ladies."

I felt oppressed by the city; its shapeless squalor as well as its new aspirations to respectability reminded me too much of the small-town India I had grown up in. Relief, along with proportion and order, seemed to lie only in the British-created cantonment, in the low red-tiled bungalows, whitewashed trees, and brick-lined flower beds and the lone guard standing stiff before long smoothly graveled driveways. It was where I often found myself in the long evenings—somehow longer in an unknown city—browsing through the boldly pirated American and British paperbacks at Saeed Book Bank and visiting newspaper offices in Saddar Bazaar.

I was never less than nervous while visiting the cantonment. My visa for Pakistan said, "Not Valid for Cantt Areas." I wasn't sure what this meant since cantt areas in the cities of the subcontinent are impossible to avoid. I was expected to stay away from "sensitive military installations," but since I didn't know what these were, I had to play it safe. I never turned my head sideways when my rickshaw passed the grander-looking buildings, never made it apparent that I was curious about anything except the dreary progression of the well-paved road and the proud replicas of new Pakistani missiles mounted on traffic islands, the missiles named provocatively after the Muslim conquerors of India.

This timidity was partly created by the three men in a beat-up To-yota Corolla who followed me every time I left my hotel. Representatives of one or all of the three major intelligence agencies in Pakistan, they seemed to show an exaggerated interest in me, a reflex from the days of the spy-infested jihad. It would have mortified the very amiable Pakistani diplomats in New Delhi who arranged for my visa and gave me, an Indian writer, what I learned later was an unprecedented liberty of travel within Pakistan. But then to be an Indian in Pakistan—or, for that matter, a Pakistani in India—is to be trapped by the prickly nationalisms of the two neighboring countries; it is to be automatically suspect.

Not that the spies did anything—or even looked—particularly ominous; the most visible amongst them, a plump, rosy-cheeked man in a pink shalwar kurta, could easily have been one of the shopkeepers standing idle behind open sackfuls of dry fruits in the narrow dark rooms of the old bazaar.

Still, if you are not used to being followed and watched, it can get stifling. The world seems full of a vague menace, the friendly, rather camp bellboy with slicked-down hair whom you think you have tipped generously turns into an ungrateful informer (so does, at one point, everyone else), and the liveliest street scene begins to look like an elaborate preparation for an arrest.

Paranoia was what the spies embodied and then, by their very presence, instilled in me. But there was a deeper unease I felt throughout the first three weeks I spent in Pakistan, waiting to go to Afghanistan, an unease about Islam and Muslims I had so far seen in others, something I sensed, while living in London, in the reports and outraged editorials about the Taliban and Osama bin Laden and other Islamic extremists in the British and American press and to which I thought I would be immune after my experience of Kashmir.

Tens of thousands of people—militants, soldiers, civilians—have been killed since the uprising began in 1990. The Indian press prefers to describe the situation in the valley as a spillover from the jihad in Afghanistan, the timid Kashmiris having been overwhelmed by Pakistani and Afghan terrorists looking to wage fresh holy wars. This broad picture, which depicted Pakistan and Islamic fundamentalists as the major villains, blurred and then dissolved altogether during the several weeks I spent in Kashmir last year; most Kashmiris still followed an unorthodox Sufi version of Islam, and the brutalities of the four hundred thousand Indian soldiers in the valley were what had pushed a small number of young Kashmiri Muslims into jihadi extremism.

My articles on Kashmir appeared in an American magazine. Soon after they came out, officials from the Indian IB (Intelligence Bureau) visited my retired parents in India and interrogated them at some length about my "pro-Pakistan" proclivities (which would have been confirmed for them when the Pakistani high commissioner in New Delhi praised my articles in print and then, not long afterward, arranged my exceptionally generous visa for Pakistan). Senior Indian columnists denounced me as unpatriotic and, while wondering what would lead an apparently well-to-do upper-caste Hindu to betray his country in an American magazine, concluded that I was pandering to white pro-Muslim audiences in the West.

This was optimistic. In the days before 9/11, you wouldn't have known that such audiences existed, judging from the little attention paid to Kashmir or Chechnya—another place where Muslims led a popular, but hopeless, uprising against a powerful pro-West nation-state—in the British or American press. Bereft of any recognizable context, the international news pages often seemed a kind of brisk atrocity mongering; part of their purpose seemed to be to verify the free world's privileges, as with the luxuries on display in the more expansive sections on shopping, food, sex, and celebrities, and Islam with all its diversity appeared primarily as the West's "other," in the way communism once had been: the aggressive ideology of an underprivileged and dangerously deluded people.

It wasn't a conclusion I ever expected myself to reach about Islam and Muslims, particularly when soon after returning from Kashmir, I thought of traveling to Pakistan and Afghanistan. I wanted to find out more about the CIA-led jihad in the 1980s and the rise of the Taliban, although there were related, less specific things I was curious about. One evening in Srinagar an old Muslim politician, routinely described as "fundamentalist" in the Indian papers, had spoken to me of how the West feared Islam even more since the demise of communism because it alone offered an alternative to the modern civilization of the West. It was hard for me then to work through such large generalizations. Later, when I began to read more in Islamic history, it became clearer to me how quickly, after the centuries of cultural and technological backwardness, the West had caught up with, and then begun to politically subjugate, the Islamic world in the nineteenth and twentieth centuries.

As it turned out, it wasn't very difficult to understand how people in demoralized societies could grow inflexible while trying to protect their older lifestyles. But this understanding came from the books I read in London, before I spent any time in a Muslim-majority country, and when, not long after I arrived in Peshawar from London, Jamal in Peshawar said, "They are all such fanatics here," I immediately warmed toward him. For I had found myself silently nurturing this commonplace prejudice, although I wouldn't have wanted to articulate it myself.

Jamal worked as a subeditor for *The Frontier Post*, one of Peshawar's English-language dailies, at whose offices I spent many hours on those bleak winter evenings. As I drove up to the boxlike narrow building, the three spies parked their car a few meters behind, before an empty lot where scrawny dogs loitered around mounds of assorted rubbish; these men had already ordered tea and barely looked at me as I walked past the pale mist-blurred lights of the chai shacks. Inside, at the reception, an old Pathan in a coarse-textured military coat hunched over a rickety table, a Kalashnikov leaning against the seat of his wicker chair; on the floor beside his feet squatted a bar heater, and occasionally he would bend toward its weak orange glow, palms stretched and facing outward, to gather some warmth. Upstairs, low doors led in and out of one cramped smoke-filled room after another, and in the room where I usually sat, a windowless cube really, the cigarette smoke stayed suspended in the air, the delicately curled plumes outlined against green walls and brown paper files and aging computers with grimy screens.

It was a difficult time for the newspaper. Its owner, a local Pathan businessman called Rahmat Shah Afridi, had been arrested in 1999 on a charge of drugs trading. His son, a young, easily distracted man who ran the paper now, told me that the small amount of cannabis found in his father's Mercedes had been planted there by agents of Mian Nawaz Sharif, then prime minister of Pakistan. It seemed like a typical Pakistani story: big men pursuing small private feuds and vendettas—and perhaps not entirely inaccurate. A few weeks after I left Pakistan, a special antinarcotics court in Lahore sentenced Afridi to death. In any case, the smaller people were suffering; the staff had been working without salaries for three months.

But the shared austerity had made people jollier; the door to the room opened every two minutes to reveal a newcomer, announcing his presence with a joke, an anecdote, a filched cigarette, and a curious friendly glance at the visitor from India. A teenage boy, his oversized brown shalwar flapping around his ankles, kept bringing trays full of chipped cups steaming with thick milky tea; the rim of the cup's bottom would be already wet by the time you took your cup, and there were so many visitors that at the end of three hours the broad, dusty table glistened all over with small overlapping circles.

Jamal was as much of a cigarette cadger and tea drinker as anyone there. But he looked restless amidst the bonhomie of his colleagues, among whose ruddy handsome Pashtun, or Pathan, faces his swarthy, blunt features, so much like that of a South or East Indian, looked alien. I often felt his dull yellow eyes fixed upon my face; there was, I sensed, something he wished to tell me in private, and when the moment came early one evening, it was this difference that he was so keen to establish.

I hadn't been misled by his appearance. He was a Bengali, from Bangladesh. In 1975, when the country was just four years old, he had, as a young captain in the Bangladeshi Army, taken part in the military coup against the government. He had been present on the morning when the prime minister, Sheikh Mujibur Rahman, and his family were gunned down at their official residence. "An accident," he said, "we didn't mean to kill him." Whether accidental or not, the moment was firmly in the past, part of Bangladesh's history. But Jamal had spent the quarter century since then dealing with the consequences.

After the 1975 coup, he spent four more years in Bangladesh, waging a futile insurgency against the government, before finally escaping to Pakistan. There was no other choice; Pakistan, still bitter about its lost province, was the only country that wouldn't deport him straight back to Bangladesh, where he was sure to be executed for Rahman's murder.

Jamal hadn't liked his new country one bit, however. He had arrived in Pakistan just as General Zia-ul-Haq was beginning his program of Islamization; there was enough of the liberal Bengali, the reader of Tagore and Nazrul Islam, in Jamal to be repelled by the brutal imposition of religion on everyday life. But he couldn't object too loudly; as a political refugee he had to be grateful that he wasn't being hanged or shot. He had to manage as best he could, and so he had done, moving from job to job, city to city, from one kind of meanness to another.

Jamal's story was refined and embellished over several evenings. I wasn't always sure how to respond to it, especially when he added that he had a wonderful book inside him. After all, he had been eyewitness to the murder of Rahman, and the world was still waiting to hear the truth behind those events in Bangladesh in 1975.

The heaviness in his yellow eyes disappeared briefly when he said this. I didn't feel like telling him that all he had was a story, that a book was something else, and that the world wasn't much interested in what had happened that morning in Dacca all those years ago.

I didn't want to discourage or alienate him. He had known such a damaged life and then only a kind of survival in Pakistan. Besides, he was on my side, a fellow stranger in Pakistan, adrift among the fanatics with whom Pakistan appeared, during my first days there, alarmingly replete. There were the black-turbaned heavy-bearded leaders of the Taliban, arriving at their embassy in Islamabad in gleaming new Pajero cars; the retired general in Rawalpindi declaiming on the nobility of jihad; the crudely painted donation boxes for the jihad in Kashmir in the bazaars; the fundamentalist demagogues in small towns threatening to march upon Islamabad if the Sharia and interest-free banking weren't immediately introduced; the tribals in the so-called self-administering areas near the Afghan border cutting off a few arms in their attempts at proper Islamic justice. Almost every day, Sunnis murdered Shias and vice versa; a few young mujahideen achieved *shahadat* (martyrdom) in Indian Kashmir, and the newspapers alone, while reporting on all-consuming religious obsessions, could take you to the point where you began to sense something hard and fierce in even the simple devotion of the skull-capped men half prostrate, on chilly evenings, on the streets of Peshawar.

But here I had to look out for my own prejudices. There had been many Muslims in the railway towns of North and Central India I had grown up in. I couldn't distinguish them from the low-caste Hindus among the railway labor gangs my father supervised. My father certainly had Muslim colleagues. But I cannot remember identifying any among the exhausted men in sweat-drenched white shirts and gray pants who returned home with my father for a cup of tea after a long day out on the tracks, although the tea would have been served to them not in cups but the special glasses kept aside in our kitchen for Muslims and low-caste Hindus.

Most Muslims in the towns of my childhood were, in fact, very poor—much more so than we—and this was the reason I noticed them. They lived in ghettos inside the older parts of the town, where, after the expansiveness of the British-built cantonment and Civil Lines and railway colony, the streets and houses suddenly shrank and were edged with open drains, the women disappeared behind sinisterly black burkas, flimsy rags curtained off the hanging carcasses at the butcher shops, and the gaunt-faced men with pointed beards standing outside dark houses looked quite capable of the brutality that our prejudices ascribed to them.

The prejudices were bred partly by our own lower-middle-class deprivations, the anxieties about money, status, security that came to be related, in the usual unreflective way, to the alien-looking community in our midst. We weren't the kind of people who incited or ever took part in Hindu-Muslim riots. But we did believe the stereotype that fueled these brief explosions of rage and despair; we had no trouble imagining the bearded Muslim as a fundamentally violent aggressor, who could murder a Hindu with as much avidity and relish as he slaughtered the cow whose chopped-up flesh, thrown inside temple courtyards, usually inaugurated the savagery.

Another, quite common, and somewhat subtler cliché presented Muslims as backward-looking, as a drag on modernizing India, if not fifth columnists for Pakistan. Of course, the blunter dismissal was: Why don't these Muslims simply go to Pakistan? After all, India had been partitioned in 1947 in order to create a new homeland for Indian Muslims. Pakistan was what most of them had asked for, so what were they doing in India?

It seems a crude question now, but it wasn't easy to answer, although politicians and other privileged men tried. However, their assertion that India was a secular country which was open to people from all religions didn't convince those of us—upper-caste Hindus—who lived in straitened circumstances and practiced as well as suffered discrimination. And so, feeling frustrated and demoralized ourselves, we redirected most of the pity and scorn with which we would have seen, if we could, our own lives. Most Hindu women probably deserved as much sympathy as was expended, in any cursory discussions of the minorities, on Muslim women, who were imagined to be leading terribly oppressed lives, forced to breed like rabbits and wrap themselves in heavy burkas.

The clichés bubbled up only when we noticed the Muslims. For the most part this depressed minority was invisible and remained so for me even after I left home and went to university in Allahabad, where Hindu caste politics in the 1980s managed to overshadow Hindu-Muslim discord.

In the late 1980s, when I moved to a university in Delhi, the Hindu nationalist agitation to demolish the Babri Mosque in Ayodhya had just picked up all over North India. There was much opposition to this inside my university campus; in fact, it was there, in the isolated and artificial world of university politics, that I became slightly more aware of the peculiar status of Indian Muslims. The student politicians organized almost daily protests inside the campus, which many of the Muslim students, most of whom came from the nearby riot-prone town of Aligarh, joined, and where one speaker after another denounced the Hindu nationalists for attempting to destroy the great Indian traditions of tolerance and accommodation.

The student leaders were eager to make themselves known; they worked hard to make their protests as noisy and disruptive as they could, and the library, where I spent most of my time, was often closed early in the evenings.

The fuss over a disused tottering mosque in the middle of nowhere seemed excessive. Then came the day in December 1992 when the mosque was demolished by a frenzied Hindu mob.

The student politicians in the campus raged for some weeks afterward, but the Muslim students stayed away from their rallies. They appeared bitter and haunted. I began to look differently at them as they huddled around the dining table and spoke in low voices, eating swiftly all the while with their fingers.

I still couldn't feel involved. I had my own anxieties to deal with; the university degree I was working toward was only the first stage in what then seemed a long, slow climb out of the relative poverty my family had lived in for much of my childhood. Occasionally I would attend the after-dinner lectures by visiting left-wing journalists and academics, articulate, suave men who discussed the historical bonds between Hindus and Muslims and the uniquely syncretic civilization of India. These ideas about India's past and present didn't always match my experience, the sense I had of the distrust and hostility between Hindus and Muslims and the keener sense I'd had, in the course of my travels through small-town India, of the stagnant resentments of the Muslim ghettos. But I didn't have the courage to contradict them then and even now feel insecure before such powerful liberal pieties.

Pakistan has its own marginalized but vigorous liberals; indeed, its small English-language press is intellectually more adventurous and engaging than its Indian counterpart. This is probably because the country seems to have few pieties left over from its fifty years of existence. The bookstores are full of such titles as *The Years of Disillusionment* and *Whither Pakistan?*; the newspapers carry long letters by retired army men expressing concern over the number of educated Pakistanis wanting to emigrate.

Very early in Pakistan's history, its foundational myth had been broken; a shared religion, it turned out, couldn't solve the problem of how people with different ethnic and linguistic backgrounds were to live together. Urdu-speaking Muslims from India, arriving in large numbers in Sindh, found themselves resented by the poor Sindhis, who in turn felt oppressed by the rich and dominant majority of Punjabi speakers in the north. The Bengalis revolted and broke away in the early 1970s, the Baluch attempt to secede was put down with a lot of difficulty, and the disastrous Pakistani imperative to control events in Afghanistan grew out of the urgent need to pacify the Pashtun separatists of the North-West Frontier. The country, which many Hindus in India still imagined to be the natural home of Indian Muslims, had created its own ghettos, where resentments were anything but stagnant.

India has had its share of restless minorities—the Tamils, the Sikhs, and the Nagas. But it has also had a consistent political life, the semi-democratic institutions it inherited from the British. Since partition, elected politicians themselves have wrecked Pakistan's frail democratic structures when given half a chance by the army officers and the bureaucrats, who have otherwise been the real rulers; the major newspaper story in Pakistan when I was there early in 2005 offered details about how a few army officers, working for the ISI, cobbled together a coalition of quasi-Islamic political parties under Nawaz Sharif in order to overthrow the government of Benazir Bhutto in 1990.

The rulers of course lived separately, in well-fortified enclaves, indifferent to all the associations of third world sleaze they gave off. There wasn't much subtlety in the town houses, with their many carpets and chandeliers and servants and guards with automatic rifles, or the large farmhouses outside cities, whose brick-walled boundaries meandered far and invisibly into the countryside and where cheap French wine bootlegged by African diplomats flowed by the glimmering pool and people discussed the latest article on Kosovo in *The New York Review of Books* and grew very worried about the "bearded fundos" and the imminent—or, depending on whom you talked to, ongoing—Talibanization of Pakistan.

The phrase "Talibanization of Pakistan" was one I heard often. It was a new way of referring to troubles that had begun much earlier, in 1979, in fact, when Soviet troops entered Afghanistan, and the United States responded by arming anti-Communist Afghans with the help of the military dictator of Pakistan, General Zia-ul-Haq.

Although something of a tyrant, Zia was not without his Pakistani supporters. His Islamic zeal was admired by those religious parties who received government patronage for their largely unsuccessful attempt to Islamize Pakistan. He was popular too among senior officers in the military. As he himself described it, Lieutenant General Hamid Gul was one of the early jihadis in the military and much loved by Zia, who first made him director of military intelligence and then director general of the ISI. While holding these positions in the 1980s, Gul was one of the three or four most powerful men in Pakistan, who, under Zia's patronage, could get away with just about anything.

But then, in 1988, Zia and other senior army men died in a still-mysterious air crash. Benazir Bhutto, the daughter of the man Zia had hanged, became prime minister of Pakistan and got rid of Gul at the first available opportunity in 1989. Gul turned into an intriguer; he led the frustrated power-hungry officers of the ISI in a successful conspiracy to bring down Bhutto in 1990.

Retirement from the army diminished Gul. He attempted to reinvent himself as a full-time jihadi, writing columns in the Urdu papers and sending long faxes, as an exasperated editor told me, to the offices of the English-language press, usually denouncing the new military government for surrendering before India and America.

Gul's awareness of his lost authority seemed present in his swift response on the telephone when I told him that the men shadowing me might stop me from traveling to his home in the Chaklala air base near Rawalpindi. "I'll see," he said, in a controlled voice, "who dares stops you from visiting my home."

Palladian columns—the mansions of military officers in Pakistan are always grand—guarded the front of Gul's house, which was otherwise remarkably un-Roman. On the walls of the living room, framed photos of the Kaaba seemed to look away from the suffocating excess in the middle: the huge crystal decorations on the center table, the shiny life-size brass deer, the satin green upholstery, the animal skin rugs, and the glittering trophies.

Beardless, and sporting a trimmed mustache, a Western-style tweed jacket, and vigorously polished brown moccasins, Gul seemed closer to his background as a cavalry officer than to the austere world of jihad. His English was mostly Urdu-accented and only occasionally, when he ceased his loud declamations, lapsed into the Sandhurst inflections and phrases of an older generation of army men. He dealt awkwardly with my more personal questions, revealing only, with obvious irritation, that his family was originally from the hilly district of Swat and that he had gone to a village school before attending a government college in Lahore.

These were humble origins when compared to the "brown sahabs" Gul was known for attacking at every available opportunity, the men Anglicized and groomed to assume power at influential establishments like Aitchison College, Lahore, and St. Patrick's College, Karachi.

They partly accounted for Gul's immodest ambitions and claims. In February 1989, when the Soviet Army withdrew from Afghanistan, he was, as director general of the ISI, leading the jihad. As he described it, his role in the jihad had begun even while he was a lowly brigadier. Three weeks after the Soviet intervention in Afghanistan in 1979, he wrote and circulated a policy paper in which he advocated Pakistani support for a low-intensity guerrilla war against the Soviet Union and its Afghan allies, gradually extending it right into the Muslim-majority Central Asian provinces of the Soviet Union.

The paper reached Zia, who was impressed by Gul's energy and ambition. A meeting with the general followed. "I told General Zia," Gul said, "that if we defeated the Russians, and I was very optimistic that we would, then there was no reason that the borders of our great Islamic world should stop at the Amu Darya" (Amu is the Oxus River, which formed the boundary between Afghanistan and the former Soviet Union).

The paper, Gul claimed, was read carefully by high-placed officials of the CIA and formed the basis of later incursions into what William Casey, the director of the CIA under Ronald Reagan, described as the "soft underbelly of the Soviet Union."

Much of this seemed like boasting, however. The cold warriors of the Carter administration had long been waiting for the Soviets to slip up in Afghanistan. Zbigniew Brzezinski, national security adviser to President Carter, who wanted to "sow shit in the Soviet backyard," had arranged for clandestine aid to the radical Islamists in Pakistan a few months before Soviet troops arrived in Afghanistan. The Soviet intervention gave them the pretext they needed to raise the ante. In the letter Brzezinski wrote to Carter on the day the Soviet Army entered Afghanistan, he was exultant: "Now, we can give the Soviet Union its Vietnam War." It was this trap for the Soviets that the CIA, under Casey, deepened through the early and mid-1980s by providing billions of dollars' worth of arms and aid.

In fact, Casey, a veteran of the OSS, and a fanatical cold warrior, wanted the ISI to involve the Muslims of the Soviet Union in the jihad, and he wasn't satisfied with the ISI-arranged smuggling of thousands of Korans into what is now Uzbekistan and Tajikistan or with the distribution of heroin among Soviet troops. One officer of the ISI, and a critic of Gul, told me that the ISI received plenty of unofficial encouragement from Casey himself to attempt operations more damaging to the Soviet Union, but nothing that could be traced back to the CIA or the government of the United States. The senior officers of the ISI, flush with unaudited funds, were running their own little battles by the mid-1980s, and one of them arranged for the mining and bombing of military installations a few kilometers deep inside Soviet territory. The Soviet ambassador in Islamabad immediately left some ominous messages at the Pakistan Foreign Office, and Gul, confronted with the possibility of a Third World War, had to hastily withdraw the saboteurs from Soviet territory.

When I met him, Gul had nothing but abuse for his former bankrollers in the CIA: "A self-serving people. All they wanted was to turn Afghanistan into a Vietnam for the Soviet Union; they used us for this purpose, and then they lost interest after the Soviets withdrew."

This was a commonplace sentiment in Pakistan. You heard it from liberal journalists, who had from the very beginning highlighted the folly and risk of fighting other people's wars; you heard it from the jihadis, hoping to fight for another day. American involvement in Afghanistan and Pakistan had become the story of the cynical arrogance of cold warriors like Brzezinski and Casey.

The jihad that Gul imagined himself to be leading turned out to be under neither his nor the ISI's control. Many different realpolitik interests had brought it to Pakistan and would, in time, take it away. The Americans wanted to rouse the Muslims of the world against the Soviet Union; the Saudi royal family, which matched the American assistance dollar to dollar, wanted its own version of Sunni Islam, Wahhabism, to triumph over the then-resurgent Shiism of Ayatollah Khomeini of Iran. For these larger battles, Pakistan was merely a base, where CIA operatives could, for a while at least, mingle happily with such rich Arab jihadis as Osama bin Laden.

After the Soviet withdrawal was agreed to in Geneva in 1987, the American interest in both the jihad and Afghanistan dwindled. The CIA promptly scaled back and soon ended its aid to Pakistan and the mujahideen.

Left pretty much to their own devices, the ISI and Gul began to flounder. In 1988 came the still-mysterious fire in Ojhri, halfway between Islamabad and Rawalpindi, in which the ten thousand tons of arms and ammunition supplied by the CIA to the ISI for the Afghan mujahideen exploded in a spectacularly violent fireworks visible in a twelve-mile radius that many people took to be the beginning of a war between India and Pakistan; the rain of rockets and missiles lasted a whole day, killing a hundred people and injuring thousands of others.

Then, in 1989, Gul abandoned the usual mode of guerrilla warfare in Afghanistan and conceived and supervised what turned out to be a disastrous frontal assault by the mujahideen on the Communist-held city of Jalalabad in Afghanistan. Four months later the mujahideen had lost three thousand men and were further away than ever from taking Jalalabad. The Afghan Communist government in Kabul lasted another three years, during which the mujahideen turned to declaring jihad against each other.

The divisions among the seven mujahideen parties recognized by the ISI had been deepening since 1979, caused less by ethnic and linguistic differences than by the inequitable way in which the ISI parceled out the largess from America and Saudi Arabia. The ISI under Gul was most generous to a particularly brutal mujahideen leader called Gulbuddin Hekmatyar, whose aggressive Islamism remained apart from the production and smuggling of heroin that created his wealth and power. The ISI expected Hekmatyar to install a pro-Pakistan government in Kabul after the fall of the Communists. But Hekmatyar turned out to be unacceptable to most other mujahideen leaders, especially those who had fought the Soviets without much American or Pakistani assistance.

When the Tajik mujahideen commander, Ahmad Shah Massoud, finally drove out the Communist government of Kabul in 1992, a full-scale civil war broke out in Afghanistan. Hekmatyar, backed by the ISI, rocket-bombed Kabul for months. More people died in the city during the fighting in the early 1990s than during the decade-long jihad against the Russians. International powers stepped in once again to bankroll various factions: The Saudis supported the Sunni fundamentalists, Iran backed the Shia Hazaras, Tajikistan and Uzbekistan had their own favorites among the Tajik and Uzbek mujahideen, and the ISI hadn't lost faith in Hekmatyar when in 1994 the student militia of the Taliban suddenly emerged out of nowhere and conquered most of Afghanistan.

Gul, still trying to prop up Hekmatyar, initially denounced the Taliban as CIA agents. These actions were more than personal or professional misjudgments and failures; they undermined whole societies. Reckless but high-placed adventurers like Gul, pursuing absurd fantasies of a pan-Islamic empire, had taken a largely poor and illiterate country to the edge.

Gul himself had done well out of it all. There was the Palladian-fronted house in Rawalpindi; there were a farmhouse and, rumors said, more properties elsewhere; there was the lucrative transport business that apparently his daughter ran in Islamabad.

And there were new jihads and jihadis to root for. "These Americans now accuse Osama bin Laden of terrorism. Once upon a time they used to call upon him in Peshawar and ask him to recruit more Arabs for the jihad," said Gul, anxious, like all jihadis I was to meet in Pakistan, to claim a special intimacy with bin Laden. "I met him in Sudan in 1993. Such a wise and intelligent man. So much spirituality on his face. But this is the effect of jihad. It is a very noble state to be in. That's why I look so young, although I am sixty-four years old. Jihad keeps me young, gives me a great purpose in life."

Gul's enemies in Pakistan—and there were many—scoffed at his Islamic fervor; it was, for them, another kind of opportunism, a private pipeline to power and to at least some of the money flowing in from rich Muslim countries for organizations devoted to Islamic causes. And listening to them, you could easily begin to think of jihad as another racket in a poor, backward country. Certainly, renewed faith alone doesn't account for the many sectarian groups that have sprung up over previous years, whose exploits—shoot-outs, bomb explosions, arson—dominate the national news.

Many sects and ideologies of the Islamic world have traveled to Pakistan. The Muslim Brotherhood in Egypt influenced the leaders of the Jaamat-i-Islami, the biggest of the religious parties, several of whom had studied at Cairo; the Saudis arrived late, but their open-fisted generosity has ensured a speedy embrace of Wahhabism among the poorer members of the clergy. A wall of Sunni madrassas partly funded with Saudi money lies alongside the borders Pakistan and Afghanistan share with the Shia-majority Iran.

Among these imported Islamic schools, the Deobandis are the most powerful and closest to the Wahhabis. The name comes from the original madrassa set up in 1866 in a small town near Delhi called Deoband. The madrassa was part of the insular Muslim response to British rule in the nineteenth century, the work of men who felt that Western-style education of the kind proposed by the British, and embraced by the Hindus, would fracture the Muslim community, men who were convinced that a training in the fundamentals of the Koran and the Sharia would shield Indian Muslims from the corruptions of the modern world.

A couple of years ago I read an American academic's book about Deoband; then one hot summer day, while I was on my way to the hill station of Mussoorie, I saw a sign for the town itself alongside the rutted road. The madrassa building, a wide, low quadrangle supervised by minarets, seemed shrunken in the vast dusty land. I wasn't welcome inside; the thin timid-looking young men in skullcaps didn't want to talk to me; wouldn't even let me in. I later discovered that Muslims had recently been massacred in a town not far from the madrassa.

The image of Deoband after that was of the fearful Muslims marooned among the Hindus of the Indo-Gangetic plain. In Pakistan, however, this image dissolved fast. The large courtyard of the Binori Town madrassa in Karachi, one of the largest and oldest of Deobandi institutions in Pakistan, has marble floors. Students from Africa, Central Asia, the Philippines, and Malaysia swarmed confidently through the large complex, its several hostels, kitchens, although in the classrooms a Koran-oriented syllabus first created in India in the nineteenth century was still being used. The notice board displayed beautifully typed appeals for volunteers in various jihads in Kashmir, Chechnya, the Philippines, and Afghanistan. The Taliban seemed a big draw, and quite appropriately; most of the Taliban's leadership as well as many of the foot soldiers of the Taliban have emerged from the Deobandi madrassas in Pakistan and southern Afghanistan.

It was Jamal who said, "You must go to the Deobandi madrassas. That's where a lot of the Taliban were trained, and a lot of Pakistani young men there also go to Afghanistan to fight for the Taliban. You'll find lots of fanatics there."

I did want to find a few fanatics; I also wanted to travel to Afghanistan. On both fronts, however, my attempts were being thwarted. At the Taliban's chaotic embassy in Islamabad, where gruffly inefficient former soldiers in black turbans ran or limped in and out of rooms furnished with peeling paint and dusty rugs, my visa application, deposited and redeposited several times, seemed as much of an illusion as the existence of an Afghan state or government. It wasn't easy to find the jihadis. The names Jamal sold me—at quite a high rate; he said he hadn't been paid his salary, he needed the money, and I didn't argue— turned out to be those of men long retired and living now in isolation. All the leads offered to me by the other English-language journalists I knew came to nothing. A Pakistani acquaintance in London had warned me that this might happen, that the jihadis knew too well how the English-language press in Pakistan felt toward them and were suspicious of anyone carrying its references. I began hanging out at the offices of the Urdu publications, many of which were sympathetic to the jihadis, and it was at the office of a plump young editor in Islamabad, one of the professional cheerleaders of the jihad and another self-proclaimed friend of Osama bin Laden, that I ran into Shafiq.

Shafiq looked old, although he was only in his mid-forties. When the editor introduced him as a veteran of the jihad in Afghanistan, he raised the sleeves of his kurta and displayed a bullet wound in his left arm. He didn't speak much; his Urdu was a low growl, the furtive tone, it turned out, of a fixer. His demands for money were more extravagant than Jamal's, and we were forced to meet early in the morning or late at night, the only time when my spies were off duty. It was difficult to arrange these meetings, for Shafiq's mobile phone, he claimed, was tapped by the ISI. But he usually had the information I required.

It took him some time to come up with someone to meet in Karachi; it wasn't his "area," he said. And then he said, with the glint in his eyes that always appeared in expectation of more money, that he had found someone special for me, an activist from the Sipah-e-Sahaba, one of the most dreaded anti-Shia groups in Pakistan, whose acronym, SSP, featured often in the daily papers, usually regarding attacks on or by Shias. He would, Shafiq promised, using the English words, provide me with "good material." All I had to do was shake off the spies and show up at the madrassa.

One early morning, when the spies were still asleep, I took a flight from Peshawar to Karachi, relieved to find no strange men in beaten-up cars awaiting me at the other end. Everywhere on the wide swift boulevard leading to the city center there were signs of Karachi's financial eminence: the billboards, the glass-fronted boutiques, and the fancy patisseries. I had expected a meaner place, acting out its reputation as the setting for violent battles between militant groups of Muslim migrants from India and the police, and instead, with the spies gone, in this port city—its warm, sea-scrubbed air and clear light and colonial buildings so much like Bombay, and so unlike the ingrown seediness of Peshawar or the diseased grandeur of Lahore and the wide suburban vacancies of Islamabad—suddenly I felt freer than I had ever before in Pakistan.

I felt, I think, as a Pakistani visitor to the city might, and it was as a Pakistani journalist from London that I introduced myself to Rahmat. The deception was necessary, Shafiq had told me. The connection to India would throw Rahmat; he would not want to talk. In any case, it gave me a new assurance the evening I went to the Binori Town madrassa: in my shalwar kurta that I had bought earlier in the day, I could have been one of the hundreds of young men heading in and out of the evening *namaz*.

Rahmat was waiting for me, as Shafiq had said he would be, at the small shop selling Afghan caps and Korans just inside the tall gateway to the madrassa. He was younger than I had expected, and the white, grimy kurta, the worn plastic slippers, and the dense beard that framed his face only highlighted his exceptional good looks, the wide, delicate cheekbones and shyly quizzical eyes.

We sat and talked in one of the garishly lit shops and cafés that hemmed in the madrassa. Shafiq had exaggerated: Rahmat wasn't a student but an odd-job man at the madrassa, and he had never been a member of the Sipah-e-Sahaba. He wasn't even sure whether the madrassa he had gone to near the city of Faisalabad was Deobandi; he only remembered that the teachers emphasized jihad as the primary duty of Muslims. As for the SSP, some members of the group had helped him and his family after his brother had been charged with murdering a Shia landlord.

The murder had happened near Rahmat's ancestral village in the Punjab, where his father had an auto repair shop. Rahmat had been languishing there after his stint at the madrassa along with his parents, four brothers, and two sisters, waiting for a job to come his way. Things hadn't been bad in the 1980s, in the days of Zia-ul-Haq's Islamization, when you could still get a job after a madrassa education. But Rahmat had gone to the madrassa at the wrong time and had come out of it to join the hundreds of thousands of unemployable young men in Pakistan. Some of his friends had mustered enough money to travel to the Gulf, and he was hoping to follow them when one day his brother murdered the landlord.

The landlord was a much-hated figure among his tenants, despised for the mistresses he kept in semiservitude as well as his financial crookedness. When he had falsified the records of Rahmat's family's ownership of a piece of fertile land, Rahmat's father and brothers had been too powerless to argue. But then he had tried to manipulate the mortgage on Rahmat's father's auto repair shop. This had enraged Rahmat's brother.

Rahmat said, "*Zamindar bada powerful banda tha*; the landlord was a powerful man." The many relatives of the dead man arrived in a Pajero and flogged Rahmat's father in front of the family, before destroying the auto repair shop. The police ransacked his house a few times, even locked Rahmat up for a few days, although he himself had been in the fields with a friend at the time of the murder.

The revolving discolike lights on the ceiling glistened on Rahmat's perspiring face as he spoke. The shop was busy. It seemed, rather incongruously, part of the celebration of wealth and leisure I had seen elsewhere in the city. The solemn-faced skull-capped visitors to the mosque inside the madrassa were easily outnumbered by the paunchy men in tight jeans and T-shirts who staggered out from badly parked Mercedes cars, strode fast to the shops, and then returned holding minimountains of shiny cellophane-wrapped sweet boxes.

Shoe polish urchins, their thin arms slinging wooden boxes, lapped at their knees. It was them Rahmat watched, turning his head away from me. His heavy-lidded eyes were even more unreadable when he turned back, and then, as if out of habit, he wiped his mouth and then his forehead with the sleeves of his kurta, already damp from his pre-*namaz* ablutions.

Only the men at the mosque in the nearby town, Rahmat said, had been able to help his family. They had employed his teenage younger brother at their own madrassa; they had worked through their contacts in the police to ease the pressure on Rahmat's family. Rahmat knew vaguely that they were members of the SSP and opposed to the Shias, but he hadn't given it much thought. Then one warm evening in 1995 one of the SSP men, someone not much older than Rahmat, who often led the *namaz* on Fridays, called for him.

When Rahmat got to the mosque on his bicycle, he found a small crowd of young men already there, including a couple of men from his village, people who had been tormented by the now-dead landlord. None of them them knew why they had been summoned. Then the man who had called them arrived, accompanied by an Afghan wearing a black turban, and addressed them briefly.

He said that the guest with him had come all the way from Afghanistan, where a new jihad had commenced. There were many corrupt men like the landlords of Punjab in Afghanistan. They called themselves mujahideen, the man said, as though they were engaged in jihad, but they were no worse than bandits and rapists, and now a new force had arisen to vanquish them and establish the law of the Prophet. The soldiers fighting the jihad were young Talibs, students, but Allah was with them.

It was the first time Rahmat had heard about the students, or the Taliban. There had been several Afghans at his madrassa, but he had kept away from them. The Afghan refugees had had a bad reputation in his part of Pakistan; they were seen as liars and thieves. His father dealt with them all the time in his auto repair shop. Their heavy trucks that they had brought from Afghanistan damaged the roads, and the drivers were often high on opium.

And so when the Afghan man began to speak, Rahmat was skeptical. He spoke Urdu with a heavy Pashtu accent that, Rahmat remembered, made some of the men smile. But the Afghan remained serious, and he didn't waste much time. He said he had come to ask for volunteers for the jihad in Afghanistan. He couldn't promise much in return, except food and shelter; the way of jihad was not strewn with roses; it was a holy duty for Muslims, and *shahadat*, martyrdom, was all they could expect from it.

Most of the young men weren't interested. But Rahmat, with a brother in jail and the auto repair shop, the sole source of his family's income, now gone, couldn't so easily disregard what the Afghan had offered. His father and his brothers wondered what he was getting into but didn't try to stop him. Rahmat remembered riding with other young men in a chartered bus to Quetta in Baluchistan and then crossing the border illegally one night. On the other side there were, along with Pashtun Afghans, many more Pakistanis. There were even Pakistani Army officers at the training camp where Rahmat learned to fire an automatic rifle, and also men from Chechnya, Kashmir, and Uzbekistan. It was in this training camp, in a rocky valley near the border, that he had grown his beard, not under any pressure—although men in Afghanistan were required to wear four-inch-long beards—but because of his desire to be a good Muslim.

Rahmat and other people in his group had been at the camp for less than two weeks when they were summoned to the western provinces, where the Taliban were fighting to capture the city of Herat. By the time Rahmat reached Herat, it was already under the control of the Taliban. He and his fellow mujahideen were like conquerors in the city. But it was a strange place. It was very cold; the locals spoke Persian, not Urdu or Pashtu; they even looked like Iranians. Even more alien were the young Pashtun men of the Taliban who went around shutting down schools, smashing TVs and VCRs, and tearing up photos. One of them discovered a seminude photo of an Indian film actress in the tent Rahmat shared with eleven, twelve other Pakistanis, and there was some awkwardness between the Afghans and the Pakistani volunteers for some time after that.

Rahmat hadn't liked the rough ways of the Taliban; they were backward people, he thought. They were cruel to their women and religious minorities and military opponents; someone in his village had been forced to participate in the massacre of civilians belonging to the Shia Hazara community in central Afghanistan. Rahmat was a bit frightened of them. But he couldn't deny that they had brought peace to Afghanistan, and when the Pakistanis he was with spoke of imposing a similar peace in Pakistan, where there was so much injustice and banditry, it seemed like an attractive idea.

Rahmat hadn't stayed long in Afghanistan as he was wanted as a witness at the trial of his brother. He hadn't returned to Afghanistan after that, although other young men he knew in his village had gone and were still going to fight with the Taliban.

Back in his village Rahmat met up again with the men at the mosque. It was with one of them that he had come to the Binori Town madrassa three years ago and then stayed on. There was some money to be made doing small menial jobs for the students and teachers; Rahmat could eat cheaply, and he could always find a place to sleep. Things were better here than in the Punjab, where his brother was still in jail and his father close to death.

R ahmat had shaken his head when I first asked him if he wanted to eat anything. But when I ordered another plate of *halwa*, he was quick to reach out and place his hand on the arm of the waiter, startling him slightly. After the food came, an oily plateful of what looked to my furtive eyes like mutton, Rahmat became more expansive, his Urdu, replete so far with Punjabi slang, became more formal, full of difficult Arabic and Persian words. He began to speak with his mouth full, of the greatness and necessity of jihad, of how Muslims were being oppressed everywhere, in Kashmir, Afghanistan, Chechnya, Egypt, Palestine, how the Jews in Israel could get away with anything because they were supported by Western powers.

I had heard, and was to hear, a lot of this talk from both the leaders and the foot soldiers of the jihad. It wasn't without its quota of truth, and you had to be careful neither to dismiss nor to swallow it whole. It was easier to see through the self-aggrandizement and deceptions of people like Hamid Gul. But the idea of oppression and injustice that Rahmat spoke of was more than just rhetoric he had picked up from the teachers at his madrassa and the ISI officers at the training camp in Afghanistan; it had a basis in his own experience of the world.

Rahmat was like the young men of my own class in the Indian small towns of the 1980s and early 1990s, people for whom the world didn't seem to have much place. The idea of religion as redemption, the unquestioning submission to one creed or philosophy—this was what my background had required of me, and it had taken some effort, and much luck, to be able to move away from it, to redefine myself as an individual, and to enter new, more complicated affiliations with the larger world.

Others weren't as lucky; these were people whose frustration and rage over their many deprivations could easily be appropriated into ideological crusades, for whom hallucinations of great power allayed their crushing sense of a very real powerlessness. It was among the young unemployed men in small towns that the Hindu nationalist movement, also funded primarily, like the jihad, from abroad, from rich Hindus in the United States and U.K., had found its foot soldiers, the men who formed the faceless mobs, who were in charge of the dirty stuff, of the necessary lynchings and destruction.

The Hindu disaffection, however, was of a different order. The young Hindus I knew were frustrated by their exclusion from the middle class; they did not, despite their rhetoric of an Indian golden age, seek to radically change the ways of the world or hold up alternative visions, as Mahatma Gandhi once had, of what a good and true life was and could be. Even the most extreme Hindu ideologues did not, in the end, wish, like the jihadis, to challenge or reject the knowledge and power of the West. They were content to take the world as they found it, dominated by the West, and then find a niche for themselves in it; they were, above all, sly materialists. This pragmatic collaboration with the West is what has produced the new Hindu renaissance of the last 150 years, a regeneration of which the software tycoons of Silicon Valley and the Indian writers in English are related aspects. Gandhi's ambition—to form a society as different as possible from the one in the West—has few takers left in India. Ironically, his distrust and fear of Western modernity are now amplified best by the radical Islamists of Pakistan, where a Westernized postcolonial elite—those men from the posh colleges that Hamid Gul despised, who now spoke helplessly in

their farmhouses of the Talibanization of Pakistan—had discredited
itself.

It is why, while India daily moves closer to the West, Pakistan seems
much further away. It is also why Rahmat, although he imagined me to
be a Muslim, saw me essentially as an alien, someone very removed
from him—the resident of London, the city of Sodom and Gomor-
rah—and why I was startled when looking up from his hectically ravaged plate of mutton and rice, Rahmat asked me if the women in
London went around with their legs exposed.

This was a question that came from my own past, the kind of thing I
would turn around in my mind, when I was still a boy in isolated
towns, with no TV or cinema around to inhibit my imagination. It was
strange and unsettling to think how quickly that past, along with all its
peculiar material and sensory privations, had vanished, how dramatically my circumstances had changed. No one before me in my family
had ever left India, while I spent much of the year in London and traveled to many different parts of the world. I published in American and
British newspapers and journals; depended upon them, in fact, for a
living.

Globalization had also opened up the West; there was more space
there for people like me, people who would have had to struggle harder
for a similar space in their native countries. I still felt myself on the
margins, writing about subjects that appeared remote from the preoc-
cupations around me, the obsessions with food, sex, money, movies,
celebrities that I saw reflected in the weekend papers in Britain. But the
first cultural shock had worn off. As a colonial I was a child, however
distinctly, of the West. England was, after all, the place where I as
an adult had chosen to be, and I had, in time, come to see something
brittle and self-righteous in my exasperation over the articles about
boyfriends and hemlines.

In any case, I spent most of my time in London at my desk, had only
a shallow relationship with the world around me. In the beginning I
was unsettled by the devout Muslims I would often see on Brick Lane,
quite near my flat. However, as often happens, the more money you
have, the more liberal you become, more in tune with the cosmopolitan city and its bland middle-class tolerance. In London, where I knew

security and stability for the first time in my life, I became someone without a past, and as the months passed, the Muslims faded into the promiscuous bustle of the gay discos, leather retailers, Balti restaurants, music halls, coffee and bagel shops.

But this kind of Westernization can also be superficial; you can quickly lapse into an older cultural conservatism. Your political loyalties can be more mixed up than what you and other people assume. It explains my unease at the American Embassy in Islamabad a few days after meeting Rahmat. There stern experts on the Taliban and Islamic fundamentalists kept using the words "us" and "them" impressing upon me the urgency of forcing "those guys," the Taliban, to give up their special guest, Osama bin Laden. Although I, with my beard and Afghan cap, looked like one of "them"—the desperate men just outside the embassy's fortlike walls—the Americans had no doubt where I belonged. I was one of "us," part of a powerful imperial civilization that, in this remote, vulnerable outpost, was denoted by bowling alleys, cocktail bars, and the framed photos of suburban barbecues on office walls.

No ambiguities existed for the diplomats. They defended the government they worked for with as much passion and vigor as the jihadis—the "them" of their vocabulary—spoke of jihad, and they could make you feel that the war they were fighting was also your war and the side we were all on had both truth and power behind it.

It was hard to demur when you considered the opposition. Far from offering a blueprint for a new civilization or society, the Taliban seemed perversely intent on annihilating the few bits and pieces of Afghanistan's cultural heritage that had survived the long war. I was in India when I heard about the news about the Taliban's intention to destroy all Buddhist statues in Afghanistan. At that point I'd still not visited the country, and I wasn't sure what was going on. I rang a Pakistani journalist in Peshawar. He confirmed some of the theories I had seen in the Pakistani papers on the Internet. The Taliban were frustrated by the sanctions imposed on them by the UN and wanted to draw international attention to the plight of Afghans facing drought and starvation; there was a struggle between the hard-liners and moderates with the Taliban, and the former had won this time.

The journalist wasn't sure about the statues, however. The tall, exposed Buddhas in Bamiyan had been around for centuries; they could not be removed. And the museum in Kabul, which held the best representatives of Indo-Greek sculpture, had been looted long ago, first by the mujahideen who took over the city after the fall of the Communist regime in 1992 and then by the Taliban in 1996. There was not much left; foreign journalists who toured the museum were only shown some rubble, although that could have come from anywhere. For years now, statues had been smuggled out of Afghanistan and transported as far as New York and Tokyo; you could still find a few with the antiques dealers in the bazaars of Peshawar.

I had already seen some of these statues, almost by chance, in the somewhat banal setting of a house in an upper-middle-class suburb of Peshawar, where they stood in glass cases before a large fake fireplace. They belonged to General Naseerullah Babur, another of Pakistan's powerful military men and Benazir Bhutto's "favorite uncle." He wouldn't say how he had got hold of the statues, most of which I recognized from photos I had seen, and only mumbled something about finding them during excavations. It wasn't hard to guess, however, and subsequently I discovered that the manner in which he had acquired the statues was as much of an open secret as his original sponsorship of the Taliban.

He was also responsible for suppressing a particularly savage civil war in Karachi between local Sindhis and Muslim migrants from India. In fact, Babur told me many such stories himself, his broad face often cracking into childlike smiles; he appeared every bit the retired man, who had made his little pile, albeit rather dubiously, and was eager to establish his role in great events, the brave Pashtun of legend, as an admiring taxi driver described him to me, who would patrol Karachi during the worst violence in an open, unescorted Jeep.

Babur's connection with Afghanistan had begun when he was the governor of the North-West Frontier Province in the 1970s. It was then he first met the Afghan Islamists, who became famous names in the jihad, and introduced them to American diplomats in Islamabad.

In 1993, Benazir Bhutto returned to power, three years after being overthrown by the ISI and Hamid Gul, and Babur became interior minister. By then Afghanistan was in chaos. The roads, bridges, schools, orchards, and irrigation systems lay in ruins. But even more disastrous was the moral breakdown that occurred in the years after the Soviet withdrawal in 1989. The modern state with its law enforcement policies had barely existed outside the cities while civil war and the consequent displacement of millions of people further undermined the tribal and religious codes that had previously governed the lives of ordinary Afghans. Warlords and gangsters flourished in the vacuum. Gulbuddin Hekmatyar, the mujahid favored by the ISI, had already branched off into heroin manufacturing and smuggling; many other mujahideen commanders took to smuggling and highway robbery. Men with guns stood at improvised checkposts on all major roads. The situation was particularly bad in the Pashtun-majority provinces of southern Afghanistan, where several commanders raped young boys and women and plundered at will.

One day in 1994, in a village near the city of Kandahar, a Pashtun man in his thirties called Mohammed Omar heard about two women who had been abducted and raped by some local commanders. Like many young Pashtuns from his village, Omar, the son of landless peasants, had participated in the jihad against local and foreign Communists. He had been wounded several times and lost his right eye. After the Soviet withdrawal he had recommenced teaching at his village madrassa. He was deeply aggrieved by the anarchy around him and often spoke with his friends in the village about ways to end it and establish the law of the Koran. The news of the raped women finally incited him into action. He went out to the local madrassas and raised a band of thirty students for a rescue mission. The students mustered around sixteen rifles among themselves. They then went and freed the girls and hanged the commanders from the barrel of a tank. A few months later there was another incident in which two commanders fought a gun battle in the streets of Kandahar over a boy both wished to rape. Once again Omar showed up with his students, releasing the boy and executing the commanders.

These were the stories Rahmat had heard in his mosque in the Punjab; they were also the stories Babur heard in Islamabad. The fame of the Taliban had grown very fast. Afghans everywhere began appealing to them for protection from the warlords. Very soon these requests for help, along with large cash donations, came to the Taliban from the traders and smugglers who needed peace and open roads in southern Afghanistan to ensure the transport of goods to Iran and the Central Asian republics.

Babur himself had long been looking into roads and oil and gas pipelines through Afghanistan to these Central Asian republics. There had also been much interest from multinational oil companies. But Kabul was still being fought over. The ISI, which both Babur and Bhutto distrusted, insisted on supporting Hekmatyar, who was far away from imposing the stability needed to conduct business in Afghanistan. The only other route to Central Asia ran through southern Afghanistan, but anyone taking it risked an infinite number of tollbooths and other forms of banditry.

Babur produced a plan to rebuild the road from Pakistan to Herat with funding from international agencies; in October 1994 he took a group of Western and Chinese diplomats on an exploratory trip to Herat. Later that month he attempted something riskier; he arranged for thirty Pakistani trucks to drive through Afghanistan to the capital of Turkmenistan, Ashkhabad.

Babur told me that he was advised against this. The commanders who controlled the roads in southern Afghanistan were reportedly very angry with him. They hadn't been told about the visit with the diplomats and thought it meant Babur was supporting the Taliban, which just a few days previously had captured a massive arsenal built up during the days when the CIA sent arms to the mujahideen.

Babur said, "I went ahead. It was an experiment. I thought, let's see what happens."

A few miles outside Kandahar the convoy was stopped by local commanders. They ordered the Pakistani drivers, including some army officers, to park in a nearby village. The men were outnumbered and so did not resist, merely passing on to their superiors in Islamabad the demands from the commanders: money, share of the goods on the convoy, and a promise to stop supporting the Taliban.

For three days Pakistani officials in Islamabad wondered what to do; a commando operation to rescue the convoy was discussed and finally dropped. Then Babur asked the Taliban to help.

The students assaulted the village where the convoy was parked and chased out the commanders and their men. That same evening they attacked Kandahar and after two days of fighting conquered the city and expelled the remaining warlords from the area.

This was the absurdly successful beginning of the military campaign that brought the Taliban almost the whole of Afghanistan in just two years. Early in 1995 they took Herat; a year later they were in Kabul. They didn't do it all by themselves. Thousands of Pakistanis like Rahmat volunteered to fight with them while cash bribes fund-raised by transporters and smugglers neutralized most of the warlords, and Babur put considerable Pakistani expertise at their disposal.

He sent Pakistani engineers to replace the phone system, to repair Kandahar airport, and to improve the roads, and although Babur wouldn't deny or confirm it to me, and only broke into his impish smile again, Pakistani Army regulars allegedly fought alongside the Taliban, and high-ranking officers planned their campaigns. Babur himself in 1996 closely monitored the capture of Kabul, from where he was to carry away, like the invaders of the past, his own booty, the statues of the Buddha and bodhisattva that now adorned his living room.

F ive years later the "boys," as Babur called the Taliban, had grown more ambitious. They weren't content, as in the old days, to expel the warlords and institute a kind of rough-and-ready justice. They wanted to create the purest Islamic society in the world. Their leaders called themselves mullahs, although few had had the necessary educational qualifications; Mohammed Omar had gone a step further and anointed himself *amir-ul-momineem*, commander of the faithful. They had designed a new flag for Afghanistan. Men from the Ministry for the Promotion of Virtue and Prevention of Vice were responsible for checking the length of beards and beating up women without male escorts.

Babur disapproved of the Taliban's restrictions on women. But they no longer turned to men like Babur for advice. They had their own boosters, the mullahs of rural Afghanistan and the jihadis, Islamist politicians, and ISI officers of Pakistan.

And they had their sympathizers. Ishrat was one of them, although he hadn't lived in Afghanistan since 1981, when as a sixteen-year-old refugee he had made the long journey from the southern province of Helmand to Pakistan. He had gone to a school in Peshawar during the anti-Soviet jihad and picked up enough English to be able to act as a guide and interpreter to foreign journalists. Ishrat was, Shafiq said, the best person to take to Afghanistan. His English was excellent; he knew his way around not only the police and customs men but also the potentially troublesome tribals in the border areas.

"You must write the truth," he kept saying, "and see things in context. Don't be influenced by what you read in the Western media." There was, he said, nothing unprecedented about the Taliban's restrictions on women, their harshness toward petty criminals, their religious strictures; the tribal system that had ruled the lives of the majority of Afghans had always been severe.

Ishrat was a short man; the beard hanging from his small face seemed very long; the shalwar kurtas he wore were always too big for his thin body. I thought his admiration for the Taliban contained something of the fascination that the physically unprepossessing have for demonstrations of brute power and strength.

It made me uneasy, but I was stuck with him. And there was that discomfiting kernel of truth in his wildest assertions. In the two months that had lapsed since my first trip to Pakistan, the Taliban had destroyed the giant Buddha statues in Bamiyan, and Ishrat was obsessed with the attention given to the event in the West. "Why do Western people care so much about old Buddhist statues no one worships? Why are they not writing front page articles about millions of starving and dying people in Afghanistan? They want to give money for the statues and take them to their museums, but what about human beings?"

It was hard to respond to Ishrat, partly because I wasn't sure of my own feelings. I had visited the refugee camps near Peshawar where whole families huddled under tiny plastic tents erected between narrow lanes muddied with soapy water and urine. I had read the alarming NGO (nongovernmental organization) reports about famine and mass starvation in Afghanistan. I knew about the UN's failure to fund-raise even $221 million as humanitarian aid for Afghanistan.

I had also just started writing a book about the Buddha and had been reading about the way merchant caravans had traveled with his ideas from North India to Central Asia. In Pakistan, I had traveled to some of the sites where the merchants had built great monasteries. I hadn't been much interested in Bamiyan; the giant statues looked ugly in the photographs, and there was Robert Byron's testimony, offered in the early 1930s, about their lacking "even the dignity of labour." Nevertheless, their antiquity gave them a kind of poise; for fifteen centuries, standing quietly in a broad mountain valley, they had weathered the change of seasons and religions around them, and the news of their defacement appalled me.

But then, as the days passed, I grew somewhat weary of the outrage and scorn; there seemed something too easy and glib about the demonizing of the Taliban. In India the loudest protests had come from those Hindu nationalists who had demolished the Babri Mosque in Ayodhya in 1992. In the angry editorials in London, the Taliban once again appeared as particularly vicious barbarians from the Middle Ages instead of the bastard children they increasingly seemed to me of the West's arrogant meddling in Afghanistan in very recent times. Much history was either forgotten or ignored in even the more ambitious denunciations: the earlier Muslim attempts to destroy the Buddha statues, British vandalism in Herat, and the relative newness of the West's reverence for monuments from the past. And when Ishrat said, "It is all hypocrisy, the Western people are afraid of Islam, they want to protect the statues, but they had never heard of these statues, they don't know anything about Afghanistan, they are not interested in whether people live or die there," I kept quiet.

In Afghanistan, I had an argument with Ishrat. He wanted me to go to Jalalabad and talk to Hindus and Sikhs who would confirm his account of the great peace and stability brought to the country by the Taliban. But it wasn't what I wanted to do; the story had been done by twenty journalists. I wanted to go to the villages.

"What will you do in the villages?" Ishrat asked. "There is nothing there." I thought he resisted me only because his contacts were all in the cities. But in the end he backed down. He said he knew someone I could talk to. He kept up the propaganda inside the taxi. "During the jihad against Russia," he said, "the whole place was full with drugs smugglers. You have heard of the Afridis? Pashtun tribe people. They control the drug business. Poppy grown in Afghanistan, turned into heroin in Pakistan, and then smuggled out to Europe and America through Iran and Karachi. No one was writing about that. America's favorite mujahid, Hekmatyar, was running dozens of heroin laboratories. Now Taliban has banned poppy, the smugglers are angry at them, but they say heroin is against Islam. They lose money because of their faith. But still no one is writing. They all talk about Osama bin Laden. But who is bin Laden? He is America's man; America made him who he is."

Ishrat pointed to the ancient-looking cassette of Indian film music on the dashboard and said, "See, Afghans can listen to music. All you Western journalists are saying Taliban banned music." But then a checkpost approached in the distance, and the driver reached for the cassette and stuffed it quickly into the pocket of his frayed jacket before the boys with black turbans and Kalashnikovs could strut over to the car, poke their tender-skinned faces through the open window, and ask severe questions.

Ishrat was quiet after that. The sun rose higher; the light steadily grew harsh, draining color even out of the roadside tents of the nomads; a pall of white dissolved the sky, veiled the high distant mountains, and then hung over the barren fields overrun with bush and the low mud houses set against stone-littered hillsides. There was little traffic: big trucks that small, straggly families by the road would try to wave down—Ishrat identified them as Pakistan-bound refugees from the Tajik-majority northern provinces—and, more frequently, the Toyota pickups, fast and dangerous on the broken road, black-turbaned men with Kalashnikovs and blank stares crammed uncomfortably in the back.

The Toyotas—famously the vehicles with which the Taliban had achieved their military victory in Herat—kicked up vast swaying clouds of dust that were then quietly absorbed into the stubborn white haze. There was more dust once we turned off the road to Jalalabad, and the car began to rock and shudder through a rutted dirt path; it blew in through the rolled-up windows and settled in a film on the battered brown leather of the car seats, powdered the beards of Ishrat and the taxi driver, blotted out the occasional groups of children and chador-draped women carrying dung cakes on their head, and scared off the scrawny goats sitting in the narrow shade of the mud wall before which we suddenly stopped.

Yellowed grass sagged from the weblike cracks in the wall. But then the low wooden door opened; a tall man with a long white beard came out and embraced Ishrat, and his quick quizzical glance at me modulated into a smile as Ishrat explained my presence, suddenly speaking fast and unintelligibly in Pashtu.

He took us, not saying much, either to Ishrat or to me, through the empty hay-littered courtyard to what seemed like a special room for visitors. He then brought me water in a shallow trough; he indicated the place in the courtyard—before a furrowed drain that ran around the compound—where I was to wash my face and hands. He came back with green tea shortly afterward. The tea tasted slightly of dust and made the bone china cup, an unexpected touch of luxury in the bare room, seem as if it had been sitting unused in one of the dark low-roofed rooms around the courtyard, in one of the little niches in the wall, for a long time.

I felt expectant, also slightly exhausted by the drive, by the nervousness that the Taliban men in the Toyotas forced in me. Ishrat hadn't promised much in the car. He had given me the name of our host, Faiz. He had told me about his involvement in the anti-Soviet jihad and the injuries—always glamorous items in these accounts of the mujahideen—he had sustained from a mortar attack by the Communists.

And it was of that life Faiz spoke to me intermittently that afternoon and evening in that cool bare room, Ishrat translating, the driver looking on blankly, and he spoke not as a man who thought himself successful would, with pride or nostalgia. He spoke, leaning against the wall, his knees drawn up, narrow eyes wandering restlessly across the room, with the neutral air of a man who had simply lived his life in the only way he could.

He could barely remember his childhood, when his father owned a few cows and goats. But he spoke vividly of the time in the 1970s when the desertlike area around him was irrigated with Soviet assistance, and orange and olive orchards came up on previously infertile land. Faiz's family was one of the beneficiaries. There had been a brief moment of relative prosperity. The house we were sitting in had been built then; Faiz's elder brother had been sent to Kabul for higher education.

Very soon afterward, there was trouble. Faiz couldn't remember the date, but his brother was probably killed in 1978, during the purges that followed the Communist coup. He was suspected of being an Islamist, although he was only a student and kept away from politics altogether.

The Communists had even come to the province, had rounded up and killed a few mullahs, and arrested anyone they suspected of being counterrevolutionary. And then the Russians had arrived.

Ishrat, translating and embellishing at the same time, told me of the Afghan rage and contempt for foreign invaders and how every Afghan spontaneously joined the uprising against the Russians. But this didn't match what he translated immediately afterward, how Faiz had stayed away from the young men in the province who came together to fight the Russians. He was married by then; he had a young son; there were the orchards to look after.

But then the bombing began, from the Russian helicopters, in response to guerrilla attacks on Communist convoys. Many of the cultivated fields near the highway to Kabul were mined, and once the canals were destroyed it became harder and harder to keep the orchards going.

Faiz's parents, on their way to Jalalabad for a wedding, died when the bus they were traveling on was hit by a stray mortar. There were other tragedies. Faiz's son turned out to be "insane"; Ishrat used the Urdu word, *paagal*, and I didn't feel I could ask him to clarify. Faiz took him to various shrines and *pirs*, including one near Jalalabad famous for curing insanity, and made him wear various amulets. But none of these attempts worked.

Faiz's two brothers were already with the mujahideen when he began fighting alongside them. It wasn't a full-time job. There were specific expeditions he joined, mostly ambushes of government convoys. He was home the rest of the time, taking care of his diminishing farmland.

It was Ishrat who volunteered the information in Urdu, while Faiz looked on uncomprehendingly, that Faiz had earned a reputation as a brave man very early in the war. It was why he was smuggled across the border and into a hospital in Peshawar when he suffered serious injuries in the abdomen during a mortar attack on his position in the mountains around Jalalabad.

Pakistan, where he first met Ishrat, was a revelation for Faiz. It was where he first saw how the jihad against the Communists had become a big business. Some of the so-called leaders of the Afghan mujahideen, living in grand villas in Hayatabad, were not even known to him by name. But there they were, handling the disbursement of arms and aid to the refugees and the mujahideen. They made him think with pity and rage of the poor young men he was fighting with, people who started out with just a few .303 rifles among them until they managed to ambush an arms convoy and equip themselves with the latest Soviet equipment.

By the time Faiz returned to Afghanistan, the jihad against the Russians was almost over. A local mujahideen commander was already ruling over his home province, and so peace came quickly and lasted longer in his part of Afghanistan. White men from UN agencies came to repair the canals; many of the destroyed orchards and fields were got going again.

Faiz wasn't one of the lucky farmers. None of the canals close to him were repaired. He had to go back to where his father had started out, making a living by selling the milk of the few cows and goats he had left over from the days of the jihad; he also made a bit of money by working as a laborer.

This was at a time when great wealth was being created all around him. Most of the restored fields grew poppy, under orders from the mujahideen commander, who lived in a mansion and maintained a private army. He wasn't as bad as the warlords in Helmand Province; he wasn't a bandit or rapist. In fact, he was quite helpful to people who had fought in the jihad. But everyone knew he was involved in smuggling and drugs; the big business Faiz had seen in Pakistan had come to Afghanistan. Planes arrived in Jalalabad from Dubai loaded with color TV sets that were then smuggled into Pakistan on big trucks. The opium went out to labs in southern Afghanistan and then, as heroin, to Iran.

This was why Faiz had first thought well of the Taliban when they came from the south and chased out the commander. He didn't mind their severity; only people in the cities chafed at their restrictions on women. But they hadn't altered the essential things. The smuggling had gone on; the poppy cultivation was stopped only recently, and he knew of people who were still at it. A few well-connected merchants and traders in Jalalabad had grown rich. Most other people became poorer; his own two brothers had left with their families for Pakistan, where they worked as truck drivers. And there was the harassment. Some young men had shown up at his own house in order to draft his son into the war against the Tajiks in the north and had to be persuaded that he was unfit to be a soldier. Faiz also didn't like the Taliban's dependence on Arab and Pakistani jihadis, many of whom he saw in the province. Foreigners had done enough damage in Afghanistan; it was time for them to leave the country and its people alone.

Dismay appeared on Ishrat's face as he translated this, and a brief argument now broke out between him and Faiz. I couldn't follow most of it, and I didn't trust the account I heard from Ishrat, who claimed to be arguing that the Arabs and Pakistanis helping the Taliban were fellow Muslims and not infidels like the Russians and Americans.

I had wondered all afternoon about the emptiness of that large house, the absence of Faiz's wife and his son. I now saw two emaciated cows stumbling into the courtyard, followed by a thin, stubble-faced man with a stick; this was, Ishrat said, Faiz's "insane" son. He tethered the cows to an iron pigot and then walked out of sight. A little later I heard the shuffling of pots and pans in an adjacent room, and then I saw a chador-clad figure move briskly across the courtyard to throw some hay before the cows and then swiftly retreat. She had been there all through the afternoon, possibly sleeping or lying down silently on the ground.

When Faiz left the room briefly, I asked Ishrat if it was possible to talk to her for a few minutes. He was quick to catch the hesitation in my voice. "Why do you want to talk to her?" he asked, slightly aggressively.

I didn't have time to respond. Faiz, who had gone out, came back to the room at that very moment; the lantern he held filled the room with the smell of kerosene. Ishrat explained my request to him in Pashtu while I looked on with some apprehension.

I saw Faiz's face go tense; I felt his narrow, shrewd eyes on me before they turned toward Ishrat.

The answer was no. Ishrat, speaking once again on his own, said that local custom did not permit strange men to talk to women.

Faiz suddenly interrupted him; he said that he could convey my question to his wife and bring me her reply.

It was better than nothing, so I asked the obvious question about life for women under the Taliban. It took a while for Ishrat to translate this, and I wasn't sure if he had done so accurately until the answer came back with a slightly more relaxed Faiz.

Faiz laughed as he spoke, revealing childlike teeth, and Ishrat himself smiled as he translated. The one thing she disliked most about the rule of the Taliban was the traveling in buses to nearby towns. The roads were broken, the buses were few, and the journeys were roughest for women, who were forced to sit squashed at the back, separate from the men in the front of the bus.

The light outside the room grew softer, and it was in the gray-blue dusk that Faiz and Ishrat went out to offer *namaz*. I watched them from the room: two silently vigorous figures on the scruffy floor of the courtyard, bending and straightening almost in unison, expressing a common faith, but so apart in their experiences, the fixer for foreign journalists in Peshawar, in touch with and amplifying ever new ideologies and passions, and Faiz, the retired fighter, all his previous disappointments and griefs bleached by his present struggles for survival, by the bare house and courtyard, and the greater blankness outside.

Later I went outside myself and climbed up to the flat roof. Night had descended swiftly, and it was very quiet. The air carried a mysterious soft tinkling, and then a couple of goats became clear in the distance. A bright half-moon outlined the mountains in the south and north, bestowed calm upon the stony, treeless plain between them.

In the morning, when the convoys of the Taliban had raced across it in great trails of dust, the plain had seemed a staging post for countless conquerors and marauders. Alexander the Great himself had crossed it on his way to India; I had picked up the fact from the books, and it had given the flat, futile land a kind of aura.

I saw it differently now. Faiz's story had animated it with many different human achievements and disasters: the irrigation systems, the olive orchards, the helicopter bombings, the mines, the poppy cultivators, and the drugs smugglers.

And you could, if you wanted, connect them to larger histories and geopolitics, to the cold war strategists in comfortable suburban retirement in America and the generals in their mansions in Pakistan still fantasizing about pan-Islamic empires, trade routes, and oil pipelines. But when you saw it from Faiz's point of view, the events still lacked a redeeming pattern. They spoke—in the house with the emaciated cows and the mad son and the unseeable woman with her silent sufferings— only of the dwindling of human possibilities and the steady grinding down of individual lives.

In Peshawar later in 2001 I heard about Jamal from one of the other men I had met at the offices of *The Frontier Post*. Terrible things had happened to both Jamal and the newspaper. Just a few days after my previous visit, a letter had come by e-mail. It started innocuously enough but then insulted Prophet Mohammed in the grossest terms. Jamal approved it for publication without reading through to the end. No one else noticed it, before it was pounced upon by one of the fundamentalist organizations, always waiting to undermine the English-language press. A mob of bearded men emerged from nowhere and burned down the press. The police sealed the offices and arrested several journalists; the editor I had met managed to escape the police and was hiding with his fellow tribesmen somewhere near the Khyber Pass. Most of the journalists had now been released, but Jamal was in prison, awaiting trial for blasphemy.

The punishment for blasphemy in Pakistan is death. But Jamal was already close to dying; the journalist was surprised to discover that I didn't know, or hadn't guessed from his dull yellow eyes, about his heroin addiction. It had begun soon after Jamal arrived in Peshawar and got to know some drugs dealers; he had been in and out of several hospitals.

No one could do anything for him now, the journalist said. I was shocked at first at the callousness, and then I felt slightly guilty myself. In London I had received a couple of e-mails from Jamal about the book he wanted to write. I hadn't responded; the book had seemed to me a doomed idea.

The journalist, who himself had barely escaped the fury of the fundamentalists, was only being truthful in a brutal, unarguable kind of way. I didn't feel that I could even offer to help. My own situation in Pakistan, as a Hindu and Indian, was already complicated. It would have been too risky to get involved with an assassin, a heroin addict, and a blasphemer.

T hey are all such fanatics here!" Jamal had said at our first meeting, and I had been grateful for the sentiment, even though I knew it to be a commonplace exaggeration, because the words stoked something I felt during my early days in Pakistan, that deeper anxiety about Muslims I began to acknowledge to myself only after I left Pakistan and felt safe again in India.

The unease had never entirely gone. But I had felt myself change during the weeks in Pakistan, and there had been an unexpected moment toward the end of my stay. I had gone to see a Moghul mosque in Peshawar. The spies hadn't followed me into the courtyard, where a few men sat in the late-afternoon sun, and I felt I was alone until I saw an old man sleeping in one dark corner. He was obviously an Afghan refugee. His long white beard and sharp features made me think he was from Herat or the western provinces close to Iran. His head, resting on a silk-wrapped bundle, displayed the fine profile of monks and wayfarers in Persian and Moghul miniatures, and watching him in the decaying old building, where the inlaid tiles were all faded or chipped, the broad-blade fans swayed dangerously as they spun, and birds invisibly chattered somewhere above in the dark domes, I suddenly felt myself pulled centuries back. I had a sense, fleeting but vivid and exhilarating, of the greatness of the old global civilization of Islam, the glory and splendor of once-famous and now-devastated cities—Herat, Balkh, Baghdad—of the whole life and world the religion had once created.

That world was now in turmoil; it had been broken into by the invincible modern civilization of the West. From the outside it seemed capable only of producing fanaticisms of the kind that had crushed Jamal, and it was hard not to be repelled by it.

"The foreigners should leave us alone," Faiz had said. "We will find our own way." But countless men had tried and failed, many societies had been exposed to new kinds of pain, and it still wasn't clear what that way could be, whether the new versions of Islam could bring justice and peace and prosperity to the faithful, whether they even stood a chance against globalization.

In any case, I could always feel myself distant from these debates and struggles. None of them had touched my own life before I went to Pakistan and Afghanistan. I belonged to another, more fortunate world. The American diplomats in Islamabad had guessed correctly: I already had my side chosen for me.

But I was confused. I had thought Jamal an ally. His fate, however, was tied to the faceless people on the other side, people who were persecutors as much as victims. I couldn't see how things, given the way they were now, could work out for them. But the thought of their failure was painful. I wanted these people to flourish. I wanted them to have as much dignity and freedom as I had been allowed in recent years, even though I couldn't but feel the absurdity of my wish and increasingly doubted whether the kind of life I lived was what these apparently deprived people longed for or could be content with.

AFGHANISTAN

Communists, Mullahs, and Warlords

Much of Kabul is built of mud. And when it rained before the Christmas of 2004, relieving a long and severe drought, the whole city seemed to melt. The piles of slush on its unpaved lanes rose, as though in a slow-moving tide, until it spattered everything: the big white Land Cruisers of aid agencies and Afghan ministers, the beat-up yellow taxis, the bombed-out palaces of western Kabul and the bullet-pocked huts on steep hills, the fortified foreign embassies and UN offices, and even the high billboards exhorting Afghans, in idiosyncratic English, to "national reconciliation and peace."

Despite the rain and the cold, the bazaars were crowded. Shopkeepers representing almost all of Afghanistan's ethnic groups—Pashtuns, Tajiks, Hazaras, Uzbeks, and Turkmens—hawked oranges, carpets, Chinese-made windbreakers and electronic goods, while beggars, mostly disabled children and widows in burkas, squatted beside the sewers and tugged at the wide trousers of passing men. Thousands of refugee families huddled around small bonfires at the abandoned Soviet Embassy, amid bomb-shattered slabs of concrete and open manholes.

It was strange to see no white faces in these crowds. Even in the modern part of Kabul, where thousands of Europeans and Americans—mostly soldiers, diplomats, aid workers, and businessmen—live, the streets were empty. Afghan guards with Kalashnikovs stood in front of iron gates set in high concrete walls topped with barbed wire. The gates occasionally opened to reveal a new or renovated mansion and to release or admit a Land Cruiser with tinted windows.

To be a foreigner in Afghanistan, it seemed, is to move from one protected enclave to another. An Indian journalist I met soon after arriving in Kabul that December told me that security had deteriorated soon after the presidential election in October, which the Taliban had failed to disrupt and which Hamid Karzai had won convincingly. That same month a suicide bomber, apparently from the Taliban, had killed an American woman and injured three European soldiers at a shopping district a few meters away from my hotel.

The Indian journalist seemed lonely, frustrated by the restrictions on both his travel and social life. For some months now he had wished to set up a FCC (Foreign Correspondents Club) in Kabul, on the lines of one in Hong Kong. One cold, rainy evening I traveled to his home with one of the foreign journalists he had invited to join the club. When we arrived, we found several other potential members already there.

As usual, there was no power. A diesel generator spluttered outside the journalist's fortresslike home, one of the thousands simultaneously going on in Kabul, giving to the city its characteristic low rumble. Inside, Afghan servants, chauffeurs, and bodyguards, part of the new service economy of Kabul, bustled around, replenishing bowls of dry fruits. The journalist opened a case full of alcohol; smuggled bottles wickedly gleamed in the dim, flickering light. Sipping scotch whiskey and German beer, the journalists loudly exchanged local gossip I would hear repeatedly in the next few days from Afghans, about kickbacks from an Afghan mobile phone operator to a cabinet minister and about one million dollars allegedly missing from the coffers of Ariana, the Afghan national airline. They speculated about whether Karzai would be confident enough to exclude the most corrupt and powerful warlords—Defense Minister Mohammed Fahim and his deputy, Abdul Rashid Dostum—from his new cabinet. There were complaints about extravagant UN agencies and NGOs pushing up rents in Kabul (up to three thousand dollars for a dingy two-bedroom apartment); about the arrogant employees of the American company DynCorp who worked as Karzai's bodyguards.

The Indian journalist abruptly called for silence and read out what he said was a draft constitution, adopted from the FCC in Hong Kong. He then asked for suggestions. As it turned out, almost every idea proposed that evening ran into an obstacle. The club needed a permanent home. But this seemed possible only when rents in Kabul were less extortionate. High-paying corporate members? Perhaps, when there were many more multinational corporations in Afghanistan. Honorary membership for such visiting foreign dignitaries as Dick Cheney or the powerful U.S. ambassador to Afghanistan, Zalmay Khalilzad? Possibly, once the American Embassy had become more accessible. Even a bar, indispensable to foreign correspondent clubs, seemed unobtainable. Seeking official permission for the consumption of alcohol in Kabul could only cause offense in what was still a deeply religious and conservative country.

Returning to my hotel late that night, past the sandbagged, barbwire-topped compounds of foreign embassies and UN offices, I felt sorry for the journalist. He had seemed right to argue, as his cherished project collapsed, that Kabul had advanced greatly since the collapse of the Taliban and that with its new, one million–strong population of repatriated refugees, many of them rich people who had spent decades in liberal societies, it was poised for a social revolution.

Earlier that evening I had seen two Afghan girls at a pizza parlor. They wore tight blue jeans, their faces were uncovered, and they sipped Pepsi-Cola as they watched American women playing softball on ESPN. They would have been an unthinkable sight in the Taliban-ruled Afghanistan I had visited in early 2001. Almost four years later, Kabul was full of such surprises: new walled-off villas with mock-Palladian façades, well-stocked supermarkets, Internet cafés, beauty parlors, restaurants, and stores selling DVDs of Bollywood as well as pornographic films. Sitting in one of Kabul's great traffic jams caused by the Land Cruisers, surrounded by the vivacious banter of Afghanistan's new radio stations and children hawking newspapers, I felt as if I were in a small Indian city, among people prospering under the globalized economy.

In brightly lit and heated offices, diplomats, NGO workers, and government officials radiated optimism as they offered facts and figures attesting to progress in Afghanistan. The first ever presidential elections in the country had been successfully conducted without any major disruptions. Three million Afghan refugees in Pakistan and Iran had expressed their confidence in their homeland by returning to it. More than three million children had been enrolled in schools, as compared with nine hundred thousand under the Taliban. The eight thousand–strong International Security Assistance Force (ISAF) under NATO command was beginning to cover regions beyond Kabul. A Human Rights Commission had been established. The $4.4 billion pledged by international donors in Tokyo in 2002 for Afghanistan was coming in—albeit slowly.

There was finally a tarmac road, stretching from Kabul to Kandahar, three hundred miles away to the south. More roads linking major Afghan cities were being constructed and renovated. Small civil-military provincial reconstruction teams (PRTs), which repaired schools and roads and were run by the United Kingdom, Germany, and the Netherlands, existed in the northern provinces and were expected to cover the entire country by 2007. Japan was at the forefront of the DDR (demobilization, disarmament, and reintegration) program, targeting warlord armies, and had disarmed about 25,000 of the more than 150,000 fighters in private militias. The United States was creating the Afghan National Army, with 10,000 soldiers already trained. The United States and Germany had trained 18,000 police officers. The U.K. was leading antinarcotics efforts. The Italians were reforming the judiciary.

To hear this litany of efforts was to feel the words "international community," which Afghans commonly used, acquire a moral dimension in Afghanistan. With one of the lowest life expectancies and the highest infant mortality rates in the world, Afghanistan seemed to need all the help it could get. But three years after the United States brought together several nations to rebuild Afghanistan, many Afghans tended to blame rather than praise that international community.

Where was much of the money for reconstruction going? they asked, pointing to the Land Cruisers and the high-rent houses and offices of the expatriate community. Disarmament was a failure and would remain so until there was better security and rule of law in the country; most militia fighters had simply concealed their best weapons and turned in those that were old and ineffective. The new Afghan Army was already afflicted with desertions. There was no comprehensive plan to house and feed the millions of repatriated refugees. And though Afghans had turned out enthusiastically for their first-ever direct elections, they were disappointed to see U.S.-backed warlords still ruling much of the country.

One evening, early in my time in Afghanistan, I went to see Dr. Massouda Jalal. In October 2004 she'd been in the news as the lone female candidate in the presidential elections. She had got only 1.2 percent of the votes cast, as compared to 55.4 percent for Karzai. But the very fact that a woman could stand for high office hinted at the immensity of the changes occurring in Afghanistan.

So it was disconcerting when Dr. Jalal, sitting in a very cold dark room and speaking in slow, precise English, denounced the elections, and the registration process preceding it, as a fraud perpetrated upon Afghans, largely a show put on by the U.S. government to impress American voters in the year of the presidential elections.

The international community, Dr. Jalal kept saying, believed in "quantity," statistics about elections and registration processes but was indifferent to "quality." The elections had not been free and fair. Many people had registered more than once, she claimed, and voted several times. Often men with guns had forced people to vote for Karzai; they had also tried to intimidate Dr. Jalal herself during her election campaign.

Western nations, she said, had not given her a single dollar while pouring millions into Karzai's campaign. Worse, they had forgotten about women's rights, which Laura Bush and Cherie Blair had so ardently embraced in late 2001 and which were trampled daily across Afghanistan by men hired by the United States in its war on terror. Educated women like herself were not allowed to participate in political decision making. Karzai's cabinet was dominated by corrupt warlords and had hardly any "qualified people"—people with the training and experience, she explained, to translate Western concepts of democracy into Afghan terms.

As with other Afghans I had met, I felt unable to assess much of what she said. Given that there were only 250 international monitors for the elections in Afghanistan, caution does seem necessary while considering claims that 10.5 million people registered to vote and that 70 percent of them actually voted in October 2004. However, the scale of Karzai's victory suggests that a better-organized election would have had the same overall result. It seemed to me that the election, though flawed, had been a positive step.

As it turned out, within a few weeks, Dr. Jalal was appointed minister in charge of "women's affairs." It again occurred to me that in places like Afghanistan outsiders like myself bring their own assumptions of what constitutes progress and risk being limited by them.

But to know, as the days passed and I traveled around Afghanistan, that the new mansions with the architectural adventurousness of Los Angeles belonged to corrupt government officials, often built upon lands stolen from poor Afghans; to learn that the provincial governor, who spoke fluently of "peace," "reconstruction," "international community," and "poppy eradication," was a drug lord; to find out that the Revolutionary Association of the Women of Afghanistan (RAWA), which was briefly famous in the West for highlighting the Taliban's harsh treatment of women, was too fearful of radical Islamists to announce its presence in Kabul—to know this was to begin to have a different sense of the change that had come to Afghanistan in the last three years. It was also to realize that like the millions suffering from contaminated water, power and housing shortages, warlords, and disease, a club for foreign journalists would have to wait for better days.

Few countries in modern times have had to wait for better days as long as Afghanistan. A bright future seemed imminent in late 2001, when the United States overthrew the Taliban regime. But the past seems hard to shake off in Afghanistan, and no events more so than the Soviet invasion of the country in 1979 and the American decision to help radical Islamists wage a jihad against Soviet communism.

In the decades before the Soviet invasion, Afghanistan had been slowly making its own way into the modern world. It is hard to imagine now, but for students at Kabul University, 1968 was no less a hectic year than it was for students at Columbia, Berkeley, Oxford, and the Sorbonne. A king, Mohammed Zahir Shah, had been presiding over the many ethnic and tribal enclaves of Afghanistan since 1933. But he knew enough of the world elsewhere to attempt, cautiously, a few liberal reforms in his capital city, Kabul. The university was set up in 1946; a liberal constitution was introduced in 1964; the press was technically free; women ran for public office in 1965. By the sixties many students and teachers had traveled abroad, and new ideas about how to organize the state and society had come to the sons of peasants and nomads and artisans from their foreign or foreign-educated teachers.

In the somewhat rarefied world of modernizing Kabul, where women were allowed to appear without the veil in 1959, communism and radical Islam attracted almost an equal number of believers; to these impatient men, the great Afghan countryside with its antique ways appeared ready for revolution. It was from this fledgling intelligentsia in Kabul that almost all of the crucial political figures of the next three decades emerged.

Less than five years after 1968, King Zahir Shah was deposed in a military coup by his cousin, the ambitious former prime minister Mohammed Daoud. Daoud initially sought help from the Communists, whose influence in the army and bureaucracy had grown rapidly since the 1960s; together, they went after the radical Islamists, many of whom were imprisoned or murdered for ideological reasons. But when Daoud, wary of the increasing power of the Communists, tried to get rid of them, he was in turn overthrown and killed. In April 1978, the Communists, themselves divided, confusingly, into two factions, Khalq and Parcham, that roughly corresponded to the rural-urban divide in Afghanistan, assumed full control of the government in Kabul, and in their hurry to eliminate all potential opposition to their program of land redistribution and indoctrination—an attempt, really, to create a Communist society virtually overnight—they effectively inaugurated the brutalization and destruction of Afghanistan.

Within just a few months, twelve thousand people considered to be anti-Communist, many of them members of the country's educated elite, were killed in Kabul alone; thousands more were murdered in the countryside. Thousands of families began leaving the country for Pakistan and Iran. A significant number of radical Islamists of Kabul University were already in exile in Pakistan by 1978; some of them had

even started a low-intensity guerrilla war against the Communist government. Several army garrisons across the country mutinied, and people in the villages, culturally very remote from Kabul, began many
separate jihads, or holy wars, against the Communist regime.

In 2001, in Peshawar, I met Anwar, whose father and uncle were
among the earliest Afghans to take up arms against the Communists.
Neither was an Islamist. Anwar's father, a farmer, lived in a village
north of Kabul, near the border with what is now Tajikistan; although a
devout Muslim, he knew little about the modern ideologies of Islam
that had traveled to Kabul University from Egypt, Pakistan, and Iran. It
was Anwar's uncle, an officer in Zahir Shah's Finance Ministry in
Kabul, who was a bit more in touch with them. He was friendly with
Gulbuddin Hekmatyar, one of the prominent radical Islamists at Kabul
University, who sought refuge in Pakistan in the mid-1970s after a
failed uprising against Daoud and the Communists.

Initially, the Russians were busy consolidating the Communist hold
over Kabul and securing the country's main highways and seemed very
far from rural Afghanistan, which in any case had had for years relative
autonomy from the government in the capital city. But later, with the
aggressive campaigns of land reforms and Marxist indoctrination emanating from Kabul, resistance built up swiftly throughout the country.
Anwar's father and uncle joined one of the mujahideen groups that,
though equipped only with .303 Lee Enfield rifles, managed to keep
their region free of Communist influence. Then, in December 1979,
the Soviet Army entered Afghanistan in order to protect the Communist Revolution, which was being threatened by factional fighting
among Afghan Communists and rebellions by the army, and the position of Anwar's family became more precarious.

In 1983, Russian planes bombed the villages where Anwar and his
relatives lived, in retaliation for attacks on Afghan Army convoys by the
mujahideen. Although Anwar's father and uncle stayed to fight and to
look after the animals and fields, there was no choice for many of the
women and children but to leave.

Anwar, seven years old at the time, couldn't recall too many details
of the long walk that took him and his mother and young brother to
Pakistan. He did remember that it was very cold. There was snow on

the ground and on the hills, and Anwar and his family walked all day, resting at night in roadside mosques. The 350-mile-long road to Pakistan was busy with thousands of refugees, but they had to avoid moving in large groups, which Russian helicopters buzzing ominously overhead liked to fire upon. They also had to stay as close as possible to the main road, for there were mines in the fields and on the dirt tracks, tiny "butterfly mines" that floated down from the helicopters and then lay in wait for unmindful children and animals.

I still heard about the mines when I traveled in the spring of 2001 on the road that links Kabul to Pakistan, through Nangrahar Province. The land seemed vacant, and the stubborn bareness of rock and desert was relieved only occasionally by a green field and a black-tented encampment of nomads. In the days of Zahir Shah this land was reclaimed, with Soviet assistance, for cultivation, and orchards and fields, watered by broad canals, sprang up. In a half-abandoned village, rusty padlocks hanging from the doors set into long mud walls, an old Afghan was startled when I mentioned that time. Rasool had been in his late teens then, had known some of the prosperity that came to the region, could even, with some prompting by me, remember the white men—Russian experts—traveling through the fields.

Unlike Anwar's father and uncle, Rasool wasn't a mujahid. He hadn't revolted against the Russians or the Communists; he had been content to tend his land. The jihad had almost bypassed him, and he had known hard times only when, sometime in the mid-1980s, Russian planes bombed the canals that brought water to his land. There had been another recovery after the Russian Army withdrew in 1989, when white men, this time from the UN, came and supervised the repair of the canals. By then the local mujahideen commanders were in charge. They taxed all the traffic on the roads; they took over the land that had once belonged to the Afghan state, forcing the farmers to grow high-yield poppy.

There was no point in Rasool's defying the commanders; he wouldn't have got cash credit from the traders in the town for anything other than opium. Not that the poppy growing had improved his circumstances. It was the mujahideen commanders who had grown very rich from converting the poppy into heroin and then smuggling it across the border into Iran and Pakistan.

And then, suddenly, before Rasool had even heard of the Taliban, its young soldiers arrived from the southern provinces, banished the mujahideen commanders, and claimed the checkpoints. They supervised, and profited from, the drug business until 1999, when they abruptly banned the cultivation of poppy, leaving most farmers with no sources of livelihood and the option only of migrating to Pakistan.

Rasool still lived in the vast, now arid land, enduring, in just three decades, a whole fruitless cycle of Afghan history. The long reign of Zahir Shah was no more than a faint memory. All the slow, steady work of previous generations was canceled out; Afghanistan was even further away from its tryst with the modern world.

But then, as in many Muslim countries suddenly confronted in the nineteenth century with the rising power of the West, Afghanistan's route to modern development could only have been tortuous. The Afghan empire of the eighteenth century had reached as far as Kashmir in the east and up to the Iranian city of Mashhad in the west. Like present-day Afghanistan, it contained many different ethnic groups, the dominant Pashtun tribes in the east and south, Tajiks and Uzbeks in the north and west, and the Shia Hazaras in the central provinces. Almost all of them were Sunni or Shia Muslims. Fiercely autonomous and proud, they had successfully resisted the British attempt to extend their Indian empire up to Kabul, but after two Anglo-Afghan wars, 1838–1842 and 1878–1880, the Afghans had been sufficiently subdued to serve as a buffer state between the expanding empires of Britain and Russia.

The British were content to exercise influence from afar without troubling themselves with direct rule. It was under their supervision that the present-day boundaries of Afghanistan were drawn, leaving a lot of Pashtun tribes in what is now Pakistan. The British also subsidized the Afghan Army. Until 1919, when the Afghans won complete independence from the British, the ruler in Kabul reported to Delhi in matters of foreign policy, which essentially involved keeping the Russians out of Afghanistan.

The British-backed rulers of Afghanistan in the nineteenth and early twentieth centuries were insecure and ruthless, obsessed with protecting their regime from any local challenges as well; Afghanistan's continued isolation was in their best interests. During the twenty-one-year rule of Amir Abdur Rahman (1880–1901), one of Afghanistan's more pro-British rulers, only one school was built in Kabul, and that was a madrassa. Condemned to play a passive part in an imperial Great Game, Afghanistan missed out on the indirect benefits of colonial rule, the creation of an educated class such as would supply the basic infrastructure of the postcolonial states of India, Pakistan, and Egypt.

Afghanistan's resolute backwardness in the nineteenth and early twentieth centuries was appealing to Western romantics. Kipling, who was repelled by the educated Bengali, commended the Pashtun tribesmen—the traditional rulers of Afghanistan and also a majority among Afghans—for their courage, love of freedom, and sense of honor. These clichés about the Afghans, which would be amplified in our own time by American journalists and politicians, also had some effect on Muslims themselves.

One such man was Jamal al-Din al-Afghani, a polemicist of the nineteenth century, who sought to alert the Muslim peoples to their growing subjugation to the imperial powers of the West. The radical Islamists I spoke to didn't remember that in 1968, while student groups at Kabul University were organizing large demonstrations, distributing fiery pamphlets, and fighting one another on the streets, a huge mausoleum for al-Afghani went up inside the campus, to honor someone who, although born in Iran and educated in India, adopted the pen name al-Afghani and even began to tell other people that he was from Afghanistan.

The increasing influence of the West, and the related undermining of Muslim power, were the inescapable reality of al-Afghani's lifetime; he witnessed it more closely than most Muslims during long stints in India, Iran, Egypt, France, England, and Turkey. But Afghanistan had hardly been affected by the lifestyles and new knowledge of Europe, by the passion and energy of white men from the West who were transforming old worlds elsewhere in the nineteenth century. This resistance to Western-style modernization would have impressed al-Afghani, who, while stressing the need to modernize Muslim societies, disapproved of the wholesale adoption of European ways of the kind Kemal Atatürk would impose upon Turkey just two decades after al-Afghani's death in 1897.

Nevertheless, al-Afghani failed to see how even small but strategically placed countries such as Afghanistan were being drawn into the great imperial games of nineteenth-century Europe and then sentenced to isolation and backwardness as buffer states. Behind his romantic attachment to Afghanistan lay fear and defensiveness, his painful awareness, shared by many other educated people in once-great Asian societies, that they had fallen behind the West and that they had not only to catch up but also to keep in check its increasing power to alter their lives, mostly for the worse.

For many educated people in premodern societies, communism offered a way of both catching up with and resisting the West, and the ideology had a powerful and often generous sponsor in the Soviet Union. But the hasty, ill-adapted borrowings from Soviet communism—the simplistic notion, for instance, of Afghans as feudal people who had to be turned into proletarians—more often than not imposed new kinds of pain and trauma on such a traditional society as Afghanistan and helped to push the country even further away from the modern world.

The Soviet Union had supported the Communist coup of 1978 in Kabul and subsequently grown concerned about the clumsy and brutal way in which the Khalq faction of the Afghan Communist Party, led by the fanatical ideologue Hafizullah Amin, a onetime student at Columbia University, had hijacked the coup and then had tried violently—and, as spontaneous revolts across the country proved, disastrously—to weld the incoherent ethnic-tribal worlds of Afghanistan into a Communist society.

As records of Politburo conversations reveal, the aging leaders of the Soviet Union at first resisted military intervention in Afghanistan. However, they feared that the United States, unsettled by the fall of the shah of Iran, was hoping to find, with the help of the wily Amin, an alternative anti-Soviet base in Afghanistan. They suspected Amin of being "an ambitious, cruel, treacherous person" who "may change the political orientation of the regime."

This sounds like cold war paranoia. It wasn't softened by the mutinies against the Communist regime by Afghan military garrisons, one of which, in the city of Herat, ended in the deaths of several Soviet and East European advisers. In the last days of 1979, when the Communist regime looked close to collapse, a contingent of Soviet soldiers flew into Kabul, stormed Amin's palace, and killed him. A more moderate leader, Babrak Karmal, who belonged to the urban-based Parcham faction, took his place and attempted to avert the collapse of the Afghan state and bring an end to the brutalities.

Karmal was only partly successful in restoring order, however. In 1986, the Soviets replaced Karmal with Mohammed Najibullah, the head of KHAD, the Communist intelligence agency. Najibullah, known for his role in the execution and torture of anti-Communists, tried even harder to win Afghan support. He toned down the Communist rhetoric, emphasized his faith in Islam, and began reaching out to the refugees and mujahideen, speaking all the time of compromise and national reconciliation. But his government couldn't possibly acquire legitimacy among Afghans while being beholden to a foreign power. And in any case, things were out of his control; Afghanistan had already begun fighting in a new proxy war that would kill a million or more Afghans over the next decade.

In the derelict Pashtun village I visited east of Kabul in the spring of 2001, five months before the attacks on the World Trade Center and the Pentagon, in an area heavily bombed and mined by the Soviet military, people talked, as they did elsewhere, of the irrelevance, indeed the nonexistence, of the Taliban government. They spoke too of the good deeds of the white men from the foreign NGOs and the UN, who were active throughout the previous two decades of war, supplying seeds, food, and health care, despite the constant danger of being kidnapped and beaten up by the Taliban.

There were three Afghans sitting on the floor of the bare, low-roofed room, all of them in their late forties, variously disabled during the anti-Communist jihad, and prematurely aged, even the dim light from the lantern seeming harsh on their sunburned wrinkled faces and wiry gray beards. Only men like these remained in the village. The soldiers in black turbans came regularly to look for fit young men. Those young men who had escaped the draft had fled to Pakistan, where many of their relatives already lived in the much worse conditions of the refugee camps.

The conversation inside the room was of the quality of seeds, the lack of fodder and drinking water for the livestock, and the refugees from the war in the north, who, turned away at the border with Pakistan, were now draining away the already meager supply of food and water in the province. The three-year-long drought and ongoing civil war had created more than half a million internal refugees. It wasn't as severe here as in central and northern parts of Afghanistan, but most of the land was still uncultivated. The harvest from last year's seeds had been poor, just enough to feed a few families. The news had come of white men, most probably volunteers from the World Food Program, distributing seeds in a nearby town. The news was good, but there remained the complicated negotiation about how to divide the subsequent harvest; there remained the long journey to the town, on foot and on trucks, past many checkpoints where the bribes—corruption, despite draconian Islamic punishments, flourished as usual—could be very steep.

Outside, in the courtyard, where tufts of grass grew wild in the cracks of the mud walls, an emaciated cow slumped on the ground, and somewhere inside the rooms around us I could sense the presence of women, could hear occasionally the rustle of thick cloth and the clink of pots and pans. I could imagine them: brisk, silent figures in the dusk, whose shapeless heavy chadoris, with the narrow mesh across their eyes, resembling the habit of a viciously persecuted medieval sisterhood.

But this was the outsider's vision; the chadori, I learned later, has usually been worn by village women as a status symbol—a sign of their husbands' education or employment—and was more common in the towns and cities. Under the Taliban you could still glimpse women without it in the villages, where everyday life was traditionally autonomous of what went on in the cities. Women in rural Afghanistan, where 90 percent of the country's approximately twenty million people still live, were less vulnerable to the Taliban's arbitrary brutality. Nancy Hatch Dupree mentions instances of women being beaten and killed outside Kabul, but on the whole they weren't as affected by the restrictions and controversies arising out of the Taliban's harsh gender policies as women in the cities. Of the minuscule 3 percent of school-age Afghan females who went to school during Communist rule, the majority came from the urban areas. It was the women in the cities, encouraged into education and employment by Zahir Shah, the Communists, and, most recently, the UN agencies, who suffered most.

The rural-urban divide has always complicated the process of change in Afghanistan, as it has in many underdeveloped countries. So too have the heavy-handed ways in which change has often been imposed upon the countryside from above, by Afghanistan's tiny, Westernized, and mostly non-Pashtun, Persian-speaking urban elite in Kabul. The rural elite of religious and tribal leaders has tended to respond to their efforts at modernization by retreating even further in time. In 1929, conservative mullahs bullied women back into thicker chadoris and sacked museums and libraries after overthrowing the liberal-minded king Amanullah, who had abolished the veil, opened coed schools, and ordered Afghans in Kabul to wear Western clothes. Not until 1959 did women appear without the chadori on the streets of Kabul, and this continued for over thirty-five years, until they faced the cruelest restrictions yet on their freedom of movement and dress.

The Afghan Communists had encouraged women in Kabul to wear skirts and employed them in the government. This was part of their plan to modernize Afghanistan. New textbooks sent out to the villages carried an image of three men in European suits leading a traditionally dressed crowd to a glorious future. Volunteer teachers in the literacy campaign forced old men and girls to attend classes while at the same time, and often in the same villages, the Communists were arresting and massacring tens of thousands of young Muslim men.

Much of the chaos and violence suffered in Afghan villages during the Communist era was engineered by a Westernized elite at the head of an active government in Kabul, a city which, with its Persian-speaking population and apparently liberated women, was already alien to most Pashtuns. This may partly explain why the sons of Pashtun peasants and nomads who made up the Taliban imposed their harshest laws upon the women of Kabul soon after driving out the moderate Islamist Tajik commander Ahmad Shah Massoud from this most Westernized of Afghan cities in 1996 and forcing him to the north.

Suddenly, in yet another Afghan regression, women found themselves sentenced to the chadori and confined to their homes. They could neither educate themselves nor work; Dupree estimates that the prohibitions directly affected anywhere between 40,000 and 150,000 workingwomen and about 100,000 girls at school. Women had to be accompanied by male relatives outside their homes, where the possibility of public humiliation, usually beatings with sticks but also harsher punishments, by the religious police was ever present.

The Taliban claimed they were shielding women from the sexual predation they had suffered in the days of the mujahideen warlords. A Taliban official, who had studied at a madrassa in Pakistan, told me that he couldn't trust his men with unveiled women, and in any case Mullah Omar, whose original mission had allegedly been to protect women from rapists and bandits, had to preserve at all costs the Taliban's reputation as uncorrupted men who had brought peace and security and "true Islam" to Kabul.

The Taliban official wouldn't be drawn into a discussion of what "true Islam" was or could be. But then what he really seemed to be articulating was the deep and long-standing fear and resentment of Western lifestyles, particularly the independence of women, among Pashtun men in the countryside, the modern ways that the Communists had brutally imposed upon Afghanistan and that Kabul, with the presence of foreign nationals there, represented. Mullah Omar expressed his contempt by staying away from what remained the official capital of Afghanistan and living in Kandahar. For the rural men who dominated the Taliban, the women in Kabul and other Afghan cities, the relatively modern Shiite and Persian-speaking minorities, the Communists of the past, and the foreign aid workers of today were all part of the same large, undifferentiated threat to the Pashtun dictatorship that they, with some help from the Sharia, or Islamic law, wished to maintain.

These complex social and economic resentments help to explain why the Taliban, while ruthless with the Shiites and NGO workers, did not curtail the religious practices of the five thousand or so mostly poor Hindus and Sikhs in Afghanistan, even though the latter were briefly required—to avoid harassment from the religious police, the Taliban claimed—to carry yellow identification badges at all times. They also help to explain the many incidents such as the one in which the religious police, who were answerable only to Mullah Omar in Kandahar, closed down an Italian-funded hospital in mid-May 2001 after they caught women workers dining with the male staff.

There were fewer such problems in the rural areas, where women, confined to looking after their families, already appeared part of the premodern moral order Mullah Omar apparently wished to re-create. You sensed that there was paradoxically a slightly greater freedom available to the women you saw traveling in the same buses as men, albeit in segregated rows, than was available to the women in Kabul, where the lines were clearly drawn.

UNESCO had supported the Communist literacy campaign that was opposed by many Muslims, and during the anti-Communist jihad in the eighties many UN agencies and other NGOs carried on, among other development projects, the tasks of women's education and empowerment in Communist-controlled Kabul. When the UN agencies argued that the Taliban had to allow Afghan women to work — particularly as nurses and doctors, since under the Taliban women could not be treated by men — the hard-line leaders of the Taliban interpreted such insistence as further proof of the UN's complicity with the various forms of Western imperialism — cultural, social, military — they imagined were arrayed against them.

This is where some earlier exposure to the outside world might have helped; one can't overestimate the value, in these circumstances, of the small educated Afghan middle class that twenty years of war dispersed across the world. But the Pashtun village mullahs who formed the central leadership of the Taliban knew little else besides the Koran. This is why the Taliban, unlike such radical Islamist groups as the Muslim Brotherhood of Egypt and Pakistan's Jamaat-i-Islami, offered no coherent ideology or doctrine, as distinct from the fatwas that emanated randomly from Kandahar against women, idolatry, kite flying, football, music, dancing, squeaky shoes, and American hairstyles.

The outlay for the Taliban's powerful Ministry for the Promotion of Virtue and Prevention of Vice, which punished those whose beards were not the prescribed eight centimeters long and those who did not observe prayers and fasts and worked hard to ensure that male minds remained free of the sinful thoughts incited by the presence of unveiled women, was three times as much as that for development. For Mullah Omar and his advisers from the rural clergy, it was enough to be pious and virtuous, and a healthy Islamic society would be created by itself. And the punishment for those who strayed from virtue was draconian: adulterers were stoned to death, while women were known to have the tips of their thumbs cut off for wearing nail polish. Not surprisingly, such cloud-cuckoo-land ideas—partly the result of their limited madrassa educations—and their brutal consequences made the Taliban increasingly unpopular among even the Pashtuns in the countryside, who, oppressed by the mujahideen, had initially welcomed them as liberators.

Their aggressive puritanism, which includes a distrust of Shiite Muslims, hundreds of whom were massacred by Taliban soldiers, is far from the twentieth-century modernist ideologies of Islam that influenced an earlier generation of Afghan Islamists. Professor Burhanuddin Rabbani, the president of Afghanistan for two years in the early 1990s, was a graduate of the al-Azhar University in Cairo, while Mullah Omar doesn't have the basic educational qualifications required to be called a mullah.

The harsh arbitrariness of the mullahs in Kandahar and the religious police was justified under the name of "true Islam" but sought for the most part to reconfigure the Pashtun dominance over Afghanistan's ethnic minorities, a new alignment of power that imposed Pashtun tribal ways over most of the country and made unassailable the Pashtun religious elites in the villages that had been, over the last century, continuously threatened and undermined by the modernizing rulers of Afghanistan in Kabul.

The obstinacy and destructiveness of the Taliban now appear part of the history of Afghanistan's calamitous encounter with the modern world. Afghanistan missed the nineteenth century, which was a period of new beginnings for many old societies in the region. No country was less equipped to deal with the twentieth-century ideologies of communism, anticommunism, and radical Islam. No country was less prepared for the assortment of strategists and adventurers, people alien to and uncomprehending of Afghanistan, who managed to enlist the country's already great inner turmoil, the tragic violence and disorder of a near-primitive society modernizing too fast, into the wider conflict of the cold war, who managed to introduce more effective means of destruction and left behind a ruin more extensive than any the Afghans had known in their war-weary history.

The past two decades had probably weighed most heavily on the women in the country's small middle class, which had briefly flour-ished in the decade before 1979. In Kabul in Christmas 2004, I met Hawa Nooristani, a popular state TV anchor in Afghanistan. We sat in a damply carpeted room at the Ministry of Women's Affairs in Kabul. Pale light came through the windows, illuminating the dust on an old fax machine. A valentine in the form of a screen saver pirouetted on the screen of one of the two desktop computers in the room; the other screen displayed a message advising that its Norton antivirus subscrip-tion had expired. Two young women in head scarves appeared after five minutes or so with a large samovar and replenished our cups of green tea.

Born in Nangrahar Province, Nooristani had gone to a local school and then in the late seventies passed the entrance test for the medical faculty at Kabul University. But the antimodern backlash had already begun in the country. Islamist mujahideen attacked schools in the provinces; they often kidnapped female students from the university in Kabul. Nooristani's father, a tribal leader, was "open-minded" enough to educate his daughters, but he was worried. "What will I do if they kidnap you?" he asked her. "I will have to kill you."

Nooristani joined the faculty of journalism at Nangrahar University. After three years, she married a government official and moved to Kabul, where she began to work for a women's magazine run by the Communist government. She rose to be the magazine's deputy editor, reporting on such social issues as the marriage of minors and profiling famous women singers and writers. She also wrote fiction and poetry in Pashtu and raised a family of five children. This apparently placid life continued for twelve years, even as the war went on in Afghanistan. Then, in 1996, the Taliban came to Kabul and closed down the maga-zine. They also detained her husband in Kandahar on false charges. Since the Taliban allowed women to work only in the health sector, Nooristani had to go underground while working for UN-Habitat, which was running a big project for widows. When the Taliban found out and began looking for her, then began a fearful phase for Nooris-tani. She and her five children had to seek shelter with friends and rel-atives and move from house to house in order to avoid arrest. By now her father and other relatives had already left for Pakistan. But she couldn't leave the country as long as her husband was in prison.

Nooristani smiled often, a sweet, guileless smile, while describing her life, but tears suddenly appeared to brim in her eyes as she said, "While I am talking to you, I remember those days and feel insecure once again. I realize again how weak were the foundations of our lives."

The overthrow of the Taliban had given her fresh hope. She had restarted the women's magazine. She anchored news programs on both TV and radio. She was also doing a computer course. Her teacher had told her, "You are an intelligent student," and as she reported this to me, she burst into girlish laughter. She was also working on a new collection of poems on a computer. She had written her two previous collections in longhand and lost both manuscripts. A friend had misplaced the first, and the other was destroyed when the Uzbek warlord Dostum bombed her home during the civil war in Kabul in 1992–1994.

The United States lost interest in Afghanistan soon after the Soviet withdrawal from the country in 1989, although Afghans continued to pay a high price for having hosted one of the bloodiest battles of the cold war. In late 2001 the United States was faced with fresh responsibilities in Afghanistan after overthrowing the Taliban regime. It was obliged not only to engage in nation building, a task President Bush rejected during a presidential debate with Al Gore in 2000 as unsuitable for the United States, but also to provide basic security to more than twenty-five million people in a country as big as Texas. As it turns out, the way the Bush administration conducted the war, and dealt with its aftermath, has complicated both tasks.

Apart from Americans serving at bases in countries near Afghanistan and aerial bombing, the United States committed only about 110 CIA officers and 316 Special Forces personnel to the overthrow of the Taliban. The Bush administration may have feared a stalemate in Afghanistan, where the armies of the British Empire and the Soviet Union fared poorly in the past. Or it may have planned to save ground troops for future military operations in Iraq. In any case, Defense Secretary Donald Rumsfeld preferred using small, highly mobile forces supported by precision bombing in Afghanistan.

This forced the United States to recruit proxies on the ground. The most easily available of these turned out to be the anti-Taliban warlords in the so-called Northern Alliance, which consisted mainly of Tajiks,

Hazaras, Uzbeks, and Turkmens and which the Pashtun-dominated Taliban had defeated repeatedly. The CIA had helped arm many of these warlords during the anti-Soviet jihad. As the jihad ended, the CIA and the State Department deferred to the Pakistani ISI and Saudi princes who had encouraged Muslims all over the world to join the jihad against the godless Communist regime in Kabul and who now tried to install the most extreme radical Islamists in power. Thus, billions of dollars of American taxpayer funding went into supporting a ruthless anti-American cabal of Islamists and Pakistani intelligence officers.

After the Soviet withdrawal in 1989, these uprooted mujahideen used brutal violence to assert their authority over the territories they controlled—hence the name *jang salar*, warlord, that Afghans came to use for many of the anti-Soviet mujahideen. Local mujahideen "commanders"—the word in Afghanistan refers to men with guns and bands of their loyal supporters—also set up toll tax checkpoints on roads. Extortion, arbitrary arrests, killings, kidnapping, and rape had become commonplace in many parts of Afghanistan in the early 1990s. Not surprisingly, many Afghans, including Hamid Karzai, initially welcomed the puritan Taliban as they arose in 1994 from the Pashtun-dominated southern and eastern provinces of Afghanistan to subdue by 1996 most of the warlords.

In the fall of 2001 Operation Enduring Freedom brought many of these mujahideen out of exile and retirement. In what President Bush has called one of the biggest "bargains" of all time, CIA and Special Forces officers handed out hundred-dollar bills totaling seventy million dollars to such regional commanders of private militias as Ismael Khan in the west; Abdul Rashid Dostum, General Mohammed Fahim, and Mohammed Ustad Atta in the north; and Hazrat Ali in the east.

Seeing that they were indispensable to the U.S. war on terror, the warlords moved quickly and boldly as the Taliban regime collapsed. In November 2001, soldiers of the Tajik-dominated Northern Alliance raced into Kabul as soon as the Taliban abandoned it and occupied important government buildings, despite being told by their American supporters to await an orderly transition. Elsewhere in Afghanistan, the former mujahideen swiftly regained the power and influence that they had previously lost to the Taliban. Ismael Khan declared himself governor of the western province of Herat and began to siphon away custom tolls on imports from Iran that then amounted to nine million dollars every month; he also reinstituted many Taliban-era restrictions on women.

Warlords in such border provinces as Nangrahar, Kandahar, Khost, and Balkh resumed their battles to control the lucrative businesses of poppy cultivation and smuggling; fighting between the militias of Dostum and Atta Mohammed caused scores of civilian deaths in Balkh in 2002 and 2003. They were soon associated with the kinds of human rights abuses—extrajudicial killings, kidnapping, torture, rape, and human trafficking—that had caused the Taliban to be established in the first place. Warlords working with U.S. Special Forces also committed atrocities, the deaths in the northern province of Shebarghan of up to three thousand Taliban prisoners crammed by Dostum in sealed cargo containers.

In December 2001, the so-called Bonn Agreement, an accord signed by militia leaders who fought with the United States against the Taliban, called for the UN to deploy an international security force in Kabul and stipulated that all militias leave the city before the arrival of the UN-mandated forces. But this was never enforced. When Hamid Karzai arrived in Kabul in late 2001 as the U.S.-backed interim president, he had to contend not only with General Fahim of the Northern Alliance and his tens of thousands of militia fighters ensconced in Kabul but also with the newly empowered warlords in the rest of the country.

Hazrat Ali is one of the more flamboyant and, with eighteen thousand armed supporters, most powerful of these warlords. He became briefly famous in late 2001, when U.S. Special Forces hired him to hunt down Osama bin Laden in the caves of Tora Bora in the eastern province of Nangrahar. It is no longer clear whether bin Laden was in Tora Bora as American B-52s pulverized the area and commanders dazzled journalists with stories of high-tech terrorist caves inside the mountains. But Hazrat Ali continued to flourish. Backed by General Fahim in the Northern Alliance, and apparently favored by U.S. Special Forces, he threatened his rivals with American aerial strikes and, after forcing out Karzai's candidate, appointed himself "security chief" of the province of Nangrahar.

Such job titles in Afghanistan are rarely without grim irony. An investigator for the Afghan Independent Human Rights Commission in Nangrahar sighed before he went on to recite the cases of kidnapping, torture, and rape of women and young boys in which Ali's men were implicated. Since Tora Bora, Ali had also become one of the powerful men in Afghanistan involved in the drugs trade.

The farmers I met in Nangrahar Province, among the 2.3 million Afghans employed in the drugs industry, described how Ali had encouraged and closely supervised the production and trafficking of opium. His men came to villages in pickup trucks and bought the poppy harvest, which, previously taken to Pakistan for processing, was now turned into heroin in laboratories within Nangrahar itself before being smuggled through Dubai and Pakistan to the streets of London or Paris.

The new freedoms enjoyed by U.S.-backed warlords like Hazrat Ali partly explain why Afghan opium poppy cultivation, abruptly curtailed when the Taliban enforced a ban in 2000 and 2001, jumped 64 percent between 2003 and 2004 and why Afghanistan last year supplied 87 percent of the world's heroin. Just as the CIA-sponsored radical Islam once connected Afghanistan to the modern world, so U.S.-backed warlords have initiated Afghanistan into the globalized economy.

When I met Hazrat Ali in Jalalabad, the capital of Nangrahar, near the Khyber Pass, in December 2004, at a compound teeming with Land Cruisers and heavily armed bodyguards, he had just returned from a tour of some poppy-growing districts. His assistant, a young swarthy man with wild eyes, was disappointed to see me. He had expected a white journalist, and he grew suspicious when I spoke to him in Urdu.

Hazrat Ali himself pleaded humility in the way a small-town hoodlum-turned-politician in India might. He was a "very simple man," he said. Sitting cross-legged on a divan at one end of a long room, bare except for chandeliers, Ali repeatedly slapped the soles of his feet as he detailed his success in eradicating 95 percent of the poppy grown in Nangrahar. He had not received clear enough instructions from Karzai, he said; otherwise he would have stopped poppy cultivation long ago. Now, within three days, there would no poppy plant left in his province.

These claims were not entirely "bullshit," as a Western diplomat in Kabul later described them. The efforts at eradication were largely successful in Nangrahar. But opium poppy can be stored for a long time, and many farmers in Nangrahar told me that Hazrat Ali was most likely waiting to sell his reserves after shortages caused by crop eradication in Afghanistan had inflated the international prices.

I asked him how farmers whom he had forced to stop growing poppy would find another way of feeding their families. He said he didn't worry about that. Opium was immoral, banned by the Sharia; it had to be eliminated. As for farmers in his province who complained about American soldiers breaking into their homes, searching for terrorists and poppy, they needed, Ali said, to reform themselves, to stop growing poppy and supporting terrorists.

In his elegant mansion in the northern city of Mazar-i-Sharif, some fifty miles from the Uzbekistan border, the former warlord-turned-governor Atta Mohammed described to me, as a television crew hovered around us, how hard he had worked to eradicate poppy in Balkh Province and how as a man of peace he had asked hundreds of his fighters to voluntarily disarm. Feared locally as an extreme Islamic fundamentalist, and previously seen in dirty camouflage khakis, Mohammed had recently trimmed his long beard and taken to wearing pinstripe suits while meeting foreign visitors in his wood-paneled office.

Balkh TV news that evening showed Mohammed discussing the progress of Afghanistan with a visiting writer from America. On television, Mohammed looked suave, even persuasive. But Miriam, a longstanding American aid worker I had met the previous evening had already told me that Mohammed's militia had stashed away large amounts of arms. Afghans in Mazar spoke casually of his role in smuggling drugs across the nearby, largely unguarded border with Uzbekistan. In July 2004, Mohammed had locked the Karzai-appointed local police chief in his own home after the latter seized a consignment of opium. British troops stationed in Mazar as part of the ISAF (International Security Assistance Force) -run provincial reconstruction team had to supply the besieged police chief with food and water until the standoff ended.

When I met the military commander of the PRT in December, he had just returned from what he described, with British euphemism, as "a frank talk" with Mohammed. Apparently, there was little else that he and his few dozen troops in an area as large as Scotland could do.

Certainly, Afghanistan's weak central government is even less equipped to tackle the fact that twenty-eight out of the country's thirty-two provinces now grow poppy, often with the support and involvement of local officials, such as the chief of police in the remote northern province of Badakshan, who until recently was running the largest heroin factory in Afghanistan in his garden.

Karzai had initially offered cash incentives to poppy farmers in an attempt to make them destroy their crops. But many farmers never saw the money, which was swallowed by corrupt government officials. Others accepted it and continued to cultivate poppy. Karzai later admitted his payments were a mistake.

The availability of high-yield seeds, cold storage facilities, and microcredit may wean Afghan farmers away from what has become their most reliable source of income, poppy, which grows easily, even in areas without adequate water, and which can earn twenty-five times more than the traditional crops of wheat, rice, and cotton. But this will take years, if not decades. And long-term schemes for making Afghan agriculture and horticulture more profitable do not seem as important to the U.S. counternarcotics program in Afghanistan as aggressive, quick-fix schemes for poppy eradication, which seem certain to invite resistance. In 2004, the American security company DynCorp trained a four hundred–strong Afghan eradication team in just two weeks, and sent it out to the central province of Wardak, where it destroyed a thousand hectares, but only after fighting off farmers who fired rockets and sowed their fields with land mines.

In November 2004, farmers in Nangrahar reported seeing a plane spraying poppy fields with chemicals. The governor of the province, Din Mohammed, who had to pacify the angry farmers, told me that only the Americans could have sent the plane, but U.S. officials denied all knowledge of it. A European diplomat told me that "very senior" members of the Bush administration had resolved to aerially eradicate poppy in Afghanistan, much to the consternation of Karzai, who feared that farmers would be incited to armed revolt by planes or helicopters destroying their fields.

It seems unfair to target, manually or aerially, hundreds of thousands of small poppy farmers without ensuring that they have alternative means of survival, especially while warlords and corrupt government officials continue to build great fortunes out of the narcotics business.

Many Afghans have asked why the eighteen thousand U.S. troops in the country were unable to arrest the more notorious drug traffickers. When I put this to a Western diplomat, he said that Al Capone was known as a Mafia don for years before there was enough evidence to convict him. He then promised arrests of some big traffickers in early 2005. But no such arrests have happened, and until they do, it will be hard to dismiss Afghans as conspiracy theorists when they claim the United States ignored the extraordinary growth in poppy production over the last three years because it expected the money from drugs, Afghanistan's only major export, to spare it some of the costs of rebuilding the country's economy. Such shortcuts, after all, have been taken before in Afghanistan, during the anti-Soviet jihad, when the CIA was complicit in the drugs trade.

Growing evidence that the Taliban and Al Qaeda were funding themselves through the narcotics trade may have finally alerted the Bush administration to the possibility that as Antonio Maria Costa, executive director of the UN antinarcotics program, wrote in a report in October 2003, "Afghanistan will again turn into a failed state, this time in the hands of drug cartels and narco-terrorists." In his more alarming survey published in November 2004, Costa warned that if the drug problem in Afghanistan persists, "the political and military successes of the last three years will be lost."

But Afghanistan will be unable to avoid this fate as long as the Bush administration considers warlords indispensable to its war on terror and thus undercuts President Karzai's authority. Much of the country appears to be run largely by these warlords and their private militias, whom Karzai himself described, in a recent interview with *The New York Times*, as the greatest threat to Afghanistan's security, even more dangerous than Taliban insurgents, who killed more than nine hundred people in 2004, including reconstruction and aid workers, but are still largely confined to the southern and eastern provinces.

Defense Secretary Rumsfeld and his former deputy, Paul Wolfowitz, consistently refused to involve U.S. troops in peacekeeping efforts in Afghanistan. More surprisingly, they opposed, until September 2003, expanding the UN-mandated ISAF beyond Kabul, especially in areas where, as the Human Rights Watch report for 2004 puts it, "there are no real governmental structures or activity, only abuse and criminal enterprises by factions." The eight thousand–strong ISAF, which is under NATO command, will expand across Afghanistan over the next three years. But its presence will still compare poorly with forty thousand NATO soldiers in Bosnia, which is one-tenth the size of Afghanistan. Moreover, the ISAF has no mandate to take on drugs traffickers or even to intervene militarily in factional fighting.

In July 2004, Médicins sans Frontières (MSF), which had remained in Afghanistan through the hard years of the civil war and the Taliban regime, finally withdrew from the country after five of its workers were killed by unknown gunmen. MSF claimed that Afghan officials gave it evidence that warlords in northwest Afghanistan were involved in the killing but did nothing to arrest the suspects. MSF had previously "condemned the distribution of leaflets by the coalition forces in southern Afghanistan in which the population was informed that providing information about the Taliban and al Qaeda was necessary if they wanted the delivery of aid to continue." It accused the United States of consistently using "humanitarian aid to build support for its military and political ambitions" and thus compromising the neutrality of Western aid agencies in war zones.

In a response published in *The Wall Street Journal*, the novelist Cheryl Benard, who is married to the U.S. ambassador, Zalmay Khalilzad, advised MSF that "it is a different world out there" and that "humanitarians will have to operate under the cover of arms—or not at all." But it is not clear whether the large-scale and expensive military offensives (costing one billion dollars per month) against the Taliban and Al Qaeda are working, especially when compared to intelligence and police operations in Pakistan, where many senior Al Qaeda members have been captured.

Both bin Laden and Mullah Omar are still at large after the highest bounties and most rigorous manhunts in history. This may attest not only to the difficulties of fighting a shadowy enemy in a vast and mountainous territory but also to the strength of tribal and religious loyalties and growing anti-American sentiment in the Pashtun-dominated provinces of Afghanistan and Pakistan. In October 2002, popular resentment of America helped a coalition of radical Islamist parties win elections in the Pakistani provinces bordering Afghanistan, where the Taliban appear to find ready support. More people in southern and eastern Afghanistan are likely to be drawn to radical Islamists as aerial bombings and raids on villages continue and the U.S. military places itself further beyond international law. No one among the thousands of Afghans detained by the U.S. military at mostly unknown locations across Afghanistan since 2001 has been given prisoner of war status. Often released as arbitrarily as they are arrested, they have no access to legal counsel. Mistreatment during interrogation—beatings, sexual humiliation, and sleep deprivation—appears common. Eight Afghans have died in American custody. In 2004, two of these deaths were ruled homicides by U.S. military doctors at Bagram Air Base near Kabul.

In Jalalabad, I met a diplomat from one of Afghanistan's powerful neighbors. He described in some detail his encounters with American diplomats and military officers whom he termed intellectually limited but very arrogant. He said, "The Afghans in the south and east hate the Americans as much as they hated the Russians. They are too tired after twenty-five years of war. But give them two more years of Operation Enduring Freedom and they will start another jihad."

Later that same evening, I was at the governor's mansion in Jalalabad, formerly a summer palace of the king of Afghanistan, when a delegation of tribal elders arrived. They had walked for much of the day from a remote district; mud covered their slippers and scaly feet. The governor attended to them immediately, after postponing his meeting with me. They sat on a terrace in two long rows, and the scene— long-bearded, turbaned men before their solicitous potentate, against a backdrop of gardens and pavilions—could have been that of a Moghul miniature painting.

The men had come to complain to the governor about heavy-handed American soldiers in their villages. After their leader spoke briefly and somberly, the governor attempted a joke, possibly in order to hide his own inability to influence his American patrons. Afghanistan, he said, had become a petri dish in which foreigners could throw in whatever they liked. Some of the men laughed, revealing toothless gums.

When their laughter subsided, one of the elders began to speak. From where I sat, I couldn't see his face. I only heard his deep, urgent voice. He spoke about the dishonor caused to Afghan families by American soldiers barging into women's quarters, about the frustration and rage felt by him and others, and he spoke for a long time, his voice growing in passion until it broke, and I began to believe that the diplomat, whom I'd thought too embittered by his own encounters with powerful and abrasive Americans, may not have exaggerated much.

Many Afghans I spoke to felt that people in the West, absorbed with Iraq, had already grown indifferent to their fate or saw in Afghanistan only what they wished to see, the dawn of democracy and freedom. But as Dr. Sima Samar, the leading human rights activist in Afghanistan, suggested recently, "Democracy and freedom are meaningless without justice and the rule of law." The parliamentary elections may appear another milestone in the grand march to democracy and freedom, but they are also likely to give greater legitimacy to warlords, who are presently better placed than anyone else in Afghanistan to form political parties and influence voters.

For many Afghans, however, the future still appears to be full of opportunities. When I returned to Kabul, Karzai had announced his new cabinet. He had managed to exclude the more powerful warlords, Fahim and Dostum, and to choose what Massouda Jalal called "qualified people," including of course Dr. Jalal herself, who was asked to be the minister for women's affairs two weeks after I met with her. The job seemed to have little political or financial power, and it would last only until the parliamentary elections, but she had accepted it.

I went to see her on her first day at work. On the afternoon I'd first met her it had been intensely cold and damp in her apartment in a Soviet-style housing estate. There was no power, and when she spoke of the "dark ages" of the Taliban, a time that she spent largely at home, it had been hard to imagine a bleakness more lowering than the one she lived with. Now, at the ministerial chambers, brilliantly lit and expensively carpeted, her husband queued with many women waiting to be received by Dr. Jalal.

The minister was busy, her assistant said, but granted me time for one question. As she stood smiling and chatting with bouquet-laden visitors, I asked Dr. Jalal what she thought the international community, which she had previously criticized, ought to do. It was the wrong question. Dr. Jalal had yet to adjust her political opinions to her new official role, and she struggled briefly while the Afghan women around her stared at me. Then she blurted out, "Don't forget us." As I left, she appeared slightly embarrassed by the sentimental words. But they expressed well, I thought later, the weary but still hopeful mood of many Afghans as they compete for the attention and goodwill of an easily distracted world.

PART THREE

NEPAL

The "People's War"

In Kathmandu in March 2005, I met a Nepalese businessman who said he knew what had provoked Crown Prince Dipendra, supposed incarnation of Vishnu and former pupil at Eton, to mass murder. On the night of June 1, 2001, Dipendra appeared in the drawing room of the royal palace in Kathmandu, dressed in combat fatigues, apparently out of it on Famous Grouse and hashish, and armed with assault rifles and pistols. In a few frenzied minutes, he killed his parents, King Birendra and Queen Aishwarya, a brother, a sister, and five other relatives before putting a pistol to his head. Anointed king as he lay unconscious in hospital, he died two days later, passing his title to his uncle Gyanendra.

Dipendra's obsession with guns at Eton, where he was admired by Lord Camoys as a "damn good shot," his heavy drinking, which attracted the malice of the *Sun*, his addiction to hashish, and his fondness for the films of Arnold Schwarzenegger—all this outlines a philistinism and a potential for violence, commonplace among scions of third world dynasties (Suharto, Nehru-Gandhi, Bhutto). And it is not so hard to believe the semiofficial explanation for his actions: that his parents disapproved of his fiancée. However, the businessman, who claimed to know the royal family, had a more elaborate and intriguing theory.

We sat in a rooftop café in Thamel, Kathmandu's tourist center, a few hundred feet from the royal palace. March, the businessman said, was a good season for tourists in Nepal. "But look," he continued, pointing to the alleys below us, where the bookshops, trekking agencies, cybercafés, bakeries, malls, and restaurants were empty. In recent years, the tourist industry has been damaged by news in the international press about the Maoist guerrillas, who model themselves on the Shining Path in Peru, and whose "people's war" has claimed more than eleven thousand lives since 1996. Even fewer tourists have ventured to Nepal since February 1, 2005, when King Gyanendra, citing the threat presented by the Maoists, grounded all flights, cut off phone and Internet lines, arrested opposition politicians, and imposed censorship on the media.

A portly man wearing a cotton tunic, tight trousers, and a cloth cap, the businessman had the prejudices of his class, the tiny minority of affluent Nepalese whose wealth comes largely from tourism and foreign aid, and that morning, the spring sun growing warm and burning off the smog over the Kathmandu Valley, the vendors of carpets, Gurkha knives, pirate DVDs, and Tibetan prayer flags sullenly eyeing a stray tourist in tie-dye clothes, he aired them freely.

He said that Maoists had bombed the private school he sent his children to; he worried that his servants might join the guerrillas, who controlled 80 percent of the countryside and were growing strong in the Kathmandu valley. He said that he was all for democracy—he had been among the protesters demanding a new constitution in the spring of 1990—but peace and stability were more important. What the country needed now, he declared, was a strong and principled ruler, someone who could crush the Maoists. He said that he missed Dipendra; he was the man Nepal needed at this hour of crisis.

According to him, Dipendra's three years as a schoolboy in Britain had radicalized him. Just as Pandit Nehru had discovered the poverty of India after his stints at Harrow and Cambridge, so Dipendra had developed a new political awareness in England. He had begun to look, with mounting horror and concern, at his homeland. Returning to Nepal, he had realized that it would take more than tourism to create a strong middle class, accelerate economic growth, build democratic institutions, and lift the ninth-poorest country in the world to the ranks of modern democratic nations. As it turned out, he had been thwarted at every step by conservative elements in the royal palace. He had watched multiparty democracy, introduced in 1991, grow corrupt and feeble while enriching an elite of politicians and bureaucrats; equally helplessly, he had watched the new rulers of Nepal fail to tackle the Maoists. Frustration in politics rather than love, the businessman claimed, had driven Dipendra to alcohol, drugs, guns, and, finally, regicide.

It's often hard to know what to believe in Nepal, the only Hindu kingdom in the world, where conspiracy and rumor have long fueled a particularly secretive kind of court politics. Independent newspapers and magazines have been widely available only since 1990, and though intellectually lively, the press has little influence over a largely illiterate population easily swayed by rumor. In December 2000, news that a Bollywood actor had insulted Nepal incited riots and attacks on Indians and Indian-owned shops across the country. Little is known about Dipendra, apart from his time at Eton, where his fellow pupils nicknamed him Dippy. There is even greater mystery surrounding Pushpa Kamal Dahal, or Prachanda, the middle-aged, articulate leader of the Maoists, who has been in hiding for the last two decades.

King Gyanendra appeared on national television to blame the palace massacre on a "sudden discharge by an automatic weapon." A popular conspiracy theory, in turn, blamed it on the new king himself, who was allegedly involved in smuggling artifacts out of Nepal, and on his son, Paras, much disliked in Nepal for his habits of brandishing guns in public and dangerous driving; he has run over at least three people in recent years, killing one. More confusingly, the Maoists claimed that they had an "undeclared working unity" with King Birendra and accused Gyanendra, and Indian and American imperialists, of his murder.

This atmosphere of secrecy and intrigue seems to have grown murkier since February 2005, when Gyanendra adopted the Bush administration's rhetoric about "terrorism" and assumed supreme power. Flights to Nepal were resumed after only a few days, and the king claimed to have lifted the emergency on April 30, but most civil rights are still suspended today. When I arrived in Kathmandu, fear hung heavy over the street crossings, where soldiers peeped out from behind machine-gun emplacements. Men in ill-fitting Western suits, with the furtive manner of inept spies, lurked in the lobby of my hotel. Journalists spoke of threatening phone calls from senior army officers who tended to finger as Maoists anyone who didn't support the king. Many of the people I wanted to meet turned out to be in prison or in exile. Appointments with underground activists, arduously made, were canceled at the last minute, or people simply didn't turn up.

Sitting in her gloomy office, a human rights activist described the routine torture and extrajudicial killing of suspected Maoists, which had risen to a startling average of eight a day. Nothing was known about the more than twelve hundred people the army had taken from their homes since the beginning of the "people's war," the highest number of unexplained disappearances in the world. She spoke of the "massive impunity" enjoyed by the army, which was accountable only to the king. She claimed that the governments of India, the United States, and the U.K. had failed to understand the root causes of the Maoist phenomenon and had decided, out of fear and ignorance, to supply weapons to the Royal National Army: twenty thousand M-16 rifles from the United States; twenty thousand rifles from India; helicopters from the U.K.

She said that the "international community" had chosen the wrong side in a conflict that in any case was not likely to be resolved by violence. Though recently expanded and mobilized against the Maoists in 2001, the army was no more than eighty-five thousand strong and could not hold the countryside, where, among the high mountains, ravines, and rivers—almost perfect terrain for guerrillas—it faced a formidable enemy.

She spoke with something close to despair. Much of her work, particularly risky at present, depended on international support. But few people outside Nepal cared or knew enough about its human rights record, and the proof lay in her office, which was austerely furnished, with none of the emblems of Western philanthropy—new computers, armed guards, shiny four-wheel drives in the parking lot—that I had seen in December 2004 in Afghanistan.

"People are passing their days here," she said as I left her office, and the remark, puzzling at first, became clearer as I spent more time in Kathmandu. In the streets, where all demonstrations were banned and any protest was quickly quashed by the police, a bizarre feeling of normality prevailed, best symbolized by the vibrant billboards advertising mobile phones (banned since February 1). Adverts in which companies affirmed faith in King Gyanendra appeared daily in the heavily censored newspapers, alongside news of Maoist bombings of police stations, unverified reports of rifts between Maoist leaders, promotional articles about Mercedes-Benz cars and Tag Heuer watches, and stories of parties and fashion shows and concerts in Kathmandu.

Thamel opened for business every day, but its alleys remained empty of tourists. Months of Maoist-enforced blockades and strikes were also beginning to scare away the few foreign investors who had been deceived by the affluence of Kathmandu into thinking that Nepal was a big market for luxury consumer goods. Interviewed in a local newspaper, a Dutch investor described the Nepalese as an "extremely corrupt, greedy, triple-faced, myopic, slow, inexperienced and uneducated people" and declared that he was taking his hair replacement business to Latvia. Western diplomats and United Nations officials, darting in their SUVs from one walled compound to another, speculated about a possible assault on the capital by guerrillas.

But it is the middle-class Nepalese, denounced by the Maoists as "comprador capitalists," who appear to live most precariously, their hopes and anxieties echoed in the newspapers by royalist journalists who affirm daily that Nepal needs a strong ruler and Gyanendra is best placed to defend the country, by means of a spell of autocratic rule, from both Maoist "terrorists" and corrupt politicians.

Often, while listening to them, I would remember the businessman I had met in Thamel and what he had told me about Dipendra, and I would wonder how the crown prince, if he had indeed been sensitized to social and economic distress during his three years in Thatcher's England, had seen his strange inheritance, a country where almost half of the twenty-six million people earned less than a hundred dollars a year and had no access to electricity, running water, or sanitation, a country whose small economy, parasitic on foreign aid and tourism, had to be boosted by the remittances of Nepalese workers abroad, and where political forces seen as anachronisms elsewhere—monarchy and communism—fought for supremacy.

Histories of South Asia rarely describe Nepal except as a recipient of religions and ideologies—Buddhism, Hinduism, communism—from India; even today the country's sixty ethnic and caste communities are regarded as little more than a picturesque backdrop to some of the world's highest mountains. This is partly because Western imperialists overlooked Nepal when they radically remade Asia in the nineteenth and twentieth centuries.

While a British-educated middle class emerged in India and began to aspire to self-rule, Nepal remained a country of peasants, nomads, and traders, controlled by a few clans and families. Previously dependent on China, its high-caste Hindu ruling class courted the British as they expanded across India in the nineteenth century. As in the so-called princely states of India, the British were keen to support despotic regimes in Nepal and even reward them with territory; it was one way of staving off potentially destabilizing change in a strategically important buffer state to Tibet and China. The country was also a source of cheap mercenaries. Tens of thousands of soldiers recruited by the British from the western hills of Nepal fought during the Indian Mutiny, the Boxer Rebellion in China, and the two world wars. The Gurkhas also helped the British suppress political dissenters in India and then, more violently, Communist anticolonialists in Malaya in the 1950s.

As the movement for political independence grew in India, Nepal came to be even more strongly controlled by Hindu kings and the elites they created by giving land grants to members of the high castes, Bahun and Chhetri, which make up less than 30 percent of the population. The end of the British Empire in Asia didn't lead to rapid change in Nepal or end its status as a client state. Indian-made goods flooded Nepalese markets, stifling local industry and deepening the country's dependence on India. In the 1950s and 1960s, as the cold war intensified, Nepal was the forward base of the CIA's operations against China.

American economists and advisers trying to make the world safe for capitalism came to Nepal with plans for "modernization" and "development," then seen as strong defenses against the growth of communism in poor countries. In the so-called Rapti Zone, west of Kathmandu, where, ironically, the Maoists found their first loyal supporters in the 1990s, the U.S. government spent about fifty million dollars "improving household food production and consumption, improving income-generating opportunities for poor farmers, landless laborers, occupational castes and women."

Modernization and development, as defined by Western experts during the cold war, were always compatible with, and often best expedited by, despotic rule. Few among the so-called international community protested when, after a brief experiment with parliamentary democracy in the 1950s, King Mahendra, Dipendra's grandfather, banned all political parties. A new constitution in 1962 instituted a partyless Panchayat system of "guided democracy" in which advisers chosen or controlled by the king rubber-stamped his decisions. The representatives of the Panchayat, largely from the upper castes, helped themselves to the foreign aid that made up most of the state budget and did little to alleviate poverty in rural areas. The king also declared Nepal a Hindu state and sought to impose on its ethnic and linguistic communities a new national identity by promoting the Nepali language.

Such hectic nation building could have lulled Nepal's many ethnic and linguistic communities into a patriotic daze had the project of modernization and development not failed, or benefited so exclusively and egregiously an already privileged elite. During the years of autocratic rule (1962–1990), a few roads were built in the countryside, infant mortality was halved, and the literacy rate went up from 5 percent in 1952 to 40 percent in 1991. But Nepal's population also grew rapidly, further increasing pressure on the country's scarce arable land, and the gap between the city and the countryside widened fast.

What leads the sensitive prince to drugs and alcohol often forces the pauper to migrate. Millions of Nepalese have swelled the armies of cheap mobile labor that drive the global economy, serving in Indian brothels, Thai and Malaysian sweatshops, the mansions of oil sheikhs in the Gulf, and, most recently, the war zones of Iraq. Many more have migrated internally, often from the hills to the subtropical Tarai region on the long border with India. The Tarai produces most of the country's food and cash crops and accommodates half of its population. On its flat alluvial land, where malaria was only recently eradicated, the Buddha was born twenty-five hundred years ago; it is also where a generation of displaced Nepalese began to dream of revolution.

In Chitwan, one of the more densely populated districts in the Tarai, I met Mukti Raj Dahal, the father of the underground Maoist leader Prachanda. Dahal was one of the millions of Nepalese to migrate to the Tarai in the 1950s. His son was then eight years old. He had traveled on to India, doing menial jobs in many cities, before returning to Chitwan, which American advisers and the Nepalese government were then developing as a "model district" with education and health facilities. In Chitwan, Dahal bought some land and managed to give his eight children an education of sorts. Though he is tormented by stomach and spinal ailments, he exuded calm as he sat on the veranda of his two-roomed brick house, wearing a blue T-shirt and shorts under a black cap, a Brahminical caste mark on his forehead.

He had the serenity of a man at the end of his life. And given the circumstances, he had not done too badly. I had spent much of that day on the road from Kathmandu to the Tarai, shuffling past long queues of Tata trucks from India, through a fog of dust and thick diesel smoke, ragged settlements occasionally appearing beside the road: shops made of wooden planks, selling food fried in peanut oil and tea in sticky clouded glasses; mud houses with thatched roofs, a preindustrial bareness in which only the gleaming automatic guns of young soldiers and the tangle of barbed wire behind which they sat spoke of the world beyond Nepal.

The jittery soldiers who approached the car with fingers on their triggers were very young, hard to associate with stories I had heard in Kathmandu, stories no newspaper would touch, of the army marching men out of overcrowded prisons and executing them. My companion, a Nepalese journalist, was nervous. He knew that the soldiers in the countryside attacked anyone they suspected of being a Maoist, and journalists were no exception. Many of the soldiers barely knew what a journalist was.

There are few places in Nepal untouched by violence—murder, torture, arbitrary arrest—and most people live perpetually in fear of both the army and the Maoists, without expectation of justice or recompense. Dahal, however, appeared to have made a private peace with his surroundings. He told me that he spent much of his day at the local temple, listening to recitals of the *Ramayana*. He said that he still believed the king had good intentions. He appeared both bemused by, and admiring of, his famous son, whom he had last seen at the funeral of his wife in 1996. The ideas of equality and justice, he thought, had always appealed to Prachanda, who was a sensitive man, someone who shared his food with poor people in the village. He couldn't tell me how his son had got interested in Mao or Marx in such a place as Chitwan, which had no bookshop or library. But he did know that Prachanda had got involved with Communists when he couldn't find a good job with the government and had to teach at a primary school in his native hills of Pokhara.

In his speeches, which claim inspiration from Mao and seek to mobilize the peasants in the countryside against the urban elite, Prachanda comes across as an ideologue of another era; he's an embarrassment to the Chinese regime, which is engaged in the un-Maoist task of enriching Chinese coastal cities at the expense of the hinterland and feels compelled to accuse Nepalese Maoists of besmirching the Chairman's good name.

In the few interviews he has given, Prachanda avoids answering questions about his background and motivation, which have to be divined from details given by Dahal: the haphazard schooling, the useless degree, the ill-paid teaching job in a village school, all of which seem to lead inexorably to a conflict with, and resentment of, unjust authority.

The "modernization" and "development" of Nepal during the 1950s and 1960s created millions of men like Prachanda, lured away from their subsistence economies and abandoned on the threshold of a world in which they found they had, and could have, no place. Nepal's agricultural economy offered few of them the jobs or the dignity they felt was their due, and they were too aware of the possibilities thwarted by an unequal, stratified society to reconcile themselves to a life of menial labor in unknown lands and an old age spent in religious stupor. Educated, but with no prospects, many young men like Prachanda must have been more than ready to embrace radical ideas about the ways that an entrenched urban elite could be challenged and even overthrown if peasants in the countryside were organized.

Growing up in Nepal in the 1960s, Prachanda watched these ideas grow in the Naxalbari movement in India. Communist activists lived and worked secretly in parts of Nepal during the Panchayat era; in the 1950s, a famous Communist leader called M. B. Singh traveled in the midwestern hills and acquired followers among the Magars, one of Nepal's more prominent ethnic groups now supporting the Maoists. But Prachanda says that the "historic Naxalbari movement" of India was the "greatest influence" on the Communists of Nepal.

In the late 1960s, thousands of students, many of them middle class and upper caste, joined an armed peasant uprising led by an extremist faction of the Communist Party of India (Marxist) in West Bengal and Bihar. Known as Naxalites, after the Naxalbari district where the revolt first erupted in 1967, they attacked "class enemies"—big landlords, policemen, bureaucrats—and "liberated" territories which they hoped would form bases for an eventual assault on the cities, as had happened in China. The Indian government responded brutally, killing and torturing thousands. Driven underground, the Naxalite movement splintered and remained dormant for many years.

In the 1990s, when India began to move toward a free market, the Naxalite movement revived in some of the poorest and most populous Indian states. Part of the reason for this is that successive Indian governments have steadily reduced subsidies for agriculture, public health, education, and poverty eradication, exposing large sections of the population to disease, debt, hunger, and starvation. Almost three thousand farmers committed suicide in the southern state of Andhra Pradesh after the government, advised by McKinsey, cut agricultural subsidies in an attempt to initiate farmers into the world of unregulated markets. In recent years, Naxalite movements, which have long organized landless, low-caste peasants in Bihar and Andhra Pradesh, have grown quickly in parts of Uttar Pradesh and Madhya Pradesh—where an enfeebled Indian state is increasingly absent—to the extent that police and intelligence officials in India now speak anxiously of an unbroken belt of Communist-dominated territory from Nepal to South India.

The Naxalite uprising in the late 1960s invigorated the few Communists in Nepal, who, like the members of the Nepali Congress, the main underground political organization, sought guidance and encouragement from India. In 1971, some Nepalese Communists living across the border from Naxalbari declared a "people's war" against the monarchy. They killed seven "class enemies" before being suppressed by the king. As fractious as their Indian counterparts, the Nepalese Communist parties split and split again over petty doctrinal or personality issues. In 1991, after the restoration of multiparty democracy, several of them contested elections and even did well; a Communist coalition became the biggest opposition party and briefly held power in 1994. In the early 1990s, however, few people in Nepal could have predicted the swift rise of Prachanda and the obscure faction he led.

The Maoists under Prachanda resolved as early as 1986 to follow Mao's strategy of capturing state power through a "people's war." They did not start the war until the mid-1990s, however, when disillusionment with parliamentary democracy created for them a potentially wide popular base in the countryside. Still, hardly anyone noticed when on February 4, 1996, the Maoists presented the government with a list of forty demands, which included abrogating existing treaties with India, stripping the monarchy of all power and privileges, drafting a new constitution by means of a constituent assembly, nationalizing private property, declaring Nepal a secular nation, and ending all foreign aid. These demands were not likely to be met, and as though aware of this, the Maoists began their "people's war" by attacking police stations in six districts four days before the deadline.

For the next five years the Maoists forced their way into the national consciousness with their increasingly bold tactics. They financed themselves by collecting "taxes" from farmers, and they exacted "donations" from many businessmen in the Kathmandu valley. They indoctrinated schoolchildren; they formed people's governments in the areas they controlled and dispensed rough justice to criminals and "class enemies." But much of the new power and charisma of the Maoists came from their ability to launch audacious attacks on the police and the army.

The military wing of the Maoists initially consisted of a few ill-trained men armed with antique rifles and homemade weapons. But they chose their first target cannily: the police, nearly the only representatives of the central government in much of Nepal. Poorly armed, often with little more than sticks and .303 Lee Enfield rifles, the police retreated swiftly before the Maoists, who also attacked roads, bridges, dams, administrative offices, power plants, anything they felt might aid the counterinsurgency efforts of the government.

In recent years the Maoists have grown militarily strong, mostly through conscription in the countryside, and regular training, allegedly provided by Indian Naxalites. They have acquired better weapons by looting police stations and buying from the arms bazaars of India: they have also learned how to make roadside explosives, pipe and "pressure cooker" bombs. In November 2001, the Maoists launched forty-eight attacks on the army and the police in a single day, forcing the Nepalese government to impose a state of emergency. More than five thousand people died in the next fifteen months, the bloodiest period in Nepal's modern history.

But violence is only a part of the Maoists' overall strategy. In an interview in 2000, Prachanda criticized Indian Communist groups for their lack of vision and spoke of the importance of developing "base areas." Since 1996, the Maoists have spread out from their traditional home in the midwestern hills of Rolpa and Rukum districts. Their cadres, estimated to number as many as a hundred thousand, travel to deprived areas, addressing, and often recruiting from, the large and growing mass of people deeply unhappy with Nepal's new democratic dispensation.

Some measure of democracy was inevitable in Nepal by the 1980s. In previous decades the state's halfhearted efforts at development had produced many low-level bureaucrats, small businessmen, teachers, students, and unemployed graduates. This new class resented the continuing dominance of upper-caste clans and families. The conflict between the old elite and its challengers was aggravated by a series of economic crises in the late 1980s. In 1985 and 1986, Nepal had negotiated a loan with the IMF and World Bank. The bank's euphemistically named (and free market–oriented) structural adjustment program, which was then causing havoc in Latin American economies, forced the Nepalese government to cut farm subsidies and jobs in the public sector. GDP grew as a result, but the gains were canceled out by inflation of up to 10 percent and a trade and transit embargo imposed by India in 1989, which caused severe fuel shortages and price rises.

The protesters who filled the streets of Kathmandu in the spring of 1990 were convinced that the decaying Panchayat system could not deal with the shocks of the new world and needed to be reformed. In acceding to demands for multiparty democracy, the king appeared to acknowledge the strength of the new educated class and to recognize that the old political system needed a degree of popular legitimacy if it was to survive. It's clear now that what happened in 1990 was less a revolution than a reconfiguration of power, sanctified by elections, among the old royalist oligarchy and an emerging urban middle class. Many courtiers and sycophants of the king managed to reinvent themselves as parliamentary politicians, often joining the Nepali Congress, the political party that ruled Nepal for all but one of the next thirteen years. There were few ideological differences between the Nepali Congress and the main opposition party, the radical-sounding Communist Party of Nepal (United Marxist-Leninist), both of which continued to be led by upper-caste men motivated largely by a desire for money and power. Elections were held frequently, and a procession of governments—thirteen in as many years—made Nepalese democracy appear vibrant. But the majority of the population, especially its ethnic communities, went largely unrepresented.

In 1992, when democracy still promised much and Maoism was no more than another rumor in the streets of Kathmandu, Andrew Nickson, a British expert on Latin America, wrote prophetically: "The future prospects of Maoism in Nepal will . . . depend largely on the extent to which the newly elected Nepali Congress government addresses the historic neglect and discrimination of the small rural communities which still make up the overwhelming bulk of the population of the country. As in the case of Peru, this would require a radical reallocation of government expenditures towards rural areas in the form of agricultural extension services and primary healthcare provision."

Needless to say, this didn't happen. In 2002, Dalits, low-caste Hindus, had an annual per capita income of only $40, compared to a national average of $210; fewer than 10 percent of Dalits were literate. The upper-caste men who dominated the new democratic regime were competing among themselves to siphon off the money pouring into Nepal from foreign donors. A fresh convert to the ideology of the free market, the Nepalese government dedicated itself to creating wealth in urban areas. Trying to boost private investment in Kathmandu, it neglected agriculture, on which more than 80 percent of the population depend for a living. Not surprisingly, absolute poverty continued to increase in the late 1990s, even as the Kathmandu valley benefited from the growth in the tourist, garment, and carpet industries and filled up with new hotels, resorts, and villas.

In such circumstances, many people are likely to be attracted to violent extraparliamentary groups. The Maoists in Nepal had their first ready constituency among rural youths, more than a hundred thousand of whom fail their high school examinations every year. Unemployed and adrift, many of these young men worked for other political parties in the countryside before becoming disillusioned and joining the Maoists.

Mohan was one of the young men who joined a newly legitimate political party after 1990 and found himself remote from the spoils of power. He then worked with the Maoists for almost five years, living in jungles, once traveling to the easternmost corner of Nepal, before deciding to leave them. He couldn't return to his village, which lay in the Maoist-dominated region of Rolpa, and had gone to India for a while. He was now trying to lie low in Kathmandu, and although he didn't say so, he seemed to be "passing his days" and making a living through odd jobs, like so many other people in the city.

We had arranged to meet in Boudhanath, Kathmandu's major Buddhist site. Sitting in the square around the white stupa, among monks in swirling crimson robes and often with white faces, Mohan spoke of "feudal forces" and the "bourgeoisie"; their corruption had paved the way for the Maoists, whom he described as "anarchists." He used the foreign words with a Nepalese inflection. He said that he had picked them up while accompanying a Maoist propagandist on tour, and it occurred to me, as he described his background, that he still used them despite having left the Maoists because he had no other vocabulary with which to describe his experience of deprivation and disappointment.

He was born and brought up in a family of Magar shepherds in a corner of Rolpa District that had no proper roads, schools, or hospitals. Educated at a school which was a walk of several miles from his village, he had joined the Nepali Congress in 1992, when still in his late teens, and become a personal aide to a prominent local politician. There were many such young men. They received no money for their services but slept in the politician's house, ate the food prepared for his family, and traveled with him to Kathmandu. Mohan said that it was a good time, the early years of democracy. He liked being in Kathmandu, especially with someone who had a bit of power. But he couldn't fail to notice that the politician returned less and less often to his constituency in the hills and often refused to meet people who came to his door asking for jobs, money, and medical help. He was surprised to hear that the politician was building a new house for himself in Kathmandu. Soon he felt he was not needed, and one day the politician's wife told him to eat elsewhere.

Clashes between Nepali Congress activists and the Maoists were common in his area; Mohan felt that he could be useful to the Maoists with his knowledge of politics. He was also attracted to the idea of ethnic autonomy that the Maoists espoused. He had seen in his time with the politician how the upper-caste–dominated government in Kathmandu possessed an unjust share of the country's wealth and resources. Many people he knew had already joined the Maoists, and in 1995 one of his friends introduced him to the Maoist "squad commander" in the region.

As he spoke, I wondered if this was the whole truth, if he hadn't joined the Maoists for the same reason he had joined the Nepali Congress, the reason many young men like him in India joined political parties, for food and shelter. In any case, he joined the Maoists at a bad time; it was in 1995 that the Nepalese government launched Operation Romeo.

This scorched earth campaign is described as an instance of "state terror" in a report by INSEC (Informal Sector Service Center), Nepal's most reliable human rights group. According to the report, the police attacked in the Rolpa and Rukum districts, killing and torturing young men and raping women. When I mentioned this to Mohan, he said that things weren't as bad as they were made out to be by the "bourgeois" intelligentsia in Kathmandu, who, he thought, were soft on the Maoists. He said the Maoists were simply another opportunistic political group; this was why he had left them. They were interested in mobilizing ethnic communities only to the extent that this would help them capture "state power"; they weren't really interested in giving them autonomy. He had also been repelled by their cruelty. He had heard about, if not actually seen, instances of Maoists punishing people who refused to pay taxes, defied their alcohol ban, or were suspected of being police informers. Using rocks and hammers, they often broke all the bones in their victims' bodies before skinning them alive and cutting off their tongues, ears, lips, and noses.

Many of these stories appear in reports by Nepalese and international human rights groups. The Maoist leaders were, I often heard in Kathmandu, riding a tiger, unable to prevent their angry and frustrated cadres from committing torture and murder. Criminals had infiltrated their movement, and some Maoists now made a living from extortion and kidnapping. When confronted with these excesses, Maoist leaders deny or deplore them. They probably realize that they are losing many of their original supporters, who are as tired of the organization's growing extremism as of the years of indecisive fighting. Nevertheless, these leaders can often seem constrained in their political thinking by revolutionary methods and rhetoric created in another time and place. Prachanda, for instance, is convinced that "a new wave of revolution, world revolution is beginning, because imperialism is facing a great crisis."

When the subject is not world revolution but the specific situation of Nepal, he can be shrewdly perceptive. A police officer in India told me that many of the Indian Communists he interviewed confessed to learning much from the Maoists in Nepal, who were not as rigidly doctrinal as Communists in India and Afghanistan. As Prachanda put it, "The situation in Nepal is not classical, not traditional. In the Terai region we find landlords with some lands, and we have to seize the lands and distribute them among the poor peasants. But in the whole mountainous regions, that is not the case. There are smallholdings, and no big landlords . . . How to develop production, how to raise production is the main problem here. The small pieces of land mean the peasants have low productivity. With collective farming it will be more scientific and things can be done to raise production."

It is not clear how much collective farming exists or what nonmilitary use the Maoists make of the taxes they collect. In fact, there is little reliable information about what goes on in the countryside. Few journalists venture out of their urban bases, and the Maoists aren't the only obstacle. Most of the very few roads outside Kathmandu are a series of large potholes, and then there are the nervous soldiers at checkpoints. And once you move away from the highway, no soldiers or policemen appear for miles on end. In Shakti Khor, a village in the Tarai region populated by one of the poorest communities in Nepal, a few men quietly informed us that Maoist guerrillas were hiding in the nearby forest, where no security forces ever ventured and from where the Maoists often escaped to India. At a small cooperative shop selling honey, mustard oil, turmeric, and herbal medicines, two men in their mid-twenties appeared very keen to put in a good word for the Maoists, who the previous night had painted red antimonarchy slogans on the clean walls.

In the other Maoist-dominated regions I visited, people seemed too afraid to talk. At Deurali Bazaar, a village at the end of a long and treacherous drive in the hills near Pokhara, a newly constructed bamboo gate was wrapped with a red cloth painted with a hammer and sickle and the names of Maoists either dead or in prison. The scene in the square appeared normal at first—women scrubbing children at a municipal tap, young men drinking tea, an old tailor hunched over an antique sewing machine, his walking stick leaning against his chair— but the presence of the Maoists, if unacknowledged, was unmistakable. When I tried to talk to the men at the tea shop, they walked away fast, one of them knocking over the tailor's stick. The shopkeeper said that he knew nothing about Maoists. He didn't know who had built the bamboo gate; it had simply appeared one morning.

When I got back to Pokhara that evening, the news was of three teenage students killed as they tried to stop an army car on the highway. The previous day I had seen newspaper reports in which the army described the students as "terrorists" and claimed to have found documents linking them to the Maoists. But it now seemed clear that they were just collecting donations for Holi, the Hindu festival of colors. There were eyewitnesses to the shooting. The parents of the victims had exhumed their corpses from the shallow graves in which the army had quickly buried them and discovered that two of them had been wearing their school uniforms. Like much else in Nepal, this would not appear in the newspapers.

The bloody stalemate in Nepal may last for a long time. The army is too small and poorly equipped at present decisively to defeat the Maoists. In some areas it has recently tried arming upper-caste villagers and inciting them to take action against the Maoists. In the southern district of Kapilavastu, vigilante groups organized by a local landlord and armed by the government claim to have killed more than fifty Maoists in February 2005. Such tactics are likely not only to lead to a civil war but also to increase support for the Maoists in areas where the government is either absent or disliked.

Though unlikely at present, talks may offer a way forward. The Maoists have shown themselves willing to negotiate and even to compromise; in July 2001 they dropped their demand that Nepal cease to be a monarchy. More recently, Prachanda hinted at a flexible stance when he called for a united front of mainstream political parties against the monarch. He probably fears that the guerrilla force might self-destruct if its leaders fail to lead their more extreme cadres in the direction of moderate politics. But any Maoist concessions to bourgeois democracy are unlikely to please Gyanendra, who clearly wants to use the current chaos to help him hold on to his power.

If he periodically evokes the prospect of terrorists taking over Nepal, Gyanendra can count on the support of India, the United States, and the U.K. In late 2001 the U.S. ambassador to Nepal, Michael Malinowski, a veteran of the CIA-sponsored anti-Soviet jihad in Afghanistan, said that "these terrorists, under the guise of Maoism or the so-called 'people's war,' are fundamentally the same as terrorists elsewhere—be they members of the Shining Path, Abu Sayaf, the Khmer Rouge or Al Qaeda." The then Hindu nationalist government in Delhi, just as eager to name new enemies, also described the Maoists as "terrorists."

The present Indian government has a more nuanced view of Nepal. But it is worried about India's own Communist rebels and their links with the Nepalese Maoists, and it believes that as Malinowski put it, "all kinds of bad guys could use Nepal as a base, like in Afghanistan." Responding to fears that the army in Nepal was running out of ammunition, India resumed its arms supply this year, partly hoping to contain the Maoists and wanting too to maintain its influence over Nepal in the face of growing competition from the United States.

There is no evidence that bad guys, as defined by the Bush administration, have flocked to Nepal, the Maoists are far from achieving a military victory, and the Communists in India are unlikely to extend their influence beyond the poverty-stricken districts they presently control. The rise of an armed Communist movement in a strategically important country nevertheless disturbs many political elites, who believe that communism died in 1989 and that history has arrived at the terminus of liberal-capitalist democracy.

A European diplomat in Kathmandu told me that although Western countries hoped the political parties and the king would put up a joint front against the Maoists, they knew they might at some point have to support the king and his army if he alone was left to protect the country from the Maoists and keep alive the prospects for democracy. I did not feel that I could ask him about the nature of a democracy that is protected by an autocrat. Perhaps he meant nothing more by the word "democracy" than regular elections, the kind of democracy whose failure to contain violence or to limit systemic poverty and inequality does not matter so long as elections are held, even if, as in Afghanistan and Iraq, under a form of martial law, and in which the turnout of voters does nothing but empower and legitimize a native elite willing to push the priorities of its Western patrons.

Such a form of democracy, which is slowly coming into being in Pakistan, could be revived again in Nepal, as the king repairs his relationship with the mainstream political parties. It is possible too that the excesses of the Maoists will cause them to self-destruct. Certainly the international revolution Prachanda speaks of will prove a fantasy. Yet it's hard to wish away the rage and despair of people who, arriving late in the modern world, have known its primary ideology, democracy, only as another delusion, the disenchanted millions who will increasingly seek, through other means than elections, the dignity and justice that they feel is owed to them.

TIBET

A Backward Country

In 1992 I left Delhi and began living in a small village in the Indian Himalayas. It was spring when I arrived. Every cloudless morning I got up and walked out onto the balcony of my cottage to see the white mountains toward the east straining high on their plinth of deep blue air. I could gaze upon these mountains for hours on end, especially in the long evenings, when the distant snow would refuse to disappear beneath the encroaching darkness, glowing an imperious red late into the night. My landlord often joined me on the balcony. One evening he asked me if I knew what lay beyond the mountains. I shook my head. "Tibet," he said.

When I finally traveled to Tibet in 2004, I remembered how surprised I had been by my landlord's reply back then. How had I managed to lose sight of this basic geography—Tibet, the broad high plateau between India and China, bigger than even western Europe, and the source of most of the great rivers of Asia (the Indus, the Yangtze, the Brahmaputra, and the Sutlej)—something so immediately obvious in all the atlases I had? How could I not have known that the Indian Himalayas bordering Tibet, a bus ride away from my own village, were predominantly Tibetan in culture and Buddhist in religion?

But then, Tibet was to me, as it had been to many others, a fantasy rather than a real place, a resonant cliché, "the roof of the world," rather than a clearly defined area on a map.

Growing up in a Hindu Brahmin family in India, I had inherited a religious idea about Tibet: It was the sacred homeland of great seers and sages, people capable of levitation and astral travel. Later, while reading nineteenth- and early-twentieth-century travelers and explorers from the West, I came across similarly romantic, if more apparently rational, notions of Tibet: It was the isolated, inaccessible country that had remained untouched by the drastic transformations imposed by railways, roads, steamships, and industries in the nineteenth century, a civilization where religion and tradition were a living force and whose peoples radiated a serenity and gentleness long extinct in the frantically modern and aggressive societies of Europe and America.

Living in the Himalayas, remote at last from the squalor of Delhi and the small towns where I had spent most of my life, I had little trouble entering this Virtual Tibet. It became more compelling as I began to travel to the Indian border with China/Tibet. In the cold deserts and high valleys, where monks and hermits lived in tiny caves cut into steep hillsides, dressed in cotton vests in sub-zero temperatures, I could easily believe in the miraculous powers attributed to lamas and other spiritually exalted people, the benign, medieval religiosity that many Western travelers found in Tibet and recently commemorated in such Hollywood films as *Seven Years in Tibet* and Martin Scorsese's *Kundun.*

There was little place in this vision for the hundred thousand or so Tibetan refugees in India, people who had escaped the country's Chinese Communist rule. Expelled from their ostensible paradise of Tibet, they stood on the narrow, broken pavements of Indian hill towns, selling woolen jackets, socks, gloves, calculators, Walkmans, and wristwatches.

I had read of how the Chinese, who first invaded Tibet in 1950, had killed hundreds of thousands of Tibetans and destroyed many hundreds of monasteries and temples. I had read that the traditional society and culture of Tibet were gravely threatened. But I still didn't know what to make of the Tibetan refugees and their oddly Westernized ways. In their jeans and American college sweatshirts, most young Tibetans didn't seem the heir to a traditional culture, not with karaoke bars and video game parlors standing next to Buddhist temples in Dharamsala, the home of the Dalai Lama, the spiritual leader of the Tibetan community in exile.

Our modern fantasies of a simple and whole past are fragile. Perhaps, that's why we hold on to them so tenaciously. In Tibet, I sought to confirm everything I had imagined about it, and for the first few days at least, I was not disappointed.

The magic began on the flight to Lhasa from Kathmandu when defying predictions of bad weather and low visibility, Mount Everest unexpectedly emerged, all sheer rock and ice, looming well above the thick cloud cover at twenty-five thousand feet, and then, after a long, snow-bound mountain range, the Tibetan plateau revealed itself in all its purity and vastness.

Chinese military officials supervised our arrival at Gongkar Airport. Their stern faces and green uniforms were the first reminder of the political status of Tibet. Outside, tour guides with Land Cruisers waited to attach themselves to tourists, and bilingual banners, on which Chinese ideograms dwarfed the elegant Tibetan script, proclaimed Tibet as part of the rapidly progressing Chinese "motherland."

But less than a mile outside the airport, the empty countryside began: barley fields next to a very broad river, whose still surface reflected with spellbinding clarity the deep blue sky, the surrounding bare hills, and, occasionally, the white massifs guarding the remote horizon.

This was the Yarlung Valley, the cradle of Tibetan civilization, where the first known ruler of Tibet emerged in the seventh century, and from where the Tibetan Empire once spread as far as Afghanistan and Bengal. At Yambulagang, the site of the first known building in Tibet, yaks with smooth black horns and bushy white tails waited to carry us to the hilltop temple where monks pored over open manuscripts of rough paper, amid an overpowering aroma of rancid yak butter and sandalwood incense. After the blinding light of the valley, the chapels were dark and mysterious, crowded with gilded statues of the Buddha and Tibetan kings, the walls hectic with murals of the sharp-toothed multiarmed demons that the Tibetans revere as protector deities.

In these first few days it seemed to me that many centuries happily coexisted in Tibet. On the small ferry that took us next morning across the Tsangpo River to the eighth-century Samye monastery, the oldest in Tibet, there were two yaks and a young monk wearing blue jeans and sneakers under his habit.

The sun was warm, dazzling when reflected in the water and on the snow peaks and sandy banks. A handsome old man in a trilby hat twirled a prayer wheel. Two young women sat silently, holding stylish parasols with one hand and rosaries with the other; they turned out to be pilgrims, like most people on the ferry. A young couple in jeans and embroidered boots sat on the floor with their lively red-cheeked baby.

At the ferry beach, a ramshackle bus waited to take us across sand dunes to the monastery. I spent the long afternoon walking around the circular walled compound of the recently renovated monastery, which was designed originally to represent the Tibetan Buddhist cosmos and was once fringed with 1,008 gold-encrusted chortens (reliquary mounds). Chinese, Indian, and Tibetan architectural styles rendered distinctive each of three floors of the central building, whose wide assembly hall was full of the guttural chants of monks sitting amid riotously colorful silk drapes and shafts of sunlight.

In one of the darker chapels, a young monk whispered to me in Hindi. In our brief hurried conversation—Chinese spies were everywhere, he said—he explained that he had left Tibet illegally in order to spend a couple of years in Dharamsala. Educated at Samye, he had not taken his vows until after his visit to the Dalai Lama. And now his younger brother was planning a risky journey to Dharamsala.

To travel from Samye to Lhasa, past ruins of hillside monasteries and fortresses, was to enter a more fraught world. It was to confront the knowledge that had shadowed me at Yambulagang and Samye: that I was looking at ghosts of buildings almost entirely destroyed by Chinese and Tibetan fanatics before and during the Cultural Revolution (1966–1976).

"Religion is poison," Mao Zedong had told the Dalai Lama in 1955, early during the Chinese occupation of Tibet. After 1959, when the Dalai Lama fled to India, the Chinese had moved swiftly to undercut the power of the monasteries, which owned most of the arable land and loaned money to and educated poor villagers. At Samye, where the first Tibetans were ordained as monks, and from where Buddhism traveled to the rest of Tibet, Red Guards, fired up by Mao's denunciation of religion and tradition, had pounded chortens and statues into dust. Some of the chortens have been restored, and with their mix of concrete and gold-leaf encrusting they embody well the tawdry kitsch produced by Chinese-led restoration efforts in Tibet. The destruction was most extensive in the region of Lhasa, where all the major monasteries— Drepung, Sera, Ganden—were reduced to ruins, and only the seventeenth-century Potala Palace, the traditional home of the Dalai Lama, escaped the fury of the Red Guards.

The Communist leadership in Beijing now admits, if grudgingly, to "excesses" and "mistakes" during the Cultural Revolution, when tens of thousands of Tibetans were condemned as "reactionaries," "rightists," and "capitalist roaders" and imprisoned, tortured, and murdered. Ambivalence now clouds the official memory of Mao, "the Great Helmsman," who steered his country into famine and chaos. This is partly because in the early eighties the Chinese regime embraced the free market after scorning "capitalist roaders" for decades and decided that "to get rich," as the late Communist leader Deng Xiaoping described, "is glorious."

It wasn't easy, however, to get rich in Tibet. The hard ground and extreme cold precluded extensive agriculture—most Tibetans still depend on yak meat and barley flour—and little infrastructure for heavy industries existed outside Lhasa. The high altitude, an average elevation of thirty-five hundred meters, and low oxygen deterred many outsiders. The only thing that Tibet seemed to possess in great quantity was its religion and an exotic past that the Chinese discovered could be packaged and sold to tourists.

Since the early eighties the Chinese authorities have promoted tourism in Tibet, despite occasional setbacks, such as the anti-Chinese riots and demonstrations in Lhasa in 1987 and 1989. They remain suspicious of the growing popularity of Buddhism among young Tibetans and even Chinese; in eastern Tibet in 2001 they partly demolished a monastic encampment that had attracted thousands of Tibetan and Chinese students of Buddhism. But they hope to attract visitors to the more famous old monasteries and temples and have rebuilt and renovated a few of them. They have also improved telecommunications, built roads and even a new railway that in a few years will link Lhasa with China.

New government hotels aiming, not always successfully, at an international style have appeared in Lhasa and the towns of Shigatse and Gyantse. There are fewer visa and travel restrictions for foreigners, and groups of nouveau riche tourists from the rich cities of coastal China throng the monasteries, posing with monks, clambering up steep metal-lined ladders to peer eagerly at the murals depicting Tantric sex.

Encouraged by the government in Beijing, which wishes to open up Tibet, like the rest of China, to private enterprise and consumerism, hundreds of thousands of Han Chinese, the ethnic majority of China, have moved to Tibetan cities in order to take opportunity of tax breaks and incentives to small businesses. Han Chinese are said to outnumber the Tibetans in Lhasa by two to one.

With its wide avenues, billboards with neon ideograms, shopping malls, discotheques, Sichuan restaurants, and brothels (usually disguised as massage parlors, as I discovered with some embarrassment), Lhasa now resembles a Chinese city on the make, as fanatically devoted to consumerist excess as it had previously been to Communist austerity.

The Lhasa of my imagination—pilgrims with rosaries shuffling through a mist of incense, past old mud houses with painted wood window frames in narrow alleys—existed only for a few blocks around Jokhang Temple, the most sacred spot in Tibet. Here at least the hustling that gives much of Lhasa the raw vulgarity of a frontier town was relatively absent. Tibetans dominated the crowd of pilgrims, tourists, policemen, and trinket sellers flowing clockwise around the temple. The women from eastern Tibet, magnificently adorned with turquoise headdresses, necklaces, brooches, and bangles, mingled with young Tibetan city slickers in reversed baseball caps.

But at the monastery of Sera, tourists clicked their cameras frantically as young monks debated Buddhist philosophy in the traditional way, underscoring their point by leaning forward and bringing their hands together with a loud clap. But the event seemed staged; an American woman with a money belt around her waist moved slowly through the crowd of tonsured men.

The Potala Palace still appears fabulous, as it abruptly rises, tier by tier, above the city on its own steep hill and gazes equably at the mountains surrounding Lhasa. But looking directly down from the roof of the palace, I saw ugly squat blocks of concrete stretching to all four corners, and the palace with its vast magnificent hulk suddenly appeared marooned in the city. As I stood there one afternoon, a shampoo salesman harangued passersby on a megaphone in the huge Chinese-built square below the Potala, a desert of tarmac created out of razing the old quarters; the echo penetrated the melancholy empty apartments of the present Dalai Lama, still touchingly preserved.

From this transplanted China that is modern-day Lhasa, I was relieved to return to Tibet. I rode in the ubiquitous Land Cruiser—essential vehicle in a country where there are hardly any paved roads. And every step of the way, trailing clouds of dust across barren white valleys, past the black tents of nomads, from which children emerged, waving, holding their happy mucus-smudged faces up to us, on the high passes where prayer flags rippled in the strong wind, and then bowling alongside a turquoise lake cradled by yak-encrusted hills, I again felt the enchantment of Tibet's immense empty spaces.

It was evening when we drew into the town of Gyantse, the place where Tibet had first encountered the modern world, in 1903 and 1904, in the shape of invading British troops. The British claimed that the Tibetans and the Russians were conspiring against the British Empire in India and that there were Russian guns in the capital, Lhasa. This turned out to be yet another imperial self-deception, reinforced in equal measure by arrogance, paranoia, and flawed intelligence. The Tibetan government, mostly run by monks, had geopolitical ambitions only to the extent that it wished its country to be left alone by its powerful neighbors. Certainly, the small Tibetan Army possessed no Russian guns and was armed with nothing more dangerous than matchlock rifles, stones, sticks, and amulets blessed by the Dalai Lama.

Near Gyantse, the British trained two Maxim machine guns on the hapless Tibetan defenders. As one of the gunners later wrote, "The slaughter was terrible . . . the Tibetans fell in heaps where the Maxims struck them." Instead of ducking out of sight from the hail of bullets, the remaining Tibetans slowly walked away from the battlefield, their heads bowed as if in mourning. The sight confused the British. As a journalist embedded with the British troops tried to explain later, "they were bewildered. The impossible had happened. Prayers, and charms, and mantras, and the holiest of their holy men, had failed them."

More than four hundred Tibetans were killed, and many more wounded, in what was only the first of several massacres in Tibet enabled by the Maxim gun, whose usefulness to imperial conquest was commemorated by Hilaire Belloc ("Whatever happens, we have got / the Maxim gun, and they have not"). As Francis Younghusband, the Central Asian expert and leader of the punitive British expedition, acknowledged, it was a "terrible and ghastly business." He forgot to add, probably because he took it for granted, that it was also a necessary business, the work of empire, intimidating weaker peoples, preempting present and potential enemies.

Tibet's isolation had not been much disturbed during the nineteenth century, when the imperial states of Europe—Britain, Russia, Germany, France—exported their rivalries to Asia and Africa and conquered native peoples in the name of a superior civilization. As the Europeans saw it, the country was too big and sparsely populated, and nothing much seemed to grow in its empty spaces apart from a ritualistic, lama-ridden Buddhism. Its importance was, and has remained, largely strategic.

The massacre near Gyantse initiated Tibet into the modern world, its new rivalries, and its newfangled weapons of mass destruction. After the British invaders imposed humiliating terms upon the Tibetans and withdrew, Tibet suffered another invasion in 1910, this time by the doddery Manchu rulers of China. It recovered its independence the next year, as the Manchu Empire collapsed, and then held on to it for almost four decades. In 1950, however, it was invaded by Chinese Communists attempting to "unify" a China they claimed had been carved up by foreign imperialists.

As part of the Chinese "motherland," the area once controlled by the Dalai Lama and his government in Lhasa is now called the Tibetan Autonomous Region (TAR), and its past is partly rewritten by Chinese ideologues. At the fort of Gyantse, a Chinese-built "Memorial Hall of Anti-British" describes the bloody events of 1903 and 1904. It lauds, in broken English, Tibetan soldiers for their efforts on behalf of the "motherland" and denounces Tibet's British violators. A tombstone marks the spot from where Tibetan soldiers, bewildered by the superior firepower of the British, allegedly plunged to their death.

The suicides, which have never been proved, seem a figment of the Chinese nationalist imagination, designed to reinforce the idea that the Tibetans were a weak, barbarian race and uniquely vulnerable to greedy foreigners. This is a common theme in Chinese writing about Tibet: that before its "peaceful liberation" it was a benighted country where "feudal" and "reactionary" aristocrats together with monasteries and monks oppressed a majority population of serfs and slaves, mostly by addling their minds with ritual and religion. This unholy ruling elite was unable to modernize and develop Tibet and didn't even learn the lessons of the rout near Gyantse, the importance of secular education, a modern army, transport, administration, and a productive population.

Before the Chinese invasion in 1950, Gyantse had been an important town on the trading route to India, then Tibet's closest trading partner. Now, cheap Chinese-made goods fill the shops and the stalls that spill onto the dusty pavements, and in the lobby of my resoundingly empty hotel, very young Chinese girls stood smiling vacantly in identical red silk dresses under a barbershop sign offering "24-hour massage service."

China is developing and modernizing Tibet, taking the country into a glorious future; it was hard to get away from this message, which was garishly advertised on the welcome arches and billboards along the empty roads, and which my Tibetan guide always pointed to with a wry smile. But the extreme youth of the prostitutes was proof that although the future might be glorious, the present was an ordeal for many people, the Tibetans as well as the large number of drifting Chinese, who sought work in what to them was a remote, strange, and inhospitable land.

I had read in several books and articles on the post-Mao China about its "floating population," estimated to be over a hundred million, looking for work away from home. Such large-scale uprooting was said to be one of the effects of the country's economic policies. However, Chinese-led modernization and development appeared to have affected only the few urban areas in Tibet, where most economic migrants from China lived. It seemed to have left untouched the laborers repairing the roads, the farmers in the small villages, and the idle Tibetans playing pool everywhere in roadside dwellings. And it had not diminished, and may even have reinforced, the role of religion in Tibetan society.

Almost all reports about contemporary Tibet attest that despite being under continuous assault for almost three decades, Buddhism remains central to most Tibetan lives. For most Tibetans, the Chinese liberalization that began in the early eighties primarily meant the freedom to worship their old gods rather than play the new stock market in Lhasa. Some of the pilgrims I saw at Gyantse's famous octagonal stupa had traveled hundreds of miles. Half bent under the weight of their wooden-frame rucksacks, they walked around the monastic complex, feeding the mangy dogs, reflexively doling out money to the beggars, while spinning their prayer wheels. Inside the dark chapels, they squeezed yak butter out of yellow plastic bags into lamps burning at altars, and with greasy hands they stuck one- and five-yuan notes in the shrines, their small-denomination notes with idealized pictures of Chinese peasants easily outnumbering the big-denomination notes left by tourists from Buddhist Taiwan, Japan, and Thailand.

The Chinese overlords of Tibet weren't without good intentions. It is mostly due to them that many Tibetans enjoy better education and health care. But the majority of Tibetans are still peasants and nomads, and even the educated Tibetans I spoke to seemed discontent with Chinese rule. Like all traditional people faced with modernization, their choices are drastically limited. To embrace the glittering new world of China is to become as ruthlessly materialist and secular as the post-Communist Chinese. It is to lose what was still precious to them, their religious and cultural identity.

The fear of "Sinicization" seemed to weigh most heavily on the Tibetan refugees I met in Dharamsala after returning from Tibet. They were convinced that Han Chinese settlers would overwhelm the Tibetans with their alien ways and that soon, with the new rail connection to China, Tibetan society and culture would cease to exist.

Although these Tibetans are a politically diverse group, they mostly agree that since the Chinese Communists invaded Tibet in 1950, they have killed—mostly through execution, torture, and starvation—up to

1.2 million people and have destroyed tens of thousands of Buddhist monasteries and temples.

In May 1980, four years after Mao's death, the general secretary of the Chinese Communist Party, Hu Yaobang, visited Tibet, where he apologized for these "earlier errors" and promised Tibetans greater religious freedom and economic development, along with a measure of political autonomy. But the Tibetans insist that the Chinese regime in Beijing continues to treat Tibet as a colony and has consistently sought to undermine its society and culture, and exploit its economic resources without much regard for its physical environment. They were supported by the Human Rights Watch report in 2004, which claims that the Communist regime in Beijing continues to behave brutally in Tibet, often detaining without trial, torturing, and executing those it suspects of being separatists or sympathizers of the Dalai Lama.

Many of these Tibetan exiles see their political leaders as being constrained by too many religious scruples. They may be right. As Samdhong Rinpoche, the prime minister of the Tibetan government in exile, explained to me in an interview in the spring of 2004, he has reservations about even such a commonplace tactic of resistance groups as economic boycott since this hurts ordinary people more than the governments. He pointed out that the Dalai Lama supported a ban on Chinese toys only because they were produced by force in prison camps and boycotting them did not impair the livelihood of Chinese laborers.

Religion is poison," Mao Zedong informed the Dalai Lama in 1955. He probably meant that religion saps a nation's will to struggle and succeed in a competitive world. Rupert Murdoch, one of the overeager investors in the liberalized Chinese economy, seemed to agree with Mao when he asserted that "the main problem in Tibet is that half the population still thinks that the Dalai Lama is the 'son of God' [sic]."

Such dismissals of Tibetan religion and culture are not confined to ultraleftists or free market libertarians. The Indian prime minister Nehru once confided to a British diplomat that the Tibetans "were rather difficult people to help, for they were so ignorant of the modern world and its ways." In a speech in 1997, Chen Kuiyuan, one of the hard-line Chinese technocrats to have ruled Tibet in recent years, pointed out that "when the Dalai ruled Tibet, there was not a single regular school; children of the working people had no right or opportunity to receive an education, and more than 90 percent of the Tibetan people were illiterate."

When I quoted this speech to Samdhong Rinpoche, he did not fundamentally disagree with it; he readily admitted that Tibet under the ancien régime was no Shangri-la. In 1959, Samdhong Rinpoche was twenty years old and training for a degree in philosophy at the Tibetan monastery of Drepung, when he heard that the fourteenth and present Dalai Lama had fled Chinese-occupied Tibet to neighboring India. Samdhong Rinpoche joined the thousands of Tibetans who followed the Dalai Lama and has not been back to Tibet since. In India, where he has spent most of his life, he is known for his learned advocacy of nonviolent politics and his admiration for Gandhi and the Indian freedom struggle against the British.

In 2001, his election as prime minister, with an impressive 80 percent of the votes cast, signaled the growing democratization of the Tibetan community in exile, of which the Dalai Lama has been the undisputed supreme leader. His vigorous self-criticism reveals the depth of introspection among the Tibetan community in exile.

As a young monk from the provinces in Lhasa, Samdhong Rinpoche saw how "members of religious order failed to follow their moral codes and in both public and in private they were mostly occupied with sales, profits, usury, economic affairs, and other unspiritual matters." Much of this occurred in his own monastery in Lhasa, Drepung. He also has little time for the Tibetan aristocracy that collaborated with the Chinese. "Most of our leaders were involved in immoral practices aimed simply at fulfilling their own self-interests." Predictably, when the Chinese came, "Tibetans unhesitatingly sold off their country, for the sake of money and goods and their own narrow self-interests." Samdhong Rinpoche attributes the sufferings of the Tibetan people to their "collective negative karma."

Dressed in a maroon robe, Samdhong Rinpoche spoke softly and precisely, in unaccented Hindi. He described to me how as a young, inexperienced refugee monk in India he first came across Gandhi's writings and began to clarify his political thinking. He said that he did not oppose the Chinese people or even Chinese sovereignty over Tibet. What he objected to was the quality of Chinese rule, its injustice and violence, which he called upon all Tibetans to actively reject through acts of noncooperation and disobedience, without hating or harming the Chinese people.

Nonviolence, he said, wasn't a tactic or a means to a predetermined end. As a form of self-control and carefully measured action, it was an end in itself. A whole way of being in the world, it entailed respect and compassion for all living things.

He sees a free Tibet as a demilitarized zone of peace, devoid of nuclear, chemical, and biological weapons. He claims his government will do all it can to restore Tibet's ecological balance, which has been upset by Chinese-built dams and mining projects. He also said that one of his priorities was to educate more Tibetan refugees in the philosophical underpinning of satyagraha, the respect for human life, and the natural environment. He has already made a beginning by reorienting agriculture-based Tibetan settlements in India to organic farming.

This sounds appropriately small-scale and achievable. But it is still hard to avoid the question, Can Buddhistic nonviolence have any role in a world ultimately shaped by brute force and economic interest?

In 1987, the Dalai Lama dropped his earlier demand for full independence for Tibet, describing it as "unrealistic" and saying that he was willing to negotiate an autonomous status for Tibet within China. His desire to seek a "middle way" of compromise did not result in any significant concessions from the Chinese; it also angered and alienated many Tibetan intellectuals and activists, who want to settle for nothing less than independence.

In Delhi in 1998, a former monk called Thupten Ngodup publicly immolated himself after Indian police forcibly ended a fast unto death undertaken by six Tibetan activists. The Tibetan Youth Congress, a radical group, had organized the hunger strike, despite the initial disapproval of the Dalai Lama and Samdhong Rinpoche.

Many Tibetan exiles I met concede that the Dalai Lama has internationalized the Tibetan issue and helped make Buddhism more popular in the West. But they increasingly question his effectiveness against a political opponent as apparently hard-nosed as the Chinese regime in Beijing, which becomes more ever more respectable and attractive internationally as China's economy grows at the extraordinary rate of 10 percent each year.

The award-winning novelist Jamyang Norbu, one of the founders of the Tibetan Youth Congress, is one of these Tibetans who believe that the Dalai Lama's religious commitments diminish his political role and that his Buddhistic desire to compromise with the Chinese does not serve the Tibetan cause.

"Some people don't want to be enlightened, at least not immediately," Norbu said in a PBS television documentary on Tibet; "they are really happy in their landscape and in Tibet. They have a kind of affinity to their place they live in. And, they don't want the Chinese there. And his Holiness cannot understand this. . . ."

Norbu rejects the Western stereotype of Tibetans as an innately nonviolent people, a romantic notion which he thinks gratifies many Western people discontented with the aggressive selfishness of their societies but obscures the political aspirations of the Tibetan peoples and the variety of means available to them to achieve independence. In 1989, he published a book about one of the Khampa warriors of eastern Tibet, who fought the invading Chinese Army in 1950 and then initiated the bloody revolt against Chinese rule that eventually led to the Dalai Lama's departure for India.

"We are ordinary Tibetans," Norbu told PBS. "We drink; we eat; we feel passion; we love our wives and kids. If someone sort of messes around with them, even if they're an army, you pick up your rifle."

In the early seventies, Norbu dropped out of boarding school in Darjeeling and picked up a rifle and joined the Tibetan guerrillas operating out of Mustang, a piece of Nepalese territory that juts into Tibet. The CIA secretly funded these guerrillas and arranged for them to be trained in Colorado. American support was halfhearted at best, intended to undermine Communist China, not to achieve Tibetan independence; it ended in the early seventies after Kissinger and Nixon decided to befriend Mao, initiating the appeasement of China which culminated in 1994, when Bill Clinton decided to separate trade with China from the problematic issue of human rights.

Abandoned by their sponsors, many Tibetan guerrillas were attacked and killed by the Nepalese Army. Finally, the Dalai Lama told the Mustang guerrillas in a taped message to give up arms and return to India.

Lhasang Tsering, who is now a bookseller in Dharamsala, was one of the Tibetan guerrillas in Mustang. He later headed the Tibetan Youth Congress and even worked for the Tibetan government in exile before resigning in protest against the Dalai Lama's decision to drop the demand for full independence.

He told me what I have heard from many other Tibetans, that in the last decade, the Chinese government has encouraged Han Chinese, the ethnic majority of China, to migrate in large numbers to Tibet, with the result that the Tibetans are a minority in their own country. Tibet faces a cultural genocide, Tsering said, and will be wiped out unless some radical and quick action is taken.

He didn't specify what form that action should take. But he reminded me that Tibetans had fought fiercely for their rights even during the exceptionally fearful days of the Cultural Revolution. Armed with swords and spears, Thrinley Chodron, a young nun, and her followers had attacked their local Communist Party headquarters, killing Chinese officials and their Tibetan collaborators. Tsering was convinced that the freedom struggle for Tibet would become militant after the Dalai Lama, who will be seventy next year, passes away.

Many younger refugees I met in Dharamsala also stressed the need for immediate and extreme action; they complained that the Buddhist methods of dialogue and negotiation advocated by the Dalai Lama had proved futile. They pointed to the world attention given to the radical Islamists in Palestine and elsewhere after their spectacular acts of violence.

I knew that such views were popular among many Tibetan refugees; they were part of their Westernized general outlook. But I didn't argue with them; I didn't feel that I had earned the right to do so. My own views were as timid and mixed as those of any traveler to a beautiful country under a despotic regime.

When I think of Tibet now, I first remember that morning on the Tsangpo: the austere landscape, where small things—the water slapping against the boat, the bare hills brown against a blue sky, and a man in a trilby hat twirling his prayer wheel—possessed the power to bestow happiness.

I remember watching snow blow off the rocky summit of Mount Everest one chilly and windy evening on the half-collapsed mud roof of Rongbuk Monastery. I remember the peasant Tibetan women in Lhasa, the garish symbol of Chinese capitalism, slowly circumambulating the Potala Palace, measuring the miles of concrete in a series of energetic prostrations, lying on their bellies on the ground one moment and then rising up, their bangled arms outstretched before them, ready to plunge again onto the hard ground.

These images are commonplace in the books I read before visiting Tibet; the Tibetan landscape and people always appear in them with a religious aura of humility and compassion. I liked to think that I was immune to these stereotypes, which often managed to hide Tibet's harsh political reality. I didn't believe that all Tibetans were apogees of loving-kindness and nonviolence. But it was hard not to feel that I had traveled to the heart of a unique civilization, one whose achievement lay not in imposing monuments and museums but in the refined personal culture—the humility and warmth—of its men and women. I had little doubt that Buddhism had helped create a distinctive and sophisticated civilization in Tibet.

I had become aware too of the great dignity and inner strength with which Tibetans have protected their tradition and identity while living amid the physical rubble of this civilization, the rubble of destroyed monasteries and temples over which a profit-driven and still repressive Chinese regime is building a Disneyland of Tibetan culture.

Many dejected Tibetan exiles probably agree with Jamyang Norbu when he says that the Chinese are turning the Tibetans into a "sort of broken third-rate people, who like ten, twenty, thirty, forty years from now will just be someone who's begging from tourists."

Samdhong Rinpoche too is convinced that time is running out for the Tibetans. But he firmly rejects using violence as a tactic against the Chinese, saying that it couldn't be an option even if he was certain that it would win independence for Tibet overnight. "You cannot achieve a good end through the wrong kind of means."

He added that it would be wrong to think of an armed struggle as the difficult option and satyagraha as the weapon of the weak. It is easy to respond to injustice with hatred and violence, but harder to persuade one's adversary of the wrongness of his actions. Nonviolent protest isn't for the fainthearted, he said; it is an arduous practice, requiring much effort and discipline.

Perhaps, this is why monks and nuns currently form the most visible resistance to Chinese rule in Tibet. According to Tsering Shakya, the leading historian of modern Tibet, monks and nuns "command the loyalty and respect of the local population," which sees them as "defenders of Tibetan culture and traditions." In September 1987, monks from Samdhong Rinpoche's alma mater, Drepung, unfurled the Tibetan flag in central Lhasa, the first major political demonstration in Tibet in years. Monks and nuns from other monasteries followed. They were arrested and severely beaten, sparking clashes between Tibetans and the police, which in turn provoked Hu Jintao, the Chinese administrator in Tibet, now China's president, to declare martial law in Tibet.

Correctly identifying monasteries as a source of trouble, in 1996 the Chinese government began to subject them to "patriotism education," asking monks and nuns to denounce the Dalai Lama. But in Tibet, as I talked to ordinary Tibetans and watched the great crowds of pilgrims in the rebuilt monasteries and temples, it seemed clear to me that despite official restrictions, Buddhism was flourishing in Tibet.

Chinese heavy-handedness merely confirms the Dalai Lama's political and spiritual authority in Tibet. But it is not easy for Tibetan exiles to translate this reverence for the Dalai Lama into political advantage. It looks unlikely at present that the Chinese Communist Party will suffer the fate of its counterparts in the Soviet Union and Eastern Europe. In any case, its successors may not look too kindly upon the prospect of an independent Tibet, the likely playground of "foreign imperialists" on China's border. Given this, the Dalai Lama's scaled-down demand for Tibetan autonomy within China appears based on a realistic assessment of the strength of Chinese nationalist feeling. For even such Chinese dissidents as Wei Jingsheng, who have suffered greatly at the hands of the current regime in Beijing, assert that Tibet is and will remain part of China.

This is partly why Tibetan leaders in exile rule out a militant nation-alist movement, despite the fact that Buddhism in Tibet is "a powerful nationalist ideology," as Tsering Shakya acknowledges, and has the "ability to mobilize the public and to contest the authority of the [Chi-nese Communist] Party." As Samdhong Rinpoche explained to me, vio-lence against China is likely to make it harder for the Dalai Lama to persuade Chinese dissident intellectuals to support autonomy for Tibet. And the Chinese government would be likely to severely punish the en-tire Tibetan population for the acts of a few armed dissenters. This seems a fair supposition; the Chinese regime has dealt brutally with its restive Muslim minorities in the northwestern province of Xinjiang.

In any case, as Samdhong Rinpoche sees it, the Tibetans are fight-ing not so much to gain political freedom as to preserve their unique Buddhistic culture. "What will we gain," he hold me, "if we win politi-cal freedom but lose the culture that gives value to our lives? It is why we reject violence, why the Dalai Lama has said he will resign his lead-ership of the Tibetan community if it took to violence. For nonviolence is an inseparable aspect of the Tibetan culture we are fighting for."

He explained that the Gandhian political method of satyagraha wasn't aimed so much at achieving large-scale results such as national independence and autonomy as at helping powerless individuals achieve dignity and confidence in their daily encounters with repressive authority. He said that satyagraha properly begins with small, achiev-able things, at the grassroots level; it seeks large-scale structural change through a profound change in basic human attitudes.

This, he said, had already happened in Tibet, where many monks and nuns saw nonviolent politics as a spiritual duty, a form of self-control and carefully measured action. Samdhong Rinpoche said that it is partly because of the Dalai Lama's principled adherence to nonvio-lence that Tibet remains a presence in the world's consciousness and that Buddhism grows attractive to many people in the West.

This sounds right. But although many people see Tibet as a distinc-tive nation with an admirable religion and culture, no Western government dares lose lucrative business in China by recognizing the Tibetan right to self-determination. As China grows economically stronger, the great Tibetan dream—that the Dalai Lama will return to his homeland—appears unlikely to be fulfilled soon.

The Dalai Lama himself seems to know this. In a recent interview he said that he would die happily in India if Tibet's political status did not change in his lifetime. Such statements are what make him seem insufficiently political. But the Dalai Lama's stance is in line with his Buddhistic distrust of immoral means and imaginary ends, the distrust, essentially, of violence and utopias, which another great exile, Alexander Herzen, expressed when he asserted that "the end of each generation is itself" and that no generation should be asked to sacrifice itself for the sake of an unknown future.

In September 2004, the Dalai Lama's representatives visited China for the third time in two years and discussed Tibetan autonomy with mid-ranking Communist leaders. The meetings between Tibetan and Chinese representatives were held again in June 2005. It is not clear whether these talks will lead to anything other than some diplomatic respectability for China as it prepares for the Beijing Olympics in 2008. However, given that they face a notoriously prickly opponent, the Tibetans have done well to keep alive the possibility of dialogue and negotiation.

And perhaps the Dalai Lama's insistence on nonviolence will appear more fruitful over time, especially if China experiences democratic reform. It has been the strange fate of Tibet, once one of the most isolated places on earth, to function as a laboratory for the most ambitious and ruthless human experiments of the modern era: the Great Leap Forward, the Cultural Revolution, and now a state-imposed capitalism. After having suffered totalitarian communism, Tibetans now confront a dissolute capitalism, one that seeks arrogantly, and often violently, to turn all of the world's diverse humanity into middle-class consumers. But it seems wrong to think of Tibetans, as many outsiders do, as helpless victims of large, impersonal forces.

It is no accident that the Tibetans seem to have survived the large-scale Communist attempt at social engineering rather better than most people in China itself. This is at least partly due to their Buddhistic belief in the primacy of empathy and compassion. And faced with an aggressively secular materialism, they may still prove, almost alone in the world, how religion, usually dismissed, and not just by Mao, as "poison," can be a source of cultural identity and moral values; how it can become a means of political protest without blinding the devout with hatred and prejudice; how it can help not only heal the shocks and pain of history—the pain that has led people elsewhere in the world into nihilistic rage—but also create a rational and ethical national culture, what may make a freer Tibet, whenever it comes about, better prepared for its state of freedom than most societies.